# SAFARI
# RIFLES

# SAFARI RIFLES
## Doubles, Magazine Rifles, and Cartridges for African Hunting

**Craig Boddington**

## SAFARI PRESS, INC.

Long Beach, CA 90803, USA.

The trademark Safari Press ® is registered with the U.S. Patent and Trademark Office and in other countries.

Boddington, Craig

Safari Press Inc.

1990, Long Beach, California

ISBN 0-940143-49-6

10 9 8 7 6

Readers wishing to receive the Safari Press catalog, featuring many fine books on big-game hunting, wingshooting, and sporting firearms, should write to Safari Press Inc., P.O. Box 3095, Long Beach, CA 90803, USA. Tel: (714)894-9080 or visit our Web site at www.safaripress.com

# CONTENTS

# INTRODUCTION

In his preface to *African Hunter* James Mellon recalled an earlier masterpiece, H.C. Maydon's *Big Game Shooting in Africa*, published in 1935. Mellon evaluated the Maydon classic precisely with the remark that "in the forty years since its publication, not a single work of comparable depth, magnitude, or detail has appeared on the fascinating, endlessly various subject of safari." He then pointed out that Maydon's contribution to African hunting literature would remain "an inexhaustible mine of hunting lore and advice" but was, of course, inevitably outdated. Mellon and his many collaborators set out to produce a modern version, even more comprehensive, and in doing so they surpassed their own vision, creating a new masterpiece.

The comparison between those two peerless authorities, Mellon and Maydon, can now be applied to Craig Boddington and John Taylor. As *African Hunter* was (and is) to *Big Game Shooting in Africa*, Boddington's *Safari Rifles* is to Taylor's *African Rifles and Cartridges*. Published in 1948, Taylor's work became a classic in its own time. He offered an enormous trove of technical information, conclusions based on field experience, and sound, practical advice for any safari-bound hunter, whether newcomer or old African hand. Until now, Taylor probably has been the most quoted, most reliable and relied on, reference to African sporting rifles, especially the medium and big bores. But like Maydon's great work, Taylor's has become inevitably outdated.

For example (and an obvious one it is), Taylor could not have foreseen the effects of the Weatherby magnums and their successors, nor did he have available a great many other powerful, high-speed rounds that have proved their value in our bolt-action rifles for plains game and assorted big game. For that matter, the scopes adorning our bolt-actions would have astonished and delighted him. The same can be said of the better synthetic stocks and recoil-taming advances.

Even in the realm of big double rifles, where far fewer innovations have appeared in the last four decades, we now see possibilities, experiments, and improvements no one dreamed of in 1948. We have the .700 Nitro-Express, new sources of ammunition and components. There are also new doubles such as George Caswell's Champlin-Famers .450 No. 2, which has been proven capable of handling a variety of bullet weights—a versatility rarely achieved in the past for double rifles. And I wonder what his reaction might have been to the .460 G&A No.2, built by Holland & Holland to the specifications of Bob Petersen.

As Editor of Petersen's *Hunting*, Craig Boddington's long association with that magazine and other Petersen publications has afforded him an outstanding opportunity to assess the potential of rifles and cartridges both old and new, and to evaluate their terminal-performance characteristics. Of course, controlled range testing for velocity, trajectory, accuracy, energy, penetration, and expansion, valuable as such research is, can divulge only part of what a hunter must know for the sake of safety and success.

How does a given rifle or type of rifle handle in a situation that may bring the trophy of a lifetime—or the death of a misguided hunter? Is the rifle dependable? Will a second shot (or perhaps even the first) be rendered useless because the recoil is too much for the shooter? Will two shots be enough? Will the sighting equipment be as quick and sure in the bush on moving game as on those paper targets back in California? Will a bullet be effective on plains game at 300 yards? On a charging lion or buffalo at a tenth of that distance? Will two rifles suffice for a given assortment of game in a given part of Africa or is a three-gun battery needed? And where game may range in size from tiny antelope to elephant and rhino, which two or three rifles will cover the spectrum? Is there reason to bring a shotgun and, if so, which shotgun?

Range testing reveals much but, in the end, cannot answer all the questions. The author has discussed these matters and more with many African professional hunters. His wide acquaintance with these pros (as well as with rifle and cartridge designers) has added an important dimension to his on-the-job experience, but he has gone much further than that in amassing knowledge of his subject. Though still a young man, he's a veteran of twenty African hunts, encompassing an enormous range of habitat, conditions, and game. Thus, he speaks with authority based on solid field experience. He has taken the trophies he describes and has had the successes, failures, and scares that can teach a man more about rifles and cartridges than a lifetime of controlled range experimentation and testing.

Craig is surprisingly humble about his qualifications; and in this regard, too, his approach, built on the firm Taylor foundation, is comparable to Mellon's enlargement and modernization of Maydon's African treatise. Mellon, like Maydon, combined his knowledge with that of collaborators who were specialists in one area or another. Craig enjoys an advantage over his spiritual forebears—computer programming to help him survey the recommendations of professional hunters throughout Africa, and to tally and analyze their responses.

Using mailing lists of the International Professional Hunters Association and the Professional Hunters Association of South Africa, he sent questionnaires to several hundred active pros who, collectively, hunt all across Africa. To me, the responses incorporated into Chapter 36 (and related tables and appendices) are among the most fascinating sections of this unique reference work. Even the disagreements—and the differences between their own preferences and their recommendations to clients—are revealing in a most useful, practical way.

On the other hand, I'll admit to some difficulty in choosing what's most fascinating. Like any firearms buff, I'm captivated by the history of rifles and cartridges that have made their mark in Africa. Chapters 13 and 15, historical perspectives on double rifles and bolt-actions, and Chapter 35, on "The Professional's Choice in the Good Old Days," will enthrall even those readers who plan no safari and perhaps never will.

This, then, is an encyclopedic reference work with an aura of armchair adventure. I, for one, haven't tired of vicarious adventure after thirty years of editing and reading it. It's here in Craig's modest accounts of his experiences—encounters with buffalo and elephant, difficult long shots on antelope, the admirable admission of fear in the presence of lion—but you'll find that he presents such experiences not to exploit a sensation of excitement but rather to illustrate practical points about right (and wrong) arms and cartridges for the game, for the country in which it's hunted, for the kind of situation that can be expected, and for the inevitably unexpected.

Above all, this is a *practical reference work*, and a quick perusal of the table of contents will tell you where to find what you must know about how many rifles to take, which ones, what's best for various kinds of hunting and game in widely different parts of Africa, how to care for and transport your equipment, where to obtain what you need—and a great deal more.

I've been editing books and articles about firearms and hunting for three decades—works by Larry Koller, Jim Carmichel, Bob Hagel, Charles Askins, Elmer Keith, the late great arms historian Harold L. Peterson, and others. And I've been reading them ever since I was hooked as a youngster when a family friend gave me Jim Corbett's *Man-Eaters of Kumaon*. I've known and admired Craig Boddington for years, too, and I've read his previous books. When I was given the opportunity to edit this one, I was delighted; and as I got into it, gleaning page after page of solid fact I'd never learned from John Taylor or any other writer, I was astounded.

Craig has created far more than a modern incarnation of Taylor's standard reference. He has produced, I believe, the most comprehensive, detailed, and useful work on the subject ever to see print. Taylor's was a tough act to follow. Another four decades may pass before anyone follows Craig's.

—Robert Elman

# DEDICATION

To Musili and Muindi, Wakambas; and Willem F. van Dyk, Afrikaner, with thanks for first introducing me to Africa—and to all professional hunters of all tribes.

# CAUTION!

This book contains data on handloading and firearms that reflect the particular experiences of the author. The author used specific firearms, ammunition, and reloading equipment under conditions not necessarily reported in the book. Under NO circumstances should the reader try to copy the loads mentioned in this book. The handloading of ammunition and the discharging of a firearm should never be attempted without the supervision of an adult experienced in both handloading and firearms. The publishers cannot accept responsibility for the firearms and handloading data in this book.

# Part I

# Big-Game Cartridges

# Chapter 1

# Light Cartridges: .22 through .270

S afari" is a magical word that must stir the imagination of even the most apathetic among us. For the hunter, the soft Swahili word conveys the adventure, excitement, and even danger that are the essence of African hunting. The meaning of the word has continued to expand ever since Theodore Roosevelt's historic 1909 African expedition, but in truth the word "safari" simply means "journey." And every journey must have a beginning—including the safari we are now undertaking through the myriad sporting rifles and cartridges available and suitable for today's African hunting.

Those who have chanced across my writings will know I am fascinated by the heavy calibers intended for use on dangerous game—and I'm certainly not alone. In the 30 years since the introduction of the .458 Winchester Magnum, its sales in America have far exceeded the number of hunters who travel to Africa to hunt the game for which it was intended. Witness, too, the current surge of interest in the .416 caliber, with no less than three major American gun manufacturers currently producing .416 rifles. It's tempting, therefore, to begin our journey with the big rifles and cigar-sized cartridges that are so fascinating to so many of us.

We aren't going to do that, though. We're going to start at the opposite end of the spectrum and work our way up, giving due consideration to cartridges as small as the .22 rimfires. Since Africa holds a greater variety of game than any other continent, the spectrum of useful arms and loads is very broad. There is, indeed, a wide array of large and dangerous game—two kinds of rhino, four varieties of buffalo, plus elephant, lion, hippo, and leopard. Nevertheless, what really gives Africa its flavor and provides the greatest part of its hunting thrills isn't the big stuff, but rather the hundred-plus species and subspecies of plains game—the zebras, the wild pigs, and the antelopes great and small—that make Africa the world's greatest hunting ground.

On almost any safari today (except very specialized quests for big elephant), the majority of hunting hours and the vast majority of the cartridges expended will be devoted to members of the antelope clan. And a varied and fascinating clan it is. African antelope range from the jackrabbit-sized dik dik, suni, and royal antelope up to moose-sized eland. Between these extremes there are many beautiful, interesting game animals that, in American terms, could be said to range from the size of javelina to the size of elk. More than a hundred species occupy, in some combination, virtually all of Africa's diverse habitats. There are desert antelope, swamp-dwellers, true plains species, brush-dwellers, species that have adapted to rugged mountains, and others that have found their niche in the dense forests.

These animals, collectively, are the heart and soul of African hunting, and the appropriate cartridges for them make a suitable starting point for our safari through rifles and cartridges. In this chapter we will look at the lightweights, ranging from .22 through .270 in caliber. First, though, a few more comments are in order.

I have written previously about what I consider to be a myth regarding the toughness of African game, and it's appropriate that this subject be addressed right now. In many books and articles about African hunting we have all read that the game there is much tougher than North American game of similar size. Often this is carried to such an extreme that it would seem even a whitetail-sized impala shouldn't be hunted with anything less than a .375. The toughness of African game is not *pure* bunk. Africa has a greater number of large and small predators than our domestic game must contend with, and I theorize that African animals are always on edge and alert—much closer to that surge of adrenalin that makes any animal appear super-tough.

A fatal shot will be just that: fatal. Pound for pound, African game has no tougher bones than American game, and the heart and lungs are in approximately the same places and just as vulnerable to perforation by a bullet. A bullet that reaches the vitals will be effective, period. However, a hit that is off by just a bit may well result in a longer tracking job than you would expect with similar-sized North American game. And even a perfectly placed, fatal shot, such as a behind-the-shoulder lung shot that hits no heavy bone, may result in a longer death run than you might expect with, say, a whitetail deer. The answer isn't heavier calibers; dead is dead. The answer is more precise shot placement!

Of course, there are wide differences in "toughness" among the hundred-odd species of plains game. To say that a 10-pound duiker or a 25-pound klipspringer is tough is ridiculous. Pound for pound, they may well be, but the point is moot with any centerfire rifle. Impala are hardy animals, and just a month before writing this I had a fine ram run fully 200 yards after receiving a 162-grain softpoint from a 7mm Remington Magnum precisely behind the shoulder and through the lungs. He was dead, of course—but nobody bothered to tell him. The result would have been exactly the same, I suspect, if he'd been hit with anything from a .243 to a .375. If the shot had been four inches to the left, on the shoulder, the result probably would have been an animal that dropped in its tracks.

Among the larger African antelope, there are, indeed, great differences in the relative toughness of one species or another. Elk-sized kudu, for instance, seem to me to be relatively soft. I wouldn't want to shoot at them with an inadequate cartridge, of course, and I wouldn't want to hit one in a non-vital place. But even if the shot is off slightly, my chance of recovering the animal after a short tracking job is good. Although similar in bulk to the kudu, the oryx/sable/roan clan is a different story altogether. Like the American elk, these animals are sturdy—just plain tough. A powerful rifle won't make up for poor shot placement, and if the bullet isn't squarely in the vitals, plan on an all-day tracking job with slim chance of recovering the animal.

Wildebeest, too, are tough, and perhaps it's animals like these that have given African game the overall reputation for being well-nigh bulletproof. They aren't, but they deserve to be shot properly with a cartridge powerful enough to do the job. With that, let's begin by examining the smaller cartridges that might be brought on safari.

## .22 Rimfire

With inexpensive, non-bulky ammunition that makes little noise, the .22 rimfire has become a classic poacher's arm in Africa as well as elsewhere. For this reason, the "two-two" is not legal for game in many African countries, and its importation may not be allowed. Hunters who consider taking a .22 on safari should check the regulations carefully beforehand—and be advised that the regulations may simply state ".22," making the .22 *centerfires* just as illegal as a .22 Long Rifle.

Where legal, though, a .22 is not only useful on safari, but a lot of fun. In theory the .22 Long Rifle would be quite adequate for the smallest antelope—the dik dik and the smaller duikers, and in heavy cover would be an enjoyable stalking rifle for such game. But in practice, except in very heavy cover, the smaller antelopes will have to be taken at ranges exceeding the 60-yard limit placed on the .22 Long Rifle by its looping trajectory.

Its real use on safari is twofold—plinking and practice while in camp, and shooting for the pot. Neither should be scoffed at, by the way. Any shooting practice at all, even during the course of a safari, is to the good—and a .22 makes such practice enjoyable and relatively quiet. It isn't unusual, especially for relatively inexperienced hunters, to develop a bad shooting habit during the course of a safari. Flinching, for example, can develop overnight if the hunter is unfamiliar with the heavier rifles he's using. The best cure is to go back to the basics, re-learning proper shooting through practice—and the quiet, recoilless .22 is the best tool available.

Although Africa does have a small variety of rabbit, much like our cottontail, most of the pot shooting consists of birds. If a change of diet is more desirable than a bit of sport, an accurate .22 is absolutely the best supplier of guinea fowl. With a shotgun, the flocks will often outrun you before taking flight; with a good .22 it's a simple matter to snipe two or three as they run straight away, just out of shotgun range.

The varmint shooting we enjoy in America is relatively unknown in Africa, perhaps because of the abundance of "legitimate" game animals. However, in southern Africa night-shooting for spring hares (actually more like a kangaroo rat than a hare) is occasionally done. And in rocky *kopjes* the dassie, or rock hyrax—Africa's equivalent of a rockchuck—is occa-

15

sionally shot. The .22 L.R. would be fine for the former, but totally outclassed for the latter.

Because of practical limitations on the number of guns one can take on safari, I would probably not bring along a .22 rimfire, but I would be delighted if one happened to be in camp; and if such were the case, I'd pack a few boxes of shells.

If I were to take a .22 rimfire on safari, without question it would be not the .22 Long Rifle but instead the .22 Winchester Magnum Rimfire. Although the .22 W.M.R. is a bit noisier and a good deal more expensive to shoot, it has great advantages. Propelling its 40-grain bullet at about 2,000 feet per second, the .22 W.M.R. is effective on small game to about 125 yards—and shoots flat enough to let you hit at that distance, which is virtually impossible with a .22 L.R.

The truth is that the .22 rimfires, whether Magnum or Long Rifle, are much more deadly than I'm allowing for. It's been reasonably well documented that an elephant was killed with a carefully placed between-the-ribs shot with a .22 L.R., and John Taylor himself said that he would walk from the Cape to Cairo with a .22 rifle and a heavy revolver and never go hungry. With precise shot placement, the .22 could certainly be used for impala, reedbuck, and a wide variety of similar game. Indeed, a resident hunter shooting for the pot might well use a .22 for such purposes.

But this book is primarily for the visiting sportsman, the hunter in search of the best trophy he can find. Such a hunter can't always wait for the animal to stand just so and can't always get as close as he would like. For him, the .22, if used at all, is a fun gun only—for the pot and for a few practice shots in camp.

## .22 Centerfires

The high-velocity .22 centerfires are primarily an American institution, developed by and for the American varminter who needed to reach out considerable distances to dispatch small pests and small predators such as fox and coyote. Their British ancestor was the rook rifle, a class of cartridge typified by the .300 Rook and .310 Cadet cartridges. The former started life as a blackpowder cartridge, firing an 80-grain bullet at 1,100 feet per second, while the .310 Cadet, a smokeless load, fired a 120-grain bullet at 1,200 feet per second.

Rook rifles were used for target shooting and for shooting rabbits, hedgehogs, foxes and such. "Rook," incidentally, is an archaic English word for a type of crow. In the well-populated English countryside long-range cartridges weren't desired, and the relatively large bullet diameter of the rook cartridges ensured quick kills without the need for velocity. In America, oldies but goodies such as the .25-20 and .32-20 served—and continue to serve—the same purpose.

In America, however, the woodchuck hunter wanted to reach out across wide-open fields, and he needed the flat trajectory that only comes with high velocity. And, of course, there was also the early fascination with the incredible velocity made possible by smokeless powder. With actions and steels just making the adjustment to the much higher pressures of smokeless powder, initially the only way to achieve high velocity was to reduce caliber and bullet weight.

The .22 Savage High Power, designed by Charles Newton and introduced by Savage in 1912, is a classic example—and is certainly the first of the high-velocity commercial .22 centerfires. Firing a heavy-for-caliber 70-grain bullet at 2,800 fps, it was a real sizzler, and was actually intended for use not necessarily on varmints but on game up to deer. The large-caliber, heavy-bullet boys damned it, as they would today. But those who used it often swore by it. I recall a photo of a 1920s missionary in China posing with two very large tigers taken with his Savage 99 in .22 High Power—and he thought the cartridge was perfectly adequate! Karamojo Bell himself, guru of small bores, wrote of shooting buffalo with the .22 Savage High Power—but he mentioned that he was very, very careful!

Although a few single-shot rifles were chambered for it, the .22 High Power in typical lever-action form didn't have the accuracy needed for varmint hunting, and therefore wasn't a true forerunner of today's super-accurate, flat-shooting .22 centerfires. Those honors go to the 1920s-vintage .22 Hornet.

With a 45-grain bullet leaving the muzzle at about 2,690 fps, the Hornet is relatively flat-shooting, and it was originally offered in accurate bolt-action and single-shot rifles. It achieved tremendous popularity early on; its muzzle blast wasn't too severe, and it could reach out to 150 yards and beyond with ease, even on the smallest of pests. As the decades passed, the Hornet was nearly abandoned in favor of much hotter .22 centerfires, but today it has enjoyed a rebirth, with several high-quality bolt-actions and single-shots again available for this fine old cartridge.

Before we go on to the modern .22s, for completeness we should mention two Winchester developments—the .218 Bee and .219 Zipper. They were designed for, respectively, the Model 92 and 94 Winchester lever-actions. The former employed a 46-grain bullet at 2,860 fps; the latter a 56-grain bullet at a very respectable 3,110 fps. Both have been chambered in custom single-shots, and the Bee has been offered in bolt-actions. In those forms, they can be real tack drivers, but in their original lever-actions, just like the old Savage High Power, they don't normally offer the kind of accuracy desirable in a .22 centerfire.

The Hornet, in Winchester Model 54 and Savage 23-D bolt-actions, really got interest going for .22 centerfires that would shoot flatter and reach out harder. In 1935, the .220 Swift answered that need with a commercial cartridge that's still at the top end of the velocity scale. The original loading boasted a 48-grain bullet at 4,110 feet per second, and our modern concept of the varmint rifle was born.

The Swift is still around, and with it are later developments such as the .222 and .223 Remington, .224 Weatherby Magnum, and .22-250. Equally good .22 centerfires that have gone by the wayside are the .225 Winchester and .222 Remington Magnum.

Most writers tend to divide the .22 centerfires into three groups: the relatively low-velocity .22 Hornet; the medium-velocity cartridges (3,000 to 3,250 fps or so) typified by the .222 and .223 Remington; and the hot .22-250, .224 Weatherby, and .220 Swift. To this group could be added the ultra-fast .17 Remington.

For the sportsman visiting Africa, all three groups are limited in use. Personally, of all the .22 centerfires I would judge the .22 Hornet as the most useful on an average safari. Relatively quiet, with compact ammo, the Hornet can perform all the functions of the .22 rimfire. It can also perform like a champ on the smaller antelopes and furbearers such as jackal, especially in thornbush country where the shots rarely exceed 100 yards. And it would be a lot of fun to pack around in the hills to pot the occasional dassie or a klipspringer.

Although they're certainly more powerful, I see less potential use for either the .222-.223s or the red-hot centerfires. They make a bit too much noise, and the ammo is a bit too bulky, to allow use for casual plinking and target practice. They're also much too destructive to consider using on edible small game and birds. The Hornet with solid bullets is absolutely the upper limit for such use. The resident hunter who is willing to pick his shots could put these cartridges to good use on even very large antelope, but the visiting sportsman would be handicapping himself unnecessarily.

If I could manage a very light rifle in my kit, I'd take a .22 Magnum or a Hornet and forget the rest. However, this is not to say that the hotter .22s aren't effective on game. I haven't used them in Africa, but I have taken several deer (where it was quite legal) with a .22-250. These cartridges, and the rifles that chamber them, make precise shot placement a joy. With head and neck shots, the outcome is certain. And I've never seen one-shot kills more dramatic and instantaneous than behind-the-shoulder heart-lung shots with a .22-250.

If one is a serious varmint shooter, and if the proposed African hunting menu will include such shooting along with a few species of smaller antelope, there's nothing wrong with packing along a favorite .223 or .22-250.

If such a cartridge is chosen, pay attention to bullet selection. Until just a few years ago, virtually all the centerfire .22 cartridges were loaded with varmint bullets—thin-jacketed bullets designed to expand explosively on impact, virtually disintegrating in small varmints and reducing the potential for ricochet. Such bullets are not designed to penetrate at all; they will be too destructive on the very small antelopes and may fail to penetrate with body shots on game even the size of impala and warthog.

Readers of Africana will recall Ruark's trouble with the .220 Swift in *Horn of the Hunter*. He was undoubtedly using the original 48-grain bullets—very fast and very frangible—and he experienced classic failure to penetrate, caused by premature expansion. The same thing will happen today with the typical varmint bullets. Fortunately, the bulletmakers have recognized this problem, and have responded with heavier bullets, up to 70 grains, with heavier jackets. If I were to take one of the hotter .22 centerfires on safari, I'd use a mixture of these heavy-for-caliber bullets for the mid-sized antelopes and pests, and full-metal-jacket military-type bullets for the tinier antelopes. So loaded, the high-velocity .22 centerfires would indeed serve a purpose, but given a choice I'd opt for a .22 rimfire or a Hornet.

## The 6mms

Three 6mms (.243 bullet diameter) are in common use today, and all three are American developments: the .243 Winchester, 6mm Remington, and .240 Weatherby Magnum. It would be easy to deduce that this bore diameter, so popular in the United States, was strictly an American concept. That's true, but not strictly. The 6mm Lee Navy was introduced as an experimental military cartridge in the Lee straight-pull bolt-action rifle clear back in 1895, and both sporting rifles and ammo were also available for some years. But the cartridge died out, and there was no commercial American 6mm until the advent of the .243 Winchester and the .244 Remington (the original designation of the 6mm Remington) in 1955.

Most of the credit for the 6mm's place as a sporting cartridge must be given to the British and Europeans, who developed about eight 6mm sporting cartridges prior to 1925. The best known of these was the .240 Belted Rimless Nitro-Express, a long-cased cartridge that was loaded to push a 100-grain bullet at 3,000 feet per second. It was a very popular plains-game cartridge, and is still encountered occasionally.

American engineers went to work on a modern, domestic 6mm, certain that the older British round could be brought up to date. Winchester saw the .243 as a dual-purpose cartridge that could perform as an excellent varmint cartridge with light bullets and as a deer and antelope cartridge with heavier bullets. Remington, on the other hand, envisioned the .244 as a long-range varmint cartridge and gave the rifles so chambered a one-in-12-inch rifling twist—great for light bullets but unable to stabilize bullets over 90 grains. Winchester selected a compromise one-in-10-inch twist to stabilize both 80-grain varmint bullets and 100-grain big-game bullets.

Apparently, the American public saw things the same way as Winchester; the .243 was instantly popular, while the .244, in spite of its longer case and slightly greater velocity, darn near faded away. Later, Remington realized its mistake and renamed the cartridge the 6mm Remington—at the same time changing the rifling twist to one-in-nine and adding a 100-grain loading. The .240 Weatherby Magnum came along in 1968. Although

19

offered only in Weatherby Mark V rifles, it's a true short magnum that will fit in any .30-06-length action.

Although the 6mm was viewed as a dual-purpose varmint/deer round, I have a feeling that relatively few 6mm rifles (in any of the three calibers) are often used as varmint rifles. Rather, they're extremely popular with America's deer and pronghorn hunters—and rightfully so. The .243 and 6mm are very similar in performance; the .243 pushes a 100-grain bullet at about 3,070 fps, while the 6mm edges that by about 50 fps in factory loads and as much as 100 fps with good handloads. The .240 Weatherby is much hotter, pushing a 100-grain bullet at nearly 3,400 fps. All three are flat-shooting, mild-recoiling cartridges that are extremely efficient on game up to the size of large deer.

With the incredible size range of African antelope, the 6mms are limited. They aren't kudu cartridges, much less cartridges for the hardy oryx tribe. On the other hand, they're nearly ideal for a tremendous range of game: gazelle, springbok, impala, bushbuck, reedbuck, and the list goes on. A good, accurate .243 would be extremely useful on many African safaris that involve such species—but such safaris also generally include larger game such as kudu, oryx, zebra, wildebeest, hartebeest, sable, and such, so a 6mm could not be the only accurate, flat-shooting rifle chosen.

As to which of the three common 6mms is best, well, it doesn't make much difference. The 6mm Remington is indeed a slightly better cartridge than the .243, and the .240 Weatherby Magnum is clearly the most powerful of all. But all three are accurate and flat-shooting, and no amount of added velocity will turn any 6mm cartridge into an all-purpose plains-game rifle.

The 6mm Remington and .240 Weatherby are essentially American cartridges, while the .243 has achieved universal acceptance—which says nothing about its comparative worth, but *is* a factor in ammo availability. The .243 is one of the most popular sporting cartridges in South Africa, used extensively for hunting the pronghorn-like springbok and also used without reservation on game up to kudu. I will admit I have never taken a .243 to Africa, but I have borrowed one on numerous occasions for impala, warthog, springbok and such. In this country, my own .243s have worked wonders on antelope and deer. And over there, the fast, efficient 100-grain slug has worked just as well.

I have never used the .243 on American game such as black bear and elk, though many hunters do. Nor have I used it in Africa against the largest plains game. With precise shot placement, it would do just fine—but there are much better tools available for the bigger jobs.

## The .25s

Bore designations become extremely confusing because there are no hard and fast rules to govern what the makers call their cartridges. Americans, for example, are very likely to use the bullet diameter to name a cartridge—as is the case with the .257 Roberts and the .308 Winchester.

Failing that, the approximate *groove* diameter is often used. The British have used these systems, but out of what seems sheer perversity they quite frequently use the *land* diameter. So they have often called a 6.5mm cartridge (.264-inch bullet diameter) a .256. That's really misleading, because neither the British nor the Europeans have any history of true ".25-caliber" sporting cartridges. This bore diameter is American, and it goes back to the very beginning of the smokeless era with lever-action cartridges such as the .25-20 and .25-35, and Remington's rimless .25 Remington for their turn-of-the-century semiautos.

In terms of general-purpose hunting cartridges, there are just four .25s, and three of them are real old-timers. The .250-3000, or .250 Savage, was a Charles Newton cartridge introduced by Savage in the Model 99 before World War I. Its original loading, with an 87-grain bullet, was the first commercial cartridge to break the 3,000-fps barrier. The .257 Roberts, based on the necked-down 7x57 case and offering a good deal more powder capacity, came along as a wildcat cartridge in the 1920s and was legitimized as a factory cartridge in 1934. The .25-06 is, as its name indicates, a .30-06 case necked down to take .257-inch bullets. In wildcat form it's been around for decades, but it didn't become a factory cartridge until Remington adopted it in 1969. Hottest of all is the .257 Weatherby Magnum, developed by Roy Weatherby in 1944.

All four are extremely fine hunting cartridges. The .250 Savage and .257 Roberts are relatively mild cartridges, pushing 100-grain bullets at, respectively, about 2,800 and 3,000 fps. The .25-06 adds about 200 fps; the .257 Weatherby another 200 to 250—making it very fast and very flat-shooting, indeed. The .250 Savage lacks the powder capacity to push 117- and 120-grain bullets at useful velocities, but in ascending order the other three can handle the heavier bullets nicely.

I have never been a heavy user of any of the .25s, but it certainly isn't for lack of respect. All four are very fine game getters, and although the bore diameter lost much of its popularity when the modern 6mms came along, the added bullet weight and increased frontal area of the .25s make them extremely efficient game cartridges.

The little .250 Savage fills approximately the same niche as the 6mms, but the other three almost reach into the general-purpose plains-game category. I took a lovely .250 Savage on a Mexican Mauser action to Rhodesia in '79, and had a wonderful time with it. I used it to take a number of impala for the pot, plus warthog, duiker, and such. In that role it was pure joy, but I didn't attempt to take any of the larger antelope with it. The other three cartridges have enough more going for them so they could indeed be used for somewhat larger game.

The .257 Weatherby Magnum was Roy Weatherby's personal favorite, and he used it on game up to Cape buffalo on several African safaris. I don't think I would go that far, but I have used the .257 on enough game to agree that its extreme velocity gives it a lightning-bolt effect on fairly good-sized plains game. Petersen's *Hunting* publisher Ken Elliott (my boss) has taken a .257 to Africa twice now, and reports incredible results on plains game up to the hefty lechwe.

The bottom line? If you have a good, accurate .25 you're comfortable with, don't leave it at home. But, like the 6mms, it should *not* be the only scoped, flat-shooting rifle you have if your game list includes the larger or tougher plains species.

## The 6.5s

The 6.5mm, shooting a bullet of .264-inch diameter, has never been popular in America, despite the fact that a number of very fine European 6.5s have attained tremendous popularity. I will cover some of these in the chapter on metrics, and here we'll address just the American 6.5s. There aren't many. The .256 Newton, really a 6.5, was a fine cartridge on the order of the .270 Winchester. Although loaded commercially, it never really made the grade—and there wasn't another 6.5 until Winchester introduced the .264 Winchester Magnum in 1958. A short magnum able to function through .30-06-length actions, the .264 was a very hot number. It arrived in—and to some extent heralded—the magnum mania that extended through the 1960s, and it achieved almost instantaneous popularity.

The original factory specifications suggested a 100-grain bullet at 3,700 feet per second and a 140-grain bullet at 3,200. Velocity was enhanced by the 26-inch barreled Model 70 "Westerner"—the rifle for which the cartridge was introduced—but those original figures were somewhat inflated. Even so, with the 140-grain bullet the .264 was and is extremely flat-shooting and tremendously effective. Shortly after its introduction, several writers took the new cartridge to Africa and wrung it out on a variety of species—and wrote glowingly of it. (And the reports of .264 performance in the Western United States and Canada were equally impressive.)

I'm not surprised. I got my first .264 in 1965, and I believed it to be a death ray. Never mind that the 24-inch barrel on my rifle never approached the velocities I thought I was getting in those innocent pre-chronograph days! I really believed in that .264, and it performed magnificently on a wide variety of North American game. Even though today's factory ballistics have been adjusted to reflect more accurate figures, the .264, in ascending caliber progression, would be the first American cartridge I would consider as an all-round rifle for African plains game. Or, to put it another way, the lightest rifle I would choose to handle *all* the nondangerous species.

I have had a couple more .264s since I had that 24-inch-barreled Remington, and these have been original Winchesters with 26-inch tubes. I worked up a load with a 129-grain Hornady spire point that yielded more than 3,300 feet per second (over a chronograph!), and ballistics like that do indeed make the .264 one of the very best cartridges for wide-open country. I don't have one right now, but to tell the truth I'd like to have one for country such as the Kalahari, the East African short-grass plains, or Ethiopia's Danakil. Optimally I'd like a bit more caliber and a bit more bullet weight for game such as zebra, sable, and gemsbok—and certainly for eland—but the .264 will do the job.

It had a short blaze of glory, and then the introduction of Remington's 7mm magnum blew it out of the limelight. The 7mm is indeed a more effective all-round cartridge, but with careful selection of loads and that longer barrel that the .264 needs, it remains one of the finest long-range cartridges for open-country hunting.

The other domestic 6.5 is hardly worth mentioning. The 6.5mm Remington Magnum was an ultra-short cartridge, able to work through .308/.243-length actions. Introduced in Remington's short, light Model 600 carbine, it was and is a decent cartridge, propelling a 120-grain bullet at about 3,200 feet per second. It just plain didn't catch anyone's eye, and although ammunition is still loaded, it must be regarded as one of the great losers in recent gunmaking history.

Still, as the Europeans have long known, the high sectional density of the 6.5mm bullet has tremendous advantages. I wouldn't hesitate to take a .264 to Africa as the light rifle. The next rifle I have built just might be in that caliber.

## The .270s

The .270—bullet diameter .277—is another uniquely American development. There are just two cartridges that use this bullet—the .270 Winchester and .270 Weatherby Magnum.

The .270 Winchester was, as everyone knows, one of Jack O'Connor's favorites. To some extent, he created its popularity—and to some extent, it created his. Jack was undoubtedly the finest gunwriter America ever produced in terms of literary skill, and he was also one of the most experienced hunters in the outdoor-writing field. He didn't need a gimmick, so I'm not being derogatory when I say the .270 was his gimmick. He liked it, to be sure—but he privately admitted that the .30-06 was more versatile. But lots of folks, including the great gunwriters of O'Connor's youth, were .30-06 fans. So Jack hitched himself to the .270's star—and it hitched itself to him. Proof of this is in the fact that the .270's popularity has dropped considerably in the dozen years or so since Jack passed away. All that aside, the .270 Winchester is a magnificent cartridge. Introduced by Winchester in 1925, it offers a 130-grain bullet at about 3,060 fps and a 150-grain bullet at about 2,850 fps. Both are extremely flat-shooting and extremely effective. O'Connor preferred the lighter bullet; although I'm not one to dispute the master, I personally prefer the 150-grain bullet.

The .270 is very much an American cartridge, one that few hands other than American have touched. Even so, it has been used extensively on African game from one end of the continent to another. O'Connor himself used it as his light rifle on numerous safaris, and it worked for him on game up to greater kudu and eland just as well as it worked in North America on game up to elk and moose.

My own good friend, professional hunter Willem van Dyk, has a battered .270 pre-'64 Model 70 given to him by a client many years ago. For non-dangerous game, that .270 is his rifle, period—and he has almost childlike faith in its ability to drop whatever he shoots at. In his hands, such faith is justified. A number of other American .270s have found their way to Africa—enough that this efficient, light-kicking cartridge is highly regarded by many African professionals.

I have had several .270s, and I've shot a lot of game with them, but I've never taken one to Africa. With all deference to Jack O'Connor, as good as the cartridge is it just isn't one of my favorites. If it were, and I had a rifle so chambered that I shot well, I wouldn't hesitate to use it. It is not, of course, a dangerous-game rifle. O'Connor shot grizzlies with it, and I know a couple of Americans who have shot lions with it—but it isn't a lion rifle. Nor is it optimum for zebra, eland, sable, roan, and oryx—though it would do the job if a larger rifle weren't available. Along with the .264, it meets what I consider a minimum standard for a general-purpose African light rifle.

Its close cousin, the .270 Weatherby Magnum, is everything the .270 Winchester is plus a bit more. It adds about 300 feet per second, bullet for bullet—making it extremely flat-shooting and quite deadly. The .270 Weatherby Magnum is largely an unsung cartridge, but to my mind it's one of Roy Weatherby's best.

As can be seen, cartridges in the .22-to-.270 class are mostly extremely specialized and not overly versatile in the African scheme of things. They have their uses, to be sure, and will serve for a greater range of game than I have indicated. But the visiting sportsman wants the best representatives he can find of a given species. His time is not unlimited, and he cannot always pick or predict the shot he gets. He simply must not be undergunned, which means he will often be a bit overgunned—if he's smart! Later in this book we'll look at how these very light rifles could be combined with other calibers to make an effective part of a battery, but now let's take a step up in both caliber and versatility to the 7mms.

# Chapter 2

# The Versatile 7mms

We weren't hunting kudu. In fact, we weren't hunting anything at all; high noon was approaching, and we were simply checking a leopard bait in the heat of the day. But the greater kudu is a showstopper of an animal. With his lovely white-striped gray hide, white nose chevron, and salt-and-pepper neck ruff, you'll stop to look at him under any circumstances. And if his ivory-tipped, spiraling horns are big enough, you'll be tempted to forego whatever else you're planning so you can possess those wonderful spirals.

This kudu was big enough, and he wasn't in southern Africa, where kudu are exceedingly common in many areas. He was in the hills of Masailand, where professional hunters prize him above all else and where an entire season can pass without the sighting of a good bull. He was in the company of a much younger bull, and together they flashed across a clearing. We saw the youngster first, and he drew our attention, as a greater kudu always will. Then we saw his traveling companion. This one took our breath away, and then was gone—and I knew I'd not see his like again on this trip. I followed up quickly, and the miracle continued. Both bulls had stopped over a low rise, just on the edge of the donga's thick thornbush. They paused for an instant only, for one backward look to see if they were followed.

At 60 yards my scope found the shoulder of the big bull. I could see the muscles tense for the one leap to safety, see the beginning of movement just as the rifle went off. The bull had hesitated less than a second too long; the huge antelope crumpled on the spot and never moved.

Although not so tough, pound for pound, as smaller antelope such as sable and oryx, the kudu is a large animal. A very big bull may weigh as much as 600 pounds. In other words, it's quite similar to the American elk in size. In some parts of the kudu's range, such as the northern Transvaal, northern Namibia, and much of Zimbabwe, the species is exceedingly common. Elsewhere, in Kenya, Tanzania, and Ethiopia, a good bull is a most rare prize. His beauty and his cover-loving craftiness are such that he is never taken lightly. Over the years, I have taken most of my kudu with a .375 H&H or similar cartridge, but this Tanzanian kudu—folded in his tracks—was taken with a little .284-caliber bullet weighing only 162 grains.

The rifle is a lovely custom bolt-action by Tucson gunmaker David Miller, and it's easily the nicest rifle I've ever owned. It's chambered for the 7mm Remington Magnum, one of America's most popular hunting cartridges. The rifle could well have been chambered for any of nearly 20 American, British, or European factory rounds, current or obsolete, using

25

the .284-inch bullet, and chances are the results would have been exactly the same: a well-placed, well-performing bullet and a very dead kudu.

It's a metric world today, and America is one of the very few countries still clinging to the old English system of weights and measurements. In the shooting world, we've not only clung to it but we thumb our noses at the rest of the world. We measure our powder and bullets by the relatively complex system of grains and pounds; the rest of the world uses grams. We use caliber designations in hundredths or thousandths of an inch, not millimeters—and rare is the bore diameter that's been able to overcome this bias. The 6.5s, ever so popular in Europe, have never done well in America, nor has the 8mm (.323-inch), Europe's equivalent of our .30-caliber. But the 7mm has broken all the rules—and is so entrenched in America and has so many cartridges and so many component bullets that it becomes hard to remember it's not really a domestic caliber.

The cartridge that started the 7mm on its way is still with us—and it's still wonderful. It is, obviously, the 7x57, also called 7mm Mauser, one of the first cartridges designed exclusively for use with the brand-new smokeless propellants back in 1892. The original loading used a very long 173-grain roundnosed bullet at a velocity of about 2,300 feet per second—not very impressive by today's standards, but red-hot in comparison to the blackpowder cartridges it replaced.

Americans got their first taste of the 7mm Mauser in Cuba in 1898. The battle of San Juan Hill is remembered for the charge of Roosevelt's Rough Riders (who were afoot in the battle)—and we tend to forget that the disastrously outnumbered Spanish defenders, using their 7mm Mausers, inflicted enormous casualties on the attacking Americans before the hill was taken. The British were introduced to the high-velocity Mauser at about the same time, during the Boer War. A whole generation of Englishmen learned healthy respect for the little 7mm, especially in the hands of skilled marksmen like the Boer hunters.

The cartridge was widely used in America, not only in surplus Mausers but in the unlikely Remington rolling-block single-shot, as well as factory and custom bolt-actions of many types. It had its strong supporters, including the likes of Jack O'Connor—who used it both before *and* after the introduction of "his" .270. But it would be stretching a point to say that the 7x57 achieved tremendous popularity in the States.

It had much more success in the far-flung British Empire. As early as 1907, John Rigby adopted it, calling it the .275 Rigby after the English fashion of naming cartridges by land rather than groove or bullet diameter. Rigby loaded it with a 140-grain spitzer softpoint at fully 2,800 feet per second. In this guise, the cartridge became a British standard for light to medium game. It was one of Bell's favorites for elephant—but not with the 140-grain pill. He used the 173-grain round nose in Kynoch's superb steel-jacketed-solid form. That long, heavy bullet at moderate velocity would penetrate an elephant's skull and find the brain from any angle—as it would today, of course. But the days are long gone when elephant stood in the open and allowed the kind of precision shooting that was Bell's strong suit.

The 7mm bullet diameter has a great deal going for it. Bullets of this diameter tend to have excellent sectional density—the relation of the bullet's weight to its cross-section—without tremendous weight. Combined with an aerodynamic design, this means they hold their velocity extremely well and thus tend to have flat trajectories. Whether spitzer or roundnose, that sectional density gives excellent straight-line penetration in game.

The smokeless era opened up a whole new world of velocity, and if fast was good, faster must be better. The early years of the century saw the British develop some half-dozen large-cased 7mm cartridges, all of which approach the performance of today's 7mm magnums. These include the .275 Belted Rimless Magnum Nitro-Express and its .275 Flanged Magnum counterpart, both Holland & Holland developments; the .280 Jeffery; and, of course, the .280 Ross developed for the Canadian straight-pull Ross rifle. The Ross pushed a 140-grain bullet at 2,900 fps; the Jeffery went a step further and was listed at 3,000 fps for the same bullet weight.

Early hunters were just as beguiled by high velocity as Americans were during the magnum mania of the late 1950s and 1960s. They found that the explosive little bullets at such unheard-of velocities dropped game like lightning, and the flat trajectory was a whole new world. Unfortunately, there were two problems.

First, bullet development hadn't yet caught up with cartridge development. A bullet's expansion properties at impact velocities of 2,200 to 2,400 feet per second differ enormously from its expansion at 2,600 to 2,800 fps. Bulletmakers still have trouble with this today, but at the turn of the century our concept of controlled expansion was unknown. In other words, bullet blow-up was relatively assured at closer ranges, especially if heavy bones were struck.

The other problem was that too much reliance was put on the lightning-bolt effect of all this new velocity—and the new, ultra-velocity cartridges were employed against animals that were beyond their capabilities. One of the early casualties was George Grey, a universally liked and highly respected soldier and gentleman. He was galloping for lion on the Athi Plain in Kenya Colony—a very dangerous pastime. Typically, a lion would be "tally-hoed" on horseback until it turned to charge, whereupon the rider would dismount to shoot. Grey used a .280 Ross, and died a lingering death from infection when he failed to stop the charge. By some accounts, he shot five times, and by all accounts the bullets broke up on the outside and failed to penetrate.

Hunters today would hardly consider a fast-moving 7mm the ideal choice to stop a charging lion—or a charging anything else. Obviously, that isn't the caliber's purpose, let alone strong suit. Karamojo Bell, who took many of his 1,013 elephant with the 7x57, would probably agree. If he were here today, he might or might not concede that he hunted unsophisticated, unalarmed animals. But I trust he would agree that the methodic, precise marksmanship he practiced with his 7mm is a far cry from having to stop a charge at close quarters.

A few horror stories similar to that of George Grey prevented the true high-velocity 7mms from achieving great popularity for nearly 50 years, but the 7x57 kept rolling along—and it remains a marvelously efficient killer on all but the largest of plains game, with the bonus of a relatively soft report and low recoil even in a very light rifle.

Today, excluding innumerable wildcats and a few custom rifles built for old-timers like the .275 H&H, there are nine commercial 7mm rifle cartridges. These are the 7x57, 7x64 Brenneke, 7x30 Waters, 7mm-08 Remington, .284 Winchester, .280 Remington, 7x61 Sharpe & Hart, 7mm Remington Magnum, and 7mm Weatherby Magnum. The total is raised to 11 if you add the rimmed versions of the 7x57 and 7x64 that are loaded in Europe. This profusion of .284 cartridges exceeds even America's darling .30 caliber.

Of these, it's interesting to note that only the two European numbers go back a long way—the 7x57 clear to the beginning and the excellent 7x64 to 1917. All of the early "magnum"-velocity 7mms fell by the wayside. Interesting, too, is the fact that, with the lone exception of the 7x30 Waters, developed for the Model 94 Winchester lever-action by necking the .30-30 down to .284, *all* of these 7mms are more than just acceptable for a tremendous variety of African hunting.

Although it's easy to oversimplify, there are basically three power levels among the 7mm rifle cartridges, excluding the somewhat anemic 7x30 Waters—which is further handicapped by the necessity to shoot flat-pointed bullets in the tubular-magazine rifles for which it was designed.

The first level is that of the good old 7x57 and the relatively new 7mm-08 Remington. The 7mm-08 factory load uses a 140-grain bullet at 2,860 feet per second—almost the velocity that was said to have gotten George Grey killed! Current factory loads are listed with that bullet weight for the 7x57 at 2,660 fps—and that makes the 7mm-08 look pretty good. The 7mm-08 is, indeed, a fine cartridge. It's based on the short .308 Winchester (or .243) case, so it can be used in a true short bolt-action, and in factory loads it has the advantage of being a recent development and therefore loaded to modern pressure levels.

The 7x57, on the other hand, is a very old cartridge—and the factories exercise extreme caution in producing such loads since they may be used in very old rifles. However, the 7x57 can be loaded to performance well beyond today's factory ballistics. You'll remember that the .275 Rigby—dimensionally identical to the 7x57—used a 140-grain bullet at 2,800 fps, and I've gone well beyond that with carefully-worked-up-to handloads in a modern action. The 7x57 offers more case capacity than the 7mm-08, and, all other things being equal, it must be—and is—capable of more velocity. But not in domestic factory loads. Essentially, then, unless you handload and thus can get the utmost in performance out of your 7x57, the 7mm-08 would be the best choice for a low-recoiling, extremely efficient .284-caliber rifle.

The 7mm-08, too, can benefit from judicious handloading, and of course it has available the full spectrum of 7mm bullets. But, as we shall see when we look at the .308 versus the .30-06, it lacks the case capacity to be efficient with bullets weighing over 150 grains. Beyond that point, achievable velocity is greatly reduced. Thus the 7x57 is the logical choice for the handloader—unless one is building an ultralight rifle and simply must use a short action.

The shooter who uses only factory loads might look at the factory ballistics tables for the two cartridges and immediately decide in favor of the 7mm-08—but that would be a hasty decision. The big advantage of the 7x57 is that factory loads come in a much greater range of bullet weights and styles. If you include European loads—most of which are available in the U.S.—choices run from 116 to 177 grains. The latter heavy-bullet load, from Dynamit Nobel, has an ultra-modern velocity of 2560 fps. The 7mm-08 is currently available only with the 140-grain Remington Core-Lokt bullet. That's a good bullet and a good load, but most of us would prefer a bit more bullet weight for a safari rifle that might be used on wide variety of game.

The next power level is occupied by the .284 Winchester, .280 Remington, and 7x64 Brenneke. The .284 is a marvelous cartridge, developed by Winchester for use in their long-discontinued Model 88 lever-action. It has a rebated rim and a very fat case with tremendous powder capacity in relation to its length. With handloaded 140- to 150-grain bullets, it will do everything the .280 will do—and that means a good 100 to 150 feet per second more than the 7mm-08.

Its problem is twofold. First, in the lever-actions for which it was designed, pressures must be kept moderate to ensure extraction. Second, such rifles limit the overall length, so heavier bullets begin to intrude into the powder space too deeply. In a custom-chambered bolt-action with a long throat, the .284 can actually equal one of the belted 7mms—but not in the lever-actions for which it was designed. On the other hand, the lever-actions so chambered are versatile, fast, and a pleasure to shoot. Custom .284 bolt-actions seem to be in vogue, but I can't see any reason for one. However, I'd love to get my hands on an original Model 88 Winchester in this caliber!

The .280 was introduced by Remington in the late 1950s, and it was very slow to catch on. In 1979 it was renamed the 7mm Express Remington and reintroduced—and that proved to be a real disaster when 7mm Express ammo was fired in several 7mm Remington Magnum rifles. Now it's again known as the .280, and it seems—finally—to be getting the recognition it deserves. Essentially the .30-06 case necked down to .284 with the shoulder moved slightly forward, it's also nearly identical to (though *not* interchangeable with) the popular European 7x64 Brenneke. It offers very high velocity with the lighter bullets, and has the case capacity to push bullets up to 175 grains very respectably. Factory loads are somewhat limited, but that's changing. Federal now offers a Premium load with a 150-grain Nosler bullet, and it's a dandy. With my own .280 I prefer to load a spitzer 160-grain—and I'm still waiting for a factory load along those lines. With the .280 now gaining in popularity, I think that's just around the corner.

There are three belted 7mm cartridges, but one of them, the 7x61 Sharpe & Hart, should be considered a dead issue. It was developed in the U.S. and was chambered in the Danish Schultz & Larsen rifle in the 1950's; dimensionally and ballistically it's very similar to the old .275 H&H. It achieved some following, but was blown completely off the market when Remington introduced the 7mm Remington Magnum in 1962.

The other major American manufacturers quickly adopted the 7mm Remington Magnum, as did the public—before long it was a world-standard hunting cartridge. As we have seen, it was far from a new idea. Cartridges of its performance level go back to the turn of the century, and in the post-World War II years there was a proliferation of high-performance 7mm wildcats. The late Warren Page, Shooting Editor of *Field & Stream*, was a tremendous advocate of the fast 7mm. Page, it's worth noting, was more than a passable African hand with a tremendous breadth of experience there. To give proper credit, it should be mentioned that to date he is the *only* gunwriter who could lay claim to having taken all of Africa's spiral-horned antelope.

Remington's "Big Seven" offered an inexpensive, over-the-counter, high-performance 7mm, and immediately proved there was a market for it. But it didn't exactly fill a vacuum in the ranks of .284-inch cartridges. The 7mm Weatherby Magnum had been introduced in 1944 and was (and is) an important part of the Weatherby line. Only slightly longer than the Remington, the Weatherby is also a short magnum with the characteristic double-radiused shoulder and a slightly greater case capacity than the Remington.

The 7mm Weatherby is a fine cartridge, and was quite popular until Remington's entry appeared. Like the old British proprietary cartridges, the 7mm Weatherby's only drawback is that rifles and ammo have been available only from the maker. The 7mm Weatherby will edge the Remington by as much as 200 feet per second with handloads, and that's significant. Factory loads are currently limited to 139-grain and 154-grain, while the Remington is available in a wide range of bullet weights from 125 to 175 grains.

The magnum 7mms aren't any better suited for stopping charging lions than they were in George Grey's day, although the bullets are inestimably better. Today the bullets will hold together at the high velocities and give outstanding penetration as well as the flat-shooting capabilities that the velocity offers. They will deliver well in excess of 3,000 foot-pounds of energy, which is impressive—but frontal area and bullet weight are needed when it's time to stop a charge, and that's no different now than it was in George Grey's day.

Factory loads for the 7mm Remington Magnum list a 175-grain bullet at 2,860 feet per second. That's clearly a respectable velocity, and the long, heavy-for-caliber 175-grain bullet both holds its velocity well and penetrates extremely well on game. Another good choice is Federal's 160-grain Premium load with Nosler Partition bullets. Loaded to 2,950 feet per second, it shoots even flatter than the 175-grain load, and offers the excellent performance of the Nosler bullet.

The Weatherby round is factory-loaded with the 139-grain and 154-grain Hornady spire points, excellent bullets loaded to 3,300 and 3,160 feet per second, respectively. That 154-grain load is a real screamer, but the Weatherby could benefit significantly from the use of a heavier bullet.

Where do the 7mms fit in for African hunting? Well, *almost* anywhere. With apologies to Bell, the 7mms are *not* elephant cartridges, nor are they suited for buffalo, rhino, or lion. I would also prefer not to tackle the largest of the plains game, most specifically eland, with any 7mm cartridge. With proper bullets and proper shot placement, of course, the various 7mms could all handle *all* of these animals—but if the slightest thing goes wrong, no 7mm cartridge can reliably clean up the mess.

With those exceptions, the 7mms are adequate for the full range of African plains game—given, again, proper bullet selection and careful shot placement. In thornbush country, where shots rarely exceed 150 yards, a light 7x57 (or 7mm-08) loaded with 150- or 154-grain bullets would provide excellent service on most plains game. I have never taken a 7x57 to Africa, but I have used one quite a bit in North America with excellent results, and I took one to New Zealand some time back. On that shoot I was using some Austrian Hirtenberger factory ammo, the 154-grain "ABC" bullet at a very modest 2,560 feet per second. Everything I shot went down with one shot, usually as if pole-axed—and that included a big red stag, about the same size as a kudu, and a couple of very large wild hogs.

This is typical of 7x57 performance; at its modest velocity, bullets tend to perform with consistent excellence, penetrating well and doing the job. The trajectory is plenty flat enough for most shooting, but if the country to be hunted is open or mountainous, one of the faster 7mms might be a better choice.

Personally, I'm not sure there is a significant difference between the .280 Remington/7x64 and the belted 7mms. Careful handloading can wring a very slight velocity edge out of the Remington magnum, and a bit bigger edge from the Weatherby—but hardly a significant one. Hunters who shoot factory ammo would probably be best served by the 7mm Remington Magnum, since it offers far and away the widest selection of loads.

Handloaders, on the other hand, might want to look at a current loading manual. I'm a big fan of 160- to 165-grain bullets in both the .280 and the 7mm Remington—and with good handloads, the .280 won't be too far behind. The Weatherby, of course, can be handloaded to offer a bit more. Velocities being nearly equal, the .280 offers additional magazine capacity and can generally be built into a lighter rifle than the 7mm magnum. And since it burns a good deal less powder to achieve its velocity, recoil and muzzle blast are somewhat less.

I'm a fairly recent fan of the .280, and to date my use of it has been limited to North American game. The 7mm Remington Magnum and I go back a good deal farther. Today I may not rate it as much better than the .280, at least with my loads, but it is a versatile, hard-hitting cartridge that I've used quite a lot. My favorite—and most accurate—load in three different 7mm Remington Magnum rifles has been a heavy charge of Hodgdon H870 with Nosler's 162-grain Solid Base Boattail bullet. My load yields about 3,000 feet per second (which can't quite be done in a .280), making it very flat-shooting indeed.

That's the load I used on the greater kudu I mentioned at the start of this chapter. Had I intended to shoot a greater kudu with a 7mm magnum, I would have chosen a 175-grain bullet—quite probably a Core-Lokt bullet in Remington's factory load. The reason I chose the lighter bullet, aside from the fact that I've had very good luck with it, is because we had been hunting gazelles and such on the wide-open Simanjaro Plains of southern Masailand, and lesser kudu and mountain reedbuck in the burned-off hills above. I needed a cartridge that would give me all the reach I could get—and the 7mm Remington Magnum had done that work for me extremely well. When the need arose to take a much larger animal, it did that equally well.

When choosing among the various 7mms, consider the country to be hunted as well as the game. In effect on game, the only real difference in the big-cased cartridges is that they'll reach out just a bit farther. Choose a bullet weight that will maximize the performance of the cartridge you choose. I like bullets from 139 to 154 grains in the 7x57; from 150 to 165 in the .280; and from 160 to 175 in the magnums. Any of the 7mm cartridges we've discussed would make a fine choice for an all-purpose African rifle, the rifle that will be carried the most and shot the most. None of them is suitable for lion and the thick-skinned game, but those aren't jobs one should ask the 7mm to perform. The jobs you *should* ask it to perform— light, medium, and even heavy plains game at short, medium, or long range—it will handle perfectly. Just so long as you do your part and put that little .284-inch pill in the right place.

# Chapter 3

# The All-American .30 Caliber

As with so many Americans of the past few generations, one of my first centerfire rifles was a 1903 Springfield, caliber .30-06. And like so many millions of Americans, I've found the caliber so useful that one of my favorite hunting rifles remains the .30-06—a cartridge I've hunted with in bolt-actions, single-shots, slide-actions, semiautos, and even doubles. Theodore Roosevelt's "sporterized" Springfield was one of the first .30-06 rifles to see use in Africa, and ever since then it has remained a standard choice as a light or all-purpose safari rifle. As we have seen, it isn't the only choice—but after 80-odd years it's a choice that's hard to argue with.

The .30-06 isn't the only good .30-caliber cartridge, nor was it the first or last to capture the hearts of American hunters. It may not even be the best of its kind, but it certainly is the most common throughout the world. I promised myself I wouldn't pick favorites in this book, but it's difficult not to pick one in the .30-06. Like Hemingway, Ruark, and Roosevelt—perhaps because of them—I chose the .30-06 for my light rifle on my first safari to Kenya. On game ranging from the tiny dik dik to the tough zebra, it accounted for something like 15 animals with 15 shots, quite possibly the best run of shooting I've ever had in Africa. I haven't always taken a .30-06 on safari, but one or another such rifle has accompanied me on several trips—and it's a cartridge that has never let me down. Most fans of the .30-06—and there are millions of them—would say the same thing.

Americans' love affair with the .30 caliber didn't start with the .30-06. That credit must go to its predecessor, the .30-40 Krag. Adopted as the U.S. military cartridge in 1892, chambered in the Norwegian-designed Krag-Jorgensen rifle, the .30-40 was America's first smokeless-powder military cartridge. Firing a long 220-grain round-nosed bullet at 2,200 feet per second, it seemed a real flat shooter compared to the .45-70 blackpowder cartridge it replaced.

The .30-40 was quickly chambered in the Winchester high-wall single-shot, and became a popular chambering for the same firm's Model 1895 lever-action. A later factory loading of a 180-grain bullet at about 2,470 fps flattened the trajectory significantly. The .30-40 was an extremely popular hunting cartridge in North America, and quite a number of rifles so chambered were carried to Africa by early American adventurers. Its long, heavy bullet traveling at moderate velocity was indeed effective, and I suspect that those who used it never found it wanting on mid-sized African game. An unusually short duration as the American service cartridge (1892-1903) precluded its long-term popularity—that plus the fact that it was replaced by the .30-06, a better cartridge in virtually all respects.

It did, however, have a contemporary rival that fared a bit better. Although not a true .30 caliber, the .303 British—using a bullet with a .311-inch diameter—was ballistically almost identical to the .30-40. Amazingly, the .303 started life in 1887 as a blackpowder cartridge, using a compressed load that propelled a 215-grain bullet at 1,850 fps. In 1892, the same year America adopted the Krag, the .303 was converted to a smokeless load. The velocity was boosted to just under 2,000 feet per second, not too flashy but miles ahead of the blackpowder competition.

At the start of World War I, the British changed to a spitzer 174-grain bullet at 2,440 fps—a cartridge that remained the Empire's standard for more than 40 years. The old Short Magazine Lee Enfield and its predecessor, the Lee-Metford, chambered in .303, became a fixture throughout the British Empire. This was the rifle carried by Cecil Rhodes's pioneer column into the Rhodesias, and the rifle the British used in the Boer War. It was chambered in a number of sporting rifles; and since it's a rimmed cartridge, many double rifles and single-shots have been built around it. Selous used the .303 extensively, as did Bell. With the heavier bullet, it offered adequate penetration on elephant, but it was no more ideally suited for such game than was the 7x57mm.

To this day, battered old SMLEs may be encountered throughout Africa, and to this day they undoubtedly account for a tremendous variety of game. But the .303 was never a flat-shooting cartridge, and in spite of its long-lived popularity it is one of the least useful of the .30 calibers. In a vintage double, or even a Lee-Metford, those with a taste for nostalgia would find it satisfactory as a medium-range, medium-game rifle. But it's really a part of history today.

A number of other American .30-caliber cartridges were developed over the years, primarily for use in lever-actions and early pumps and semiautos. Some of these have died away while others remain incredibly popular. A partial list would include the .30-30, .30 Remington, .303 Savage, .307 Winchester, and .300 Savage. The .300 Savage is the most powerful of these, nearly duplicating the ballistics of the .303 British. All of these moderate-velocity .30 calibers are outstanding short-range deer cartridges, and as such would be well-suited for hunting mid-sized African plains game in brushy or forested country.

I have actually seen a number of Winchester Model 94 .30-30s in use in Africa—and they do just as well over there as in America's whitetail woods. They are not, however, a sensible choice for the safari hunter who will encounter a wide range of plains game at varying ranges under varying conditions.

The cartridge that replaced the .30-40 Krag is a whole different story. Originally introduced in 1903 with a 220-grain bullet at 2,300 feet per second, the case was shortened slightly in 1906 and the loading changed to a 150-grain spitzer at the unheard of velocity of 2,700 feet per second. The .30-06 is a rimless cartridge originally designed for a Mauser-type action, and over the years its loadings have changed markedly—usually for the better.

Current factory loadings for the .30-06 run from 110- to 220-grain bullets. The most interesting loadings for the hunter are a 150-grain bullet at 2,910 fps; a 165-grainer at 2,800; the standby 180-grain load at 2,700; a Federal 200-grain bullet at 2,550; and the long, heavy 220-grain roundnose at 2,410 fps. Handloaders can beat these velocities by a little bit, but not much. They can also select from an incredible range of outstanding bullets in all of these weights, plus specialized slugs like Barnes's 225-grain spitzer and 250-grain roundnose. The truth is, though, that factory .30-06 ammunition is hard to beat in all respects. The cartridge has remained popular for so long that tremendous amounts of development have gone into today's .30-06 ammunition. And, of great importance, the majority of .30-caliber bullets available today have been developed to perform at .30-06 velocities—and most of them perform well.

The 165-grain bullet is a relatively new development in the .30-caliber field, and it just may be the best choice for open-country work on mid-sized game. Its greater sectional density, when compared to the more common 150-grain bullet, allows it to hold its velocity better, and of course its greater weight and length give it better penetration. However, for African hunting where one never knows what one might encounter next, the 180-grain bullet is probably the best choice for all-round plains-game hunting. In spitzer design, it shoots plenty flat enough for almost all purposes, and can be relied upon for all African game up to kudu, zebra, and such.

The 200-grain bullet won't shoot quite as flat, but gives tremendous penetration and is devastating on game. In a spitzer design, it's amazing just how flat it will shoot—but it isn't the best choice for open country. The heavier bullets in the .30-06 are pretty much special-purpose loads, at their best for hunting in close cover. As good as it is, the .30-06 case simply lacks the powder capacity to push bullets heavier than 200 grains at meaningful velocities. However, the 220-grain, in both solid and softnose form, has been the standby for African hunters who wished to use the cartridge on game larger than it was really intended for.

On his 1935 safari, Hemingway had excellent success on lion, buffalo, and rhino with 220-grain bullets from the .30-06. It would give the same results today; in terms of penetration, there's just no stopping that long 220-grain bullet at moderate velocity. Personally, I have shot nothing larger than zebra, wildebeest, and kudu with the .30-06. But if I happened to have that rifle in my hands, and if it was loaded with a heavy bullet, I wouldn't hesitate to tackle *undisturbed* Cape buffalo with the .30-06. I must add that I'd sure want a bigger rifle handy to tidy up the mess in case I screwed up.

The late George Parker—war hero, border patrolman, gunfighter, and one of the unsung greats in the hunting world—was a .30-06 fan. In those pre-chronograph days he preferred an Improved version with the case blown out. Today we know that most Improved versions of the .30-06 do, indeed, burn more powder, but actually achieve almost no velocity edge. Parker used his '06 exclusively on a 1952 Angolan safari, where the bag included not only large plains species such as roan, kudu, and giant sable, but also hippo and the mean little dwarf forest buffalo.

David Miller, the renowned Tucson gunmaker, uses a .30-06 as his personal rifle, and it has accompanied him around the world. David does not use it for dangerous game, but he did use it to take his superb mountain nyala in Ethiopia's high country. The mountain nyala is not only one of Africa's largest antelope, but one of the few customarily taken at very long range in the heather-covered mountains. Miller didn't find his .30-06 lacking any more than its millions of other fans have.

Fed a steady diet of 180-grain spitzers of good construction, the .30-06 will do anything on safari you ask of it short of handling the dangerous game. With a handful of heavier bullets, both solid and soft, "just in case," it remains what it was when Roosevelt used it in 1909—an ideal plains-game rifle.

Its little brother, the much more recent .308 Winchester, was developed as a military cartridge in the years following World War II. The .308 has a shorter case, better suited for use in semi- and fully automatic military rifles. It has quickly caught on as a sporting cartridge, being equally suited for use in lever-actions such as Browning's BLR and the Savage 99, and of course in short-throw bolt-actions.

Up to a point, everything I've said about the .30-06 applies to the .308 Winchester. Because of its reduced case capacity, with bullets up to 180 grains it lags about 100 feet per second behind the .30-06—hardly a significant difference. With heavier bullets, though, case capacity starts to tell and the gap widens considerably.

I do have a prejudice in favor of the .30-06, but the .308 is a fine cartridge. In a bolt-action, it can be built a few ounces lighter on a shorter action—but I've never seen any reason for owning a bolt-action .308 when a .30-06 gives so much more versatility with heavier bullets. There are, however, lots of good reasons for owning and using a slick lever-action .308 like the Browning, Savage, or the defunct Model 88 Winchester. I used a Savage 99 .308 in South Africa a few years ago; such a rifle is just as suitable on African plains game at moderate range as it is in America's deer country.

## The Magnum .30s

Belted, high-performance .30-caliber cartridges are hardly new. The first of this type was the .300 Holland & Holland Magnum, originally called the "Super .30" when it was introduced in 1925. However, it's worth noting that this Holland & Holland development wasn't the first high-performance .30 caliber. Those honors go to the .30 Newton, an unbelted cartridge designed by Charles Newton around 1913. Western loaded factory ammo for it, but only Newton offered rifles so chambered. It wasn't quite as hot as the .300 H&H, but it did offer significant improvement over .30-06 velocities with all bullet weights.

Holland's Super .30 enjoyed much more success, and retains a significant following to this day. It caught on rather slowly—until the Wimbledon 1,000-yard match was won with it in 1935. Two years later, the then-new Model 70 Winchester was chambered for it, and it quickly gathered a large following.

Modern factory loads for the .300 H&H offer fairly modest improvements over the .30-06—3,130 fps with the 150-grain bullet; 2,880 with the 180; and 2,580 with the 220. Handloaders can raise these velocities considerably. If you don't handload, there's little reason to choose a .300 H&H, and lots of reason not to. Few rifles are so chambered today, and ammunition can be damned hard to find. On the other hand, the long, tapered case makes for very smooth feeding—and it remains an extremely efficient, flat-shooting cartridge.

The .308 Norma Magnum, introduced in 1960, was a fine cartridge that really never had a fighting chance. Extremely similar to the .30-.338 wildcat so popular among 1,000-yard benchresters, it's an extremely accurate cartridge whose only factory load propels a 180-grain bullet at a fast, effective 3,020 fps. Unfortunately, it came out just behind the commonly chambered .300 Winchester Magnum, and was made available in very few rifles. Although still a fine cartridge, the .308 Norma is something of an oddity today.

The 1958-vintage .300 Winchester Magnum is a whole different story. Unlike the 2.85-inch .300 H&H, the .300 Winchester is a short magnum with a case length of 2.62 inches, meaning it will function in .30-06-length actions. With a 150-grain loading at 3,290 fps, 180 grains at 2,960, 200 grains at 2,830, and 220 grains at 2,680, the .300 Winchester Magnum clearly offers a tremendous improvement over .30-06 velocities, with significant resultant advantages in both trajectory and striking energy.

The cartridge that remains king of the .30-caliber spectrum, at least insofar as factory cartridges are concerned, is a good deal older than the Winchester. It is, of course, the .300 Weatherby Magnum, available in commercially loaded ammo since about 1948. Essentially it is one of several "improved" or blown-out versions of the .300 H&H, using the full-length case with the body taper removed. It has the Weatherby hallmark of the Venturi shoulder, and it is probably the most popular and arguably the most useful of all the Weatherby magnum cartridges.

Published velocities for Weatherby factory ammo list a 150-grain bullet at 3,545 fps; a 180-grain bullet at 3,245; and a 220-grain at 2,905. Velocities like these put muzzle energies above the 4,000 foot-pound level with all bullet weights, rivaling energy figures for the .375 H&H. The .300 Weatherby is clearly extremely powerful and just as clearly extremely flat-shooting, and it's been the choice of many of the top modern hunters.

Both Herb Klein and Elgin Gates used almost no other cartridges to hunt the world. In both cases their .300 Weatherbys, with heavy bullets, were used for game up to and including elephant and rhino. I haven't used the .300 Weatherby for such heavy game, but I have used it on a variety of game both in Africa and North America. It's a long-range cartridge without peer, and most certainly an efficient killer of almost anything that walks.

This may seem heresy, but I have not personally found the .300 magnums to be noticeably more effective on game than the .30-06. They do indeed make *hitting* game at longer ranges much easier, and they certainly extend one's practical range a fair measure. Bullet performance, however, is a real concern with all of the .30-caliber magnums. At .30-06 velocities, the velocities for which most .308-inch bullets were designed, penetration is sure and expansion is reliably controlled. Push those same bullets as much as 500 fps faster and the results are much less predictable. In fact, most lighter .30-caliber bullets—and many medium weights—become virtual bombs at .300 magnum velocity.

Of course, if one will be hunting in the Kalahari Desert, where shots are sure to be long, all that is just fine. By the time a bullet has arrived where the game is, it will have slowed down enough that its performance will be what it should be. But for general African use, forget the fancy ballistics and stay away from the lighter bullets in the magnum .30s.

As with the .30-06, a stoutly-constructed 180-grain bullet is a good choice—but it should be the minimum weight considered for any of the hot .30s. In both the .300 Winchester Magnum and the .300 Weatherby Magnum, a long, aerodynamic 200-grain bullet is quite possibly the best choice for all-round use. It won't start out as fast as the 180 (let alone the 150!) but its superior sectional density dictates that it will be moving faster than the lighter slug once distances become significant.

The .300 Weatherby also offers excellent velocity even with the 220-grain bullet, and it's perhaps the only .30-caliber that has enough case capacity to offer respectable velocities with Barnes's long, heavy 250-grain .30 caliber. I'm not very enthusiastic about using any .30-caliber cartridge on lion, but if I had to pick one it would be the .300 Weatherby with a 220-grain roundnose or a handloaded Barnes 250.

Until very recently, the .300 Winchester Magnum has been the most popular magnum .30 by quite a margin. It has the advantage of being a short magnum, able to be chambered in any .30-06-length action, while the Weatherby requires a .375-length action. The .300 Weatherby has also had the disadvantage of being offered (in both rifles and ammo) only from Weatherby—a "proprietary" cartridge, as most of the older British numbers were. That is slowly changing. The Sauer rifle was chambered in .300 Weatherby some years ago, and today .300 Weatherbys are available from Ruger, Remington, and Winchester as well as from a number of custom and semi-custom makers. .300 Weatherby ammunition, too, is now being offered by Remington and PMC. The old .300 H&H is good, and the .300

Winchester is excellent, but for maximum performance in a .30-caliber cartridge, the .300 Weatherby Magnum is at the top of the heap. It's always had a following, but with added availability in modestly priced rifles, I expect it to become increasingly popular over the next few years.

The drawbacks of the magnum .30s, compared with the .30-06, are increased recoil and muzzle blast, increased gun weight and length (a .30-06 is just fine with a 22-inch barrel, but the magnum .30s really need a 24-inch tube and do better still with a full 26 inches of barrel), and a greatly reduced selection of bullets that can be relied upon to perform at the increased velocities. The advantages are increased practical range and easier shooting at longer ranges, plus an across-the-board increase in raw energy.

Those energy increases are significant. However, in spite of what many experts have accomplished with .30 magnums, they are still not suitable charge-stopping cartridges for lion and the thick-skinned African game. No .30-caliber bullet yet designed, at any velocity, is. In terms of performance on game, none of the .300s will display a noticeable advantage over the .30-06 (or, for that matter, the .308 or .303 British) under most African hunting conditions. However, in the African deserts and open savannas, and in mountains of Ethiopia, the ranging abilities of the .300s do offer tremendous advantages.

Whether a magnum or a "standard" .30 is chosen, it's a cartridge that will provide yeoman service on a tremendous range of African game. It is ideal on game from impala up through kudu and zebra, and in a pinch, with proper bullets, it will do the trick even on massive eland. It will turn the lights out on a leopard much more quickly than a heavier rifle. And it's been used with success against lion and buffalo much too often to say it can't be done. But I can say that it shouldn't be done. To find sensible absolute minimums for such game, we'll need to take another step up in caliber.

# Chapter 4

# The Light Mediums

There has been some confusion about the capabilities of those cartridges falling between the .30s and the .375—the broad and useful spectrum of cartridges from 8mm, or .323 caliber, to 9.3mm, or .366 caliber. There is a tremendous variance in velocity, bullet weight, and power among this group, so it's most unwise to make broad statements. Generally, though, these cartridges can perform duties above and beyond what you would expect from a "light" safari rifle—but they won't stop a charge like a "heavy" rifle or as reliably as the classic "medium" bore, the .375 H&H. They're sort of in-betweeners, either "light mediums" or "heavy lights." Whatever you choose to call them, the group includes a number of wonderful hunting cartridges.

Three good ones in this class are America's trio of medium magnums: the 8mm Remington, .338 Winchester, and .340 Weatherby Magnums. The popularity of the latter two is such that, as Americans are prone to do, we have come to believe we created this class of cartridge. The truth is that the Americans, the English, and the metric-minded Europeans *all* have a long history of cartridges in this class. More to the point, the English and Continental cartridges have a long and glorious history in Africa, while the American "light mediums" are new to that scene.

For the sake of simplicity, the metric cartridges will be covered in detail in a separate chapter. To keep things in perspective, though, the 8mm Mauser, or 8x57, dates back to 1888—and remains a European standard. Although it's a fine hunting cartridge, its limited case capacity keeps the velocity down, especially with heavier bullets. It offers no real advantage over .30-06-class cartridges. The 1912-vintage 8x64 Brenneke, essentially the same as our wildcat 8mm-06, will keep pace in the velocity department—and do it with heavier bullets with larger frontal area. Better still is the 8x68S Magnum, a true rimless magnum developed in 1940. This one is extremely popular among savvy Europeans, essentially filling the niche occupied by our .338. Ballistically it is very similar to the 8mm Remington Magnum.

There have been a number of 9mm rifle cartridges, but only the 9x57 has survived. It is essentially similar to, but a bit less powerful than, our .358 Winchester. Careful handloading could take advantage of its greater case capacity, but it uses an oddball (to Americans) bullet diameter of .356. Still seen in Africa, it's considered a fine rifle for short-range work on all manner of nondangerous game—but even though it has the bullet weight, it lacks the velocity and energy to be reliable on dangerous game larger than leopard.

Another favorite European bore is the 9.3mm, caliber .366. Frank Barnes's *Cartridges of the World* lists fully 15 9.3mm cartridges, most of which are long gone. The most common survivors are the 9.3x62 Mauser, the 9.3x64 Brenneke, and the 9.3x74R. All have been available with excellent bullets ranging from 232 to 293 grains. The 9.3x62 goes clear back to 1905, and it was the most popular general-purpose cartridge in the portions of Africa settled by the Germans. Although it uses heavier bullets of the superb Brenneke designs, it's actually very similar to the .35 Whelen.

The 9.3x64 Brenneke is another story. Actually an unbelted magnum, the 9.3x64 gives up nothing to the .375 H&H, propelling its heaviest 293-grain bullet at 2,570 feet per second. Because of ammo availability, an American probably wouldn't choose it over the .375—but a European might, and he wouldn't be wrong.

The 9.3x74R is a very long, very trim rimmed cartridge for use in doubles and single-shots. It can't compete with the .375 H&H, but it's very close to the .375 Flanged—and much more available. Its 286-grain bullet at 2,360 fps has been used on all African game, including elephant, with much success. Personally, I'd want a bit more gun, but the 9.3x74R does have a great advantage in that its slim pencil-like profile allows it to be built into a double of incredible trimness and light weight.

The English, too, had a proliferation of these medium cartridges, though not as many as the Europeans. Some, like the .360 Nitro-Express, were simply smokeless adaptations of blackpowder cartridges, offering little. Others were indeed fine cartridges. Unlike their European counterparts, all of the British over-.30-and-under-.375 cartridges can be considered obsolete today—but several of them left their mark.

The first smokeless cartridge in this class was the .400/.350 Nitro-Express, a rimmed cartridge introduced by John Rigby in 1899. It fired a 310-grain .35-caliber bullet at just 2,000 fps—but that long, heavy bullet at such a modest velocity penetrated like crazy, and the cartridge had a tremendous following. A friend of mine, South African diplomat Vic Zazeraj, has a Greener .400/.350 on a Martini-type single-shot action, and he swears by it for game up to, but not quite including, buffalo.

Under the British proprietary system, other companies soon followed with the slightly less powerful .400/.360 Nitro-Express, but it never achieved any following to speak of. Better was the 1905-vintage .360 Nitro-Express No. 2, a larger-cased cartridge that propelled a 320-grain bullet at 2,200 fps. This was really a fine cartridge; a double so chambered could be put to good use today.

Farther down the caliber scale were more interesting developments. The .350 Rigby Magnum, or .350 Rimless Magnum, was developed by John Rigby for use in Mauser actions in about 1908. It remained popular clear up to the collapse of the British Empire in Africa—and is still seen occasionally today. Factory ballistics showed a 225-grain bullet at 2,600 fps, yielding 3,380 foot-pounds of energy. For its day, that was good velocity, and even heavy-rifle king John Taylor had nothing but good things to say about the .350 Rigby Magnum. Ballistically it falls far short of the .358 Norma Magnum, and is actually just about identical to the .35 Whelen. And that isn't a bad place to be; I have never shot a .350 Rigby, and am unlikely to—but I've used few cartridges that do a better job on large game than the .35 Whelen. And cartridges like that do their work without a lot of recoil.

The .350 was used rather extensively for buffalo and even elephant, with darned few complaints. I would personally use such a cartridge on buffalo only in fairly open country—the way they were hunted when this cartridge was in its heyday.

Another fine cartridge that came just a couple of years later was the .333 Jeffery, or .333 Rimless Nitro-Express. Its companion rimmed cartridge was the .333 Flanged. Firing a 250-grain bullet at 2,500 fps and a very long 300-grain bullet at 2,200, this one was also considered a deadly killer on game up to buffalo. John Taylor apparently thought little of the copper-capped 250-grain bullet, but believed in the heavy 300-grain slug. I can appreciate that; we know today what *a good* 250-grain .338 bullet will do, and I would suspect that the much longer 300-grain slug would be darn near unstoppable.

This cartridge was the inspiration for the .333 O.K.H. wildcat developed by the legendary team of O'Neil, Keith, and Hopkins, based on the .30-06 case. Later, they developed the .334 O.K.H. using the .375 H&H case blown out. Carrying it a step further, you could say that it was therefore the inspiration for the .338 Winchester Magnum. True .333 bullets are hard to come by today, but .338 bullets can easily be swaged down for use. There were enough .333 rifles built that they do come up for sale every now and again—and they're worth having. In power, the .333 is very close to the .338-06 wildcat that's becoming so popular today.

Virtually the only cartridge in this class that failed to build a good reputation was the .33 Belted Rimless Nitro-Express, a Birmingham Small Arms development. This one uses a .338-inch bullet, so its ills would be easy to cure with modern bullets. It was a belted cartridge, and thus was quite similar to the .338 Winchester Magnum. *Except* that it was offered only with a much-too-light 165-grain bullet, obviously of poor sectional density and just as obviously a dismal penetrator on game. It didn't last very long.

Saving the best, or at least the most popular, for last, that brings us to the .318 Westley Richards, or .318 Rimless Nitro-Express. Never as readily available or as commonly used as the 9.3x62, the .318 was nevertheless the most popular *and* most popularized British medium bore. Introduced in 1910, it has been called the British equivalent of the .30-06, and indeed it's similar—when I had a .318, I made brass from .30-06 cases. However, its .330-inch bullet has much more frontal area, and it was blessed with tough, deep-penetrating 250-grain softpoints as well as the excellent Kynoch solids.

Factory ballistics listed the 250-grain bullet at 2,400 fps and a 180-grain bullet at 2,700. That makes it almost the equal of the .333 Jeffery, just a tad slower—and again, about the same as our current .338-06 wildcat—provided, of course, that the factory figures published nearly 80 years ago were accurate. I had a .318, a beautiful Westley Richards Mauser, for some time, and I shot it extensively. I chronographed several batches of old Kynoch ammo, and the velocities I got weren't even close—the 250-grain loads didn't come up to 2,200 fps. One has to wonder if that was because the ammo was half a century old, or if it *ever* reached published velocities.

It doesn't really matter; the .318 was widely used and widely sworn by. Taylor rated it extremely effective, saying, "I have the highest possible opinion of it provided it's kept in its place and not abused by being taken alone against dangerous game in thick cover." Amen.

My own experience with the .318 was limited to plains game; I took it to Botswana and South Africa in 1987, and used it to take a variety of animals up to wildebeest and zebra at various distances. I was using old Kynoch 250-grain solids and softs and Barnes 250-grain .338 bullets swaged down (in two steps) to .330. It was, quite simply, one of the deadliest rifles I have ever used. There seemed to be no stopping that long, heavy bullet at its moderate velocity.

I shot a big blue wildebeest, a very tough antelope, at quite a long distance—some 225 yards. The big bullet penetrated completely through both shoulders, and literally flattened the bull in his tracks. I would not hesitate to use the .318 on an unwounded, undisturbed buffalo—and I intended to do so. It just didn't happen; we could only find our buffalo in the heaviest cover, and that was what my other rifle—a .470 double—was there for.

The .318 is a charming, charismatic cartridge with little recoil. I wish I still had that rifle, but I'm a lefty and of course it had a right-handed bolt—and, to be honest, somebody else wanted it more than I did. I found it in a gunshop in Los Angeles, and it had quite a checkered career before it got to me. Built in 1927, it had been shipped to New Brunswick originally. From there, somehow, it got to Australia—it had the "broad arrow" stencil on the stock showing it had been commandeered by the Australian military, probably during World War II. Westley Richards had reconditioned it 15 years before I bought it. After all that, it still shot like hell—and lurking in gunshops all over the world, there remain to this day a few classic British rifles waiting for someone who knows what they are and what they will do.

There is no real reason to bring back the .318, or any of the other old Britishers—we have modern cartridges with readily available bullets that duplicate their performance, though without the charisma. But if you chance upon one, buy it and go to the trouble to put together the ammo. They're as good now as they ever were, and they're a piece of history. As my good friend, professional hunter, and Anglophile (when it comes to rifles) Ian MacFarlane put it when I showed up in camp with that .318, "You just feel good about it when you shoot something with a rifle like that."

On the American side of the Atlantic there were several cartridges in this class. We had a whole slew of cartridges from .32 to .35 designed for the pump, lever, and early semiautos that were in vogue in the early days of smokeless powders. Most were low-powered rounds, very similar to the two survivors: the .32 Winchester Special and the .35 Remington. A couple are worth mentioning. The .35 Winchester, designed for use in the big Winchester 1895 lever-action, fired a 250-grain bullet at almost 2,200 fps, so it was no pipsqueak. It was loaded by Kynoch for some time and saw some use in Africa. It died along with the Model 1895, and is a real rarity today.

Also worth mentioning is the .33 Winchester, the last chambering for the great Model 1886 Winchester. It was widely used as a bear and moose cartridge, but its real claim to fame is that it used a .338-inch bullet, making it the American ancestor of the .338 Winchester Magnum.

A cartridge that really could have gone places is the .35 Newton, one of Charles Newton's excellent rimless magnums. It was offered in factory loads for a time, and they were red-hot—not just for their day, but for any day! It's said that a 250-grain bullet could be pushed in excess of 2,900 fps. I have trouble believing that, but I have no trouble with the last listed factory load, a 250-grain bullet at 2,660. That makes the cartridge faster than the .35 Whelen or the .350 Rigby Magnum, and pushing the .358 Norma, a belted magnum. It must have been really something, but it died with the Newton Rifle Company during the depression. Charles Cottar, the first American professional hunter, was one of few recorded .35 Newton fans.

All this has been background; as great as the British cartridges were, they're long gone today. And as great as some of the metrics are, ammunition for them is scarce as hen's teeth—not only in America but in much of Africa. Now let's look at the commonly available cartridges in our "light medium" class.

## Lever-Action Cartridges

These need to be mentioned, not only because of Americans' love for their lever guns, but also because they're fine cartridges. In this group we'll lump together the .348, .356, and .358 Winchesters. We'll ignore the .35 Remington, a great cartridge in the whitetail woods but underpowered for larger game. The .348 is the oldest of these. It was only chambered in the Model 71 Winchester, the last incarnation of the old 1886 lever-action. The .348 was dying, not easily or quickly, but steadily, until Browning brought out a modern replica a couple of years ago. With a 200-grain bullet at 2,530 fps, the .348 is a powerful and effective hunting cartridge. Its discontinued 250-grain load, with a muzzle velocity of 2,350, was even better. I have not taken the cartridge to Africa, but I have used it extensively on black bear and wild hogs. With handloaded flat-pointed 250-grain bullets it's simply deadly. I don't see it as an African cartridge; the only rifle ever chambered for it doesn't lend itself to scope use, and it certainly isn't a dangerous-game cartridge. But it would be deadly in thornbush.

The .358 was introduced to replace the .348. It's a short rimless cartridge based on the .308 case, and with the 200-grain bullet its muzzle velocity is identical to that of the .348. With the 250-grain loading, also discontinued, it lagged about 100 fps behind because of its smaller case capacity. However, it was offered in the box-magazine Model 88 Winchester and the rotary-magazine Savage 99—and is still available in the slick little Browning BLR. All of these guns can be scoped. They can also use sharp-pointed bullets, which a tubular-magazine gun cannot. The flat-nosed slugs hit like a freight train, but they shed their velocity like a thrown rock.

Jay Mellon mentions using a .358 in *African Hunter*, and he had good luck with it. Again, this isn't a cartridge I've used in Africa—but I've often thought a slick little Savage 99 or BLR so chambered would be a handy gun in thornbush country. Ballistics are actually a bit better than the 9x57 Mauser's, and there are no flies on its African reputation. The .356 is its ballistic twin, a semi-rimmed version developed for use in current Marlin and Winchester lever-actions. The .356's only problem is that, again, flat-pointed bullets must be used to avoid detonation in a tubular magazine.

All three of these cartridges are extremely effective, and both the .348 and .358 are particular favorites of mine. There's just one *caveat:* There is no way to get real velocity out of these cartridges, so they need the heavier bullets to be truly effective on larger game. And under no circumstances are they suited for buffalo; they're all done at the upper limits of the plains species.

## .35 Whelen

In England and on the Continent, almost all cartridges are designed by the major firearms and ammunition makers. In America, where we have many thousands of knowledgeable handloaders with good equipment and components readily available, many fine cartridges have been developed by private individuals. Sometimes these cartridges are adopted by major manufacturers, and sometimes they're kept alive—and even kept fairly popular—by handloaders without the blessing of a major manufacturer. Certainly that's the case with the .35 Whelen, a 65-year-old wildcat cartridge that never lost its steady, if small, appeal. In 1988, Remington finally adopted it as a factory cartridge—and the results were stunning beyond their wildest expectations.

Personally, although I was fortunate to take the first head of game, a moose, with the "new" rifle and its factory ammo, I questioned whether more than a few hundred people had even heard of the .35 Whelen—or its designer, the great gunwriter Colonel Townsend Whelen, long gone to his reward. Within a few months of its introduction, Remington took some

25,000 orders for .35 Whelen rifles, far more than they were prepared to produce!

Based on the .30-06 case, the .35 Whelen offers (in factory form) a 180-grain bullet at 2,700 fps and a 250-grain bullet at 2,400. To my mind that short, fast 180-grainer is useless on game larger than, say, impala or reedbuck. But the 250-grain slug is another story. Handloading can boost it to 2,500 or thereabouts, so it's right in there with the .318 Westley Richards, .333 Jeffery, and .350 Rigby. That bullet can be had in roundnose or spitzer form, and with that many rifles out there, I suspect the bulletmakers will follow with some interesting .35-caliber slugs.

I have not taken my .35 Whelen on safari yet—but I intend to. I have used the rifle on moose, elk, black bear, and wild boar, and it's one of the surest killers I've ever used. Its 250-grain bullet has the weight and the frontal area, and it does wonderful things without undue recoil and muzzle blast. Out to 200 yards, I would rate it the equal of the .338 Winchester Magnum. It would not be a good choice in open country, but in the mixed thornbush common in much of Africa, it would be ideal.

At a recent sportsmen's show, a guy asked me what I thought about the .35 Whelen for Cape buffalo. As must be obvious, I'm a heavy-caliber proponent—especially when it comes to dangerous game. But this guy had a legitimate problem. He and his wife were headed to Africa, and she wanted to take a buffalo—but was uncomfortable with recoil, even at .375 H&H levels. I thought back to my first use of the .35 Whelen, on a very large Alaska-Yukon moose. The range was about 60 yards, and that bull was as big as any Cape buffalo that walks. At the shot he simply went over backwards, landing with all four feet in the air, lights out. Yes, I would use the .35 Whelen on a buffalo, provided I was close enough—but not *too* close—and could place my shot on or just behind the shoulder. I would use a good softpoint for the first shot, but I'd try to get some solids to back it up. Chances are, now that this .35 is so popular, Art Alphin will turn out some of his A-Square Monolithic solids in .358 diameter. If he would, you wouldn't have a great buffalo gun—but you could sure get by if you had to.

## .338-06

With so many good cartridges in this category, I won't waste space on the many equally good wildcats out there. The .338-06, however, is in a slightly different class. For one thing, it's tremendously popular at this writing. For another, I'll be very surprised if it isn't a *bona fide* factory cartridge by the time these lines see the light of day. It is, of course, simply the .30-06 necked up to take a .338-inch bullet, just as the .35 Whelen is the same case necked up for a .358-inch bullet. It won't do anything the Whelen won't do, and vice versa. However, that .30-06 case is extremely efficient when necked up slightly, and the velocities are quite amazing. I'm told 2,600 fps is possible with a 250-grain bullet (but I'm told that with the

Whelen as well, and *I* can't do it!). Chances are, if it were legitimized, a 250-grain factory load would have the same 2,400 fps velocity as for the Whelen in that weight.

There are other advantages to the .338, though. Grain for grain, .338 bullets have better sectional density than .358 bullets, and there's a much larger selection of good bullets already on the market. These include Monolithic solids, Trophy Bonded Bearclaws, and Speer's 275-grain heavyweight. Had the Whelen not been legitimized, I believe the .338-06 would have been by now. But I still predict we'll see it in factory form from one of the majors. If we do, it will be another great African cartridge in the mold of the .333 Jeffery and .318 Westley Richards—light of recoil, low of report, and absolutely deadly.

## 8mm Remington Magnum

Remington's "Big Eight" is a recent development. Based on the .375 H&H case, necked down take a .323-inch bullet and with the body taper removed, it was introduced in 1978. Although there was much initial fanfare, the public didn't seem to care; the cartridge has languished since the very beginning, and I seriously doubt if rifles will be chambered for it much longer.

I think that's a shame—it's a darned good cartridge, accurate and flat-shooting. Remington's factory loads feature Core-Lokt bullets of 185 and 220 grains. The light bullet has a muzzle velocity of 3,080 fps, yielding 3,896 foot-pounds; the 220-grainer leaves the muzzle at 2,830 fps for 3,912 foot-pounds. I've taken several head of elk-sized game with the Big Eight, and I've seen it used on a variety of African game. It performs well, especially with the 220-grain bullet.

The cartridge's problems are twofold. First, no 8mm has ever achieved lasting popularity in America. And falling right between the .300 magnums and the .338 Winchester Magnum, it may lie in a nonexistent "niche." It is also a full-length magnum, meaning that only actions capable of handling .375 H&H-length cartridges are suitable. And that lets out a large number of excellent American bolt-actions.

There's also a serious bullet problem. The 185-grain factory bullet is too light and too short for serious game. The 220-grain bullet is superb, or at least it has been for me. But this cartridge cries out for a *good* 250-grain bullet—and it hasn't generated enough demand for anyone to create one. Most of the component bullets available in this country were designed for 8x57 velocities, and they're useless in the 8mm magnum. The wonderful bullets the Europeans load in the 8x68S are almost impossible to obtain. And there you have it—a great cartridge, ideally suited for open-country African hunting for the very largest of plains game. With the right bullet, it could well be used against buffalo and certainly lion. But so far, that bullet doesn't exist.

48

## .338 Winchester Magnum

Introduced in 1958 in a version of Winchester's pre-'64 Model 70 called "the Alaskan," the .338 Winchester Magnum is headed toward middle age today. It had a great deal going for it from the start. Obviously, it had the backing of what was then America's premier gun company—in a day when the Model 70 was *the* bolt-action sporter. It was also a true short magnum, able to fit into any .30-06-length action. And it had the excellent legacy of the British .33s to trade on—plus the absolute backing of Elmer Keith, who had been championing his O.K.H. .33-caliber wildcats for decades.

In spite of all these advantages, the .338 was very slow to catch on. No, it has never teetered on the edge of disaster as the 8mm Remington seems to be doing, but it's just been sitting there, or so it seems to me—at least until recently. In just the last few years the .338 appears to have caught on.

Most of this surge of interest seems to be among elk hunters, and indeed the .338 is one of the finest of all elk cartridges. There's a valley in Montana that I hunt regularly, and all the local hunters have given up their time-honored .270s and .30-06s in favor of .338s. It's become a standard backup rifle with Alaska bear guides, too, quite possibly outstripping the .375 H&H in popularity.

Chances are it will always be more of a North American cartridge than an African cartridge, but slowly and surely it's working its way into the Dark Continent as well. As it should—it's everything the old-time .33s ever were plus a lot more.

One of its prime attributes is that, with its 30-year history, it has a wonderful selection of superb bullets available. Current factory loads are 200-, 210-, 225-, and 250-grainers. Federal offers the excellent Nosler Partition in 210- and 250-grain .338 loadings, and Remington has a magnificent 250-grain loading using Speer Grand Slam bullets. I believe Winchester's 225-grain bullet is a Hornady-sourced spirepoint, but whatever it is, it's a good load. And A-Square offers a wide selection, including 250-grain Sierra boattails and 250-grain Monolithic solids. Handloaders have even more of a field day, with Trophy Bonded Bearclaws and 275-grain Speers available, as well as a full range of "standard" bullets from 200 to 250 grains.

The .338 is not exceptionally awesome when you study the ballistics. Factory figures list a 225-grain bullet at 2,780 fps at the muzzle, which yields 3,862 foot-pounds. The 250-grain bullet is listed at 2,700 fps for 4,046 foot pounds. I recently chronographed some Remington 250-grain factory ammo, and while it was extremely accurate in my rifle, the velocity was actually 2,650 fps. With careful handloading, I can reach the 2,700 fps level with a 250-grain bullet, but I can't go much beyond.

The .338 can't be considered as powerful as the .375 H&H. Its bullets have a higher sectional density and are generally more aerodynamic, so it will reach out a bit better. And that added sectional density does give them

49

slightly better penetrating powers. But they don't have the frontal area or the weight. The .338 will reach out a bit better than the .375 for open-country shooting on the larger plains animals—but up close it won't match the .375.

It will do a bang-up job for 95 percent of all African shooting, and it has bullets available that will handle the rest if necessary. But it still isn't a charge-stopper, and shouldn't be considered as such.

What it *is*, is a general-purpose safari cartridge with few equals—especially in country where some reach is required. For African use I would stick with the 250-grain bullets and ignore the lighter weights. I have taken the .338 on several safaris, and I used to swear by the 210- and 225-grain bullets. But I've had different brands in both weights come unglued on close-range shots, and you can't afford that in Africa (or anywhere else). So I've gone to the 250-grain weight, and I'd also throw a handful of Monolithic solids into my duffel just in case. Speer's 275-grain bullet also has a lot of promise. It's starting to get a bit slow; the .338 case lacks the capacity to push it really fast—but it provides wonderful penetration. The .338 is one of my favorite cartridges, a most useful safari caliber. It is not a sensible one-gun battery, but it makes a fine choice as the lighter rifle of a two-gun outfit.

## .340 Weatherby Magnum

Everything that can be said about the .338 Winchester Magnum can be said in spades about the .340. Introduced in 1962, it's one of Roy Weatherby's later creations—and in my view one of his best. Based on the .375 H&H case, it requires a full-length action—but that case capacity enables it to do wonderful things with heavy bullets of great sectional density and superb aerodynamics. And Lord, is it *fast!* I just checked a reference, and it quotes the 250-grain factory .340 at 2,850 muzzle velocity. (Another reference quotes that load at 3,000 fps, which is a bit optimistic!) Just yesterday, we chronographed a fresh batch of Weatherby ammo out of a Mark V with 26-inch barrel. The actual velocity was a full 2,900 fps and a bit of change, which translates to muzzle energy of 4,668 foot-pounds.

I'll stand on what I said regarding the .338—regardless of energy figures, the .340 won't match the .375 when it comes to stopping a charge, and it certainly can't take the place of a heavier rifle. It would be a number one choice for hunting large plains game in open country. For instance, few better cartridges exist for hunting gemsbok in the Kalahari, oryx on the short-grass plains of Tanzania, or mountain nyala in Ethiopia's high country. And just like the .338, with suitable bullets it could do it all in a pinch.

The .340's extreme velocity does have a down side, though. Bullets must be chosen with extreme care, since most .338 bullets were designed to function at .338 velocities. The .340 will add some 200 to 300 feet per second. That's great way out there, when velocities have dropped off—but it can mean bullet blowup at close range. Nothing lighter than a 250-grain bullet should be considered, and it should be a tough bullet designed for controlled expansion. Weatherby offers a Nosler 250-grain loading, and of course handloaders have a variety of good bullets to pick from. A-Square factory loads with Monolithic solids are available for this one, too, nicely rounding out the package.

It should be said that the .340 Weatherby has a perceived recoil far above that of the .338—it hits hard and fast, seemingly much worse than a .375 H&H. For most circumstances, I've found it unpleasant enough that I prefer the .338—but for those situations where you want to reach out and hit hard at long range, it's tough to beat.

## .350 Remington Magnum

This one is an oddball, introduced some 25 years ago in the Remington Model 600 carbine. It's an ultra-short magnum, able to fit into .308-length actions (but just barely, and at the expense of seating bullets very deeply). It never sold well, and is pretty much history today—but you almost never see one on the used gun racks. Those who have 'em swear by 'em, and they are indeed neat little rifles for close-range work on medium-sized game. Ballistically, the .350 Remington Magnum is identical to the .35 Whelen. As such, the 20-inch carbines it was chambered in would make wonderful walkabout rifles for thornbush or swamp hunting—but I doubt if this cartridge will ever stage a comeback.

## .358 Norma Magnum

This just might be one of very few cartridges that *will* make a comeback. A short magnum developed by the Swedish firm of Norma, it started life in 1959 as a problem child—there was ammunition but no rifles. It appears likely that Norma believed a major U.S. firm would chamber a rifle for the .358, and for good reason—it's a fine cartridge. But the .338 Winchester Magnum was brand new, and no major U.S. manufacturer picked up the .358—nor has one to this day. Schultz & Larsen and Husqvarna were the only rifles so chambered, except for custom jobs. Both of those rifles are long gone, but today a number of custom and semi-custom shops are building some .358 Normas. Most surprising, though, is that Norma, now imported by Federal, added the .358 Norma Magnum to their ammunition line here in the States for 1989. It's been several years since this cartridge was available—and it's one of the few times in my memory that a cartridge has been brought back from the graveyard of discontinued loadings.

The 250-grain factory loading is rated at 2,790 fps, delivering 4,322 foot-pounds of energy. Those figures certainly beat anything the .338 can do, and they look pretty good against the .375. A traditional problem for the .358 Norma Magnum was that the available component bullets, at their best, were designed for .358 Winchester velocities—if not .35 Remington. Quite obviously, no bullet will perform at velocities 500 fps above what it was designed for. But today, with every bulletmaker racing to bring out bullets for the .35 Whelen, the .358 Norma just might have a chance. If it survives, it would fit nicely into the top end of this "light medium" class.

Even with the best bullets, I would still not choose the .358 Norma instead of a .375 for dangerous game—but it offers an interesting alternative to a .338 or .340, especially if there's a likely possibility of having to use this light-medium rifle on game such as lion or buffalo. For real versatility in Africa, it does have a serious failing: So far no solid is available in .358 diameter. Chances are, though, that somebody will correct that in the very near future.

This has been a long chapter because so many cartridges in this group have a real purpose in African hunting—but not in close cover after dangerous game. John Taylor had it pegged a generation ago, and although the cartridges have changed, their purposes and limitations remain unchanged. "Always provided that there is a more powerful rifle at hand for use in thick cover, you could not wish for a more satisfactory general-purpose medium bore than Westley Richards' .318," wrote Taylor. Instead of the .318, he could well have applied those words to any of the cartridges we've discussed in this chapter—whether of his day or ours. All of them will provide yeoman service on the vast majority of game. And under the right conditions, with the right bullets, all of them could be used on anything that walks. But none of them will provide the margin you must have for dangerous game at close quarters.

The "magnums" in this group extend the reach, the practical shooting distance—and that's desirable. But even the fastest of this group, with the flashiest of trajectories, will fail to carry these cartridges into the realm of charge-stoppers for lion, buffalo, and elephant. That's why so many African game departments have made their use on such game illegal.

# Chapter 5

# .375: The Medium Bore

It seems in vogue today to malign the .375 H&H in favor of more modern cartridges—whether bigger or smaller, faster or slower. Introduced clear back in 1912, the .375 H&H is an archaic design—a long, sloping body with a minimal shoulder, and velocities that are hardly red-hot by today's standards. A variety of smaller-caliber cartridges shoot flatter and hit almost as hard. And a number of larger cartridges hit harder and shoot almost as flat. All of these cartridges have their places—and under certain circumstances they might be more useful than the old warhorse .375.

Indeed, as we shall see later on in this volume, the .375 may not have a place in every safari battery today. But whether in .375 H&H or some other configuration, the .375-bore remains what it was nearly 80 years ago—the single most useful rifle any African hunter could carry.

A book like this takes time to write; as these lines are being written, I have made 18 African hunts—and in two weeks I leave for Zimbabwe. By the time this volume is finished, it's possible I will have seen Africa yet again, and perhaps again. When I leave in two weeks, a .375 will not accompany me—but that's most unusual. I have taken a great variety of rifles to Africa, and have borrowed others while there. One way or another, on most occasions a .375 of some persuasion has been part of the battery. Once, when it was not, I wound up borrowing my partner's .375 at least four times!

On many occasions I have personally carried an open-sighted heavy rifle—but I've asked a tracker to carry a scope-sighted .375 "just in case." At least three times, on buffalo, I've traded the heavy rifle for the .375 so I could be absolutely certain of the shot placement I knew I must have. Yes, I've said in print that the .375 is marginal for buffalo. It is, but it's on the right side of the margin. I've hunted buffalo with the .416 Rigby, .416 Hoffman, .416 Weatherby, .458 Lott, .450 Ackley, .458 Winchester Magnum, .460 Weatherby, .470 Nitro-Express, and .500 Nitro-Express—but I've shot more buffalo with .375s than with all the others combined.

And yes, I've said in print that the .375 is only marginally flat-shooting for open-country hunting. But I have a Kafue lechwe in the top 10 that I shot at well over 400 yards with a .375 H&H. Where did this great cartridge come from, and where is it going?

The inspiration for the .375 H&H can probably be found in the 9.5mm Mannlicher-Schoenauer, called in Britain the .375 Nitro-Express Rimless. Chambered in light, inexpensive Mannlicher rifles, it wasn't much more powerful than the 9x57, but in the years before 1910 it was growing too popular for the British gun trade. Holland & Holland countered with the

.400/.375, or .375 Velopex. Although almost identical in power to the 9.5, the .400/.375 was probably the first belted cartridge.

The .400/.375, besides being anemic, apparently suffered from bad bullets as well. It didn't make the grade. Its successor, introduced in 1912, is still going strong. The .375 Belted Rimless Nitro-Express was first introduced with 235-, 270-, and 300-grain bullets. Initial loadings are listed with the light bullet at 2,800 fps; the 270-grain slug at 2,650; and the 300-grainer at 2,500. The .375 Flanged Magnum Nitro-Express, its rimmed counterpart for doubles and single-shots, was loaded slightly slower to keep the pressures down. Ballistics for this version were quoted at 2,600 fps for a 270-grain bullet and 2,400 fps for a 300-grain bullet, developing 4,060 and 3,850 foot-pounds, respectively. This was actually a very flat-shooting load for a double rifle, and it remains a good choice today.

In those pre-World War I days, it would be an overstatement to call anything an overnight success—but successful the .375 Holland & Holland was, and became so very quickly for its day. Then, as now, the wonderful thing about the .375 was that it seemed to be effective far beyond its bullet weight, energy, and recoil. Even John Taylor, who derived his own "Knock-Out" values to quantify the hitting power of a rifle, wrote regarding the .375 that his "Knock-Out value of 40 points. . . does not really do full justice to it."

Ivory hunter Pete Pearson started his career as a staunch .577 fan, but eventually switched to the .375 and never went back. Harry Manners, another of the all-time great elephant hunters, swore by his over-the-counter Winchester Model 70 .375. And, of course, the number of professional hunters who rely on the .375 as their backup rifle is overwhelming.

Some cartridges, quite possibly through accident, achieve a happy, near-perfect combination of bullet weight, bullet construction, velocity, and frontal diameter. I suspect the .318 Westley Richards, with very modest ballistics, was such a cartridge. In its class, the .30-30 Winchester is another. Certainly this holds true for the .375.

While many British cartridges remained purely proprietary rounds—and were thus eventually doomed when the I.C.L. conglomerate discontinued Kynoch ammunition—the .375 Belted Rimless Nitro-Express was eventually released to the gun trade, and many rifles of many makes were manufactured. As far as I can tell, this was not as true of the .375 Flanged Magnum; I have personally never seen one that wasn't made by Holland, while its closest competitors in doubles, the .400/.350 on one side, the .450/.400 on the other, were made by nearly everyone.

The .375 crossed the Atlantic to America quite early, and by the mid-1920s Western was loading ammunition. The first factory American rifle so chambered was the new Winchester Model 70, introduced in 1936 and offered in .375 in 1937. Prior to that, a number of American custom shops, led by Griffin & Howe of New York, had built custom .375s.

The 235-grain loading dropped by the wayside, while 270- and 300-grain bullets have remained the traditional loads. That 235-grain bullet started very fast, but lacking in sectional density, it shed its velocity very quickly. Still, I suspect it was a useful load for light game—and had the advantage of much-reduced recoil. Speer still offers a 235-grain semi-spitzer, a bullet I've used on a fair amount of African game. It was extremely effective for me on animals up to the size of kudu—and that's just what it was meant for. Trophy Bonded also offers an excellent 240-grain spitzer, and I've used that one as well. With my handloads pushed to 2,900 fps, it's a real screamer—and with that wonderful bonded-core construction, it performs extremely well on game up to kudu and elk. Just this year, Federal announced a new factory load with a 250-grain spitzer boattail, and I'll be curious to see how it works. Just so long as it isn't applied against anything *really* tough, it should be a dandy.

Even so, the mainstays for the .375 are the 270- and 300-grainers. Of these, I have always preferred a 300-grain bullet. There are some good 270-grainers around; Hornady's 270-grain spirepoint and Winchester's Power Point, to name just two. However, the standard .375 solid is 300 grains, and it always made more sense to me to have both bullets the same weight.

There's a myth that the .375 will print all its bullet weights to the same place at 100 yards, and it's a myth perpetuated by the best of writers. The occasional rifle will, it's true—but most won't. Mine won't. Don't count on it until you've checked it out!

The other advantage to the 300-grainer is its greater sectional density, which means greater penetration on game—and just as importantly, given equally aerodynamic shapes, better long-range ballistics. The 270-grain slug may start faster, but a 300-grain bullet, if also of spitzer design, will be going faster at 250 yards, and will drop less as well as carrying more energy.

The .375, with its long history, has a wealth of wonderful bullets available. And today there are more factory loads than ever before. Federal has five different .375 factory loads, including a wonderfully flat-shooting load with 300-grain Sierra boattails. A-Square, although a small company, offers four different .375 factory loads, while Remington and Winchester have three each. The handloader has even more available, with Swift partitions, Trophy Bonded Bearclaws, and the recently resurrected (at last!) Nosler Partitions. For close-cover work, there's also the real heavyweights, Barnes's 350-grain bullets in both solids and softpoints. There is more choice available right now for the .375 in both loaded ammo and bullets than ever before. It isn't that the .375 has just arrived—it arrived nearly 90 years ago. But it does appear that a whole new generation is noticing it.

If it has a disadvantage, it's that it requires a full-length action; it will not fit into a .30-06-length action. Wildcatters recognized that long ago, and there have been a number of wildcats based on the .300, .338, and .458

Winchester Magnums necked up or down to .375. Most of these cartridges will duplicate .375 H&H performance in a short action—but none have come particularly close to appearing in factory form.

Another complaint is that the cartridge is inefficient; if all that body taper were removed and the shoulder changed, significant improvements in velocity could be achieved. That's quite true. The .375 Improved was a very popular wildcat 30 years ago, and it did indeed improve the velocities of the .375. So did Roy Weatherby's .375 Weatherby Magnum, very similar to the Improved but with Weatherby's distinctive double-Venturi shoulder.

An uncle of mine, Art Popham, has had a .375 Improved since the early 1950s, and he swears by it. Gunwriter Jon Sundra has a .375 JRS, essentially a .375 Improved but based on the 8mm Remington Magnum case. And Art Alphin's A-Square Company has brought back the .375 Weatherby in both rifles and factory-loaded ammo.

I can't swear to the velocities the other versions get, but I have an A-Square .375 Weatherby. With a 300-grain bullet, 2,750 fps is a breeze, and 2,800 is touchy but possible. The current factory 300-grain loads are quoted at—and usually reach—2,530 fps. Clearly, a significant velocity advantage can be achieved, but it's only fair to compare apples with apples.

My regular handload for the standard .375 H&H chronographs an honest 2,600 fps with a 300-grain bullet. For open country, I use the most aerodynamic of the .375s, the 300-grain Sierra boattail or the new Hornaday 300-grain Spire Point boattail. The computer indicates that when it's sighted 2.14 inches high at 100 yards, it's dead-on at 200 yards and 8.67 inches low at 300 yards. Supposing I could get my .375 Weatherby up to 2,800 fps with the same bullet (I can, but its not easy, and not for warm weather!), the computer tells me I should sight 1.73 inches high at 100 yards to achieve that 200-yard zero—and I'd be just 7.32 inches low at 300 yards. Although actual shooting can't duplicate the computer's precision, it can come close enough for practical purposes. That is, I would sight a little less than 2 inches high at 100 yards, thus obtaining a 200-yard zero and a drop of only about $7\frac{1}{3}$ inches at 300.

Is 1.35 inches of difference at 300 yards worth all the fuss? Not really. Energy differences, by the way, are more significant—4,502 versus 5,222 foot-pounds. But the .375 has proven for 90 years that it has enough energy as it sits. And yet I do have the .375 Weatherby, and I rather like it. For true open-country work, every little bit does make a difference. But unless you're a fairly serious gun crank and tinkerer, you might as well stick with the .375 H&H—it will do everything you need it to do and more.

Pretty much the same thing goes for the biggest .375 of all, the .378 Weatherby. With careful handloading, you can get its 300-grain bullet clear to 2,900 fps, about the level reached by Weatherby's factory loads. Friends of mine swear by the .378—while others curse it. I have never used it, so I can't draw a conclusion, but I will make two observations. First, when you get to 2,900 fps with a 300-grain bullet, you're starting to pay a vicious price in recoil. Second, there is only so much velocity that any bullet will stand—and all .375 bullets were designed to perform at .375 H&H velocities, not 350 fps faster. With good, hard, tough bullets it will be okay—but lighter-constructed bullets at close range simply must be unreliable.

Yet these "ultra-.375s" do have a place in Africa, and that's where ranges are long and the game tough. My .375 Weatherby was obtained with two hunts in mind: the Kalahari Desert and the Ethiopian highlands. In the Kalahari it's ideal for gemsbok across an open pan, and if I ever get to Ethiopia, that's the rifle I will carry. Typically, there's just one shot at a mountain nyala, and it might be at 400 yards in dense heather where the animal simply must be anchored or lost. That's where such a gun is at its best—and of course, with proper bullet selection it can handle all the normal .375 chores as well.

What *are* a .375's normal chores? Just about anything, at any time. The .375 will not reach out over the short-grass plains like a smaller-caliber, higher-velocity cartridge will—but it will do the job in a pinch, albeit with a good deal more punch than is needed on the smaller African antelopes. It will also drop buffalo and even elephant with deadly efficiency, given reasonable shot placement. It will not do this as effectively as something over .40 caliber, but it will do it. On the upper and lower end of the African game spectrum—impala, reedbuck, bushbuck, etc., on one end, and buffalo, rhino, and elephant on the other—it's the ultimate compromise caliber.

For the largest of plains game—eland, bongo, and tough smaller animals such as gemsbok, sable, and roan—it's an ideal cartridge. And its real *forte* is lion. An unwounded lion may be taken most readily with a .30-06, 7x57, even a .270. A wounded lion may not be stopped by a big double. But taking the average of all circumstances, the .375 remains after 80 years the perfect lion gun, and for that matter it's just as perfect for brown, grizzly, and polar bear.

The beauty about the .375 is that you never know exactly what you might run into next in Africa. With a .375, you are ready for anything, if not exactly perfectly armed for everything. With a big double, you're ready for a charging buffalo, but are you ready for the 65-inch kudu that appears across a wide ravine? With a scope-sighted 7mm, you're quite ready for that kudu, but are you ready for the buffalo that waits around the next bend, the same buffalo a poacher wounded the day before? With a .375, you're just fine.

I've shot most of my kudu, half my elk, and all of my eland with a .375. Some were at very long range, and I never found it wanting. I mentioned the lechwe I shot at extreme range. Another shot I remember well was on a very fine Limpopo bushbuck. He was feeding on a sidehill quite far way, just momentarily in a small opening. I wanted him, and if I wanted him there was no time, no rest, and no choice. I sat down and wrapped into a tight sling, but I knew he'd moved into the shot and been hit way too far back. I was fortunate; he was gut-shot, and could well have been lost—but

I was using Sierra's relatively soft boattail 300-grain. It opened nicely. He was a wonderful ram, and he was dead inside of 75 yards.

That bullet is maligned a lot, but it's one of my favorites. It isn't the toughest—if I *know* I'm going up against buffalo, I'd choose a Swift or a Nosler in the .375. If consciously hunting lion, I'd choose a Trophy Bonded Bear Claw. But for general, all-round hunting, I often use that Sierra because I know exactly what it will do each and every time. It is fairly soft—and that's great on lighter game. On game the size of buffalo, I just watch the shot placement—and I've shot a number of buffalo very dead with that 300-grain .375 Sierra. If you get into a long-range situation, it is also wonderfully flat-shooting.

The .375 is not a true heavy rifle, by any means. Nor is it a light rifle. Taylor differentiated between the "large bores" and the "large medium bores," making the separation at, I believe, .450. Clearly the .375 falls far short, and thank God for that! The .375 is the ultimate medium, fully able to stand in for the heavy—not just in a pinch, as the .33s to .35s can, but with deadly efficiency. Yet it's flat-shooting, accurate, deserves the benefit of a good scope sight, and the man who knows how to use it gives up nothing to any high-velocity light rifle.

On many occasions in the African bush, I have carried a heavy rifle and wished for something with more accuracy or more reach—and, as I mentioned, at least three times on buffalo and Lord knows how many times on other game, I've been able to make that switch for a .375. Not as frequently, but on several occasions, I've carried a light rifle in search of smaller game, and wished for the weight of a double in my hands. But I've never carried a .375 and switched it for something else—nor have I ever wanted to. In its original form, or in one of its more compact or faster versions, since 1912 it's been *the* medium bore, one of the most useful of all African cartridges.

# Chapter 6

# The Lower .40s

I've always found it interesting that in Europe, America, and England, virtually no smokeless cartridges have ever existed that use bullets between .375 and .400. This is virtually the only .025-inch gap in the entire world of sporting cartridges between .220 and .500. Perhaps it's because the .375 H&H came so early, and was so good. Or perhaps it's because the next number up from the .375—which preceded it by a good 15 years—was also so good. This was the .450/.400.

Based on a blackpowder .450 case necked down to take a nominally .40-caliber bullet, the .450/.400 made the transition from blackpowder to smokeless and emerged as a classic "all-round" cartridge. In two different, non-interchangeable case lengths, it fired a 400-grain bullet of excellent sectional density at between 2,100 and 2,150 feet per second, giving penetration unequaled by many heavier calibers. It remained popular until the end of Britain's colonial era, but, as effective as it was, it had a problem: Its long, rimmed case was best-suited for use in double rifles and single-shots. However, it was chambered in a few early bolt-actions. A Canadian guide I hunted with in 1973 had a turn-of-the-century .450/.400 bolt-action, a strange-looking affair. I'd give anything to have recorded the make and taken some photos of that odd duck!

Such rifles must have been extremely rare, and are virtually forgotten today; like the other big rimmed Nitro-Express cartridges, the .450/.400 was an ill fit in a bolt-action. Jeffery offered the rimmed .500-3" Nitro-Express in a bolt-action for a time, until powerful cartridges designed for bolt-actions could be developed. And the bolt-actions were coming on strong.

Dependable, accurate, offering repeat firepower, and available at a fraction of the cost of a double, the Mauser and Mannlicher sporters were selling like hotcakes among British sportsmen in the first years of this century. Light rifles such as the 6.5x53R Mannlicher-Steyr and the 7x57, delivering unprecedented penetration with their very long bullets, were the darlings of the small-bore crowd. The 8mms and 9.3s filled the medium niche. Clearly the British gun industry had to respond, and a logical avenue was with magazine rifles that approximated the ballistics of the .450/.400.

The redoubtable .450/.400 originated as a blackpowder cartridge. This round, its blackpowder cousins, and the straight-cased, much more obscure .400 Purdey were virtually alone in the British field of cartridges between .375 and .450. Surprisingly, the Americans had a great many blackpowder cartridges in this arena. *Cartridges of the World* lists some 40 American blackpowder cartridges in the upper .30s and lower .40s. Many of these were Sharps, Maynard, and Remington cartridges for single-shot rifles, and Winchester and Marlin rounds for lever-actions. A few survived into the smokeless era, if briefly—but only one had any impact in Africa.

This lone American was, of course, the .405 Winchester, Teddy Roosevelt's "lion medicine," developed for Winchester's Model 1895 lever-action. The rifle itself was nearly 10 years old when the cartridge made its appearance. It fired a 300-grain bullet that was a bit light for its caliber, but it produced velocities of 2,200 fps for well over 3,000 foot-pounds of muzzle energy. Roosevelt found it marvelously effective on game up to lion, but lacking penetration on heavier game. Old Charles Cottar, the first American professional hunter, used the .405 extensively throughout his long career. The rifle was a heavy kicker and was considered needlessly powerful for American game; thus, the .405 chambering was never a big seller, and it died with the Model 1895 during the Depression.

Browning brought back an exact copy of the '95 a few years ago, but chose to chamber it in the available .30-40 Krag instead of the obsolete .405. I've always regretted that; especially as a lefty, I have always wanted to take a .405 to Africa—but the rifles are scarce and valuable today.

The Europeans had a few entries into the lower .40s caliber spectrum, both in blackpowder and smokeless form. The 10.75x57 was the largest variant of the 7x57 case, using a .424-inch bullet at understandably low velocity from so small a case. A bit better was the 1910-vintage 10.75x63 Mauser. Both undoubtedly saw use in the German colonies before World War I. Later developments were the 10.75x68 Mauser and the big 11.2x72 Schuler (using a .440-inch bullet). These cartridges did have an impact in Africa, but the lasting glory was to go to the British cartridges. We'll start with them as we examine the "lower .40s."

## .425 Westley Richards

The British gunmakers had a problem: fitting enough cordite to generate the desired power into a case that would fit the available bolt-actions. Until around 1910, John Rigby was Mauser's British distributor, and no magnum Mauser actions were made available to other makers. Westley Richards solved this dilemma with the .425 Westley Richards, introduced about 1909. This unusual cartridge could be called the first of the "short magnums," since it did indeed fit into a standard-length Mauser action—although not without some unusual dimensions.

Case length was 2.64 inches, a tight fit. The head diameter is a very fat .543-inch, but the rebated rim was turned down to just .467 to fit a standard Mauser bolt face. It wore an amazingly long neck, making it quite possibly the oddest-looking cartridge ever developed. Under England's system of proprietary cartridges, it was made by almost no one else, ever—yet it was quite a success for Westley Richards. And well it should have been; firing a 410-grain bullet of .435-inch diameter, it had a muzzle velocity of 2,350 fps for an energy of 5,010 foot-pounds—in other words, the same energy delivered by double-rifle cartridges from .450 to .475.

For some odd reason, the standard Westley Richards bolt-action .425 sported a 28-inch barrel. This was a common length for early double rifles, but added to the action length of a bolt gun, it made the rifle most unwieldy. Still, the cartridge retained a following for many years, and was the standard game-department issue in Uganda. The .425 was also chambered in a few W.R. doubles, and, as unlikely as it seems, was said to be satisfactory.

## .404 Jeffery

The .404 Rimless Nitro-Express, better known as the .404 Jeffery (or, in Europe, the 10.75x73mm) came along just a year later. By that time magnum Mauser actions were available, and this cartridge needs one. Introduced by Jeffery but released to the gun trade, it achieved a much more lasting popularity than the .425. Perhaps this was because several makers offered it, or perhaps because it has a more conventional shape. Certainly it isn't because of its flashy ballistics. Although it fires a fatter .423-inch bullet (and thus one with less sectional density and penetrating abilities), the .404 basically duplicates the .450/.400's ballistics: a 400-grain bullet at 2,125 fps for 4,020 foot-pounds.

The .416 Rigby is the most-remembered of the big British bolt guns, but the .404 was unquestionably the most popular. God only knows how many thousands were made by Jeffery, Westley Richards, Cogswell & Harrison, and numerous other firms in England and on the continent. Uganda being a notable exception, the .404 was the standard game-department issue in Kenya, Tanganyika, and the Rhodesias. The German firm of RWS continued loading ammunition after Kynoch dropped the .404, and indeed loads it to this day. A simply amazing number of .404s are still in service in Africa.

When I hunted Rhodesia in the late '70s, my host, Roger Whittall, had a battered Cogswell & Harrison .404, undoubtedly a game-department rifle. I didn't use it, but my partner, Ron Norman, used it on both hippo and buffalo with good results. I just now saw the same rifle, even more battered, in Mozambique in the hands of Roger's tracker, Chinkengiya. The game scout who accompanied me in Masailand, Julius Sayo Mahoo, was armed with a lovely Westley Richards .404—and although he never had to use it in my behalf, I never questioned whether he or it could do the job.

When famed gunmaker David Miller made his first safari to the Central African Republic, he built himself a .404—and used it most effectively on elephant and bongo. Since RWS ammo was always available (if hard to find), more than a few .404s have been built in America in recent years. Bullets have long been made by Barnes, and with modern propellants in a Mauser action, those mild 1910 ballistics can be upped substantially. For that matter, today's RWS load is a good deal hotter than the original Kynoch loading.

61

In the old books, you'll find the occasional whispers of .404 bullet failure. However, considering its wide use by so many game departments as well as private individuals, it's quite possible that more heavy game was shot with the .404 than any other British cartridge. If that's true, and it's at least *close* to the truth, then there must inevitably have been a few failures along the way. In all probability, most problems with the .404 resulted from using not the 400-grain bullet but rather a light, short 300-grain copper-capped bullet. With a muzzle velocity of 2,600, this bullet was designed for rapid expansion on thin-skinned game. It did that, possibly all too well; it had a reputation for explosive expansion, and was probably downright hazardous to use against dangerous game. Fortunately, the .404 has out-lasted this loading by decades.

Imported into the U.S. even today in a sturdy, inexpensive rifle by Parker-Hale, the .404 is an overlooked choice as an African rifle. Light in recoil, its effectiveness cannot be questioned.

## .416 Rigby

Introduced by John Rigby in 1912, the .416 Rigby is the most famous of the over-.40-caliber bolt-action cartridges, at least insofar as Americans are concerned. In its day it was not the most common, being offered only by Rigby—but it's possible that the great .416's heyday is yet to come.

Although it was a highly regarded cartridge in Africa, its legend outstripped its actual use; Rigby produced it in the hundreds, not in the thousands. Nevertheless, it was used, and by good hands. Commander David Blunt used almost nothing else. Harry Selby started out with a double, but when a lorry backed over it he made a quick run to Kenya Bunduki and purchased a .416 Rigby off the shelf. He's still using it today, nearly 40 years later. It's undoubtedly that very .416 that was immortalized in Ruark's fictional *Something of Value*—and quite possibly is largely responsible for today's fascination with Rigby's .416.

The great Jack O'Connor used few heavy rifles, but he owned and carried to Africa a .416 Rigby. A good friend and favorite professional of mine, Ronnie MacFarlane of Botswana, carries a much-battered John Rigby .416 for backup. . . and the list goes on.

A massive rimless cartridge with a case length of 2.90 inches and an overall length of 4 inches and more, the Rigby is an astonishingly modern case design, with sharp shoulder and little body taper. It originally propelled a 410-grain bullet of .416-inch diameter at 2,370 feet per second, delivering 5,115 foot-pounds of energy. Its Kynoch bullets, both solid and soft, were superb. From the start, the Rigby was revered as a real killer that delivered wonderful penetration.

Like all the other great British cartridges, it could have died when Kynoch quit loading the ammo—but it was too damned good and had too much charisma surrounding it. Although few actions are large enough to harness it, over the years a number of custom rifles were built around it in

America. After Kynoch ammo dwindled to collectible status, the .416 was kept alive with R.C.B.S. dies, Barnes bullets, and brass made by turning the belts from .460 or .378 Weatherby brass.

Then Jim Bell at Brass Extrusion Laboratories, Ltd. (now owned by P.M.C.) began loading ammo, and a few years later Art Alphin at A-Square followed suit. Paul Roberts of Rigby began making .416 rifles again on big Brno actions—and today he builds more .416s than anything else. Continental firms like Henri Dumoulin began building lovely rifles around big actions that would hold the .416, and suddenly the .416 Rigby was back in business. On the continent, Harald Wolf Mastergunworks in Belgium also offers rifles, cases, and loaded ammo—not only for the .416 Rigby, but for several other nearly forgotten big bores.

Today, the future of the original .416 seems more than secure. In addition to Rigby, Dumoulin, and custom rifles, the semi-production American firms of Dakota Arms, Kimber, and Gale McMillan have announced .416 Rigbys, as has the German firm of F.W. Heym. And so has Ruger. A .416 Rigby on a magnum action has long been the dream of American firearms genius Bill Ruger, and such a rifle was announced early in 1989. As the second prong in a two-pronged approach, Federal now includes the .416 Rigby in their Premium Safari ammunition line. Clearly the .416 Rigby will be more available in the 1990s than it ever has been.

Well it should be; it's a truly great cartridge. I have a Dumoulin .416 Rigby on a left-hand action, and it's a cartridge that gives you confidence. I stopped a charging lion cold with mine, and although I'm personally torn between a double and a magazine, the .416 Rigby is a cartridge I intend to use more in Africa. However, it needs to be said that, with modern propellants, the Rigby's big case isn't needed to duplicate those wonderful 1911-vintage ballistics. It could also be said that handloading can take advantage of that big case to increase velocities significantly—but it was a 400- or 410-grain bullet at about 2,400 feet per second that made the .416's reputation.

## Lower .40 Wildcats

Innumerable wildcat cartridges have more or less duplicated the performance of the .404 Jeffery, .416 Rigby, and, less frequently, the .425 Westley Richards. Most of these are long forgotten, but their common goal was to achieve the ballistics of these famed cartridges in modern cases that would fit in either .375 H&H or .30-06-length actions. Most of them used either the .375 H&H case or the .458 Winchester Magnum case, necked to appropriate diameter with various shoulder conformations. There's no reason to examine them all, but several have had significant impact on the rebirth of the .416.

The .416 Taylor was conceived by gunwriter Bob Chatfield-Taylor some 30 years ago. Using the .458 case necked down to .416, it will fit into .30-06-length actions, and it will indeed match (and beat) the original Rigby ballistics. Which makes it a wonderful cartridge, period. It's amazing that the .416 Taylor never made it into factory form; Bill Ruger considered it years ago, but as legend has it was unable to get an ammo maker to go along with him and produce the cartridges.

Nevertheless, it was and is a popular wildcat. John Wootters has used it—and written about it—widely, and although that didn't seem to help the Taylor, it undoubtedly kept the .416 pot stirring. Today, with several factory .416s, it's unlikely a major manufacturer will pick it up. But it remains a fine cartridge, and A-Square does load ammo for it.

American professional hunter George Hoffman created the .416 Hoffman, a .375 H&H case necked up to .416 with most of the body taper removed and a fairly short neck. George used it personally in the Sudan, Zambia, and Botswana, and swears by it. I have one, a fiberglass-stocked swamp rifle, and I swear by mine as well. Generally it pushes a 400- or 410-grain bullet at about 2,400 fps. George has had good luck achieving higher velocities, but in my particular rifle I start to get pressure above that level.

It doesn't really matter—2,400 is plenty. I shot my first elephant with the .416 Hoffman and a then-new 400-grain Barnes Homogenous Alloy Solid—a homogenous-alloy bullet with no lead core. I made a side-on brain shot from about 35 yards, and the elephant was down before the rifle came back from recoil. The bullet whistled through the skull in a straight line, and as far as I know it's still going.

When Remington designed the .416 Remington, they consulted heavily with George but chose to modify their case design slightly. That effectively killed the .416 Hoffman, but they're virtually identical. A-Square does offer factory .416 Hoffman ammo, and .416 Remington ammo will fit and can be safely fired in the Hoffman chamber—but not vice versa.

There have been a number of other .416 wildcats, and also several using other diameters. Hunter, outfitter, and writer Les Bowman created a .411 Magnum on a .458 Winchester Magnum case, using a .411 bullet. Years later Phil Koehne of K.D.F.—the Seguin, Texas, gunmaker—came out with the similar .411 K.D.F. in his own K.D.F. rifle, for which he also offers ammunition. The .411 uses a 400-grain bullet, thus gaining a slight (but insignificant) edge in sectional density over the .416 bore. Ballistics are the same, a 400-grain bullet at about 2,400, but, like the .416 Taylor, in a cartridge suitable for a standard-length action. The K.D.F.s I've shot have been extremely accurate, and it's certainly a fine cartridge.

It should also be said that the .411 (and the .416 Taylor, .425 Express, and all the short magnum .40s) are extremely efficient cartridges. For instance, it takes a lot more powder (and thus more recoil and noise) to achieve that 2,400 fps in a .416 Hoffman or Remington. And it takes more still in the Rigby. Yes, with sheer case capacity and a strong action, the bigger cartridges will go faster if you keep adding powder—but I believe that the shorter wildcats based around the .458 Winchester Magnum (or

.338) case are just about optimum in efficiency with regard to energy produced for powder burned.

The .425 Express is a similar, much more recent development. The brainchild of gunwriters Cameron Hopkins and Whit Collins, the .425 uses the good old .404 Jeffery .423-inch bullet in a necked-up .338 Winchester Magnum case or a necked-down .458 case. Again, it pushes a 400-grain bullet at a bit over 2,400. The larger-diameter bullet gains frontal area over a .416, but sacrifices sectional density. It is said to be very accurate, but so are the others. Once again, prior to the .416 Remington and the Ruger .416 Rigby project, it had a future, but now will undoubtedly be yet another over-.40 wildcat. A-Square makes ammunition at this writing. Good cartridges though these wildcats all are, they must be considered losers in America's .416 race. The .416 Rigby is a surprising winner, considering its antiquated case size. Let's now look at the other two winners.

## .416 Remington

Throughout the 1980s there was a persistent and apparently growing interest in .416s in America. The Hoffman was widely written about—by me as well as others—as were the .416 Taylor and the .411 K.D.F. In the past three decades, the firearms-industry rumor mill had several times hinted that a .416 cartridge might be coming along, and by 1987 the rumors finally seemed to have some substance. Aside from public interest, it also made sense—that huge gap between the .375 H&H and the .458 Winchester Magnum was the only sizable caliber gap in the entire spectrum of American sporting cartridges. Winchester had toyed with a .416 more than once, and Bill Ruger's desire to market a .416 Rigby was well known. And of course, Weatherby had the right case in their .378 and .460, and a big action to go along with it. Remington had never been involved in the .416 rumor mill, at least to my knowledge.

When they did it, they did it fast, with efficiency, and with few leaks until it was a reality. And they must get credit for being the first major U.S. manufacturer to adopt a .416. The .416 Remington was a natural for them; the standard-length Model 700 action will handle a .375-length cartridge, and their Custom Shop was well organized to handle such a project. They also had the brass; the .416 Remington is essentially the 8mm Remington Magnum necked up.

The .416 Remington's ballistics are no great surprise—nominally a 400-grain solid or soft at 2,400 fps, yielding 5,117 foot-pounds of energy. The factory ammo that I've chronographed actually does a bit *better* than that, but there's been nothing wrong with those figures since 1911.

In developing their factory loads, Remington threw another curve. Rather than spend R&D money in reinventing the wheel, they obtained the best bullets they could find that were available in sufficient quantities. The softpoint is the semi-spitzer Swift, a marvelous partition-type bullet with the front part of the core bonded to the jacket. For solids they chose the

Barnes Homogenous Alloy, the same bullet I used on that elephant I mentioned.

Performance of the .416 Remington will be identical to that of the Rigby, Hoffman, *et al.*—but it has the great advantage of being readily available, inexpensively, from a major manufacturer, and with marvelous bullets to boot. I actually had the honor of shooting the very first head of game with a factory .416 Remington firing factory Swift softpoint loads. It wasn't a buffalo, but it was a very fine record-book Alaska-Yukon moose. And of course the big bullet did its job—and retained 97 percent of its weight while it did it.

## .416 Weatherby

In the late 1980s, the time couldn't have been more ripe for a new Weatherby magnum. There had been no additions to the line since the .240 Weatherby Magnum was introduced in 1968, and the company's founder, Roy E. Weatherby, Senior, had effectively turned over the reins to his son, Roy E. Weatherby, Junior (Ed, as he prefers to be called), before he passed away in 1988. Although some thought was given to a 6.5mm Weatherby Magnum, the only major caliber gap in the entire line lay between the .378 and .460 Weatherby Magnums.

The case used by these two cartridges was also ideal; it was really a belted version of the big .416 Rigby case. Indeed, clear back in the 1950s Roy Weatherby himself had considered necking the .378 up to .416. But in those days there were no readily available American .416 bullets, and the mark he wanted to beat was the .458 Winchester Magnum. So he created the .460 Weatherby instead, and another 30 years passed before the time was right for the .416 Weatherby.

In 1989, the time *was* right. Good bullets were available from multiple sources, including indestructible Swift softpoints and Monolithic Solids that could handle Weatherby velocities. And interest in the .416-bore was at an all-time high.

The .416 Weatherby Magnum was announced at the S.H.O.T. Show in January, 1989, but it was late spring before the first rifles were available. In fairness, it must be stated that little is new about this hottest of the .416s. It's a belted version of the .416 Rigby, with case capacity virtually identical to the Rigby cartridge. However, the belt makes headspacing much simpler and makes reloading more goof-proof. Weatherby ammunition, too, is loaded for Weatherby rifles—not 75-year-old Mausers. Right from the factory it's loaded to the absolute upper limit of velocity that even the most courageous handloader would try to wring from a .416 Rigby.

If it has a drawback, it's that same belt; added to an already-fat case, the slight extra diameter added by the belt can reduce magazine capacity from what would be possible with the Rigby case. The Weatherbys never attempted a staggered-box magazine with the .378/.460 version of their Mark V; instead they opted for a two-cartridge in-line magazine, and this configuration is retained in the .416. Since I personally only carry a cartridge chambered when action is imminent, that makes the big Weatherby a two-shot rifle, pure and simple. There's no denying that's a drawback, but under most circumstances two shots is enough—and the third cartridge can always be slipped into the chamber when the tracks start getting fresh.

Regardless of all that, the .416 Weatherby right out of the box realizes the full potential of the big Rigby case. The goal was to push a 400-grain bullet at 2,700 fps, and the first batch of handloaded ammo sent to me by Weatherby's Larry Thompson beat that by some 50 feet per second. That was also close to the limit, at least with these components; extraction was sticky and the cases showed signs of excessive pressure.

At 2,700 fps, which is no problem, the energy figures for the .416 Weatherby are stunning—nearly 6,500 foot-pounds at the muzzle. A velocity like that, coupled with one of the more aerodynamic .416 bullets, also ensures trajectories as flat as many light and medium bores. Sighted just two inches high at 100 yards, the .416 Weatherby is dead-on at 200 and just $8\frac{1}{2}$ inches low at 300 yards. In effect, it's an elephant cartridge that could double for use on springbok in the Kalahari!

Yes, there's a price. Recoil is fierce, some 88 foot-pounds in a $9\frac{1}{2}$-pound rifle, whereas the Rigby and Remington are down in the low 50s. The .416 Weatherby I used was fitted with a K.D.F. Recoil Arrestor, which did tame the recoil—but the muzzle blast was shocking.

In late May, 1989, Ed Weatherby and I took the new .416 to Botswana's Chobe area to try it out on Cape buffalo. The cartridge obviously had the bullet weight, bullet diameter, and energy to be effective on buff—but the concern was equally obvious. Would the bullets hold up under such high velocities, fully 300 fps above the .416 Rigby for which they were designed?

We took several buffalo, shooting Swift softpoints, and indeed they did hold up. Did they ever! Recovered bullets were few and far between, but those we found retained over 95 percent of their original weight, with the classic Swift mushroom just like I've gotten from .416 Remingtons and .375s. I shot one buffalo with a typical behind-the-shoulder lung shot at about 60 yards. The bullet blew on through, as expected, and the buffalo was so obviously stone dead when we got to him that a finishing shot couldn't be justified—which is unusual.

More astonishingly, we followed up one of Ed's buffalo and found him standing in thick cover, very sick. Ed shot him square on the shoulder at 10 yards—and that bullet went clear through as well. The only bullet I recovered was from a steeply-angled shot on a zebra, but we were able to recover a couple of Ed's bullets from raking shots on buffalo. Although the .416 Weatherby is a real kicker, hunters who can handle recoil should give it serious consideration. It's everything all the other .416s are, plus a whole lot more. And while no conclusions can be drawn from just one rifle, it should also be mentioned that the .416 Weatherby I used was the most accurate big gun I've ever fired. One 100-yard group of less than ½-inch contained three 400-grain Swifts and two 400-grain Monolithic Solids, all factory loads, for God's sake.

Just as in 1912, there are now several entries in the lower .40 race—and I wouldn't be surprised if the sporting press gets some mileage from comparisons. In truth, there are no bad apples in the bunch. The Weatherby offers by far the most velocity and energy, but it does kick more. All the rest are pretty much even up—and collectively, they're all good choices for African hunting.

The lower .40s offer a significant edge over the .375 on dangerous game. They won't make up for sloppy bullet placement any more than anything else will, but they will stop a charge much more reliably. Some of those who have used them extensively rate them less effective on elephant than the .450-plus cartridges, but so few elephant are shot today this is a moot point. Others, like Blunt, reckoned they were better because the higher velocity gave better penetration. Taylor rated the .416 Rigby much better for lion than larger calibers because of better expansion with the softpoint bullets. And certainly they're excellent for buffalo.

With a scope, they shoot adequately flat for normal hunting ranges. They aren't true long-range cartridges, but with the semi-spitzer bullets now available, at .416 Rigby velocities they give up very little to the .375—if anything. The .416 Weatherby, with its greatly increased velocity, shoots flatter than the .375.

Unquestionably, they are needlessly powerful for plains game—but overkill, if there is such a thing, makes a lot more sense to me than being undergunned. Mounted with a scope, the .416s and their brethren easily fall into the category of all-round rifles—good guns to carry for anything that might develop. A heavier rifle would be, perhaps, a more certain choice for elephant and even buffalo, if such were the specific quarry. Certainly a .416 would be an unlikely choice to shoot impala for the pot.

In Africa, though, you never know what might develop. A kudu hunt turns into a buffalo hunt in seconds—while an elephant hunt can turn into a rare opportunity to take a bongo. It's always seemed sensible to me to pack along a rifle that could handle whatever came along—and all of the lower .40s fit handily into that niche.

# Chapter 7

# Big Bores for Repeaters

The very term "big bore" is hard to define. For our purposes, we'll say that modern big bores begin at .450. This is admittedly arbitrary; the .416 Rigby and its progeny all develop energy levels comparable to the Nitro-Expresses from .450 to .475. In fact, it wasn't until 1958, with Winchester's introduction of the .458, that a cartridge designed for repeating rifles existed at the lower end of the "big-bore" scale. Because of the proprietary system, a proliferation of nearly identical .450-caliber-plus cartridges evolved in England, but with very few exceptions they were rimmed cartridges for double rifles. Historically, there have been almost no big-bore developments, period, on the Continent. The one exception, the 12.7x70mm, is a good one, but European gunmakers don't have a long history with big cartridges.

It's interesting to speculate why, given all the rimmed cartridges for doubles, big-bore cartridges for repeaters have been so scarce. Obviously, the heavies have a limited market—but just as obviously there *is* a market, and the sales potential would have been especially good back in the pre-World War I days when most of the big-bore development was under-way.

It's quite possible that the .425, .404, and .416 were considered so effective that a really big jump upward in caliber was needed to gain any benefit. In effect, that's what happened; no British rimless or belted cartridges exist between this trio and the two big .50s, the .500 Jeffery and .505 Gibbs. The Europeans had a pair of 11.2mm cartridges, caliber .440—and then nothing until you get all the way to the 12.7x70mm Schuler mentioned above. Firing a .510-inch bullet, it just happens to be identical in all respects to the .500 Jeffery. It's uncertain whether this cartridge was actually a Schuler cartridge adopted by Jeffery—or vice versa. But whichever, it stands as the lone European big bore.

From the blackpowder era until 1958, there was no factory American big-bore cartridge designed for smokeless powder, although there were smokeless versions of several blackpowder cartridges. The .45-70 Government cartridge is the last of these, and it looks as if it will survive as long as metallic ammunition is loaded!

Starting with Winchester's Model 1876 lever-action, then continuing with the Model 1886 and comparable Marlins, we Americans had a long succession of lever-action rifles chambered for large-caliber cartridges—.45-75, .45-70, .45-90, .50-95, even the big .50-110 (which survived briefly into smokeless loading). Such rifles indeed saw some service in Africa; H. Rider Haggard included Winchesters in the armament of Allan Quatermain's party in his turn-of-the-century *King Solomon's Mines*, and the other Quatermain novels as well. However, it must be remembered that such rifles were small bores in the blackpowder era.

It wasn't until 1898 that John Rigby redefined a .45-caliber rifle as a big bore. He did it with his .450-3¼-inch Nitro-Express, and the world has never been the same. Prior to the introduction of this smokeless cartridge, firing a 480-grain jacketed bullet at 2,150 feet per second, a .450 was a light rifle in Africa. A .577 blackpowder rifle was a sort of heavy medium, and the standard heavy rifle was an 8-bore, the same designation we use in shotgun gauges; 8-bore or 8-gauge means, roughly, that eight round balls fitted to that bore diameter weighed one pound, so its round ball weighed *two ounces*. The big 8-bores varied somewhat in exact bore diameter and case design, but a bullet of conical shape weighing 1,250 grains with a diameter of .875-inch was fairly common. Velocity, with a load of 10 drams of blackpowder, was about 1,500 fps—and energy was just over 5,000 foot-pounds. During the 40-year reign of the blackpowder breechloader in Africa, this was the standard formula for stopping a charge.

It hardly seems coincidental that Rigby's .450-3¼" would achieve the same energy figures—or that the .458 Winchester Magnum would strive to do so another half-century down the road. Rigby's .450-3¼" Nitro-Express seemed to kill every bit as well as the big 8-bore. It was, perhaps, not so reliable a charge-stopper, but it penetrated better and could be built into a rifle that could actually be carried, whereas the 8-bores weighed some 16 to 18 pounds.

It's probably no coincidence, either, that both the .425 Westley Richards and the .416 Rigby developed energies just over 5,000 foot-pounds. Like the .450-3¼" compared to the 8-bore, the .425 and .416 achieved that level with the increased velocity of a lighter bullet. And, as I said, perhaps these were so effective that no demand was perceived for a rimless version of the .450-3¼".

At the turn of the century, a few magnum Mauser actions were barreled to the .500 Nitro-Express with three-inch case. A slant-box magazine was used so the rim of a cartridge rode ahead of the rim of the cartridge below it in the magazine. As mentioned, I saw a .450/.400 bolt gun once as well, undoubtedly also for the three-inch case. These fell by the wayside with the development of the .404, which became the standard chambering for a big bolt gun. Rigby, of course, kept their .416 for themselves, as did Westley Richards with the .425. And then the big .50s arrived on the scene.

## .505 Gibbs

It is generally believed that the .505 Gibbs predates the .500 Jeffery, so we'll look at it first. It may go back as early as 1913, and was almost certainly introduced by George Gibbs. It appears that the rifle was never extremely popular, and original .505s are rare and quite valuable today.

However, the .505 Gibbs is one more cartridge whose reputation outweighed its actual use, another legendary British big bore with a charisma that lasts to this day. It was written about widely, even by Ernest Hemingway, who chose it as the backup rifle for his fictional professional hunter in *The Short Happy Life of Francis Macomber*. Tony Sanchez wrote that it was J.A. Hunter's favorite, especially for elephant cropping.

Ballistics were extremely impressive: A 525-grain bullet of .505-inch diameter left the muzzle at 2,300 fps for 6,180 foot-pounds of muzzle energy. It was obviously effective on anything that walks, and friends who have shot the original Gibbs rifles rate them as the hardest-kicking firearms they've ever handled.

The ammunition was available well into the 1950s, and a number of custom .505 Gibbs rifles were built in this country, especially by long-defunct Hoffman Arms. Like the .416 Rigby, this is another cartridge that is seeing a rebirth today—though on a much smaller scale than the .416. Kimber is offering their magnum bolt-action in .505, as are European firms such as Heym and Henri Dumoulin. A-Square and B.E.L.L. make ammunition, and a variety of good bullets are available. Its big brother, the .500 Jeffery, has experienced no such renaissance today.

### .500 Jeffery

The .500 Jeffery offered several advantages over the Gibbs. It had a much shorter case, 2.74 inches versus 3.15, with a rebated rim, making it much easier to fit into a bolt-action and allowing bullets to be seated much farther forward. It was also loaded hotter, using a .510-inch 535-grain bullet at 2,400 fps for 6,800 foot-pounds of energy. The cartridge is believed to have been developed by the German firm of Schuler, who made rifles chambered for the metric version, the 12.7x70mm Schuler. It was clearly a great thumper for the largest of game, but it never achieved the reputation of the Gibbs. Perhaps it came along too late; it's believed to have been introduced in the 1920s, after most of the Nitro-Express cartridges were well-established.

This is actually a very obscure cartridge, one of the rarest of the Nitro-Express rounds. It's believed that Jeffery made just 23 rifles so chambered, although Schuler undoubtedly made many more. If you see one at a good price, buy it—but plan on having real trouble getting ammunition. According to the references I could find, the ammunition was made in Germany, not in England, and it was not available after World War II. Harald Wolf is now making ammunition and rifles in Belgium on a limited basis, although his version differs from the original in that his rim isn't rebated. So, like the .505 Gibbs, this grand old cartridge may still have a bit of life. Tony Sanchez is currently using one of Wolf's rifles to back up his clients, and he reports marvelous results on elephant. American Bill McBride has a Kreighoff .500 Jeffery; there are a few around. The most famous, C. Fletcher Jamieson's Jeffery, referred to often by John Taylor, still exists; it's now owned by Jamieson's son.

When the war ended, the .500 Jeffery was dead and the Gibbs, like all the other British Nitro-Expresses, was dying slowly. There was a real gap in powerful cartridges for repeaters, and it was not to be filled until the .458 Winchester cartridge came along in 1958. In the meantime, handloading Americans got busy.

## Big-Bore Wildcats

The first important big-bore wildcat was not a bolt-action cartridge at all; it was a lever-action cartridge designed by Alaskan outfitter Harold Johnson. Called the .450 Alaskan, it was based on the .348 Winchester case, introduced along with the Model 71 Winchester in 1936. The rifle was (and is) a big, strong lever-action, the last incarnation of the great Model 1886. The .348 proved extremely effective on elk, moose, and mid-sized bears, but Harold Johnson wanted a bit more gun to take into the alders after brown bear.

He developed the .450 Alaskan in the late 1930s, and it had quite a following—and is still occasionally seen today. Because of the tubular magazine, flatnosed bullets are required; and because of limited case capacity, a 500-grain bullet starts to sacrifice velocity. But with a good flatnosed bullet like Speer's 400-grainer, made for the .45-70, the .450 Alaskan is quite a cartridge. Velocity figures given go as high as 2,200 fps, and of course velocities in that range with a 400-grain bullet yield over 4,000 foot-pounds of energy.

There were several other versions of Johnson's cartridge, including the .450 Fuller and .450/.348 Ackley Improved, both of which removed more of the body taper and gave additional powder capacity. My own "Alaskan" is actually the Ackley version, and I've chronographed 405-grain bullets at 2,270 fps from my rifle! That proved a bit too hot. And, to be honest, given the stock style of a Winchester lever-action, the recoil was frightful. I backed off a bit, but even so a good, honest 2,150 fps is no problem—and that's a 4,000 foot-pound load, essentially the same as the .450/.400. I haven't read any accounts of the .450 Alaskan or its brethren being used in Africa, but there's no reason why it wouldn't be darn near perfect for lion and acceptable for buffalo.

In the years following World War II, a number of wildcats were developed around the full-length .375 H&H case, necked up to take .458 bullets and blown out to remove most of the taper. The .450 Mashburn and .450 Watts were nearly identical, being straight-walled cases with slight body taper. The .450 Ackley, still seen today, has almost no body taper and a slight shoulder.

After the development of the .458 Winchester Magnum, the .45 wildcats died out for a while, but today there's a resurgence based on the need—or at least the desire—to wring a bit more velocity out of the .458-caliber

500-grain bullet, a tough chore with the .458's limited case capacity. More recent wildcats on the .375 case include the .450 Barnes Supreme, straight-cased with a slight shoulder and short neck; and Jack Lott's .458 Lott, a straight-walled case with a tiny bit of body taper. The Lott was designed so that a hunter short on ammo could fire .458 Winchester Magnum ammo in his Lott chamber with no problems.

All of these cartridges are ballistic equals. With modern powders and plenty of case capacity, it's a breeze to duplicate .450-3¼" velocity, 2,150 fps. It's just as easy to push the 500-grain bullet at 2,300 fps, which yields 5,870 foot-pounds, and it's possible with most of these cartridges in most rifles to reach 2,400 fps without undue pressure. That load yields well over 6,000 foot-pounds, more than enough for anything.

Some of these wildcats are so close to one another that they're inter-changeable. I have a lovely .458 Lott, and one year I took it to Zambia on a hunt with Geoff and Rusty Broom. Midway through the hunt, Geoff and I decided to take a short holiday and go to his home at Matetsi, in Zimbabwe. Because of the gun permits, I left my .458 Lott in Zambia, but he had a .450 Ackley with no ammunition—so I packed along some ammo to help him clean up some leftover buffalo permits. The ammunition fed and functioned perfectly, just fireforming slightly to attain the Ackley shoulder in the process. I don't recommend such haphazard interchange, but the point is that all of the .458 wildcats are very similar.

At this writing, A-Square makes available .450 Ackley and .458 Lott factory ammo, so these two are the most likely choices.

The .404 Jeffery case has been another basis for .458 wildcats. The best known of these is the .460 G&A, for *Guns & Ammo* magazine. The brainchild of *Guns & Ammo*'s Tom Siatos and Jack Lott, the cartridge is essentially the .404 Jeffery necked up to .458, with the shoulder moved forward and most of the body taper removed. Again, it achieves about 2,300 to 2,350 feet per second with a 500-grain bullet. Tom Siatos, Bob Petersen, and Central African Republic outfitter Jan Schallig have used the .460 G&A with great success.

Ian Henderson, one of the pioneers of safari hunting in what is now Zimbabwe, used one of the first .460 G&A rifles, built for Californian John Pollon on a .404 Jeffery that had belonged to Ian's father. He wrote to me about it: "I used it during a cull and found the penetration superb. In fact, all the shots went clean through and we did not recover one bullet, which was a pity. My experience was hardly a true test, as we were taking head shots in mixed herds with no large bulls, so were not able to fully test the knock-down effect. I would class this rifle in the same category as the .505 Gibbs."

In a later development, Jack Lott cooked up the .450 G&A Short Magnum, again using the .404 case but shortening it so the cartridge would fit in a .30-06-length action. Ken Elliott, Publisher of Petersen's *Hunting,* has a Model 77 Ruger .458 rechambered for this cartridge, and he used it to stop a buffalo charge cold in the Zambezi Valley. In the shortened form, velocity runs about 2,200 fps, still plenty.

After the big .378 Weatherby was introduced in 1953, the wildcatters had a new, big, and readily available case to play with. John R. Buhmiller wildcatted the .450 Buhmiller on the .378 case, taking it to Tanganyika in 1955. Ultimately, this cartridge was the basis for the .460 Weatherby. Other wildcats based on this case include the .475 A&M, designed by the team of Atkinson & Marquart, using the .475-inch .470 Nitro-Express bullet; and Gil Van Horn's shortened-case .475 Van Horn. Another shortened version is the .460 A-Square Short Magnum, for which A-Square offers factory ammo.

The .460 case has been necked up further into a variety of .50-caliber wildcats using both .505- and .510-inch bullets. A-Square has both a short version, the .495 A-Square (.375 H&H-length), and a full-length version, the .500 A-Square, for which they offer factory loads. There's a .500 Barnes Supreme featuring a straight, tapered case with no shoulder. The most publicized of these is the .510 Wells, designed by Arizona riflemaker Fred Wells. Using a relatively straight case with a slight shoulder, the .510 Wells is an extremely powerful cartridge pushing a 600-grain bullet at over 2,400 fps. Tanzanian professional hunter/rancher Gary Hoops proudly showed his .510 Wells when we pitched up at his farm in the middle of Masailand to get a truck spring welded.

Professional hunter/writer Ross Seyfried is currently experimenting with yet another "ultimate" wildcat—a rimless .577 that pushes a 750-grain bullet in excess of 2,250 fps. He rates it a killer on both ends.

The drawback to all of the wildcats is the relative unavailability of ammo. In some cases this is cured by A-Square, but even so you won't find it on many dealers' shelves in the United States—and none in Africa. With the exception of the .458 Lott, the use of a wildcat entails being darn sure you have enough ammo with you—and also taking whatever steps are necessary to make sure you don't get separated from it, which can be a tall order with today's air travel.

There's another peculiar concern. Most African countries are nervous about sportsmen bringing in rifles, and some are downright paranoid. A gun permit may specify a certain number of cartridges, and in rare instances officials may inspect ammunition to make sure headstamps match. In part, this was one reason why A-Square's Art Alphin went to so much trouble to make factory ammo for so many obscure cartridges. A couple of years ago, a hunter carrying a .416 Hoffman, using necked up .375 cases, had his ammo confiscated because the headstamp didn't say .416. I've carried the .458 Lott with ammo based on the .375—but not after I heard about that. Africa is just too far away to take a chance, and anyone using a nonstandard cartridge must accept the risks associated with being tied to unavailable ammunition.

The wildcatting will go on, and for several reasons. First, powerful cartridges are fascinating—and it's always interesting to see how much power can be obtained from a shoulder-fired rifle. Witness the huge bolt-actions currently being built around the .50 Browning machine-gun cartridge! But if the .458 Winchester had done what it was designed to do and was publicized as being able to do, I doubt if we'd have nearly as many wildcats—and possibly not the current .416 craze, either.

## .458 Winchester Magnum

Introduced in 1958, the .458 Winchester Magnum is the largest of Winchester's family of short magnums, which also includes the .264, .300, and .338 Winchester Magnums. All, introduced between 1958 and 1962, were designed to function in .30-06-length actions. The original ballistics listed a 500-grain solid and a 510-grain softpoint, both at 2,130 fps for just over 5,000 foot-pounds of energy. Clearly, the objective was to achieve the ballistics of the classic .450 to .475 Nitro-Express cartridges for doubles—but in a compact, standard bolt-action.

The cartridge was and is extremely effective, but why the Winchester designers didn't make it a full-length case based on the .375 no one can say. Their Model 70 action was long enough, so perhaps it was simply because the short magnum concept was "in" in those days. In any case, it was a big mistake, and for more than 30 years shooters have been paying for it.

The initial loadings did come very close to published figures, but to achieve them the little 2.5-inch case was crammed clear to bursting with powder. It was a compressed load, and occasionally you heard about ignition failure. In the worst of these cases—and I've seen a couple of them—the bullet barely gets out the barrel and bounces on the ground halfway to the target. Enough of these stories got back to Winchester—and were finally believed—so that a number of years ago .458 Winchester Magnum ammo was quietly downloaded.

Current figures are quoted at 2,040 fps for 4,622 foot-pounds of energy. That's still respectable, but it isn't what the cartridge was designed to produce. Worse, there's a bit of blue sky in those figures, which is rare for factory ammo today. In my chronographing, I have yet to see a current .458 Winchester Magnum cartridge fired from a 24-inch barrel break 2,000 fps. A speed of about 1,975 is more usual, closer to 1,950 in a 22-inch barrel.

That puts the energy down around 4,000 foot-pounds, on a par with the .450/.400 and original figures for the .404 Jeffery. Is it enough? Sure it is, especially with the excellent bullets Americans have available. But it won't equal the old .470, .450-3¼", or their kin. Nor will it equal the modern .416s. Its greater frontal area does make a difference, but it's lost a full 1,000 foot-pounds of energy, 20 percent, from its initial figure—and that's a lot to make up for. In fairness, the .458 retains a tremendous following, including many more knowledgeable than I. These include the likes of Finn

75

Aagaard and my old friend Barrie Duckworth—who shot his thousandth elephant with a Mannlicher .458.

Handloaders can, with some difficulty, get the .458 back to 2,100 fps and a bit more with carefully selected powders and judiciously compressed loads. However, the handloader has a wealth of more versatile case designs to pick from.

The beauty of the .458 has always been the proliferation of relatively cheap, available ammo. It came about at a time when the Nitro-Expresses were being discontinued, and of course the American mass-produced rifles were serviceable and available at a fraction of the cost of even a British bolt gun. It took Africa by storm, and is unquestionably the most common big bore in use today—and probably the single most common big bore in history. Whether its bullet starts at 1,950 or 2,130 fps, it's been used, and used effectively, far too much to suggest it isn't enough gun. It is. But it's not a dinosaur killer. For the non-handloader on a restricted budget, or the professional hunter in the bush who doesn't want to worry about ammo availability, it still might be the best thing going. But Lord, how much better it would be with just a bit more case capacity! In fact, its factory ballistics can actually be duplicated by the oldest American centerfire cartridge still in existence.

## .45-70 Government

It seems almost impossible that the cartridge carried by Custer's troops at the Little Big Horn back in 1876, in countless skirmishes in a dozen Indian wars throughout the American West up until the turn of the century, and even up San Juan Hill with Roosevelt's Rough Riders, should still be a viable big-bore cartridge today. It is, but certainly not in the trapdoor Springfield rifles that made it a part of history, nor with the original loadings for that weak-actioned rifle.

The .45-70 was a traditional chambering for both Winchester and Marlin lever-actions, as well as several fine American single-shot actions that were as strong as the Springfields were weak. The .45-70 was a standard American hunting cartridge, widely used for the largest of game—bison (as long as bison remained to be hunted), moose, even grizzly. It was in America what the British .577/.450 Martini-Henry was throughout the British Empire, and it's outlasted even the Martini.

As satisfactory as the .45-70 was, handloading hunters learned in the dawn of the smokeless era that its ballistics could be significantly improved—in a strong action. Such actions included the lever-actions, the Winchester Hi-Wall single-shot, the Remington rolling block, and others. Gradually, all the rifles chambering the .45-70 became obsolete, but enough of them remained in use that the ammunition continued to be available.

Then a couple of odd things happened. In the 1970s, Marlin brought out a new, modern lever-action chambered for .45-70, and Ruger included it in the myriad chamberings for the single-shot Number One. In the Ruger, possibly one of the world's strongest actions, the .45-70 can be handloaded to equal the current factory .458 loadings. The Marlin isn't quite so strong, but a 400-grain bullet can still be pushed to nearly 1,900 fps. In a tubular-magazine lever-action, I'd be terrified of a roundnosed solid; the potential detonation isn't worth the risk. But it's ideal with the flatnosed 400-grain bullets that are available.

A sort of modern-day .450 Alaskan, the Marlin repeater can be scoped, and its .45-70 cartridge would be just fine and extremely handy for cats and even buffalo. In factory form, though, it's quite anemic—it needs a strong action and handloads, making it a sort of factory wildcat.

## .460 Weatherby Magnum

The big daddy of factory American cartridges needs no reloading to boost up its performance; it's just fine right out of the box. The .460 Weatherby Magnum, based on John Buhmiller's wildcat, was introduced by Roy Weatherby in 1958. Its stated purpose was to give Roy Weatherby the world's most powerful cartridge, and it's that for sure. A more subtle reason was the East African Professional Hunters Association's banning of cartridges under .40 caliber for use on elephant, buffalo, and rhino. His .378 Weatherby Magnum was suddenly out of the running, and Weatherby needed a cartridge that would compete in that arena with the new .458 Winchester Magnum.

The .460 can do it that in spades. Factory velocity is quoted at 2,700 fps, yielding a stunning 8,095 foot-pounds of energy. In all of my testing, actual velocities have run a bit lower, but with factory loads or handloads 2,600 to 2,650 is about right—and hardly figures to sneeze at. The .460 Weatherby has been widely maligned, and indeed with a softpoint designed to perform properly at a velocity 500 fps slower, it may not give the desired penetration. But with a good solid or a tough softpoint, it's just plain magnificent.

A good friend of mine, Bruno Scherrer, swears by a .460 for his heavy game. On a hunt in the Sudan several years ago, he had been working his tail off to get a decent elephant. Tracks, small bulls, cow herds—but nothing big. The wind shifted when they were working a very large herd, and the game was over—almost. The forest opened into a broad clearing, and they reached it just in time to watch the herd pass on the far end—much too far to shoot at an elephant. The last bull to pass was a dream elephant with long, heavy ivory. Against his professional hunter's wishes, Bruno took the shot. It was easy, really—a single lung shot with a scoped .460 Weatherby at very close to 200 yards. At that distance, it had what the .458 has at the muzzle—and the ivory weighed out at 98 pounds per side. It was also the kind of shot that is never attempted at an elephant—but whether recommended or not, the .460 Weatherby is darn near the only cartridge that makes it remotely practical.

The .460 Weatherby does bring some excess baggage with it. Recoil is fierce enough that recovery for the second shot is slowed, and the big belted case is so bulky that its Weatherby Mark V rifle holds but two shells in the magazine. (That capacity is the same for the .378 and .416 Weatherbys as well.) It's a price to pay; I've always been more comfortable with the added capacity and somewhat less recoil of something like a .416 Rigby or a .458 Lott. Still, the .460 Weatherby does fill a valuable niche as a magazine rifle that is unexcelled in sheer stopping power. A professional-hunter friend of mine told me the .460 was the most deadly rifle he'd ever seen on buffalo. I don't doubt that for a minute; on the occasions I have used it, it's been devastating.

Unlike all the cartridges we've discussed heretofore, these big bores are not multi-purpose rifles. They're stopping rifles, designed only for the largest of game—elephant, buffalo, rhino, and hippo. In bolt-action form, they do offer exceptional accuracy, and will reach out to a couple of hundred yards on lesser game—but lighter cartridges are much better suited. With softpoints, they're also devastating on lion—especially if things go sour with the first shot. But their strong suit, what they're made for, is getting a heavy bullet deep into the vitals of the largest game on earth. They're special-purpose cartridges, not jacks-of-all-trades. And in that special role, together with their Nitro-Express cousins designed for use in doubles, they're irreplaceable.

The two rimmed cartridges mentioned here, the .45-70 and .450 Alaskan, are at best very marginal in this role. The rest of the group offer difficult choices. The .458 Winchester is the standard. Most of the others beat it, and perhaps it needs to be beaten—but not by much. The .460 Weatherby and the big .500s beat it by an incredible margin, giving, perhaps, a significant charge-stopping edge. As a group, though, any of the rimless or belted cartridges from .458 up will do the job, so a wrong choice would be hard to make.

# Chapter 8

# The Big Nitro-Expresses

It's more than possible that the likes of the 9.3 Mauser accounted for more game than all the large-caliber Nitro-Express cartridges rolled into one. Double rifles—and the cartridges they fired—were always expensive and somewhat unusual. Many professionals, whether professional guides or professional poachers, did carry them, and a few still do. But many more carried cheaper, lighter, higher-capacity magazine rifles. The game rangers rarely carried doubles—they couldn't afford them. Neither could the ranchers and farmers who, as a group, undoubtedly accounted for more game than all the rest. But facts be damned; the British Nitro-Express cartridge is more than just part of the legend of safari—as a pervasive symbol, the big cigar-shaped cartridge *is* African hunting.

I succumbed to the legend early on; at about 13 I discovered J.A. Hunter and his double .500 in the school library, and it wasn't long after that I discovered Robert Ruark and his Westley Richards .470. From those days forward, I coveted a big double, something every Kansas schoolboy really needs. Eventually I traded around and got my hands on one, and in the years that have followed I've owned a variety of Nitro-Express doubles, and shot a few more. The big doubles and the cartridges they fire are indeed wonderful; pressures are kept very low by the huge cases, and although unhandy, those big cases offer a tremendous psychological lift.

Their sole job is to stop the largest and most dangerous game, whether it's inbound, outbound, or standing still. And this they do, all of them—and in nearly equal measure. Thanks, in part, to the British proprietary system whereby a gunmaker could have an exclusive right to a cartridge he designed, there exists a bewildering array of Nitro-Express cartridges ranging in caliber between .450 and .500. It's an understatement to say they're similar; many use the same basic case, and although bullet diameters may differ by a few thousandths, bullet weights and velocities are generally very close, if not identical.

Fifty years ago, good copy could be had by comparing in depth one of these cartridges to another—much the way modern scribes pit the .280 Remington against the .270 Winchester. Fifty years ago, there might have been some limited validity in such a comparison; most of the cartridges were available then, and the bullets some of them fired were also exclusive with one or another maker. Today, it borders on the ridiculous to attempt to compare the .470 with the .475 No. 2 or the .450-3¼" with the .500/.450. Original ammunition for all of them is headed toward antique status, and most of the guns are already there. Although a few new guns are being built today, the man who wants a double rifle often seeks an old one in decent condition and sound working order with a good bit of rifling left in both barrels. The exact caliber those barrels are chambered to is less important than overall condition and who the maker was.

This is today's reality, especially since original ammunition—which in some cases, by virtue of bullet shape or design, strongly influenced the cartridge's performance—is getting too old to rely upon. For many years, the value of a vintage double was predicated on whether the sale was accompanied by a supply of ammunition. Forget it; the 1990s have arrived, and the Kynoch ammunition remaining is becoming uncertain. This problem will only get worse as time goes on; I have had misfires with old Kynoch ammunition, as have most hunters who use it. In the last two years I've heard of two different failures of old Kynoch on lion—and one of them resulted in a mauling. I just now heard about a professional hunter who was nearly killed by a buffalo after old Kynoch ammo misfired. The horn went in under the third rib. After stuffing his right lung back into the wound he drove himself to the hospital.

It isn't worth it; use the old doubles, but forget about the old ammo.

The good news is that *all* of the old Nitro-Express cartridges can be reloaded. B.E.L.L. has a good, strong modern case that will work, and R.C.B.S., Huntington, and others will make dies. Bullets may be Barnes, Woodleigh, A-Square, Trophy Bonded, even common Hornadys in the case of the various .450s. Some of the bullets are better than the originals, some are not as good. But they're all we have now, the point being that all the big Nitro-Expresses share the same choice of bullets today.

There is a simple means for "aging" Kynoch ammo, at least relatively speaking. The older corrosive-primed Kynoch had copper-colored primers, while the most recent non-corrosive ammo had brass-colored primers. All of the failures I've personally had, whether misfires or hangfires, have been with ancient corrosive stuff. At this writing, I still have *some* confidence in non-corrosive Kynoch. The .470 Kynoch ammo I have now was probably loaded in the late 1950s, and it functions perfectly—but my comfort level drops annually.

The big Nitro-Expresses are dinosaurs, throwbacks to another era—but they're wonderful fun to play with, and they're still marvelously effective on the world's largest game. As noted earlier, the standard stopping rifle of the blackpowder era became the 8-bore. A fair number of hunters relied on 10- and 12-bores instead—and there were a couple of monster breechloading 4-bores—but the 8-bore ruled the roost. Of course, there was the odd eccentric who relied on a small bore—a .577 or, rarely, a smaller bore yet. Frederick Courteney Selous, not the greatest of the elephant hunters but possibly the greatest African hunter who ever lived, gave up the punishing big bores in favor of a single-shot Gibbs firing a .461 blackpowder cartridge—not because it was adequate, but because he preferred to take his time and place his bullet rather than be kicked into next week. In later years, he wrote that the muzzleloading 2- and 4-bores of his youth had adversely affected his nerves and his shooting for all time.

Also mentioned earlier was the fact that John Rigby changed all this in 1898 when he introduced the straight-cased .450-3¼" Nitro-Express. That's true enough, but the 8-bore didn't go away overnight. Many oldtimers clung to it well into our century.

Most hunters who used both reported that the 8-bore was more reliable in stopping a determined charge. However, the "little" .450 Nitro-Express delivered unprecedented penetration, and it would indeed stop anything, if not quite so spectacularly as the 8-bore's huge bullet. It also did it without the clouds of game-obscuring smoke, and with appreciably less recoil. It also did it from a 10½-pound rifle as opposed to one weighing 17 or 18 pounds. With reluctance, the blackpowder behemoths of the 19th century faded from the scene.

Most of the early Nitro-Express cartridges for doubles were based on existing blackpowder cases. In the latter part of the 19th century, the British developed a series of "Express" blackpowder cartridges, generally bottle-necked, sometimes with a compressed powder charge, and offering velocities much higher than normal for the day—sometimes by virtue of a lighter bullet. None of the Expresses approached the 2,000 fps threshold that was instantly crossed with smokeless cordite. Equally important, that velocity was suddenly possible with heavy, jacketed bullets of good sectional density—bullets that would penetrate as no others ever had.

Rigby was first, with Holland following soon after with the .500/.450 Nitro-Express, based on an identical blackpowder case. Then the race was on, and Lord knows how many .450 cartridges we would have had—except that in about 1905 .450 cartridges were banned in India and the Sudan. The reason was both simple and strange; the old British military cartridge was the .577/.450 Martini Henry, and because of unrest in those regions—and huge quantities of Martinis everywhere—the Brits wanted to keep .450 ammunition and components out of the wrong hands.

Now the race was *really* on to develop suitable replacements for the .450s in acceptably legal calibers. That 1905 ban plus the proprietary system are responsible for the great number of near-identical cartridges from the .500/.465 to the .476 Westley Richards.

As mentioned, most of the big Nitro-Expresses were derived, at least initially, from blackpowder Express cases. Obviously, they are not interchangeable. If you have any questions about the exact chambering of a rifle you're considering buying or using, find an expert. A number of blackpowder rifles were made well into the smokeless era, and in rare instances only the proof marks on the "flats" of the barrels will tell you whether the rifle was proofed for blackpowder, nitro—or both.

A second word of caution: Have the barrel slugged to determine exact caliber. For unknown reasons, the bore and groove diameters of British double rifles vary widely, especially in some calibers. Worse, some of the most respected references on the subject are just plain wrong regarding bore and bullet diameters for Nitro-Express cartridges. It's easy to be wrong, too—there are two .475 No. 2s, for instance, one firing a .483 bullet and one firing a .488 bullet. It's confusing but not defeating; there are bullets that will fit. Just slug the barrel to make sure you know what you're dealing with. Now let's take a more detailed look at the big British Nitro-Expresses.

## .450/.400

There are two versions of this fine cartridge—the original with a $3\frac{1}{4}$-inch case and a later Jeffery version with 3-inch case. Generally the former is called the .450/.400-$3\frac{1}{4}$" while the latter is called the .450/.400-3", or .400 Jeffery. The longer version, a straight transition from a blackpowder case, was one of Britain's first smokeless loadings. Neither should be confused with the .400 Purdey, a Nitro loading for a blackpowder cartridge that wasn't nearly as powerful. The blackpowder brass used for the early .450/.400-$3\frac{1}{4}$" ammo proved not quite strong enough for the Nitro loading, so initially there were reports of sticky extraction. This prompted Jeffery to develop his own cartridge, using a much heavier case designed for cordite.

Introduced in 1896, the Jeffery version was the first of the big Nitro-Expresses based on a case designed for smokeless powder. To this day, many double-rifle men will tell you that the 3-inch version is to be preferred because the cases are better. Theoretically that's true, but of course the $3\frac{1}{4}$-inch case was improved and stiffened generations ago—and today most people will be using B.E.L.L. brass in any case. In my opinion, neither one has an advantage over the other. Both versions were extremely popular, and it's too bad they are not interchangeable.

Ballistics are virtually identical, a 400-grain bullet propelled by 60 grains of cordite, yielding a bit over 2,100 fps for 4,000 foot-pounds of energy. This is one instance where it's very important to slug the barrel; .450/.400s vary from a bullet diameter of about .405-inch to .411. The $3\frac{1}{4}$" guns tend to be about .411, but you never know until you check. Champlin Arms's George Caswell, America's largest dealer in double rifles, tells me there's more variation in .450/.400s than in any other Nitro-Express.

Nominally, this is a .40-caliber cartridge with a long case and an impossibly long, skinny neck. At 2,150 feet per second (2,125 for the 3-inch version) it set the velocity pattern for all the Nitro-Expresses that followed—and it was and is a wonderfully effective cartridge. The .450/.400 was one of the great all-round cartridges, essentially filling the same sort of niche in double rifles and single-shots that the .375 H&H came to occupy in bolt-actions.

It isn't long on foot-pounds, although 4,000 is quite enough; nor, obviously, does it have a flat trajectory. However, that 400-grain .40-caliber bullet at its very modest velocity seems to be one of the accidentally perfect combinations that sometimes come along. You can check any number of references, and no one has anything but high regard for the .450/.400's performance on game—especially in terms of deep, straight-line penetration.

The cartridge was the choice among India's tiger hunters, including the great Jim Corbett. In Africa, where it was more of an all-round cartridge, it seems to have been the exclusive choice of few but saw satisfactory use by many. Major P.H.G. Powell-Cotton favored his .450/.400 in both Abyssinia and Central Africa—although he also had a .600 double available on his later trips. Even the king of the small-bore advocates, Karamojo Bell, had a .450/.400.

Today .450/.400 doubles in both case lengths are surprisingly common, and generally less expensive than doubles for the supposedly more desirable .450-plus cartridges. Although I have never seen a .450/.400 in use in Africa, a few are still around. Mark Selby carries his to this day, a wonderfully used old rifle with the inscription "To Mark from your Uncle Bob," a gift from his godfather, Robert Ruark.

A legitimate problem with many .450/.400s is that they were built on actions that would accommodate larger cartridges, thus ending up at a weight of 11 pounds or worse; thus no recoil problems but more weight than needed. At $9\frac{1}{2}$ pounds or thereabouts, I can't imagine anything more pleasant than a .450/.400 double to carry and shoot. Especially in today's Africa, when so few safaris include elephant, a .450/.400 would be a particularly sensible choice for buffalo and tracking hunts for lion.

It was also a popular chambering in Farquharson single-shots, and could easily be adapted to a Ruger No. One action. That's worth mentioning because the .450/.400 could benefit from a scope sight. I have a personal fascination for the .450/.400, and I've always wanted to own one. One of these days, by golly, I will!

## .450-3 $\frac{1}{4}$"

Variously called the .450 Rigby and .450 Straight, this was the cartridge that changed the world. Introduced by John Rigby in 1898, it's a wonderful cartridge to this day. It has a long, tapered case, not the big bottlenecked case of most of its brothers. This means the .450-3$\frac{1}{4}$" can be built into a slimmer rifle than can other cartridges of similar power. Rigby's rifles in this caliber were amazingly trim and sleek—to my taste, the best-balanced and most attractive doubles ever made.

The .450-3$\frac{1}{4}$", like almost all the Nitro-Expresses, was based on an existing blackpowder case, but it used 70 grains of cordite to propel a 480-grain bullet at 2,150 fps. This unprecedented velocity gave the cartridge nearly 5,000 foot-pounds of energy, and that remains the standard formula for heavy game to this day. Eventually, there would be three

.450-caliber Nitro-Express cartridges, and much confusion exists regarding who used what; most references just refer to a .450. Because all three were banned in India and the Sudan early on, few rifles were so chambered after 1906.

Kermit Roosevelt carried a Rigby .450-3¼" on the historic 1909 safari, while his dad had Holland's counterpart, the .500/.450. Most of the .450-3¼" rifles I have seen were made by Rigby, and there are a few Army & Navy guns (probably also made by Rigby) so chambered. The beauty of the .450-3¼", if you happen across one, is the slim, straight case and its ability to fire .458-inch bullets. Some .450s will require a 480-grain bullet to regulate properly, and that means Barnes or Woodleigh. But many will regulate just fine with 500-grain Hornadys; if yours does, you've got a great bullet readily available for peanuts.

## .500/.450

Properly called the .500/.450 Magnum Nitro-Express 3¼", this was Holland's answer to the Rigby .450 3¼". It used a blackpowder Express .500/.450 case, a larger bottlenecked case that needed more powder—75 grains of cordite—to produce its velocity of 2,175 fps. But because of the larger case, it did so with less pressure. The bullet was an identical 480-grain slug, and this one will also take .458 bullets. (At least, most rifles will—again, always slug the barrel of a double rifle!)

The .500/.450 was essentially a Holland exclusive, although it's impossible to state any firm rules regarding double rifles and their cartridges. Rifles were made only from 1899 to around 1907, when the chambering was replaced by the .500/.465. That makes the .500/.450 one of the rarest of the double-rifle cartridges, but it's usually found in best-quality rifles. Brass is easily made today by necking down B.E.L.L. basic .500 brass, and of course bullets are readily available. It's a great cartridge, and it's just as adequate today as Teddy Roosevelt found it in 1909. His rifle, by the way, was a best-quality Holland presented to him by a group of English sportsmen, including Selous. The rifle exists today, and it was taken to Africa and used by Teddy Roosevelt's grandson and great-grandson, "T.R. III" and "T.R. IV," in 1987.

## .450 No. 2

Believed to be a Jeffery development, the .450 No. 2 was introduced by Eley in about 1903. It was the first of the .450-plus Nitro-Expresses with a case designed specifically for cordite powder. It was released to the gun trade; thus a number were made by several different makers prior to the ban on .450 cartridges. The case was huge—fully 3½ inches in length—and very strong. This was in response to some early reports that both the .450-3¼" and .500/.450 had sticky extraction. Undoubtedly they did, especially since the first cartridges used soft, thin brass designed for blackpowder. The .450 No. 2 had a heavier charge, 80 grains of cordite—but with the larger case, greatly reduced pressure.

The reduction in pressure was certainly desirable, but the problem with the other two cartridges wasn't too much pressure; rather, it was poor brass. This problem was soon corrected, and at first glance the .450 No. 2 seemed to have no reason for existence. However, that extra-long case was much bigger and more impressive than its competitors, and it quickly gained popularity. The truth is that the .450 No. 2, in spite of its larger case and heavier powder charge, exactly duplicated the ballistics of the .500/.450: 480-grain bullet at 2,175 fps, yielding 5,050 foot-pounds of muzzle energy. And, obviously, that's a proven and near-perfect formula for excellent performance on the world's largest game.

The double rifle is, by the nature of its construction, one of the weakest of rifle actions. So the low pressure of the .450 No. 2 is a very real advantage. The original brass was extremely strong, and current B.E.L.L. brass is very heavy as well. Before B.E.L.L. came on the scene, the .450 No. 2 was virtually dead, being an early casualty as Kynoch began dropping the big cartridges. Today it's an extremely sensible choice. Not being as desirable as a .470 or .475 No. 2, the guns so chambered will be a bit cheaper. And .450 No. 2s were built by a variety of top makers. Today good brass is available, and .458 bullets may generally be used.

The .450 No. 2 is George Caswell's personal favorite among the big Nitro-Expresses, and he's having a few of his new Champlin-Famars doubles so chambered. With modern steels and the .450 No. 2's stout case, original velocities can be exceeded, and, thanks again to that heavy brass, case life tends to be better than with most cartridges in this class. Caswell is also having surprising success with lighter .458 bullets of 350 and 400 grains. Of course, with a double it's all a matter of getting the barrels to shoot together. Sometimes you get lucky and sometimes you don't—but usually it's a matter of matching the original velocity at which the barrels were regulated. In the final analysis, the .450 No. 2 is no better, or worse, than any of its ballistic kin—and it shouldn't be shied away from by anyone looking for a good double.

## .500/.465

Like so many of the big Nitro-Expresses, the .500/.465 is yet another cartridge based on the straight .500 case. It was a Holland & Holland cartridge that appeared about 1907, simply the .500/.450 necked up just a little, and obviously a direct response to the banning of the .450-bore in India and the Sudan.

Unlike the .500/.450, the .500/.465 enjoyed a long and successful life. Although generally (and again, *generally* is the strongest word that can be used) exclusively a Holland & Holland proposition, it was extremely popular—and many rifles so chambered are still in use. It was one of the last Kynoch loadings, with early 1960s-vintage ammo occasionally encountered.

Although the bullet remained 480 grains and the charge was 75 grains of cordite, the ballistics weren't improved by the increase in caliber; velocity is 2,125, and energy a bit under 5,000 foot-pounds. It was and is a very fine cartridge, neither better nor worse than any of the .450s or .475s.

The .500/.465 is generally encountered in fine guns, not the garden-variety working double, so it was used by relatively few "working" hunters. Taylor used it quite a bit, apparently preferring it to the .470 because he thought it had a slightly better bullet shape. Tony Sanchez, who knew Taylor well in his last years, states that in the final analysis the .465 was Pondoro's favorite.

The Portuguese nobleman, Count Vasco Da Gama, preferred his Holland .465 to both the .577 and .600, feeling the excessive recoil of the latter two caused recovery to be too slow for the second shot. Dr. Richard Sutton, an American who hunted and wrote extensively in the 1920s, preferred a .465—but his was a Purdey, quickly dispelling the myth that the .465 was strictly a Holland exclusive. Although primarily a .470 man, the American hunter/explorer/naturalist James L. Clark used a Holland .465 on his later trips. Another great American hunter, Stewart Edward White, used his Holland .465 for decades. My good friend Roger Whittall, Zimbabwe rancher turned professional hunter, has a lovely Holland sidelock .465— one of the few sidelocks I've ever seen in the field. Joe Wright, one of his young professionals, has a Westley Richards boxlock .465, a rare duck.

Today there are good cases and good bullets for the .465, and its only drawback for the hunter in search of a good double is that, because of the makers' names generally found on a .465 barrel, the guns will tend to be expensive.

## .470 Nitro-Express

This most popular of all the Nitro-Expresses made its appearance about 1907, and is believed to have been introduced by Joseph Lang. It was not retained as a proprietary cartridge by anyone, but was released to the gun trade in general. *Everybody* made .470s, and .470s may be encountered in almost any configuration.

There's nothing magical about the .470's ballistics; it fired a .475-inch 500-grain bullet at 2,150 feet per second, delivering 5,140 foot-pounds of energy. The case, again, is the .500 case necked down, with a $3\frac{1}{4}$-inch case length. Taylor felt the original bullet tapered a bit too much toward the nose and lacked the straight-line penetration of some of the other big Nitros. That may or may not be true; he wasn't emphatic about it, and many other top hunters relied upon the .470 with no reservations. In any case, it's irrelevant today since few hunters are still using original bullets, and all the Nitro-Expresses share the same bullet choices, except for the .450s with their ability to use Hornadys.

Because so many .470 rifles were made by so many makers, ammo remained available well into the 1960s. The .470 just plain outlasted most of the big Nitro-Expresses. It wasn't, and isn't, better than the others (nor is it worse), but it's the cartridge that most readily comes to mind when you think of a big double rifle.

Although .470 rifles are to be found in any persuasion, as a non-proprietary chambering they tended to be working guns—boxlocks by Evans, Lancaster, Wilkes, Hollis, Westley Richards, Lang, Gibbs, and many others. They were used, and well-used, by a host of hunters all across Africa.

H.C. Maydon, author of the classic *Big Game Shooting in Africa,* used a .470. As mentioned, James L. Clark used a .470 by Evans. Australian Andrew Holmberg, one of the great hunters of *big* elephant, used a .470. So did Roy John Dugdale "Samaki" Salmon, although he used his in conjunction with a .416 magazine rifle. It's likely the cartridge would have survived anyway, but the fact that Robert Ruark wove his Westley Richards .470 into his novels and stories, almost as a central character, didn't hurt.

John Kingsley Heath used a .470—I saw the rifle when it was for sale a couple of years ago, and I believe it was also a Westley Richards. Even Peter Capstick, more often than not, mentions the .470 when he speaks of a big double. Yes, I succumbed as well; when I started shopping for a big double, it had to be a .470. My first double was a Wilkes in that caliber, and my current is another .470 by C.W. Andrews, an unknown English maker who knew how to put together a nice rifle.

Ironically, while the .470 is really no better than the rest, its popularity is such that the value of a rifle goes up by a minimum of $1,000 if .470 happens to be its chambering. This is a point well worth considering in shopping for a used double, since that extra $1,000 or more does not buy added performance over any of the .450s or .475s. On the other hand, the .470 is the only Nitro-Express for which any number of rifles are being built today.

A couple of the English makers will build .470s today, and in Europe you can find new .470s from Heym, Dumoulin, the Ferlach makers, and several others. There are rumors of a couple of American double .470s in the works, and certainly ammunition is more commonly available than ever before. Not only do B.E.L.L. (in the future, as Eldorado Custom ammo under new P.M.C. ownership) and A-Square make cases and loaded ammo, but Federal now offers .470 Nitro-Express in both solid and soft as part of their Premium Safari ammo line. In Belgium, Harald Wolf includes .470 in his line along with several other Nitro-Express cartridges.

Personally, I love the .470; I've used it widely with Barnes, Woodleigh, A-Square, and original Kynoch bullets, and it does everything I need a big rifle to do. It's a good choice, especially with the availability of Federal ammunition. But it's important to keep in mind that it isn't a better game cartridge than its kin—and you'll pay a premium for a rifle so chambered.

## .475 Nitro-Express

Another cartridge introduced just after the .450-caliber ban, the .475 Nitro-Express is for some reason the rarest of all big Nitros. I haven't been able to find out who introduced it, but it's possible that it was Cogswell & Harrison's cartridge, since almost all of the very few .475's I've seen or heard about were made by this company. The exception is a lone Lancaster that George Caswell had in his shop.

Bullet diameter is .476, and the chambering is so rare that .475s have been a virtual pariah for decades. That's too bad, as it's really a nice cartridge. Based on the .450-3¼" case with much of the body taper removed so it will accept the larger bullet, it originally fired a 480-grain slug at 2,175 fps, delivering (you guessed it!) 5,050 foot-pounds of energy. Its advantage, like that of the .450-3¼", is the straight case which allows it to be built into a very trim rifle.

The .475 presents more of an ammunition problem than most, but B.E.L.L. .450 cases will work just fine, and Barnes will make .476 bullets. A rifle so chambered should be a half-pound lighter than a comparable .470, and can usually be found at a considerably lower price.

## .475 No. 2

This one is an obvious crib on the 3½-inch case of the .450 No. 2, and it really had no reason for existence since by the time of its introduction any problems with the smaller cases had long since been solved. Nevertheless, it was extremely popular, and a variety of makers offered .475 No. 2s over the years, including fine European makers; my uncle had a lovely .475 No. 2 by Belgium's Francotte. The common .475 No. 2 load used 85 grains of cordite and 480-grain bullet, for 2,200 fps at the muzzle and 5,170 foot-pounds of energy.

Unfortunately, Jeffery did their own thing with the .475 No. 2, using a 500-grain bullet and just 80 grains of cordite. This reduced velocity and energy somewhat, and also reduced the pressure (which was the object). Any difference in hitting power is indistinguishable, but obviously a double rifle regulated for one load is unlikely to be accurate with the other.

There's another, more insidious problem, and that's bullet diameter. Most .475 No. 2s use a .483-inch bullet. However, most (not all) Jeffery rifles use a .488-inch bullet. Most of the rifles regulated for the Jeffery load will be marked for it on the flats of the barrels, or at least will give the bullet weight and charge of cordite. The ammunition boxes should be marked "For Jeffery Rifles," and Jeffery cartridges *should* be headstamped .475 No. 2J. It's a galling complexity, and it's absolutely critical that the bore of any .475 No. 2 rifle be slugged to determine appropriate bullet diameter.

Of course, there's absolutely no doubt that, wrong diameter notwithstanding, a great many Jeffery cartridges were fed into standard rifles over the years, and vice versa. It's amazing what the old doubles will stand for—sometimes. But today the watchword is *old*, and it's important to match the bullet diameter to the rifle, for safety as well as performance.

The rifles were relatively common, and a great many hunters used .475 No. 2 rifles, including the likes of hunter/naturalist Carl Akely. My good friend Ian MacFarlane, the Botswana outfitter/professional hunter, carries a .475 No. 2 to this day. With its extra-long, impressive case, it gives the feeling of more power than it really has—but it was nevertheless a fine cartridge. It nearly died away, since that extra-long case was shared only with the less common .450 No. 2. Now that good B.E.L.L. brass is available, the .475 No. 2 makes a good, serviceable heavy double.

## .476

Generally called the .476 Westley Richards, this one is probably the least common of all the Nitro-Expresses except the .475 Nitro-Express. It's a bit of an oddball, little known and widely misunderstood. A Westley Richards cartridge, it was made by very few other makers, and is rarely encountered. Most of the references, including John Taylor himself, offer information on this cartridge that is just plain wrong. Bullet diameter has been variously quoted at .483, .510, and even .520. Bullet diameter is actually .476, and the case length is 3 inches, based on the .500-3" case necked down.

That 3-inch case makes it a very handy cartridge, and it probably should have become more popular than it was. It used 75 grains of cordite and a 520-grain bullet (also unusual, thus giving its original bullets the best sectional density of their class) for 2,100 fps velocity and 5,100 foot-pounds of energy. Elmer Keith had a rifle so chambered, and liked it. Ian MacFarlane's eldest son, Ronnie—with whom I've hunted several times—has a Westley Richards .476. The ammo is a bit of a headache, but it's a great cartridge; with its 3-inch case and heavier-for-caliber bullet, it just might be the best of the bunch, at least in theoretical terms. And certainly it's no worse than the rest.

## .500 Nitro-Express

There were actually *two* .500s, a 3-inch version (by far the most common); and a $3\frac{1}{4}$-inch. Both are straight-cased cartridges taken directly from blackpowder predecessors, and both originally used a 570-grain bullet with an 80-grain charge. The longer case had a bit less pressure and a bit less velocity, but the common .500-3" was quoted at 2,150 fps muzzle velocity for 5,850 foot-pounds of energy.

For all practical purposes, all the cartridges from .450-$3\frac{1}{4}$" to .476 Westley Richards are identical in power and performance on game. There just isn't a nickel's worth of difference between them, and if it weren't for (1) Britain's proprietary system of gunmaking and (2) the ban on .450 cartridges, most of them wouldn't exist. With the .500, we finally get to a horse of a different color. With equal velocity, yet a heavier bullet with greater frontal area, the .500, in either case length, offers a bit more.

Rifles were built by a great many makers for many years, from the 1890s until the collapse of the British Empire—and today .500s are being made again, with Heym offering both a double and a slant-box magazine bolt-action for the .500-3". Belgium's Marcel Thys, too, will make a .500, as will others. I just returned from a Mozambique elephant hunt, where I used a Heym .500-3" double. It did a good job on a fine tusker, just as .500s have for nearly a century.

Hunters who used it had nothing but praise for it, and many used it extensively. In his book, *On The Trail of African Elephant,* Tony Sanchez-Ariño, who was a friend of J.A. Hunter, states that Hunter's favorite cartridge was the .505. That must be true, since Tony knew him well, but in his most active years he often favored a .500 double, and it was a Boswell in that caliber that he used to clear Kenya's Machakos district of several hundred rhino. Geoff Broom, one of the great modern professional hunters, still swears by his German-made .500. Another modern great, Gordon Cundill, carries a double .500 almost as a personal talisman, appearing undressed without it.

The .500 gives an edge over the .450-class of cartridges, but it isn't a big enough difference to warrant giving up a .450-3¼" or .470 in favor of a .500. The difference is there, and it might even be significant, but it isn't earthshaking. And most .500s, especially older rifles, will be a good deal heavier than the .450s. If elephant is the game, a .500 makes sense—and any good double makes sense if the price is right. But unless I planned to do a lot of elephant hunting in heavy cover, I wouldn't choose a .500 over one of the .450s or .475s.

On the other hand, the .500 isn't a cartridge to stay away from. In the average 11½- to 12-pound double, the .500's added performance can be had without additional recoil, and even in a 10½-pound rifle it isn't unreasonable. The bullet diameter is .510, and although the bullet selection isn't as great as for the .450s or .470s, it's more than adequate. Those straight cases are a snap to reload, and case life is excellent.

The past few years have seen a tremendous interest in .50-caliber rifles, mostly bolt-action wildcats. But I wouldn't be surprised to see a few more new doubles like the Heym out there. Just a couple of years ago, I had an opportunity to buy one of J.A. Hunter's double .500s, and I wish I had—it was well used but still serviceable, and it would have been great fun to go on safari with a piece of history like that.

## .577 Nitro-Express

This one was the real tool of the ivory hunter. Too much gun for the casual sportsmen, too heavy for most professional hunters to carry, the .577 was for serious business with big elephant.

A smokeless version of an existing blackpowder cartridge, like the .500, the .577 Nitro-Express occurs in two case lengths, a 3-inch and 2¾-inch.

But unlike the .500, there is a huge difference between the short case and the long one. The .577-3" uses 100 grains of cordite and a 750-grain bullet, reaching 2,050 fps and 7,020 foot-pounds of energy. Even today, it stands as one of the most powerful cartridges the world has known. The 2¾-inch case is a totally different cartridge, and they must not be confused; the shorter version used a reduced charge of cordite to propel a short-for-caliber 650-grain bullet; velocity was low and energy just 5,500 foot-pounds.

Rifles for the 2¾-inch version could be built relatively light, and in this guise it had some popularity in India. However, the strong suit of the .577's 750-grain bullet was not only power but penetration—and the 650-grain bullet does not stack up. The .577-3" was far more popular—but do take a close look at the proof marks if someone offers you a good deal on a .577.

The .577 in blackpowder form was extremely popular throughout the British Empire in the last quarter of the 19th century. The transition to smokeless came early, and many of the great ivory hunters relied on the big .577. James Sutherland used the .577; F.G. Banks used one; George Rushby used one; Tony Sanchez *still* uses one; and the list goes on. American professional hunter Owen Rutherford was a good friend of mine, regrettably killed in a freak accident in 1989. One of very few Americans to have killed a hundred bull elephant, Rutherford did it in recent years—with a .577.

A great bull of a man, Owen regularly carried his .577 double on the bongo hunts that were his specialty. I couldn't do it, and few men can. Taylor recommended the .577 (and the .600) as a second rifle, to be carried by someone else while the hunter saves his strength and carries something in the .450 class. Makes sense to me; I know how heavy my 10-pound .470 gets at the end of the day, and I wouldn't care to carry a rifle half again as heavy.

The other drawback of the .577 is pure, unadulterated recoil. I've never owned one, and probably never will. But I've shot them. I've never considered myself recoil-sensitive, and indeed the .577 doesn't hurt me—but it throws me off-balance to the point where I'm much too slow for the second shot. If I were hunting elephant alone in heavy cover, I'd consider such a rifle—but it's not a sensible tool for most African hunting today.

The .577s were built by a number of makers, and they aren't all that uncommon. They are, however, more unusual than the .450 to .500s, and they command a premium price today. They're worth it as collector's pieces, but, sadly, the real need for them hardly exists in today's Africa.

## .600 Nitro-Express

Introduced by Jeffery in 1903, the mighty .600 was strictly a smokeless proposition, not based on any previous blackpowder cartridge. It used a 900-grain bullet of .622 diameter from a straight 3-inch case, and until the .460 Weatherby came along in 1958 it stood as the most powerful of all sporting cartridges. Velocity was low, 1,950 fps from 110 grains of cordite, but how much velocity do you need from a 900-grain bullet? Energy was

7,610 foot-pounds! There was a lighter load as well, the same bullet but less powder for 1,850 fps. I can't say how common this lighter load was.

Like several other Nitro-Express cartridges, the .600, in either load, had a reputation that far outstripped its actual use. It was, and is, extremely rare. When Holland built their "Last .600" rifle a few years ago, Malcom Lyell put together a monograph on the .600. In it, he reckons that less than 200 rifles of all makes, single-shots and doubles, were built. B.E.L.L. has made ammunition, but I suspect it was intended chiefly as a curiosity—original ammunition is worth over $50 a cartridge today. A very few .600s are still in use; American Bill Feldstein used one in Mozambique in 1989, and German Walter Eder has used his .600 on many of his 30-plus elephant bulls. Recently, a couple of new .600s were built in Belgium, but I doubt if we'll see a surge of interest in this caliber.

None of this is to imply that the big guns weren't used. Indeed they were. Those rifles you encounter may be of several different makes, but it appears that Jeffery made more than anyone else. Taylor wrote glowingly of a .600 he owned, and so did Major P.H.G. Powell-Cotton, both Jeffery rifles. Powell-Cotton, however, relied more heavily on a .450/.400, and, as mentioned above, Taylor recommends the big guns only for closing the final deal. Few well-known ivory hunters seem to have relied extensively on the .600. One was Bill Pridham, who used the .416 Rigby as his main rifle but backed it up with a .600 for the tough stuff. Another was Carl Larsen, a Dane who hunted Portuguese East Africa in the early years of the century. His rifle was also a Jeffery, probably the underlever hammerless design most frequently seen.

The problems with the .577 are compounded in the .600; the rifles weigh 16 to 18 pounds, recoil is indeed fierce, and, of course, the ammunition is very heavy and bulky as well. On the other hand, one shouldn't need a lot of cartridges for something like that.

## Wildcats for Doubles

The problems in wildcatting any cartridge are severe, but they're compounded with a double. First, there must be a cartridge, for the ammunition must exist in order for the barrels to be regulated. So the cartridge development must be done with a single-shot, or in a laboratory's universal receiver. Pressure data must be obtained, and it must be accurate since doubles simply can't handle the breech pressure of a bolt-action or good single-shot. Quite obviously, the costs are as enormous as the hassle, especially considering the price of *any* new double on today's market.

Even so, over the years a few determined sportsmen have created their own double-rifle cartridges. The first was probably the .600/.577 Rewa, basically a .600 case necked down to .577. Ordered by the Maharaja of Rewa, there might be two such rifles in existence.

A few years ago, Bob Petersen of Petersen Publishing Company, a serious double-rifle fancier with a marvelous collection of fine doubles, decided he wanted his own "proprietary" flanged cartridge. I don't think any of us, Pete included, realized what kind of hassles were involved. The idea was to create a flanged cartridge that, in a double rifle, could approach the velocity of the .460 G&A based on the .404 case—about 2,300 fps with a 500-grain .458 bullet. The new cartridge, with a special run of brass from Norma so headstamped, was called the .460 G&A No. 2.

A rechambered Ruger No. One was used to develop loads. The barrels were made by Holland & Holland for, as I recall, a new sidelock action originally barreled to .458. The project was a success—but there's still just one such rifle in the world.

Along the same lines, but far more complex, double-rifle fancier Bill Feldstein is currently having a .700 Nitro-Express created by Holland & Holland. I believe the finished gun will weigh 22 pounds—and the old saw, "Why do you use a .600? Because they don't make a .700," will have to be rethought. The .700 has a 3½-inch case, and a 1,000-grain bullet, and it requires 215 grains of smokeless powder to develop 2,000 fps. Energy is 9,050 foot-pounds.

These are one-of-a-kind projects, but the Belgian firm of Elko Arms, under the direction of Dr. Lauren Kortz, has proprietary flanged cartridges for which they build over/under, side-by-side, and *three-barreled* rifles. The cartridges are the .376 and .459 Elsa K Magnums and Super Magnums, in two different lengths. Respectively, they use standard .375 and .458 bullets, but the .459 is designed to fire heavy-for-caliber 600-grain bullets at about 2,200 fps. The firm has been in business for several years, and is still making guns and providing them with ammunition at this writing. It's a specialized market, but the market for double rifles of any persuasion always was.

The big Nitro-Expresses aren't in a class by themselves; bolt-action cartridges of similar performance levels are readily available. The Nitro-Expresses aren't general-purpose safari cartridges—even less so than their magazine counterparts. The double rifle, by its nature, is a short-range affair. But when you need a cartridge that will stop something, you need it badly—and every single one of the creaky old Nitro-Expresses can do that just as well today as when Africa truly was the Dark Continent.

# Chapter 9

# Some Useful Metrics

They say America will eventually make the transition to the metric system, abandoning our antiquated and complex English system of weights and measures. Perhaps we will, someday; the metric system makes a lot of sense once you understand it. But that's the rub—Americans don't understand it, and few and far between are the metric cartridges that have received any acceptance among American shooters.

The lone exception seems to be the 7mm group; the various 7mms have darn near eroded the .30-caliber's position as America's favorite. But then, they had a head start, since the 7x57 predates even the .30-40 Krag and the .30-30. But so does the 8x57, and Remington's 8mm magnum has been a dismal failure in terms of sales. The 6.5mm is a European standard, but the Remington's 6.5mm Remington Magnum went nowhere fast—and even with its English designation, the .264 Winchester Magnum had but a short day in the sun. The examples are endless; in spite of being an unquestionably better cartridge, the 6mm Remington is nowhere near as popular as the .243.

If our homegrown metric cartridges suffer so badly on the American market, it should be clear that European metric cartridges have no chance at all—and that's generally the case. But it doesn't mean there aren't a number of really excellent European cartridges, past and present, that have made their mark in Africa's game fields.

In truth, an American who wishes to own and use a currently manufactured European cartridge lets himself in for almost as much hassle as he would if he chose an obsolete Nitro-Express—and if he latches onto a rifle chambered for an obsolete metric, he may inherit virtually unsolvable ammunition problems.

However, there are good sources for most metrics in the U.S. RWS's excellent ammunition is imported, albeit in small quantities, and Federal is now the U.S. agent for Norma, which loads a wide variety of common (and some obscure) metrics. Gun South now imports the Austrian Hirtenberger ammunition, good stuff. R.C.B.S. and Huntington either offer or will make dies, and bullets can be had for most of the more common metric designations. But under no circumstances, as with the Nitro-Expresses, will it be as simple as going to the corner store and purchasing a box of .270, .30-06, .375, .458, or even .416 Remington.

In spite of the frustrations, there are good reasons for owning some of the metrics. For one thing, many of them were and are chambered in excellent rifles that just beg to be taken to Africa and used. For another, a few metric cartridges occupy a niche unfilled by a domestic cartridge. Let's take a look at some of the most useful metrics that might be encountered.

## 6.5mm

The 6.5, bullet diameter usually .264, is a European standard, and has been since smokeless powder came into being. Perhaps the most famous of all the 6.5s is the 6.5x53R Mannlicher-Steyr, originally a Greek military cartridge and sold all over the world in the fine Austrian Mannlicher sporters. The English called it the .256 Mannlicher after their manner of calling a cartridge by its bore, rather than groove or bullet, diameter.

Firing a very long, well-constructed 160-grain bullet at 2,300 feet per second, the penetration of this little cartridge was incredible. The 6.5x53R sparked the small-bore craze that swept Africa, and it was widely used by many turn-of-the-century hunters. The near-identical 6.5x54 Mannlicher-Schoenauer that followed it in 1903 (and was soon called the "new" 6.5 or .256) shared its ballistics and reputation. Sometimes it's unclear who used which cartridge. Phillip Percival loved the .256, and so did the great lion hunter Leslie Tarlton. Bell used it some, and Powell-Cotton, John Millais, and Blayney Percival swore by it. It was the favorite rifle of the great hunter/soldier Major C.H. Stigand.

The 6.5x54 M-S is still available today, but the rimmed 6.5x53R cartridge is strictly a piece of history, and most of the rifles still in existence have been shelved for lack of ammo. Roger Whittall retired his for that reason, a grand old rifle that he learned to shoot with. It was given to his grandfather by F. C. Selous himself.

The .256 wasn't a giant killer—but it was light, quiet, and gave unprecedented penetration, much appreciated by hunters who had grown up with blackpowder, low-velocity arms firing hardened lead bullets. The 6.5x54 Mannlicher-Schoenauer remains with us today, though no longer as popular as it once was—and today rarely considered as a cartridge for really large game. There are several very similar 6.5s, including the 6.5x55 Swedish, 6.5x58 Portugese, 6.5 Carcano, *et al.* All of these originated as military cartridges, and the life span of each was more or less tied to the rifles that were chambered for them. Today the 6.5x55 Swedish is probably the most popular, and with its modern loadings, it—or any of the others—is certainly an efficient, viable choice for a wide range of plains game.

More interesting is the 6.5x68, a Schuler cartridge that is a true rimless magnum. Dating back to just before World War II, it's essentially the 8x68S necked down to 6.5, and the velocities are wonderful—about the same as or better than the .264 Winchester Magnum without the magazine-capacity-devouring belt. As with many of the 6.5s, the Europeans also load a rimmed version for single-shots and the popular drillings.

Reedbuck are not hard to kill. About the same size as a Texas whitetail, they can be shot with any medium-sized caliber.

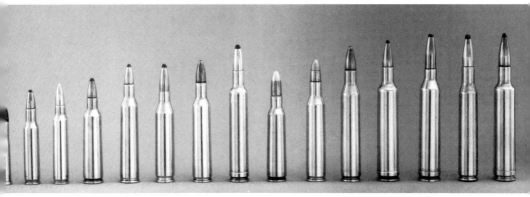

Here's a sampling of the myriad cartridges between .22 and .270 caliber. The little .22s, such as the Hornet and .222, are useful for extremely small antelope, while the larger cartridges in this group will handle a surprisingly wide variety of African game. Left to right are: .22 Hornet, .222 Remington, .223 Remington, .22-250, .220 Swift, .243 Winchester, 6mm Remington, .240 Weatherby Magnum, .250 Savage, .257 Roberts, .25-06, .257 Weatherby Magnum, .264 Winchester Magnum, .270 Winchester, and .270 Weatherby Magnum.

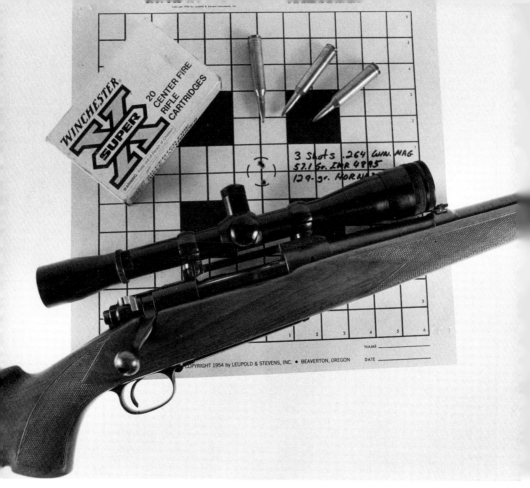

3 shots .264 Win. Mag
57.1 Gr. IMR 4895
129-gr. Hornad[...]

COPYRIGHT 1954 by LEUPOLD & STEVENS, INC. • BEAVERTON, OREGON

NAME _____

DATE _____

The strong suit of the small-caliber cartridges is their ability to reach out, so accuracy is also a requirement. Rarely seen in Africa today, Winchester's 26-inch-barreled .264 Magnum was an ideal plains rifle.

The dorcas gazelle of the Sahara is a small animal weighing around 40 lbs. A .223 was used for this very good male. As long as the distances are not too great, a .223 is adequate for these animals.

This impala was taken with a .270 Weatherby Magnum. An underrated cartridge in the Weatherby lineup, the .270 is a light-recoiling, easy-to-shoot cartridge that is astonishingly flat-shooting.

My father-in-law, Paul Merriman, used his Ruger M77 in .270 on a fine sable, felling it with one shot—proof again that the .270 is a fine game cartridge, and that shot placement really is everything.

Paul also needed but one
.270 bullet for his record-
class waterbuck, another
animal generally con-
sidered a bit large for the
light cartridges. If you
trust a rifle, and its caliber
is within reason, use it!

I used a Musgrave .243
on this springbok. Among
today's professional
hunters, the .243 is one
of the most popular
calibers for game of this
size—with good reason.

I used my David Miller 7mm Remington Magnum on this Grant's gazelle. Its power level wasn't needed, but its flat trajectory certainly was.

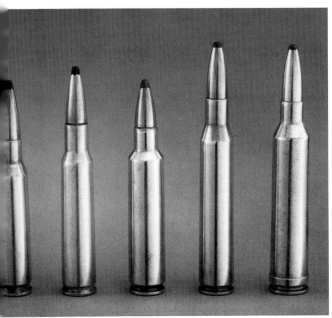

Among the most common modern 7mms are, left to right, 7mm-08 Remington, 7x57 Mauser, .284 Winchester, .280 Remington, and 7mm Remington Magnum. The 7mm magnum is the most common in Africa today, but the old 7x57 still has quite a following.

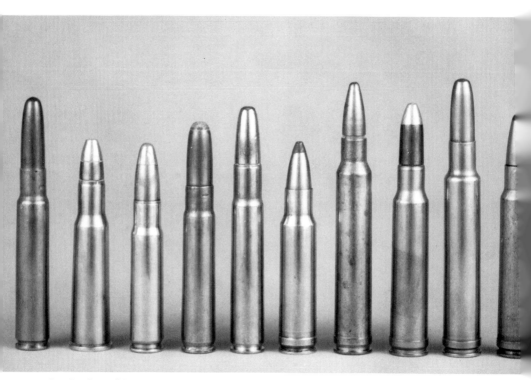

A selection of both modern and obsolete "light mediums." From left, .318 Westley Richards, .348 Winchester, .358 Winchester, 9x57, .35 Whelen, .350 Remington Magnum, 8mm Remington Magnum, .338 Winchester Magnum, .340 Weatherby Magnum, and .358 Norma Magnum.

The beauty of the larger-cased 7mms is that they retain their flat trajectory with heavy bullets well-suited for a wide range of game. A single 162-grain Nosler folded this Tanzanian kudu in his tracks.

The fringe-eared oryx weighs between 400 to 500 pounds. Calibers from 7mm on up are recommended for these tough and tenacious animals.

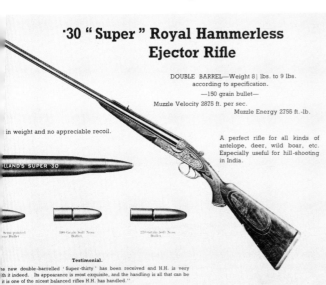

## ·30 " Super " Royal Hammerless Ejector Rifle

DOUBLE BARREL—Weight 8¼ lbs. to 9 lbs.
according to specification.

—150 grain bullet—

Muzzle Velocity 2875 ft. per sec.

Muzzle Energy 2755 ft.-lb.

in weight and no appreciable recoil.

A perfect rifle for all kinds of antelope, deer, wild boar, etc. Especially useful for hill-shooting in India.

LLAND'S SUPER ·30

Semi-pointed
our Bullet

180 Grain Soft Nose
Bullet

220 Grain Soft Nose
Bullet

### Testimonial.

he new double-barrelled 'Super-thirty' has been received and H.H. is very
th it indeed. Its appearance is most exquisite, and the handling is all that can be
it is one of the nicest balanced rifles H.H. has handled."

This Holland & Holland catalog page from the 1920s touts what we now call the .300 H&H Magnum, though in its long-obsolete rimmed form. In belted rimless style, the .300 H&H remains tremendously popular.

Roan antelope are very tough animals and resistant to bullet shock. Even an adult male lion will stay clear of them in most cases. This record-class roan was shot with a .30-06, which is enough gun. However, as in all big-game hunting, shot placement is critical.

Warthogs are medium-sized animals found over much of Africa. Not a lot of gun is needed for these animals. This one was killed with a .30-06.

Cokes hartebeest are common in Masailand, Tanzania. Well known for their toughness, the hunter must use an adequate gun to take one cleanly. A .30-06, which was used for this bull, is certainly adequate up to 200 yards.

Most famed of the "standard" .30 calibers are, left to right, .30-30 Winchester, .30-40 Krag, .308 Winchester, .30-06, and .303 British (actually a .311 caliber). All except the .30-30 made a significant mark in Africa, but the .308 and .30-06 are most common today.

It's hard to imagine a more useful African rifle than a good scope-sighted .375. Using a 300-grain Swift bullet, my old .375 absolutely flattened this zebra—as it will most of the time.

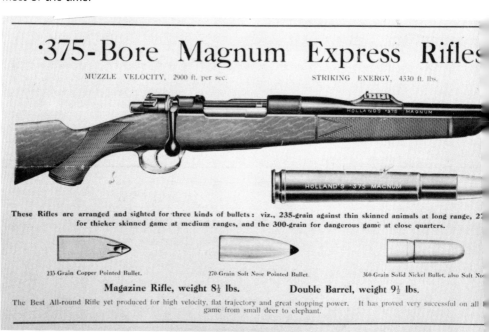

# ·375-Bore Magnum Express Rifles

MUZZLE VELOCITY, 2900 ft. per sec.

STRIKING ENERGY, 4330 ft. lbs.

These Rifles are arranged and sighted for three kinds of bullets : viz., 235-grain against thin skinned animals at long range, 27 for thicker skinned game at medium ranges, and the 300-grain for dangerous game at close quarters.

235-Grain Copper Pointed Bullet.

270-Grain Soft Nose Pointed Bullet.

360-Grain Solid Nickel Bullet, also Soft No

**Magazine Rifle, weight 8½ lbs.**

**Double Barrel, weight 9½ lbs.**

The Best All-round Rifle yet produced for high velocity, flat trajectory and great stopping power. It has proved very successful on all game from small deer to elephant.

This early Holland catalog page shows what we now call the .375 H&H Magnum. Originally, the bullet weights were 235, 270, and 300 grains, but the lightest loading fell by the wayside.

Ralph Schneider used his pre-'64 Model 70 .375 to take this fine bongo in the forests of Cameroon. The .375 remains the classic choice for very large plains game such as this. (Photo by L.J. Wurfbain)

It's important to remember that the .375 H&H isn't the only .375 cartridge. A few others include, left to right, the long-obsolete .375-2 1/2" Nitro Express, .375 Flanged Magnum, the .375 H&H itself, the .375 Weatherby Magnum, and the .378 Weatherby Magnum.

A confirmed .30-06 fan, gunmaker David Miller used one of his making to take his mountain nyala in the Ethiopian highlands. This animal probably presents, on average, the most difficult shooting in Africa.

The barrel is going quickly on my old .375, and this is about the best it will group these days—but it's an old friend that I have supreme confidence in.

When this lion was shot, somebody remarked "A .30-06 would have been good enough, but the .416 is better." No argument here!

Lighter, faster bullets are another way to get added versatility out of the .375. I used Jack Carter's superb 240-grain Trophy Bonded Bearclaw spitzer to make a very long shot on this Eastern Cape kudu.

Pachmayr's Bill Baker used his .458 Lott with Hornady 500-grain bullets to take the most beautiful buffalo I've ever seen.

In truth, the .375 H&H is a long-range cartridge. It isn't as flat as the faster magnums, but if you know its trajectory and stick with aerodynamic bullets, it will work wonders. I used a 300-grain Sierra boattail, handloaded fast, to take this lechwe at over 400 yards.

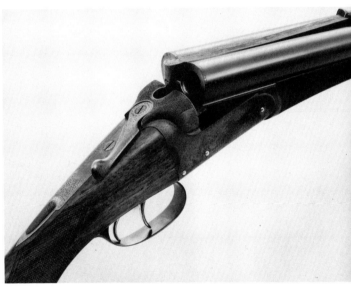

This is a first-quality box-lock by English maker Thomas Turner, chambered for the .450/.400-3", also known as the .400 Jeffery. It was this cartridge, famed for its penetration and chambered in sturdy, reliable doubles, that the old over-.40 bolt action cartridges had to compete with.

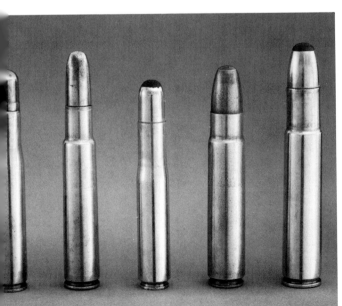

The classic British large-caliber magazine-rifle cartridges are, left to right, .404 Jeffrey, .416 Rigby, .425 Westley Richards, .500 Jeffrey, and .505 Gibbs. These are all modern loads—.404 from A-Square, .416 from B.E.L.L., and the last three from Harald Wolf Mastergunworks in Belgium.

Remington gets credit for the first modern .416 from a major American manufacturer. This is one of their original prototype rifles in .416 Remington Magnum.

From old to new and back again are these over-.40 magazine-rifle cartridges: left to right, .405 Winchester, .404 Jeffrey, .416 Remington Magnum, .416 Rigby, and, newest of all, the .416 Weatherby Magnum.

Ludo Wurfbain used his .416 Remington with Barnes homogenous solids to take this forest elephant in Cameroon. In the heavy forests the various .416s should be considered an absolute minimum.

A Swift softpoint from the .416 Weatherby penetrated completely on a behind-the-shoulder lung shot. The bull went less than 50 yards. The real question, with the Weatherby's high velocity, was whether the bullets would withstand it. They do!

A lineup of the wildcat and standard cartridges that comprise the current .416 craze includes, left to right, .411 KDF, .416 Taylor, .416 Hoffman, .416 Remington Magnum, .416 Rigby, and .416 Weatherby Magnum. All are essentially equal except the Weatherby, which offers greatly increased velocity.

Standard cartridges for magazine rifles over .44 caliber are limited to the .444 Marlin, .45-70, .458 Winchester Magnum, .460 Weatherby Magnum, .505 Gibbs, and .500 Jeffrey.

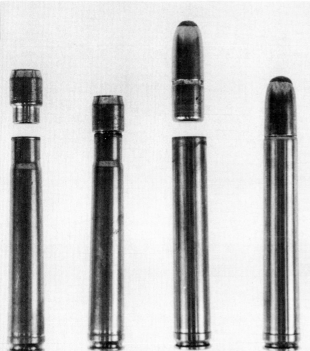

Here's a selection of big wildcats. From left: based on the .404 Jeffrey case, the .460 G&A and .450 G&A Short; based on the .375 H&H case, the .450 Ackley and .458 Lott (both in factory loads from A-Square); based on the .348 Winchester case, the .450/.348 Ackley Improved; and the .458 Winchester Magnum for comparison.

Brass for the .458 Lott can easily be fireformed by using inexpensive cast-lead plugs in a .375 case. Firing the plug results in a perfect .458 Lott case.

This is a lovely Belgian double in 7x57. Although the currency exchange makes new continental doubles quite expensive today, they are often superb bargains on the used-gun market.

A-Square's Art Alphin has a line of powerful proprietary cartridges, not true wildcats since he offers factory ammo. From left are his .338, .425, .495, and .500 A-Square rounds.

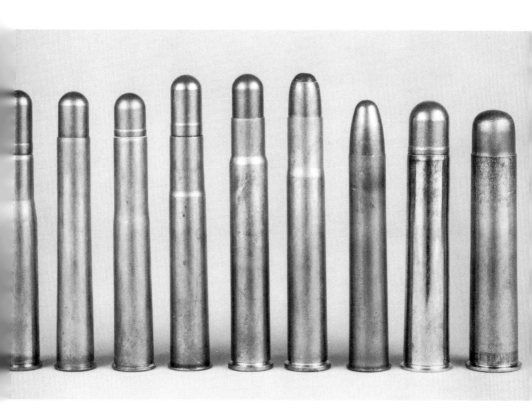

This lineup includes most of the big Nitro Expresses. From left are the .450/.400-3", .450-3 1/4, .500/.465, .470, .450 No. 2, .475 No. 2, .500-3", .577-3", and .600.

In the golden era of the Nitro Expresses, before World War II, Kynoch made available a lead-sealed metal "tropical pack" of 20 cartridges.

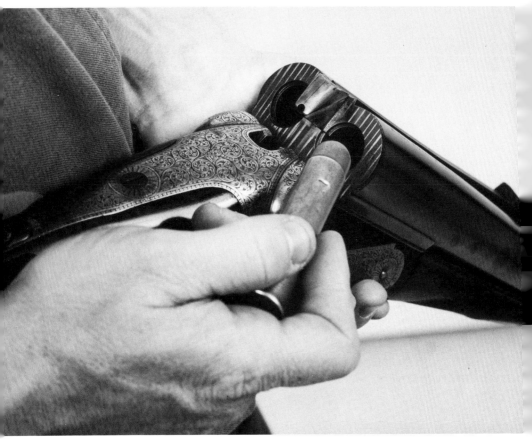

The .600 is an awesome rifle, but most of the old-timers felt it was too heavy. Not until the introduction of the .460 Weatherby did any cartridge match its power.

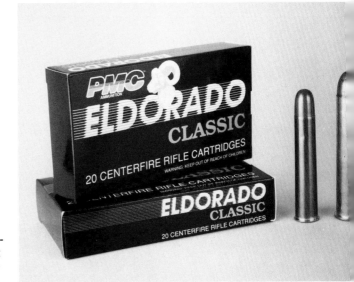

PMC's Eldorado Custom Shop has been working with Holland & Holland in the development of their new, so far one-of-a-kind .700 Nitro Express. It dwarfs even the redoubtable .577!

It was a big surprise when a major company like Federal tooled up not only for .416 Rigby but also for .470. It's good ammo, too—this 50-yard group, two shots from each barrel, is the best my .470 has ever shot with anything!

B.E.L.L., now owned by PMC, led the way in bringing back factory ammo for the Nitro Express rounds. Today A-Square offers an extensive line of factory ammo, including most of these oldtimers.

This Ferlach rifle by Winkler has an overbarrel in .22 Hornet and an underbarrel in 7x65R. Essentially the same as the .280 Remington, the 7x65R and its rimless brother, the 7x64, are fine plains game cartridges.

Here's a sampling of some fine metric cartridges: From left, 7x57, 7x65R, 9x57, 9.3x62, 9.3x64, and 9.3x74R. All of the 9.3s are excellent, with the 9.3x64 easily the equal of the .375 H&H.

CENTER FIRE
LE CARTRIDGES

8×68S

NEW!
WITH
ANVIL
PRIMERS

e Tip Bullet
Grains

amil Nobel AKTIENGESELLSCHAFT
TROISDORF · GERMANY

10 CENTER FIRE
RIFLE CARTRIDGES

8×68S

MANTLE

NEW!
WITH
ANVIL
PRIMERS

H-Mantle Copper Hollow Point Bullet
187 Grains

ATTENTION!
Only for barrels with the larger 8-caliber bores
(Bore .316 in., Groove .323 in.)

Dynamit Nobel AKTIENGESELLSCHAFT
TROISDORF · GERMANY

Little known in the U.S., the 8x68S is a formidable cartridge in the range of the .338 Winchester Magnum—but especially effective because of the superb Brenneke-designed bullets it has traditionally been loaded with.

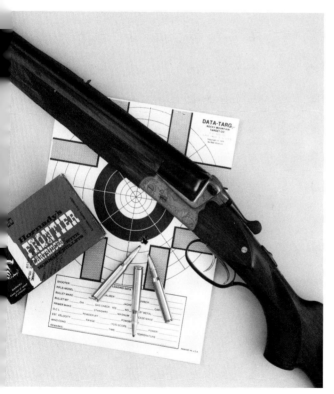

The drilling makes an interesting choice for a utilitarian African gun. This one is a Sauer with .30-06 rifle barrel under shotgun barrels. The unusual stiffness of the rifle barrels supported by the shotgun barrels tends to make them amazingly accurate.

George Rushby, gold prospector, boxer, and ivory hunter. A man of great physique, he used various rifles and calibers on elephants but concluded that he liked the .577 Nitro-Express best.

Sir Samuel Baker, possibly the earliest advocate of a large caliber gun. He used a 4-bore in Africa, which even he admitted generated a tremendous recoil.

Walter Dalrymple
Maitland "Karamojo" Bell
was the king of the
small bore fans. A Major
in the R.A.F. during
World War I, he bagged
over 1,000 elephant with
the likes of the 6.5mm,
7x57, .303, and
.318—and lived to enjoy
his retirement in Scotland.

Major C.H. Stigand was
another vociferous
small bore fan. He survived World War I to be killed in action against the
Dinkas in 1919. Though
he had a heavier rifle,
he never found his
6.5 wanting.

Jimmy Sutherland, on the other hand, used a pair of .577s. He believed in them, and he enjoyed one of the longest careers of any of the professional ivory hunters.

The hippo is a huge beast, but succumbs readily to a brain shot. This one was taken handily with a .30-06; shot placement is everything, and with it the small bores do their work.

The lump behind the shoulder of this eland bull is a 300-grain Sierra, at rest under the hide after breaking the near shoulder the way in—perfect performance. The tiny hole just to the left of the ear, on the other hand, is the exit from the second insurance shot, a solid, which quartered the other way.

In the blackpowder era, there was no way to increase velocity, so the only way to get more power was to use a bigger hammer—but there was no way to obtain the penetration that we enjoy today. Here's a conical bullet from a typical 8-bore of the late 19th Century.

Here are just a few of the superb softpoints available in caliber .375. From left: 240-grain Trophy Bonded Bearclaw, 300-grain Hornady Interlock, 300-grain Trophy Bonded Bearclaw, 300-grain Nosler Partition, 300-grain Swift A-Frame, 300-grain Sierra.

These three .416 softpoints were recovered from buffalo. All three retained over 90 percent of their weight and penetrated extremely well. On the right is a Swift; the other two are Trophy Bonded Bearclaws.

After several years in the field, A-Square's Art Alphin redesigned his "Dead Tough" softpoint. Here's the results, the Dead Tough II released in 1990. Recovered from buffalo and wildebeest, these 400-grain .416s all have weight retention between 92 and 94 percent—superb performance!

A .416 Remington was used for this buffalo. The various .416 calibers available today are ideal buffalo rifles with plenty of punch and excellent long-range ballistics. They are gaining ground rapidly with the Africa-bound sportsman.

These are .470 solids recovered from buffalo and rhino. The one at the left hit heavy bone and bent a little, but it held its course. The rest could be reloaded—and that's what you want.

This bushpig was shot at close range in impossibly thick cover, a good place for the 250-grain Kynoch solids in the .318.

Despite all the stories, snakes are actually rarely encountered during safaris. However, when sighted, caution must be taken because they are exceptionally fast and are very hard to hit with a rifle. A shotgun is ideal and this 7-foot cobra from East Africa was neatly dispatched with a 12 gauge.

## 7mm

The 7mms have been covered in Chapter 2. However, it should be noted here that the 7x57, 7mm Mauser, or .275 Rigby—whatever you choose to call it—remains one of the world's great sporting cartridges. It was one of Bell's favorites with the long, stable 173-grain solid; he once said that the barrel of his .275 had never been "polluted" by a softnose bullet. Today it would be generally illegal—and most folks would at least consider it unwise—to use the 7x57 on the kind of game Bell used it on. But it must not be forgotten that it did the job, and it still could. While modern loadings push lighter bullets fast enough to give quite flat trajectories, Bell's experience might well be remembered today. The long 175-grain loadings that are still available may well be slow, but at moderate ranges they'll outperform the short, light, fast bullets all day long.

There is, of course, a rimmed version of the 7x57, and likewise for the 7x64 Brenneke mentioned in Chapter 2. The 7x64 is virtually identical to, although not interchangeable with, the popular American .280. Its rimmed counterpart, the 7x65R, makes a wonderful light rifle in double or single-shot form, or as the rifle barrel in a versatile drilling—two shotgun barrels over a rifle barrel (or, rarely, a double rifle with a third, smoothbore, barrel underneath). The Europeans, too, have had their share of high-velocity 7mms, but the 7mm Remington Magnum has become a universal choice.

## 8mm

The 8mm bore has always been popular in Europe, and among Europeans who travel to Africa it pretty much occupies the niche the .30 caliber fills with American hunters. The good old 8mm Mauser or 8x57 dates clear back to 1888, making it one of the oldest cartridges still in use. Originally, it had a bullet diameter of .318, but in 1905 this was increased to .323. Since then, the earlier bore has been called "J" and the later version is designated "S." The "J" bore was called a 7.9mm Mauser by the English, and it was extremely popular. H.C. Maydon used his almost exclusively, as did literally thousands of sportsmen. Although the "J" bore is rare today, in the .323 configuration the 8x57 remains extremely popular to this day—and anything you say about the .30-06 could well be said about the 8x57. What it gives up in velocity it gains in frontal area, and the effect on game is about a draw.

A great many other 8mm cartridges were developed over the years. A few of them have hung on while many have died away. The most powerful, and the most interesting, is the 8x68S, a magnum-length cartridge with a case length of 2.658 inches. This is a cartridge a European might have instead of .300 magnum, 8mm Remington, or .338. And it's every bit as good as any of them. Current RWS loadings range from 180 to 224 grains, and velocities and energies are quite high, the latter well above the magic 4,000-foot-pound level.

Flat-shooting, said to be extremely accurate, the 8x68S was introduced about 1940, then reintroduced after the war. It has never been loaded in America, but is a favorite of European big-game hunters. Like so many European cartridges, the really wonderful thing about it is the fine bullets RWS loads it with; from controlled-expansion H-Mantels to full metal jackets to aerodynamic "cone-point" bullets, available ammunition runs the full gamut. The cartridge, in my view, is too light for reliable use on cats and buffalo—just like the .300, 8mm Remington, and .338—but it would do the job, and will certainly handle the full range of plains game.

## 9mm

There were something like a half-dozen European 9mm rifle cartridges, bullet diameter generally .356 instead of our more common American .358 bullet diameter. Of them, the 9x57 Mauser enjoyed a degree of popularity, even in America. Although the bore diameter has potential, the European cartridges had generally low velocity. The best of them was no better than the .358 Winchester, and most were in a class with the .35 Remington. No 9mm rifle cartridges are currently listed by RWS. Rather than spend more time on them, let's turn to some metrics that still have real importance in African hunting.

## 9.3x62

The 9.3 is a traditional European caliber. In the English system, the bullet diameter is .366, making it quite close to the .375. The forerunner of this cartridge, still loaded and occasionally seen, is the 9.3x57, based on the 7x57 necked up. The 9.3x57 is a bit of a wimp, but the 9.3x62, making good use of its greater case capacity, is a fine cartridge. Introduced in about 1905 in Mauser sporters that were far less expensive than the various English guns, it was at one time the most popular all-round African cartridge—and it's a good one to this day.

The best of the modern loadings propels a long, stable 293-grain bullet at 2,430 fps for 3,843 foot-pounds of energy, a deep-penetrating load that is available in Brenneke's TUG dual-core H-Mantel bullet, similar to the later Nosler Partition and extremely effective. Full-metal-jacket bullets and more conventional softpoints are also available.

Few Americans have played with this cartridge in recent years, but it has some interesting advantages. First, it's a relatively small, rimless case, so can be built into a light, compact magazine rifle with a full five-round capacity. That 293-grain .366 bullet also offers better sectional density, and thus better penetration, than even the 300-grain .375. Stockmaker Jim Coffin has been playing with it recently, describing it as an upgraded .35 Whelen with better bullets. Probably a good analogy.

The 9.3x62 remains an excellent African cartridge today, especially for someone seeking performance with little recoil. Where its caliber makes it legal for use, I'd rate it as the minimum for buffalo and cats—made so as much by its excellent bullets as by its power level.

## 9.3x64 Brenneke

Better yet is Wilhelm Brenneke's largest cartridge, using a fatter, longer case to drive a 285-grain bullet at 2,690 feet per second for 4,580 foot-pounds of energy, and a 293-grain bullet at 2,570 fps and nearly 4,300 foot-pounds. Although never popular among English-speaking hunters, the 9.3x64, in terms of trajectory, penetration, and bullet performance, must be considered every bit as good as the .375 H&H—and just possibly the only cartridge in the world that's better for all-round African use.

RWS still loads the ammo, and several European firms still make the rifles. It's amazing how strong the charisma of the .375 really is; here's an equally good, currently available cartridge that is forgotten and ignored throughout much of the hunting world. But it's hardly forgotten by the hunters who swear by it, and many have—for all game up to elephant.

## 9.3x74R

This long, slender, rimmed cartridge is the 9.3 that's most familiar to Americans. A perfect choice for a light, fast-handling double in either the European-preferred over/under configuration or side-by-side, a great many 9.3x74Rs have made their way into the U.S. It's also a common rifle-barrel chambering for a drilling. With two 12-gauge barrels and a 9.3x74R, such a gun is ready for just about anything.

The 9.3x74R goes back nearly to the turn of the century, but must not be confused with the still-older and much less powerful 9.3x72R, still loaded and seen occasionally. The common loadings for the 9.3x74R today are a 285- or 293-grain bullet, both at 2,280 fps for 3,291 and 3,383 foot-pounds, respectively. That puts the 9.3x74R on a par with, just slightly less powerful than, the rimmed version of the .375 H&H, the .375 Flanged Magnum.

Thanks to its excellent bullets, the same ones loaded in the other 9.3s, it has been used with great success on game up to elephant. For my money it's a bit light for such work, but has certainly proven itself adequate for cats, buffalo, and all manner of plains game. Its strength is that it can be built into a very light, very responsive double rifle. Its weakness is its low velocity, giving it an arcing trajectory and a very limited range.

Given a choice, I'd opt for the .375 Flanged over the 9.3; at such marginal levels, every slight increase in power is to the good. However, most .375 Flanged Magnum rifles were made by Holland—and thus are extremely valuable. A great many 9.3 doubles can be had for about $2,500 today, and I once had a set of 9.3 barrels on the Valmet system for literally the cost of a common over/under shotgun. Excluding blind luck, the 9.3x74R offers one of the best opportunities to find an affordable double that is adequate for dangerous game.

## 10.75x68 Mauser

The Europeans had several 9.5mm cartridges, essentially a .375, that just didn't make it; perhaps if either World War had turned out differently, those cartridges would have achieved wider use. The next bullet diameter that sparked a lot of cartridge development on the Continent was the 10.75mm, caliber .423. There were nearly a half-dozen, including a straight-cased 10.75x57, the ultimate necking-up of the 7x57 case. Of these, just two achieved some level of popularity: the 10.75x68 and the 10.75x73. This latter cartridge is identical to the .404 Rimless Nitro-Express, or .404 Jeffery—and it's still loaded by RWS.

So is the older 10.75x68, but although this cartridge has the caliber and the case capacity, it was (and still is) loaded with a too-light-for-caliber 347-grain bullet at 2,230 fps for 3,830 foot-pounds of energy. It obviously has the energy as well as the frontal area, and since it was available in inexpensive Mauser rifles it was widely used. However, it was also widely mistrusted and is rarely seen today. Apparently, that short, light bullet wasn't long in the penetration department, and gave unsatisfactory results on thick-skinned game. Chances are it was, and is, just dandy for plains game and lion—but that isn't usually what one seeks in a .423-caliber cartridge.

Though handloading with good bullets might cure its ills, the 10.75x68 is probably best forgotten, and should not be chosen over any of the 9.3s with their long, well-constructed bullets. The 10.75x73, of course, is a marvelous cartridge—as it always was; everything said about the .404 Jeffery in Chapter 6 applies, and with it should be added thanks to RWS for keeping the cartridge alive long after the British gave up on it.

There were, additionally, a couple of 11.2mm (caliber .440) cartridges, the anemic 11.2x60 Mauser and the powerhouse 11.2x72 Schuler. Both vanished during World War II, probably never to be seen again. As mentioned in Chapter 6, the famed .500 Jeffery was probably a European development, called on the Continent 12.7x70 Schuler. It's likely that more German rifles were made than English, and Taylor mentions that the only ammo available was actually made in Germany, probably by Krieghoff-Schuler.

In the realm of large, powerful cartridges, there haven't been many metrics—but several made their mark, and shouldn't be ignored by modern hunters. The German hunters of today tend to be knowledgeable and demanding of their rifles—and they're more likely to carry an 8x68S than a .300 Weatherby; or a 9.3x64 rather than a .375. They know what they're doing.

# Chapter 10

# Small Bore versus Big Bore

ampfire arguments are part and parcel of the sport of hunting. It isn't that hunters are, by nature, particularly argumentative. But we do tend to be a bit self-righteous, and certainly convinced that our own views are the proper ones. And, after all, since hunters love their rifles as much as they do their game, what better subject for campfire discussion—with each party certain that his own choice is the only sensible one?

The controversies are endless. Double rifle or magazine? Long barrel or short? Solid bullet or soft? Long Mauser extractor or the modern type? Even the heavy-caliber double-rifle crowd can argue endlessly over the choice of extractors or ejectors, hammer or hammerless. But few such campfire discussions are as fundamental as the one that rages between those who prefer small-caliber rifles and those who prefer the big bruisers.

The discussion has raged since there were hunters, and I suspect our ancestors discussed heatedly what size rock was the most effective—a huge stone that had to be dropped from above or a light, round stone that could be hurled with both velocity and accuracy. In America, the argument was characterized by the 50-year war of words between Jack O'Connor and Elmer Keith. For general hunting, Jack loved his .270 with 130-grain bullets, rarely using anything heavier than a .30-06. Elmer wanted more, and felt more was needed; he developed his .333 (and later .338) wildcats, believing that his 250-grain .33-caliber bullet was perfect medicine not only for elk, but also for deer-sized game.

It should be immediately obvious that such a discussion is relative to the size of game being considered; what is "small" for an elephant is not small for a whitetail deer. Nor can there be any absolutes about just what is "small" or "large." In the final analysis, although Keith and O'Connor remained bitter enemies to their deaths, they weren't really all that far apart. When Keith eventually got to Africa, he relied on his .33s for plains game but used a .375 for lion and a double in .476 or .500 for the really big stuff. O'Connor, too, hunted Africa extensively. He did, indeed, rely on a .270 or .30-06 for plains game, but the .375 was his minimum choice for dangerous game—and he also used a .416 Rigby. No one ever called the .416 a light rifle!

In Africa, the small bore-versus-large discussion may not have been as heated, but the lines were more clearly drawn. The king of the small bores was Walter Dalrymple Maitland "Karamojo" Bell, unquestionably one of the great early ivory hunters—and also an excellent storyteller who left behind a fine record of his exploits. Bell concentrated on elephant in a time when the great beasts were relatively undisturbed, and by all accounts he was one of the finest rifle shots of his day.

Bell used a number of rifles, including the .303 British, .256 Mannlicher, .318 Westley Richards, and even a double .450/.400. His greatest one-day bag was with the .318—19 bulls. He started with 35 cartridges, had eight misfires, and wrote that he had a couple of shells left over. Another favorite of his was the .275 Rigby—the old 7x57 Mauser, firing a long, beautifully shaped 173-grain steel-jacketed solid at a modest 2,300 fps. With it, he shot a great many of his thousand-plus elephant, and his oft quoted and most succinct analysis (from *The Wanderings of an Elephant Hunter*) goes like this:

"I have never been able to appreciate 'shock' as applied to killing game. It seems to me that you cannot hope to kill an elephant weighing six tons by 'shock' unless you hit him with a field gun. And yet nearly all writers advocate the use of large bores as they 'shock' the animal so much more than the small bores. They undoubtedly 'shock' the firer more, but I fail to see the difference they are going to make to the recipient of the bullet. If you expect to produce upon him by the use of large bores the effect a handful of shot had upon the jumping frog of Calaveras County, you will be disappointed. Wounded non-vitally he will go just as far and be just as savage with 500 grains of lead as with 200. And 100 grains in the right place are as good as ten million."

Truer words have never been written; shot placement *is* everything—but Bell was an extraordinary shot who hunted in times, if not extraordinary, certainly much different from the years that followed. Many of Bell's contemporaries started with the light rifles—but few continued with them, and he is one of the only hunters of his era who actively advocated them.

John Taylor, author of *African Rifles and Cartridges* and *Big Game and Big Game Rifles*, was another marvelously entertaining writer who knew what he was talking about. One hears the occasional rumor that Taylor, unlike Bell, shot better with his typewriter than his rifle, but who doesn't? Taylor is considered the champion of the big-bore advocates, but he was nothing of the sort. He did use .577s and .600s, the ultimate big bores—but he rated them as useful only as a second rifle for the professional elephant hunter. As you read his books, you'll quickly note that he was a double-rifle man, preferring the .450-.475 class. And in spite of that, he was lavish in his praise for the .375 H&H, .400/.350, .333 Jeffery, and certainly the .425 Westley Richards and the magazine-rifle cartridges of similar power. His "thing," if you will, was bullet performance—whether from large bore or small: "There were many occasions that convinced me of the excellence of these long heavy bullets of moderate velocity thrown by the .333 and .350."

If a bottom line is to be found in Taylor's works, he recommends something on the order of a .450 to .475 for the largest game, and few people have ever disputed such advice. Oddly enough, Bell himself might have made the same recommendation. In a letter to Denis Lyell, he wrote:

"The ordinary average city man (which we all are today when it comes to elephant and such, like it or not!), out for rhino say, will undoubtedly feel better about it when carrying a double .470 or .577 than he would with a .256 or .275. We must not forget that he has not had the opportunities of knocking rhino spinning with a .256. Therefore I take it the novice is behaving in a more sportsmanlike way when he arms himself with the deadliest weapon he can obtain, i.e., a heavy double."

A great many of the early hunters started with the great blackpowder guns, changed to small bores—and eventually went full circle to the largest of the Nitro-Expresses. Selous himself started with muzzleloading 4-bores, later giving them up in favor of a single-shot .461 by Gibbs, which he used well into the smokeless era. However, he also used the .256 Mannlicher and .303—and finished his career a great fan of the then-new .375 H&H.

Arthur Neumann is believed to be one of the three greatest elephant hunters. The other two are Bell and Captain James Sutherland. Neumann started with blackpowder 10-bores, breechloaders, and blackpowder .577s. At the end of his career, he used a .303 British, .256 Mannlicher, and a .450-3¼" by Rigby. He reckoned the .256 too light for elephant, but used the .303 on the great beasts.

Captain James Sutherland hunted from 1896 to 1932, and possibly might have been the greatest elephant hunter of all. Starting in the smokeless era, in his early years he used a .303 Lee-Metford, and later on a .318 Westley Richards. He gave up on them, eventually shooting a pair of .577 Nitro-Expresses. In *The Hunter is Death*, Bulpin quotes Sutherland saying to George Rushby:

"After all, we are in the business to kill elephants and the more efficiently and humanely we do it the better. All the hunters I know, particularly the young and cocky ones, who use small-bore weapons and consider themselves such stylish shots that they cannot possibly miss a vital point, invariably litter the bush with wounded animals, or get themselves killed before they learn any better. Common humanity demands that if we are to kill, we at least do so with maximum dispatch."

George Rushby, too, was an early fan of the .318. He was shooting elephant from a ladder, and that 250-grain bullet was just the ticket, allowing precise shot placement with little disturbance and little recoil. He tried it with a double .450 and the recoil knocked him off the ladder! In general, though, Rushby, like Sutherland, was a .577 man. In his own book, *No More the Tusker*, Rushby wrote that, for elephant, "all rifles from .400 cal. downwards should be considered small bores and from .400 cal. up to .475 cal. as medium bores and from .475 cal. up to .600 cal. as large bores."

By Rushby's classification, there were several "medium-bore" advocates. Commander David Blunt used almost nothing but a .416 Rigby. "Samaki" Salmon and William Pridham shot several thousand elephant between them, largely with .416s, although each also had a big double for backup—Salmon a .470 and Pridham a .600. And yet Bell wasn't alone with his small bore. Major C.H. Stigand, who shot in Somaliland and Central Africa between 1899 and 1919, was a true small-bore fan; although he had a double .450, he much preferred the .256 Mannlicher for virtually everything.

When Oklahoma lawman Charles Cottar fetched up in East Africa at the turn of the century, he had his Winchester .32 Special with him. Apparently nobody told him it wasn't enough gun, and he used it well until, later on, he obtained a Model 95 in .405. It could be argued that even his .405 was downright marginal for the largest game—eventually a rhino did indeed kill him.

With a current bag of 845 elephant, Tony Sanchez is one of the greatest living elephant hunters. Regarding Bell's bag of over 1,000 elephant with small bores, Sanchez wrote:

"This fact has been intensely discussed by others far more knowledgeable than me, but I would like to say that if all his elephants were killed with the small bore, and, in addition, several hundred buffalo and plenty of lion, then he was very lucky to have survived to tell the tale."

The small-bore men relied on precise shot placement, which they were capable of delivering, plus excellent performance from long, heavy-for-caliber bullets. The large-caliber advocates relied on nothing different; they also demanded topnotch bullet performance, and they staked their lives and fortunes on their ability to place those bullets. On the other hand, they wanted the large-caliber, heavy bullets as a hedge against human error and occasionally less-than-perfect bullet performance. That's the difference, pure and simple. Given that shot placement, a good bullet from a small bore will work wonders.

As I mentioned, I'm incredibly impressed by the 250-grain bullet from the .318 Westley Richards, and also the 220-grain .30-caliber and 175-grain 7mm bullets. In a pinch, I'd use them on darn near anything—but I'd prefer not to have to. Our little .30-06 has a wonderful reputation in Africa, going back to Teddy Roosevelt's 1909 safari. The old Kenya hand, Leslie Tarlton, may have held one of the highest all-time bags for lion. In a letter to Denis Lyell in 1926 he wrote, "I also think a great deal of the American Springfield, which with a 220 grain bullet is, I rather fancy, the best all around small bore in the world."

On his 1936 safari, Hemingway did wonderful work on buffalo, lion, and rhino with his Springfield—which he understood and shot extremely well. He did not so well with his double .470; he hated the trigger pull, didn't know the rifle, and just plain couldn't shoot it. Therein is the crux of the matter. Whatever rifle is chosen, whether .30-06 or .600 Nitro-Express, the bullet must be constructed so as to get into the vitals—and the shooter must be able to put that bullet there.

Today's hunter may generally shoot but one or two buffalo on a license, and a wounded animal will count. On one safari in five, he may have the opportunity to shoot one lion, and on one safari per dozen he may have an elephant on license. The ability of the small bores to take game far beyond what might reasonably be expected is there—but it seems ridiculous in this day and age to take any risk whatever that could result in a wounded and lost animal.

It should be remembered, too, that few men are alive today who have had the experience of a Bell, Selous, or Tarlton. What worked for them would indeed work today—given the time to learn what they learned and given animals in the same kind of country and unsophisticated temperament. Meeting such qualifications is impossible today.

The old East Africa Professional Hunters' Association—which counted as members several of the old small-bore gang—established .40 as the minimum caliber for elephant, buffalo, and rhino. In other countries, the .375 H&H is often the stated minimum for lion, eland, and larger game.

Even the most recoil-shy hunter should be able to learn to handle a .375—and remember that George Rushby called the .375 a "small bore" when it came to elephant. It is a game of shot placement and bullet performance—but both the large-bore and the small-bore camps always recognized that. It's just that the large-caliber advocates realized that neither would always be perfect, and they wanted the slight edge that a larger bullet of greater diameter does unquestionably offer.

# Chapter 11

# Expanding Bullets

The barrel of Bell's .275 Rigby may indeed never have been polluted by the passage of an expanding bullet. His attitude isn't particularly unusual; a fair number of professional hunters to this day shoot nothing but full-metal-jacket non-expanding bullets. For entirely different reasons, both Bell and the surviving solid-bullet crowd can make good cases for their preferences.

Bell, Stigand, Tarlton, and all the others who relied on cartridges as small as the little .256 Mannlicher for game as large as elephant had no choice but to rely on deep penetration—it was all they had going for them. In the .256, with that long pencil of a 160-grain bullet—in well-constructed solid form—they got that penetration. A long, heavy-for-caliber solid bullet at such moderate velocity simply cannot be stopped. The 7x57—.275 Rigby if you prefer—is the same kettle of fish with its original 173-grain round-nosed solid. So is the 250-grain .318, the 220-grain .30-06, and so on.

Remember, it was a light, fast, *softpoint* from a .280 Ross that got George Grey killed. The old hands never forgot it, and many never used another expanding bullet. The Ross bullet was, of course, much too light for lion in the first place, and wasn't constructed to hold up at the kind of velocity the Ross rifle produced. Failure to penetrate was predictable, and it happened—not only with George Grey, but with others using the Ross rifle. And not only with the Ross; the British made light, fast softpoints for several different cartridges, and many of them failed. A whole generation became soured on expanding bullets.

Had George Grey been shooting .275 Rigby solids in his Ross rifle, there's absolutely no question that the vitals of the lion that killed him would have been perforated. But that still leaves an unanswered question: Would those little solids have *stopped* him?

The modern professionals who rely on solids arrive at the same conclusion from a totally different direction. First, as professional hunters their primary need for a rifle is as backup—either to stop a charge or to prevent the escape of a wounded beast. Generally, they carry big rifles, .375 or larger—most likely, today, a .458 because of cost and availability. They must have penetration, whether through the brain of a cow elephant that suddenly becomes murderous or through the north end of a wounded southbound wildebeest that's heading for the Park boundary. With solids, either job can be handled.

The professional hunter who sticks with solids isn't all wrong, especially in a large-caliber rifle. There's a great deal of difference in effect between a 500-grain .458-inch solid and a 160-grain .264-inch solid. Under most circumstances, the difference is almost enough.

My Botswana professional hunter, Ronnie MacFarlane, was backing up a client who had just shot a lion. He was shooting a .500 double with Kynoch softpoints, and since the hit was uncertain and the lion was heading for heavy cover, he let drive. Both barrels misfired and the lion kept going. Now he had a mess to clean up, and he couldn't trust his softpoints to go off. The only other cartridges he had were solids of a more recent vintage—but surely in .50-caliber it wouldn't make much difference? When the lion charged from close range, Ronnie managed to hit him twice straight on, both shots going under the chin. He was dead, but not stopped; the mauling wasn't serious, but *any* lion mauling is serious enough.

Would the cat have reached him if he'd had softpoints? Who knows—but Ronnie doesn't think he would have. That's the same kind of question one could ask regarding George Grey and a solid bullet. Perhaps, perhaps not—but he wouldn't have been in any worse shape.

If there's a lesson in any of this, it's that there is a place for a softpoint bullet—but it damn well better be a *good* softpoint! Fortunately, there are plenty of good ones around.

The professional hunter may well keep his rifle loaded with solids most of the time, except possibly when after lion—but the client is better advised to keep softpoints loaded all the time except when specifically after elephant, rhino, and perhaps buffalo. As mentioned at the very beginning of this volume, the vast majority of shots fired in Africa will be fired at soft-skinned, non-dangerous plains game. A solid will do the job, but a softpoint will do it more quickly and efficiently—and may save a lot of tracking if the bullet isn't in exactly the right place.

With lion, there's absolutely no argument: tough, reliable, expanding bullets are the only projectiles that make sense. Although I have personally killed lions very dead with solids, it's not an experience I want to repeat. With elephant, it's just the reverse; a good solid is the only sound choice—but I have seen an elephant bull killed very dead with a center-of-chest shot from a .458 softpoint. There are just no absolutes in bullet performance or choice of caliber.

When it comes to buffalo, every jury will render a different verdict. In toughness as well as size, a buffalo is just on the edge of pure solid-bullet country. With lesser cartridges—the old small bores, even the .30-06—a solid is the best means to guarantee the penetration you must have. With a bigger gun, it can go either way so long as the softpoint is well-made and well-chosen. Some professional hunters absolutely insist on solids for buffalo, and they aren't wrong; a shoulder shot with a good solid will take out *both* shoulders.

However, hunters who prefer softpoints aren't wrong, either. A good softpoint, properly placed, will generally do a quicker job—and you don't have to worry quite as much about overpenetrating and hitting a buffalo on the far side. I generally hedge my bets; in a bolt gun I'll have a softpoint up the spout and solids underneath. In a double I'll normally have a softpoint in the right barrel, the first one, and a solid in the left. With a double, you can always use the solid if you're presented a going-away shot. I've done that; a 500-grain solid angled properly through a buffalo's hip does nice work. On a bad angle, you can't count on a softpoint to penetrate enough.

Except for the bad-angle shots, I prefer a softpoint for the first shot on buffalo. And on this animal, there's a legitimate question of whether a bad-angle shot should be taken at all! Excluding spine shots, the quickest one-shot kill I've ever had with a buffalo came with a "little" 300-grain Swift A-Frame bullet from a .375 H&H. It was a lung shot, pure and simple—and the bull died in 40 yards.

On the other hand, one-shot kills on buffalo are extremely rare. The animals are too strong, and nobody wants to go after a wounded buff if it isn't necessary. So the first shot, fatal or not, is generally followed up. That's when the solids really come into play; those follow-up shots are usually at a retreating rump. My best buffalo was shot in Zambia's Kafue region with a 300-grain Sierra boattail from a .375. The distance was just under a hundred yards, and it was a very standard broadside heart shot. When the bull took off, I followed up with two more solids from the rear, and we heard his death bellow before we began the tracking job.

Except when specifically hunting lion, I often load a magazine rifle with a mixture of solids and softs as a matter of course; a softpoint up first, but solids below. If a stalk is being made on a specific animal, I can slip a softpoint into the chamber—giving me two softs before I get to the solid. In that fashion I'm ready for a going-away shot on a wounded animal such as a wildebeest or oryx, should the softpoints fail to do the job. I'm also ready for buffalo—and I'm always hunting buffalo, regardless of what we're really looking for.

In Africa, just like everywhere else, it's unusual to get to the second shell in the magazine. So that "insurance" solid might rest in its place in the magazine for days. The softpoint will do the bulk of the work day in and day out—and do it well.

Fortunately, expanding bullets have come a long way since George Grey's day. There's a tremendous variety to choose from—and very few bum choices. The choice generally comes down to accuracy in your particular rifle, and exactly what properties you want from your bullet.

With expanding bullets, the major controversy has traditionally been between bullets that expend all their energy inside the animal and bullets that penetrate completely. The first group wants a bullet to penetrate to the vitals, expanding explosively and spending all its energy right there. The penetration boys want some expansion, sure, but they want entrance holes *and* exit holes. Neither side is right or wrong. A bullet that expends all its energy in the vitals will certainly kill more quickly; energy expended on the ground on the far side doesn't do much good. On the other hand, I have to wonder just where all that energy is going to be expended. In the vitals, great—but what happens if it expands prematurely and fails to penetrate?

If I'm shooting a medium-weight, moderately fast bullet weighing, let's say, 115 to 225 grains in calibers ranging from .25 to .33, I expect—and demand—complete penetration on average broadside shots on average-sized animals. That, of course, is a wide range of caliber and bullet, but you know the bullets I'm talking about—the general-purpose bullets such as 130- and 150-grain .270s; 165-grain .30-calibers; 140- to 160-grain 7mms; 200-grain .338s; and so forth. On game such as impala, whitetail deer, hartebeest, mountain goat, blesbok, and the like, I expect complete penetration on a normal behind-the-shoulder shot. If I don't get it, and the bullet comes apart in the vitals, the results will be spectacular. But what happens when you have to take bad-angle shots, or the opportunity arises to take a much larger animal?

When you get complete penetration on a similar behind-the-shoulder shot, you might have to follow a blood trail for 100 yards or so. But seeing that kind of result on a regular basis gives me confidence in a bullet; I know I can take a raking shot on animals of the same size—and I can take a good shot on a larger animal if the opportunity arises.

Several years ago, Remington—a company that I hold in highest esteem—held a writers' seminar in south Texas. The featured new product was the M700 Mountain Rifle in .280, with a hot new 140-grain load. I shot a deer in the heart with that load at about 60 yards; he went straight up in the air and came down with all fours sticking up. *But there was no exit.* I rode along with another group that was attempting to shoot nilgai, the big 600-pound Indian antelope, with the same load. The penetration just wasn't there for so large an antelope. I recovered a wounded bull the next day by spine-shooting him from behind, and he had been hit with a center-on shoulder shot from the .280. The shoulder was broken, but the inside of the ribcage wasn't even bruised.

Is that a bad bullet? Of course not. But it's a *deer* bullet, not a bullet for Africa where the size of the game varies so much. As far as I'm concerned, all of the factories are loading very good bullets today. The two types of bullet with the most consistent reputations are Remington Core-Lokt and Winchester Power-Point. The latter is essentially a conventional softpoint, nothing fancy at all. However, it seems to me that the Power-Points are well-matched to the velocities at which they're pushed, and I have a lot of faith in them. Likewise the Core-Lokt.

For every hunter who swears by the Winchester Silvertips, you'll find another hunter who curses them. When they work, they work like a charm—but when they fail, they fail spectacularly and usually at the worst moment.

Federal's line of softpoint ammo isn't one you hear about a lot in Africa—but I suspect that's because there isn't a darn thing wrong with it. The "red box" Federals are loaded with their own Hi-Shok bullets, a conventional softpoint that works extremely well. The "gold box" Premiums are loaded with "name brand" bullets—at this writing either Sierra boattails or Nosler Partitions.

The Nosler Partitions, of course, are designed for controlled expansion and deep penetration. The front part of the jacket expands normally, peeling back to the partition. Sometimes the front part stays attached, and sometimes it blows off—but it's a cinch that the rear of the bullet will stay together and keep penetrating. If the Nosler has faults, they could be the facts that expansion is limited, and accuracy, though acceptable, is generally not the best that can be had.

The Sierra bullet is essentially a conventional softpoint with lead core and copper jacket. Expansion is controlled by thickness of jacket, taper of jacket toward the nose, and amount of lead exposed. Sierras are thought to be soft bullets, and certainly they are not hard bullets. However, I have had extremely good luck with Sierras, particularly the 300-grain .375 boattail. They are also consistently the most accurate bullets I have used.

Hornady's line of loaded ammo as well as component bullets are excellent. All Hornadys now feature the "Interlock" belt that locks the core to the jacket. Whether it works or not I can't say—but for whatever reason, Hornadys stay together well. Their spirepoint bullet shape is one of the most aerodynamic going, and accuracy is excellent. Hornady has just introduced a boattail spirepoint 300-grain .375 bullet. I haven't yet used it on game, but so far it's very accurate and it looks good.

Conventional Speer bullets are just fine, as far as I'm concerned—but their premium line, the Grand Slams, are even better. If the Grand Slams have a fault, it's that they're available in few calibers. However, they can be had in .338 and .375—and they're a good choice. One day I was looking for a Cookson's wildebeest in the Luangwa Valley, shooting 285-grain Grand Slams in a .375. We found a fine bull in a herd, but just as I was ready to shoot, a very good waterbuck stepped from behind a tree some 200 yards off to the left. I dropped the waterbuck in his tracks, then swung onto the wildebeest just as he started to run. It was a "mixed double" I'll never forget, and the Grand Slams performed perfectly.

For light to medium African rifles, hunters using factory ammo can choose literally any brand their rifle likes and they'll be in good shape. The one rule is to choose heavy-for-caliber bullets. Forget the lightest bullets, and sometimes even the most popular. Ignore the 150-grain .30-06 in favor of 165s or, better, 180s. Find some 200-grain loads for the .300 Magnum. By going to a heavier bullet, you'll lose a bit of velocity and thus insure you'll have the penetration you need when the chips are down.

You see, there's rarely a problem with a bullet; failure is most likely when a bullet is pushed faster than it was designed to travel. A .30-caliber bullet designed to function at .30-06 velocities may or may not perform at .300 Weatherby Magnum velocities, especially up close when those velocities are very high. So, if you're using the faster magnums, go to heavier bullets of controlled-expansion design—Noslers, Grand Slams, even the custom bullets we'll discuss later.

One of the most spectacular failures I've seen—and I haven't seen many because they're quite rare—was with a 400-grain .423 caliber. The bullet was A-Square's Dead Tough, a conventional softpoint but a good, heavily jacketed bullet. The problem was simple; the bullet was designed to perform at .404 Jeffery velocities. It was fired in a wildcat .425 Express at some 400 feet per second faster than it was designed for. It came completely unglued in a zebra's paunch on a quartering-away shot, and all we found were fragments.

On the other hand, I just witnessed one of the most spectacular performances I've ever seen from a softpoint bullet. The bullet was a Barnes 350-grain softpoint fired in a .411 KDF. Velocity wasn't high—about 2,450 fps at the muzzle. I took a going-away shot on a big bull nilgai, centering him so precisely that the bullet cut his tail on the way in. I expected to break him down, but he got behind some brush before I could shoot again. We found him piled up 75 yards away, stone dead with an exit hole on his brisket.

Now, that bullet didn't expand very much—it couldn't have to penetrate like that. But in my view, no bullet does you any good if it doesn't reach the vitals. Somewhere there has to be a trade-off between explosive expansion and the total penetration of a solid. For my money, I'd rather have the penetration, even if I have to sacrifice some expansion. But so long as the bullet can reach the vitals from any angle at which you care to take a shot, your choice can't be wrong.

Bullet choice is more limited in the larger calibers, but it's quite adequate for the more common bullet diameters. Hornady, Speer, and Sierra make very fine .375 bullets, and now Nosler is back in the game with the wonderful .375 Partition, which was discontinued for many years. In .416, Hornady is the only major company currently offering bullets. Their 400-grain roundnose softpoint is a fine bullet, but the .416 screams for something more aerodynamic. Speer makes an excellent 400-grain .458 bullet, a dandy lion load, but Hornady has the lock on 500-grain bullets, both solid and soft. This picture is going to change. Recently announced is Speer's African Grand Slam Series which will include solids and softs in .375, .416, and .458

There's not a thing wrong with any of these bullets, but it's nice to have a selection. It's into this arena that the custom bulletmakers and smaller ammo companies have jumped with both feet—and they're making some of the finest bullets to come down the pike.

Barnes, of course, is the company that kept us shooting the Nitro-Expresses and so many other long-obsolete cartridges. Their standard expanding bullets are just conventional softpoints, lead core and pure copper jacket of varying thickness depending on the velocities at which they're to be fired. They work well, especially at the moderate velocities of the big bores. New from Barnes is the X-bullet, a homogenous-alloy bullet with a nose cavity that creates expansion. It works, and could well be the bullet design of the future.

Art Alphin of A-Square offers quite a line of loaded ammunition with his own Lion Load and Dead Tough expanding bullets, essentially conventional softpoints with expansion controlled by jacket thickness. The Lion Loads are thin-jacketed and are quite literally designed to be bombs—providing explosive expansion for use on thin-skinned dangerous game like lion and leopard. The Dead Toughs are designed to penetrate. I've already stated my opinions regarding softpoints, so it shouldn't be surprising that I find the Lion Loads too soft. The Dead Toughs are a bit soft for my taste in some calibers, but in .375 and .470 I've found them to work just fine. His second-generation Dead Tough II bullets are just now proving themselves, and they seem to offer it all—expansion, penetration, and weight retention.

Bill Steiger's Bitterroot Bonded Core bullet has been famous for decades; with the core chemically bonded to the jacket, it simply cannot shed weight, and penetrates incredibly. The problem has always been supply—you just can't get the darn things.

A few years ago, Corbin swaging equipment became available, and a number of small custom and semi-custom bullet companies sprang up. The best-known and most successful of these suppliers have been Lee Reid of Swift Bullets and Jack Carter of Trophy Bonded. Both Lee's A-Frame bullet and Jack's Bearclaw are magnificent bullets. They're twice to four times the price of a conventional bullet—and worth every cent. But don't ask me to tell you which one is best. I can't.

The Bearclaw is a bonded-core design with no other gimmicks besides good engineering. It's accurate, dependable, and in game will generally retain something like 95 percent of its weight. It expands incredibly, often to three times its original diameter—and it does so with razor-sharp flanges, the "bearclaws." It's a devastating bullet, but it must be remembered that the radical expansion will eventually limit penetration.

Lee Reid's Swift A-Frame is essentially a partition-type bullet, its major difference being that the front part of the core is bonded to the jacket, so weight retention is incredible. Ninety percent is below average for a Swift. I shot the first .416 Remington Magnum Swift bullet into a big Alaskan moose at maybe 35 yards, and that bullet retained 96 percent.

Unfortunately, these wonderful bullets are generally available only in the most common diameters. They aren't made for most of the Nitro-Expresses, but that's actually all right; at the moderate velocities of the big boomers, it's a simpler chore to achieve good performance. The bonded-core feature is nice, but not nearly as beneficial as with higher velocities. Furthermore, there are other options for the big bores. The Barnes bullets that kept us shooting for years remain very good, particularly the softpoints.

Even better in some ways are the Australian Woodleigh bullets. The Woodleighs don't necessarily perform better than Barnes—but they are made to duplicate the shape and bearing surface of the old Kynoch bullets, thus making the regulating of a double a bit simpler.

Bullet performance is everything. With it, cartridges with really marginal ballistics—such as the .333 Jeffery, .318 Westley Richards, 9x57 Mauser, even our own .30-30 Winchester—can achieve reputations as giant killers. With poor bullets, cartridges that could have been very fine—like the .280 Ross and 10.75x68—have been damned for decades.

I'm sure glad I'm not in the bulletmaking business, because it's impossible to please everybody. This guy wants the bullet to stay in the animal, but that guy (like me!) wants an exit hole. Problem is, if all you're getting is exit holes, then nobody gets to see what your bullet looks like—and it's impossible to photograph all those pretty, mushroomed bullets we like to show in magazines. The best compromise has to be for the bullet to stop just under the hide on the far side of the animal—but how to program exactly that performance time after time may take those poor guys a bit more work.

# Chapter 12

# Full Metal Jackets

Making a good solid bullet may not be easier than making a good softpoint, but at least everyone is in agreement on the requirements. A solid bullet's task is simple. All it has to do is stay intact, penetrate until it runs out of velocity, and stay in a straight line.

Getting one to do that—well, we've come a long way from the hardened lead balls of Cornwallis Harris's era. In those days, it didn't take a great leap of genius to harden lead with antimony, tin, or even pewter; nor was it long before it was discovered that a conical bullet of much greater weight penetrated better than a round ball. But the lead bullets covered with a jacket of harder metal that accompanied the development of smokeless powder were a tremendous step forward.

Even better were the steel-jacketed solids that followed, with the steel covered by a thin layer of gilding metal to take the rifling. These bullets withstood the velocities at which they were pushed—moderate, practical velocities that are ideal for the utmost penetration. It was bullets like these that enabled Bell to practice his legendary marksmanship, and with little change it's bullets like these that are relied on to this day.

The steel-jacketed Kynochs are gone, if not forgotten. But Hornady solids (also steel-jacketed) remain in .375, .416, and .458. Woodleigh solids, like the softs, are available in diameters suited for almost all the Nitro-Expresses. Barnes solids are, too, but Barnes's original copper-tubing solids do have a tendency to rivet at higher velocities, squirting the core out the front of the jacket. Better are the homogenous-alloy "true" solids, either the Barnes alloy solid or A-Square's Monolithic Solid. These bullets are not necessarily better than the Hornadys or Woodleighs—but they are unstoppable.

I shot my first elephant with an experimental Barnes homogenous-alloy solid, a 400-grainer from a .416 Hoffman rifle. It was a side-on brain shot. The bullet zipped in and out in a dead-straight line, and that bull was down before the rifle came down out of recoil. You can make penetration comparisons in a variety of test media, and you'll learn some interesting things. You'll learn, for instance, that the .416s (higher velocity, less frontal area) will out-penetrate the .458s; the .375 will out-penetrate darn near *anything;* about 2,100 to 2,500 feet per second seems to be the magic velocity for deep, straight penetration. But the bottom line is that today's solids are very good and very reliable—and they will reach an elephant's brain from any angle. And yes, they can fail. Every once in a while you hear about a conventional solid—lead core, metal jacket—coming apart. Of course it can happen. Fortunately, it's rare—but with the homogenous alloy solid, it's impossible. That makes such bullets an extra-good piece of insurance!

Still another solid worth mentioning is Jack Carter's Sledgehammer Solid. Several years ago, I tested some prototypes of this bullet in a particularly tough kind of duct sealant. They blew up like varmint bullets—and Jack went back to work. The production Sledgehammer has a lead core surrounded by a thick naval-bronze jacket. It won't come apart, it won't bend, and it won't deviate from its course. Its unique feature, though, is its flat nose, like an exaggerated .30-30 bullet. There's some unusual feature of energy transfer with that flat point. It doesn't expand, but it hits as if it does. If I were a professional hunter who loaded with solids every morning, these are the solids I would load with. I don't think anything makes a solid into a sensible load for lion—but in a pinch that sledgehammer shape just might save your tail.

Suppose you're not a professional hunter but rather, like me, a client hunting a variety of African game. Where does the solid bullet fit in? Its applications are admittedly limited—but when you need a solid, there's no substitute whatsoever. In that regard, a solid is the most versatile bullet; it will kill anything, from any angle. The expanding bullet has its limits.

When it comes to elephant, there's no argument—solids all the way. Likewise rhino; I gave a big bull two .470 Woodleigh solids right behind the shoulder at close range, quartering away, then a third quick shot by the base of the tail as the bull ran off. *There were no exits!*

Hippo, too, are game for solids. There's no trick and little sport to shooting a hippo in the water; just aim carefully for the soft spot above and between the eyes, and I suspect a .22 Hornet would do nicely. But on the ground, with body shots, the hippo is a whole different ballgame—a ballgame for the best solids and the largest rifles. I got into one in a thicket one time, and it seems like I was dumping shells in and out of my .470 for ages. All bullets fired were solids, all good body shots—and *no exits!* In my opinion, if a reliable solid bullet didn't exit, it's a damn good thing a softpoint wasn't used!

As mentioned, it can go either way with buffalo. I much prefer a softpoint for the first shot, provided that shot can be picked. But a solid is a nice ace to have up your sleeve. I absolutely dumped a running bull with a .470 solid one time. We'd been tracking him for hours and it was getting hot. He jumped at close range in some heavy thorn, but ran quartering toward our backtrail. I had a soft in the right barrel, but a solid in the left. I got a touch ahead of him and hit the rear trigger. It was as if all four feet hit a hidden cable; he slid on his nose for 20 yards and never moved again. I wouldn't have fired that shot with a softpoint of *any* make.

With the marvelous controlled-expansion bullets available today, there is no reason to choose a solid for any other type of African game, with the possible exception of eland. Personally, I can't imagine shooting an un-wounded 2,000-pound animal up the rear—so for my eland I've always

148

used a softpoint for the first shot. But I'm not shy about backing it up with a solid.

I was up on the Palala River, just south of the Limpopo, hunting seriously for a Cape eland. We'd been at it for a week, and time was running out. Willem van Dyk and I were tracking a good herd, a herd that we'd bumped three times. It was time to give up, and then we ran smack dab into them. After a Mexican standoff that lasted two eternities, the bull stepped out. I shot him quartering slightly away at about 40 yards with a 300-grain Sierra. He bucked like a stallion, and when he came down quartering away a bit more, I hit him with a 300-grain Hornady solid. He went 15 yards, maybe 20.

When we rolled him over, we found the solid's exit on the point of the off shoulder, perfect performance. But just a couple of inches away, making a huge bulge under the hide, was the Sierra boattail. And that, too, was perfect performance on a very large, very tough animal.

I habitually carry solids in the bottom of my .375's magazine, likewise in a .416. Because they're there, I have used them to drop departing wildebeest and such. They work, but I wouldn't suggest that you must have them for plains game. One good use solids do have is pot-shooting smaller antelope, whether literally for the pot (damaging as little meat as possible) or to minimize trophy damage. For this to be practical, though, it's essential that your solids shoot to *exactly* the same point of impact as your chosen softpoint load. With factory loads, that's a matter of luck. With handloads it's usually a snap.

When shooting plains game—or anything else, for that matter—with solids, watch carefully. The last time I shot a solid at a small animal I was looking for an impala for meat, and I also wanted the skin. I lined up very carefully with my .375, but at the shot nothing happened except normally running impala and the whine of a departing ricochet. No sound of the bullet hitting, no nothing. We walked up to check, and a few yards into the brush were *two* very dead impala.

It seems that fewer and fewer hunters rely exclusively on solids. A number of Zimbabwe professionals do, and in the thick bush they hunt I can understand that; a solid is believed to hold its course best in brush. There's some truth behind the myth, but just by virtue of being a solid a bullet won't buck brush better than anything else. Solids tend to be long, parallel-sided bullets that are heavy-for-caliber with high sectional densities. *These* are the properties that help a solid remain on course through flesh and bone—and they're the properties that make it hold its course in brush. A softpoint so configured would behave in the same way, but the myth persists. When it comes to solids, sheer size is meaningless. Goof-proof, consistent performance is what matters. Walter Eder told me he was having a problem with elephants getting up after being brained with solids from his .600. He didn't need a bigger hammer; he was shooting the biggest one there is. He needed a better bullet, as proven when he did a post-mortem and found that the huge 900-grain bullets were breaking up in the skull without penetrating. He wound up having some custom .620-inch bullets made, and the problem appears solved.

Down in the eastern Cape, out of Port Elizabeth, I was invited to a bushpig hunt with dogs, to be conducted in the impossibly thick coastal thornbush. The rules were simple. I must keep up; I must not shoot a dog; I must not use a scoped rifle; and I must not use an expanding bullet. I had my Westley Richards .318 along on that trip, and it seemed a job made to order for that famous 250-grain Kynoch solid. After crawling through those hellish thorns to the dusty battle between pig and dogs, I shot my pig where the neck joins shoulder at 30 feet. *I did not get an exit!*

# Part II

# Safari Rifles

# Chapter 13

# The Double Rifle—A Historical Perspective

When Cornwallis Harris headed inland from the Cape Colony in 1836, the firearms he had at his disposal were woefully inadequate. The only choice was a muzzleloader, and even percussion ignition was a few years away from common use. Heavy-for-caliber conical bullets were unusual, but it was known that the pure lead balls could be hardened with tin or pewter for better penetration.

Even rifling, though widely used, was only partially understood; rifled sporting arms were likely to have but two grooves, and the ball would often be cast with a "belt" to take the rifling. Accuracy was, perhaps, a bit better than a smoothbore musket could offer—but not much. Many concepts for repeating firearms had been tried, but until the self-contained metallic cartridge came along, the necessity of using loose powder, bullet, and priming separately made repeaters impractical. Multiple-barrel arrangements—usually two, but occasionally three and even four—were the only way to obtain additional shots. Doubles were obviously the most practical; two locks and side-by-side barrels made an attractive, well-balanced arrangement, while additional barrels made the whole affair too heavy and unwieldy.

Calibers were large, but even so penetration was sketchy. On the really large game, first encountered by Englishmen such as Harris, William Cotton Oswell, and Roualeyn Gordon Cumming, multiple wounds were normal. These early adventurers hunted on horseback, galloping close to fire and dashing away—sometimes, according to their accounts, charging their muzzleloaders at the gallop from a bag of loose powder! With our modern concept of sportsmanship and the humane one-shot kill, the accounts the early hunters left behind seem barbaric. With game such as buffalo, giraffe, rhinoceros, and elephant, it wasn't unusual for dozens of balls to be fired before the game was finally brought down. It was exciting, dangerous sport—and many of the early hunters paid for it with their lives.

Velocities were quite uniform—somewhere between 1,300 and 1,600 feet per second. Conical bullets were occasionally seen, but they tended to be relatively stubby and light-for-caliber; the aerodynamic and penetrating potentials of a long, parallel-sided heavy-for-caliber bullet weren't yet known. In other words, the only way to increase killing power was to increase caliber. Bore diameters were expressed in gauge, or balls to the pound. For instance, the first British military *rifle* was a round-ball gun bored "20 to the pound," or 20-gauge, caliber .615.

In common use as sporting rifles during the middle years of the 19th century were 10- and 12-bores, both considered "general-purpose" rifles.

For larger game, the 8-bore was most common. However, 4-bores (quarter-pound round-balls) were relatively common as a "big bore," and 2-bores were occasionally seen. Sir Samuel Baker's "Baby" was a gargantuan single-shot 2-bore. Weighing 20 pounds and firing a half-pound explosive shell, "Baby" was indeed awesome. Baker confessed to being afraid of it, and reckoned he fired it altogether just 20 times. "I very seldom fired it, but it is a curious fact, that I never fired a shot with that rifle without bagging. . ." *Curious* because, in those days, the really large game was often brought down by sheer weight of lead.

Ballistics of these rifles were nothing to sneeze at, even by today's standards. The 10-bore generally fired an 875-grain ball at 1,550 fps, yielding 4,660 foot-pounds. The 12-bore fired a 750-grain ball at the same velocity for about 4,000 foot-pounds. Both were used on dangerous game, and obviously they possessed the foot-pounds—but not the penetration. The 8-bore, with a 1,257-grain bullet at 1,500 fps, could do the job. In foot-pounds, it delivered just under 5,300—the same energy level that "elephant cartridges" produce to this day. The 4-bore, just for comparison, fired its 1,880-grain bullet at some 1,330 fps. It produced 7,400 foot-pounds of energy, a level unmatched in the smokeless era until Weatherby's .460 came along!

The 4-bores were almost invariably single-shot arms; the weight was far too excessive if built into a double. The 8-bores and smaller bore sizes could go either way, in single-shot or double form. By the middle of the 19th century, James Purdey, Westley Richards, and Holland (singular at that time) were all building double-barreled percussion rifles. William Cotton Oswell, who hunted from 1837 to 1852, had a smoothbore Purdey double 10-bore as his favorite arm. Gordon Cumming hunted for five years, from 1843 to 1848, and his favorite also was a Purdey, a double 12-bore—but for larger game he had better luck with a single-shot 4-bore.

Although they were beautifully made, the muzzleloading double rifles were not doubles as we know them; they were in essence two rifles—two barrels and two locks—put together on one stock. For a double rifle's barrels to shoot together, the first essential criterion is consistent ammunition—and this would not be possible until the invention of the metallic self-contained cartridge.

British gunmaker Joseph Lang saw the French pinfire self-contained cartridge as early as 1851, and was impressed. But this system was fragile and unsuited for powerful arms. The centerfire cartridge developed by George Daws, circa 1861, was the answer. By 1870, brass cartridges in 4-, 8-, 10-, and 12-bore were readily available—and so were double rifles very much as we know them today.

These big-bore blackpowder breechloading doubles were exposed-hammer underlever guns, opened by a lever surrounding the triggerguard. When the lever was swung to one side, the barrels were released and dropped open. Underlever doubles were made well into the smokeless era, including a few hammerless guns. Jeffery's underlever design is one of the most common versions of that firm's .600 Nitro-Express rifle.

James Purdey himself invented the top lever, and in 1875 W. Anson and John Deeley, both employees of Westley Richards, patented the Anson & Deeley hammerless action, to this day easily the most common hammerless boxlock action in the world.

By 1890, just before smokeless powder came into widespread use, hammerless double rifles were starting to take over. To this day, however, a few double-rifle men will argue in favor of exposed-hammer guns. Indeed, a sound argument can be made; a hammer gun can be carried in greater safety, since a hammerless gun is always cocked and ready and must rely on a mechanical safety. The exposed hammers on the older variety can be lowered to the safety position. On the other hand, they *are* exposed and there's always the possibility that a chance blow to the hammer could cause an accidental discharge. A non-ejector hammer gun is also said to be—and undoubtedly is—the most silent of all rifles to get into action. By holding the trigger back while the hammer is cocked, total quiet can be maintained. But by the time the cordite Nitro-Express cartridges were introduced, hammer guns were already an anachronism. Though rare, nitro-proofed hammer doubles do exist. Jack Lott has a wonderful .577 hammer gun, and Zimbabwe professional hunter Steve Alexander uses an Army & Navy .450 No. 2 hammer gun.

In its heyday, the underlever blackpowder hammer gun could have been a big bore—an 8-, 10-, or 12-bore, or, rarely, even a monstrous 4-bore—or it might have been more of a general-purpose rifle chambered for something like the .577, .500, or one of the .450s.

Bullets had changed; conicals had almost universally replaced the round ball, and hunters were well aware of the increased penetrating qualities. In the 1870s, the blackpowder "express" cartridges began to make their appearance, possibly the first velocity fad to hit the world's hunters. The blackpowder expresses, another development credited to James Purdey, took their name from the then-new "express train." Using a bottleneck cartridge such as the .500/.450, a very heavy charge of blackpowder was used to drive a light-for-caliber conical bullet at unprecedented velocities. The bullets were often made light by a cavity in the nose, thus also inducing very rapid expansion—especially in the soft, unjacketed lead. The weight of a caliber .450 "express" bullet might be as light as 270 grains—and velocities ran just shy of 2,000 feet per second.

These expresses flattened trajectories tremendously, and they became very popular for light game. On large game, as would seem obvious, the bullets failed to give needed penetration. As the century wound down, serious hunters of large game clung to their 8-bores. The small-bore fans, of which there were many, stuck with blackpowder .577s.

In 1876, Holland became Holland & Holland when gunmaker Harris Holland took his nephew, Henry Holland, into the business. In 1886, they introduced a new wrinkle in double guns—the Paradox. The Paradox was essentially a smoothbore gun except that the last few inches of the barrel were rifled. The idea was to give an instant choice between ball or shot, with the recommendation that one barrel be loaded with each. Powder charges were fairly light, as were the guns; although Paradox guns were made in 8-, 10-, and 12-bore, their bulleted cartridges could not be used in the big-game rifles of the same bore size, and vice versa. The concept was popular; before the Paradoxes vanished, other companies brought out their own versions under such fanciful names as Explora, Colindian, Jungle Gun, and so forth.

Although the Nitro-Expresses were yet to come, the double rifle was in its final stage of development by the mid-1890s. When, in 1898, John Rigby introduced the .450-3¼", the complete, fully developed rifle was ready and waiting. From this point to the present, the few changes that would occur would be mostly cosmetic; for instance, the shift to the Anson push-rod system to remove the fore-end, as opposed to the older lever system. By the time the switch to Nitro was made, the process of regulating the barrels was fully understood. This was and is an art—always costly and time-consuming, and mastered by very few artisans. On the surface, it would seem quite simple; surely if the barrels were exactly parallel, the accuracy would be all anyone could ask for. It isn't that easy.

The problem is that one barrel lies to the right of the center of gravity, the other to the left. If the barrels were exactly parallel, during firing the forces of recoil would pull the right barrel off to the right and the left barrel off to the left. To combat this, the barrels must have a very slight angle of convergence. Too little and they will never shoot together; too much and they will crossfire at close range.

To this day, although modern technology can help, the only way to regulate a double is by hand, through trial and error. The craftsman starts with the barrels' axes converging very slightly, the barrels firmly joined at the breech, soldered together, and wrapped with wire to hold them in place. Now begins the trial and error. Shoot, then adjust the convergence or divergence by heating the barrels to melt the tin holding them together and moving an adjusting wedge at the muzzles. Shoot again, reheat, and move the wedge until an acceptable degree of accuracy is achieved.

Considering the inexact nature of this procedure, it's simply amazing the degree of accuracy that a double rifle can offer. In general, two shots from each barrel within a four- to six-inch circle at 100 yards is just fine. Call it "grapefruit accuracy"—but I've seen doubles that would cut that in half, and once in a while you'll run into "tennis ball" or even "golf ball" accuracy. Regulating a double is a frustrating, time-consuming business. It's no easier today than it was a century ago, and there are far fewer men alive in the world who can do it.

Double-rifle actions, too, have changed very little since the blackpowder days. Toward the end of that era, double-rifle design pretty much evolved into two basic types of actions, sidelock and boxlock. The sidelock was and is a "fine gun," more expensive to create, plus offering the characteristic sideplates as perfect vehicles for embellishment. The boxlocks, though expensive when compared to single-shots or magazine rifles, were and are "working guns," plainer and less expensive.

Theoretically, the sidelock is the stronger of the two. The reason is that the boxlock's moving parts must be inlet into the steel of the action from underneath. In the sidelock, the breech is left more solid and the moving parts are affixed to the right and left sides of the action. With older steels, the original Anson & Deeley boxlock action occasionally failed in early Nitro-Express doubles—which operated at much higher pressures than any blackpowder gun. Better steels and improvements such as stronger "third fasteners" quickly corrected this, and it's fair to say that the sidelock has no *practical* strength advantage over the boxlock.

Sidelock guns are generally either bar-action or back-action. The "bar" of a double is the solid portion of the action underneath the barrels, the portion that contains the hinge pin and the locking lugs. In a bar-action sidelock, the mainsprings are in the front part of the sideplate, essentially adjacent to the bar. In the back-action sidelock, perfected by Holland & Holland, the mainsprings are to the rear, and thus more integrity is maintained in the bar. Most sidelock double rifles, with their higher pressures, are of the back-action type, while fine shotguns are often bar-action sidelocks.

The sidelock must be made essentially by hand, while a basic boxlock action, if not mass-produced, can at least be produced on a larger scale. Westley Richards had their own hand-detachable boxlock design, but most of the gunmakers (even the top names) offering boxlock doubles (and they all did) purchased their basic actions "in the white." Webley & Scott made a great many of them, and you can find Webley actions on boxlocks by Holland, Purdey, Rigby, Westley Richards, *et al.* Only slightly less common is what is often called a "trade action." A bit different from the Webley, this Birmingham-made action also appears in guns from a variety of makers. It is believed that these actions were turned out on a cottage-industry basis by a number of Birmingham craftsmen, then sold to the trade "in the white" as were the Webley actions.

Whether sidelock or boxlock, the double rifle locks up via lugs—the "lumps"—on the underside of the barrels near the breech. Sliding underbolts, originally designed by James Purdey, fit into recesses in these lumps, thus locking the action when the barrels are closed against the standing breech. On firing, the action naturally flexes and attempts to open. All doubles flex slightly during firing, and when this flexing goes too far an obviously unsafe condition has occurred. That's what happens when a double "goes off the face." To prevent this, most double rifles have some form of third fastener at the top of the standing breech. This could be some form of Greener crossbolt, or a doll's head—an extension of the barrels that, on closing, drops into a fitted recess at the top of the standing breech.

The big Nitro-Express cartridges work at what is, for modern smokeless cartridges, very low breech pressures. In recent years, with our much stronger and more consistent modern steels, doubles have been built for a number of modern cartridges, including the current version of the .375 H&H (much stouter than the old .375 Flanged Magnum) and the .458 Winchester Magnum. However, this is not a strong action design by bolt-action standards, and there are limits. I have heard of doubles being made for the .460 Weatherby Magnum, a cartridge that achieves breech pressures in excess of 50,000 copper units of pressure (C.U.P.), a good 25 to 30 percent more than any Nitro-Express cartridge. Most reports indicate that such guns "go off the face" after relatively few firings—and that should come as no surprise.

Although extremely complex to make, and thus expensive, the double rifle is a very basic tool. Few bells and whistles can be added to it, but there are several variations that remain points of argument for double-rifle men. They are: single or double triggers; automatic or non-automatic safety; and ejector or extractor.

The question of triggers is the simplest. Actually, very few double rifles have been built with single triggers; the double trigger is most common and most traditional. In theory, one of the advantages of a double is two completely independent actions in case one fails. This advantage, if it really exists, is somewhat negated by a single trigger. On the other hand, hunters who haven't grown up with double-triggered guns may *never* learn to shift their finger back for the second trigger—and if that's a problem, a single trigger is the only answer. The choice is pretty much a matter of personal preference, but you'll have trouble finding a single-trigger double rifle; very few have been made. If a single trigger is your preference, be aware that you'll lose the ability to have constant and instant availability of either softpoint or solid bullet. That's a *real* advantage, a wonderful capability, and it's one I've needed and used several times, particularly with buffalo.

More to-do is made over the question of an automatic safety. An automatic safety is basically a sliding shotgun-type safety, seen on 99 percent of all double rifles, that automatically moves to the "safe" position when the opening lever is activated. John Taylor made a fuss over this, believing it was a dangerous feature that could, in a heated moment, get you killed if you reloaded quickly and forgot about the safety when you closed the rifle.

Tony Sanchez, on the other hand, made a most rational case for the automatic safety in *On the Trail of the African Elephant*. He simply felt that sliding the safety forward to "off" as you bring the rifle up should be second nature, and indeed he's correct—putting the safety forward should be every bit as automatic, or reflexive, as shifting your finger to the rear trigger after firing the first barrel.

I must admit that I have disconnected the automatic safety on my own double rifles, a simple matter. But that act now requires the opposite reaction—after firing and loading, I must be always aware of the need to move the safety to the "on" position if I'm not going to fire again. This is an inherent problem with the double that must be taken into account; it's either fully loaded or fully unloaded, with no "halfway measure" such as a loaded magazine but empty chamber. If loaded, only that mechanical safety stands between you and an accidental discharge. Well, as I said, I've disconnected the automatic safety on my doubles—but I pay close attention to having that safety in the proper position, and I watch where the barrels are pointed.

To me, it's not important whether a double rifle has ejectors or extractors. Some of the oldtimers, Taylor included, wanted nothing to do with ejectors; the theory was that the metallic "ping" when the rifle was opened did more to pinpoint the hunter to dangerous game (especially elephant) than the actual sound of the rifle. That argument really doesn't hold water today, since no sportsman has either the opportunity or desire to wade into an elephant herd with the intention of dropping as many as possible before they spook. Regardless of who's really right, the ejectors must have won; a double rifle in any caliber is worth from $500 to $1,000 more with ejectors than without.

However, from a user's standpoint, I don't think it matters a tinker's damn. With the low pressures associated with Nitro-Express cartridges, extraction is a breeze; there's little expansion of the brass, and empties simply fall out of the chambers. All it takes to get the cases out of a non-ejector double is a flick of the wrist, turning the gun out and down. The empties fall out, and you can stick two more in just as fast as you can with an ejector double. Personally, I prefer a non-ejector; I feel I can reload it just as fast, without looking down. That hippo bull I mentioned earlier was caught away from the water in the Selous Reserve. Oddly, in that area it isn't unusual to find them in heavy thorn at midday, miles from water. I was determined to kill him with a body shot from my .470, not the easy brain shot. We got the job done, but I was dumping cartridges in and out, and ejectors wouldn't have speeded the process. Considering the price of new cases, I'd just as soon not have had to rummage around in the grass 10 feet away to find my brass when it was all over.

When the German firm of Heym—a good gunmaker—first offered their Model 88B in .470 I got hold of one. It had what seemed to me a marvelous piece of engineering, a little lever at the base of the fore-end that switched the extractors to ejectors and back again. Great idea, but unneeded moving parts are an invitation to disaster. I got four shots out of the rifle before that switch broke, leaving me with one barrel that ejected and one barrel that didn't. Since then, Heym has dropped that feature.

Barrel lengths on most doubles run from 24 to 28 inches. Although the latter figure sounds long, remember that 28 inches is a normal barrel length

159

for a double shotgun—and a double rifle with 28-inch barrel will be shorter than most bolt-action rifles with 24-inch barrels. The 28-inch barrels were more popular early on, while shorter barrels are likely to be found on later guns. But you never know. I had a wonderful Wilkes .470, a very old rifle, with 24-inch barrels. It handled like a dream, but so do doubles with 26- and even 28-inch barrels; the differences aren't significant.

Sights normally will be some kind of standing leaf on a quarter or full rib, with or without folding leaves. For my money, the folding leaves are useless. My Andrews .470 has one standing and three folding leaves marked for distances out to 300 yards. So what? I can't *see* well enough to use a double's bold bead and coarse V much beyond 150 yards, and I doubt if many people can. The main thing is to make sure the first leaf, the one you'll really use, is standing, not folding.

Once in a while, you'll find a big double with a flip-up aperture sight or fixtures for a claw scope mount. Depending on who wants the rifle, such features may add or detract. Truth is, anybody sees better and shoots better with a scope. But a scope seems so out of place on a good double that I've never been attracted to one with mounts, and I probably never will be. That doesn't make much sense, though, because a good low-powered scope would enhance a double's usefulness immeasurably.

A great many doubles were more or less standard "over-the-counter" rifles, perhaps more than you might think. But many were indeed made to customers' specifications. Most will have some degree of cast to the stock, and a few have very odd dimensions. Keep in mind that all of this can be fixed; cast can be added or taken off easily, and a comb can always be reshaped or lowered and a too-long stock shortened. However, a comb that's too low or a stock that's too short might need replacement. It can all be done, but the degree of fixing required can ruin any collector value.

The crucial thing about a double that's to be used, not just purchased to look at, is that it must fit, properly and perfectly. If it doesn't, fix it, whatever it takes. The double's stock in trade isn't accuracy or firepower—it's two shots, delivered faster than anything else can deliver them, and gun fit must be right. When the double rifle comes to the shoulder, the sights should be an unneeded redundancy—the rifle should already be there, perfectly lined up. If the sights aren't *on* when you throw the rifle up, that double simply isn't right for you. Or you aren't right for it.

# Chapter 14

# The Double Rifle Today

The double rifle could well have died away. Winchester's .458 Magnum, introduced in the excellent Model 70, then the preeminent bolt-action rifle in the world, came out at the most opportune time imaginable—1958, just when Kynoch was discontinuing virtually all the big Nitro-Express rounds. Only a couple of them made it into the 1960s, and by 1967 Kynoch was out of the ammo business altogether.

Slowly, as existing stocks of ammo dwindled, the grand old guns were sold or shelved. Many found their way into the hands of American collectors, and it was in America that double rifles got a new lease on life. As mentioned earlier, with Barnes bullets and R.C.B.S. dies, handloaders could keep shooting the big doubles. And then Jim Bell got into business with new brass and ammo.

Economics dictate that the double rifle will never be as common as the bolt gun in Africa or anywhere else. But right now the double rifle is more visible than it has been since Stewart Granger's day. Just a few years ago, when I wrote my first African book, *From Mt. Kenya to the Cape*, I stated that I had seen just seven double rifles in use in Africa. Several of those had been in my own hands! In the very few years since then, I have seen that number and more in various professional hunters' hands. It's partly chance, of course, but it isn't that I'm looking more closely today; I've always been fascinated by doubles.

More new doubles are being built right now than have been for many years. In 1989, Holland & Holland's Russell Wilkin told me his firm had more doubles under construction than at any time since World War II—including Bill Feldstein's double .700! Of course, a Holland Royal is not an inexpensive rifle; at this writing, something on the order of $45,000 might do the job.

A very few other English firms can still build doubles, but most will not. A much larger number are being built on the Continent—and some of them are very fine rifles. On the other hand, some are not very fine rifles. Now, I can no more afford a Holland & Holland than I can fly to the moon, and in my lifetime I'll never be able to afford one. Fortunately, serviceable doubles, though never cheap, don't have to cost that much. The key word is serviceable. A poorly made double, at any price, is a bad deal.

Remember two things. First, the regulation is extremely complex. A double will never be a real tackdriver in the American sense of the word, but a poorly regulated double will have trouble giving barn-door accuracy. Second, the double is not a strong action—it simply must be well-made or it isn't safe to fire. So, beware of "great deals," and obtain a guarantee that allows you to shoot the rifle before you're stuck with it!

Having said all that, I must also say that some wonderful doubles are being made in surprising places. The Heym guns are magnificently accurate, and with modern steels tend to be slimmer and trimmer than the English could make them in "the good old days." The Belgians have made fine doubles for generations; names like Francotte, Dumoulin, and Lebeau-Corally need take a back seat to no one. Such guns are hardly inexpensive, but they won't set you back like a Holland.

The various makers in Ferlach, Austria, can turn out fine doubles—and usually do. The Champlin-Famars gun, made in Italy to George Caswell's specifications, is essentially a brand new Webley-actioned English-type double. These rifles are beautiful, and they shoot.

There are also a great many smaller makers, many that I simply don't know about. It seems as if every year I hear about a couple more. Don Shrum, of Cape Outfitters in Cape Girardeau, Missouri, imports Marcel Thys doubles from Belgium—lovely rifles offered in a tremendous array of calibers from .22 Long Rifle to .600 Nitro-Express. His guns seem to average about $15,000, and look like they're worth it. I don't know the current status of the French Chapuis double, but several years ago I shot one in .375 H&H and another in 9.3x74R, both side-by-sides, and both acceptably accurate. Another French maker, Guy Ripamonti, is new to me; I just saw his guns at a recent show. His side-by-side .375 is gorgeous and very inexpensive, well under $5,000. Do they shoot? I don't know, but it would be worth finding out. The Italian Perugini-Visini, imported by William Larkin Moore, is a good-shooting double that's priced extremely well in the boxlock version. Right now there are a couple of Americans, small shops, considering building big doubles. I don't know if they have any idea what they're getting into—that regulating business is very tricky—but I hope they pull it off.

When I think about doubles, I tend to think side-by-side. However, there are many European over/under doubles, and some have been made in large calibers. Bill Illingworth, a Zambian professional I hunted with in 1983, had a German over/under .470! Regulation is a bit easier with an over/under; the yawing isn't as pronounced. However, the same principles apply except vertically rather than horizontally. The only real disadvantage to an over/under double rifle is that the opening arc is obviously much greater, so loading is a tad slower and more difficult in close quarters, such as heavy thorn. The over/under also lacks that incredibly broad plane to sight over and thus tends to be not quite so fast in the crunch. However, over/unders, particularly in 9.3x74R, are readily available from many European makers—sometimes very inexpensively. The Valmet, for instance, can be had in 9.3 for less than the cost of many bolt-actions. Over/unders are often easier to scope than side-by-sides, a real advantage that's especially nice in the lighter calibers.

For many years, the 9.3, a good enough cartridge but no powerhouse, was the only *rimmed* cartridge a new double was readily available in. As far as I'm concerned, that was a problem. There have been many very fine doubles made for the .375 H&H and .458 Winchester Magnum. That's all well and good, and such guns work—most of the time. However, rimless and belted rimless cartridges are not double-rifle cartridges, period. The better makers have excellent ejection/extraction systems that work marvelously well. But they're of necessity complex, with little spring-loaded gizmos that drop into the extractor groove. They can fail—not often, but eventually—even from the best makers.

A professional hunter friend of mine asked what I thought about a .458 double. Don't you hate it when friends ask for advice? You know they've already made their minds up, so do you tell them what they want to hear, or what you really believe? I told him to get a .470, even though the ammunition would be a bigger problem. He'd already decided; he got the .458, and a lovely gun it is. The very first time he had to stop a buffalo charge he fired both barrels, then broke the gun to reload. The ejectors slipped over the case heads, the classic failure with rimless or belted cases, and he had no choice but to try to get out of the buffalo's way. He managed. The gun was shipped back to Europe for repair, and he tells me it's never done that again. It will sooner or later, I'll wager—most of them do.

The very best news in doubles, to me, is the resurgence of the .470. The big Nitro-Express case gives the low pressures that doubles handle best, and the big rim (flange, if you prefer) absolutely guarantees foolproof extraction and/or ejection each and every time. As I said in Chapter 8, the .470 isn't necessarily the best of the Nitro-Expresses, but it is the most available. Now that Federal is loading it, that's the double-rifle cartridge that makes sense, and it's the one rimmed cartridge that most new doubles (excluding the 9.3x74R) are being chambered to. It isn't alone, though; as I mentioned, the Marcel Thys gun is available in any Nitro-Express you like. The Champlin-Famars gun can be had in .450 No. 2 as well as .470, and the Heym can be had in .500-3" as well as .470 (and .458 and .375).

Compared to bolt-actions, of course, the number of new doubles being built is a drop in the bucket. We're talking about dozens of guns worldwide, not hundreds of thousands. Even so, the big double is on a roll, and over the next few years I predict we'll see more of them.

The new-gun market is one subject, and the used-gun market is quite another. It's a basic decision a hunter must face when he contemplates acquiring a big double. There are pros and cons; prices are soaring for classic English doubles, but in general a good, sound used rifle can be purchased for a great deal less than a new rifle.

Depending on the maker, the new rifle may or may not appreciate in value like the used gun, but it will have better steel. It can also be tailored to the shooter's tastes and dimensions, while an older gun is what it is—unless you modify it, which could hurt its value. It's a tough decision, and there isn't a right or wrong answer.

In either case, there really aren't any bargains out there. A dozen years ago, you could occasionally blunder into good used doubles at modest prices, but today darn few shooters are unaware of the double rifle's intrinsic value. Worse, there are a whole lot of folks who figure they're worth more than they really are.

There aren't many pitfalls to buying vintage doubles, just so long as you don't pay a great deal more than you should. First, check the barrels. They'll show some wear, and some wear is acceptable; cordite burns very hot, and there will be some erosion in well-used guns. But the rifling should be bright and fairly sharp. The best way to spot serious wear is to see if the left barrel, the second barrel that isn't fired nearly as much, looks a whole lot better than the right barrel. If the difference is noticeable, you'd best group the rifle before you bite.

Next, check the proof marks on flats of the barrel. They're confusing, but make sure it's proofed for a full Nitro charge. *Cartridges of the World* will give the original cordite charge of a Kynoch factory load. Blackpowder guns later proofed for Nitro will most likely not have been proofed for a full charge.

Finally, unless you're buying the rifle from a reputable dealer, arrange to have a gunsmith take a look to make sure it hasn't come off the face. If it has, it can probably be fixed—but that might be expensive. Incidentally, if the barrels are worn out, consider it a wallhanger. It would have to be a very fine gun from a "name" maker to be worth rebarreling, and you don't just willy-nilly rebore a double as you might a bolt gun.

Shopping for used doubles is an interesting game. In fact, it's fascinating. I've done it several times in earnest, and in truth I'm always doing it—though I can rarely afford to. Take double rifles and divide them into two categories: "fine guns" and "working guns." Now, fine guns are certainly shootable, and there's no reason not to hunt with them. But unless price is no object, forget a fine gun if all you want to do is take the rifle on safari.

A fine gun is a sidelock. A boxlock, in rare cases, *can be* a fine gun—but a working gun *is* a boxlock. Today's prices probably won't be valid for very long, but just for a general comparison of used doubles, look at it this way: a working boxlock gun chambered for a Nitro-Express cartridge from .450/.400 to .500 has a basic value of $6,000. A nice sidelock has a basic value of $12,000. These are "getting" prices, not "asking." This assumes normal used-but-very-serviceable condition, with the normal embellishment associated with that type of gun; no gold inlay, no documentation of a famous user. Now things start to get interesting.

If the rifle happens to be chambered for .470, add about $1,000. Everybody wants a .470. The other premiums are the large bores. For .577, add a minimum of 50 percent; for .600, the really rare one, God help you. Now, if the rifle is chambered to .450/.400, subtract $1,000 to $1,500. Both .450/.400s are great cartridges, but nobody wants them. If it happens to be chambered to one of the real oddballs, either .475 Nitro-Express or .476 Westley Richards, you should be able to talk the price down a bit. Keep in mind that you can get bullets and make cases from B.E.L.L. brass, so it's no big deal. In .450 No. 2, .450-3¼", .475 No. 2, etc., the basic price should hold.

Now, if the rifle has ejectors, add $500. If it has extractors only, subtract $500. Chambering and presence or absence of ejectors are the only physical specifications that have tremendous impact on value.

*But*, the name inscribed on the barrel makes the most difference of all. If happens to say Holland & Holland, add 75 percent. If it says Rigby or Westley Richards, add 50 percent. If it says Purdey, double it. If it says Woodward, God help you. But unless you're a collector, don't get hung up on names. Once you get past the premium names, you aren't into second-class rifles. Most of the name makers made a fair number of second-class (meaning plain, not poor quality) rifles themselves.

There were dozens of small English makers, good 'smiths who just never hit the big time. Their rifles are good, but you needn't pay a premium to own one. Webley and Scott, Grant, Lang, William Evans, Boswell, Wilkes, Thomas Bland, Hollis, Fraser, George Gibbs, Charles Lancaster, Dickson, Tolley, Greener, Cogswell & Harrison, W. J. Jeffery; Lord, who have I missed? There were dozens of small makers in both London and Birmingham; it's unlikely that a complete listing exists anywhere. My own .470 was made by C.W. Andrews, a maker I've never heard of before, nor have I ever seen another rifle with that name on it. And of course, don't forget that a number of very fine rifles have *no name* on them at all. Virtually all the top makers produced rifles for the Army & Navy Cooperative Stores, Ltd. This co-op furnished rifles (and everything else under the sun) for soldiers and sailors at affordable prices. They were the epitome of the good, sound, working gun—and anybody, the name makers included, may well have made them.

For instance, a good friend of mine picked up a lovely Army & Navy .450-3¼" at a most reasonable price. Non-name maker, less desirable caliber, but a perfectly lovely boxlock rifle on a Webley action—in great shape, available quite inexpensively. Who made it? It's impossible to say. Considering the caliber, it could well have been made by Rigby—or darn near anyone else. You can find virtually identical doubles of various calibers—Webley action, similar sights and quality of wood and metalwork—with names like Rigby, Holland, Wilkes, Boswell, *et al.* stamped on the barrel. Depending on the name, you'll pay a great deal more for an identical rifle than my friend paid for his Army & Navy.

The permutations of shopping for doubles are fascinating. Take my current Andrews rifle, for instance. Made sometime in the 1920s, it was darn near unfired when I got it, and since it's chambered for .470, it's quite a desirable gun. If I decided I wanted a "name" rifle, a Rigby for instance, I could probably trade my .470 for one—if I could find a Rigby in, say, .450-3¼", and an owner crazy enough to make such a trade. A name gun in .470, though, would be a most valuable combination! It's all kind of silly, really—a good boxlock double is a good rifle, period. In any caliber from .450, up it will do the job as well as any other. Assuming the rifle fits, the maker's name inscribed on the barrel isn't important.

Sidelocks are in another world. The sidelocks were generally the makers' "best" guns, and show a good deal more of the individual maker's taste and innovative touches. Many of the smaller makers didn't produce sidelocks at all, but sourced their Webley or trade actions and assembled, barreled, regulated, and finished their boxlock doubles. Those that did make sidelocks made good ones. As works of art, they're worth every penny they cost. In terms of function, however, you won't get any more out of them than you will from a boxlock costing half to a third as much.

Enroute to your next safari, if you happen to pass through London try to spend a bit of time at Rigby's, Holland's, or Westley Richards's. Chances are you won't see an extensive selection of doubles, but generally there will be a few to look at, and there's always something to learn. But don't expect a bargain—costs in Britain, if anything, are higher than in the U.S. A select few shops over here are better places to look at a selection of used doubles. Griffin & Howe in New York usually have several. The largest selection I know of can be found at George Caswell's Champlin Arms in Enid, Oklahoma.

Considering that a double is a significant investment, when you're serious about finding the double that's right for you a trip there is worth the effort. George often has as many as a hundred good used doubles on hand—sidelocks, boxlocks, famous makers and unknowns. When you have a chance to see a number of guns all in one place, you can quickly learn to recognize a Webley action, and you can compare the weight and balance from one gun to another.

It's worth repeating here that proper fit is more important with a double than with any other type of rifle since its most important job is to deliver two shots almost simultaneously; to stop a serious charge when the chips are down. To do that reliably, it must fit its owner like an extension of his arms and eyes.

The double rifle is Gregory Peck in *The Snows of Kilimanjaro;* Stewart Granger in *King Solomon's Mines* and *The Last Safari*; Robert Redford in *Out of Africa;* it's Ernest Hemingway, Robert Ruark, and J.A. Hunter. The big double symbolizes the grand tradition of African safari—but is it really a sensible choice for today's hunter?

It would be foolish to suggest that anyone really needs a double rifle to hunt Africa; many of the great oldtimers used magazine rifles exclusively. Harry Manners never found the .375 H&H in a bolt-action rifle wanting, and Commander Blunt stayed with his .416 Rigby throughout his career. Many top hunters switched back and forth; Hunter loved his double .500s, but for control work he was more likely to use the .505 Gibbs. Samaki Salmon, too, used magazine rifles for control work, a pair of .416s; for ivory hunting, though, he used a pair of .470 doubles. For the sportsman, who has no need or desire to take a large number of animals at one sitting, it pretty much comes down to personal preference. However, it would be just as absurd to suggest that a double is not a sound choice as it would be to suggest it as the only choice!

The double does have very real advantages. It's short, handy, and its big Nitro-Express cartridges are unquestionably adequate. A good double handles like a dream, points naturally, and no matter what, *nothing* is faster for a second shot. It's also important to note that the second shot comes with absolutely no extraneous motion or noise. Now, even with much practice, the third shot from a double will come more slowly than from a magazine rifle. However, when that third cartridge is placed in a double's chamber, the fourth goes in right alongside it. I would submit that a double is just as fast for the *fourth* shot as any magazine rifle—and faster by far than a three-shot magazine rifle.

It also has serious disadvantages. The first is cost. Even a very plain, well-used boxlock from an unknown maker will cost close to 10 times what an equally plain production bolt-action .458 will cost. If you can't afford one, don't despair; they're great fun to own and shoot, but they aren't 10 times better than a bolt gun!

Yet another disadvantage is the fact that a double rifle is a very basic tool. Like a shotgun, it is what it is and there's little that can be done to change it. A bolt-action rifle can be fine-tuned, accurized, scoped or unscoped, and its ammunition can be carefully tailored for the exact job at hand. Unless you're willing to go to extremes of trouble and expense, as the double rifle comes into your hands, so it shall remain. The bullet weight and load for which it was regulated, unless you're lucky, is the only load that will deliver any real degree of accuracy.

The double's barrels were regulated for a certain bullet and a specific charge of cordite powder, and with that load its barrels will shoot together, more or less. I have seen doubles that would actually put two shots from each barrel into two inches at 100 yards, but that's exceptional. Acceptable accuracy is four inches, and sometimes six inches is about all you can get. Keep in mind that the exact loads for which older doubles were regulated haven't been loaded for 30 years or more!

How big a problem is that? Are doubles actually all that finicky? Well, it depends on the rifle. Getting the barrels to shoot together is a matter of barrel vibrations and harmonics plus that slight degree of convergence of the two barrels. There's nothing magic about Kynoch bullets and cordite powder. As in getting bolt-action rifles to shoot tiny groups, everything

167

inter-relates. Bullet weight and bearing surface are important, and velocity and barrel time are critical.

If you are shooting Kynoch bullets—or bullets identical in weight and bearing surface to original Kynoch bullets—in theory all you have to do to achieve the original regulated accuracy level of a double is to duplicate the original velocity. The Australian Woodleigh bullets (and excellent bullets they are!) are very similar to Kynochs in profile and bearing surface, and they generally match in weight. However, if you wish to shoot 500-grain Hornadys in, say, a .450-3¼" that was originally regulated for 480-grain bullets, you've got a slight problem to begin with.

Another basic problem is in knowing exactly what velocity the original regulating load developed. Kynoch's quoted factory ballistics are a good starting point, but the various lots I've chronographed over the years have indicated some amount of "blue sky" in factory figures. Most Kynoch .470 ammunition I've chronographed, for instance, is a bit below 2,100 fps—not the full 2,150 it's supposed to deliver.

All smokeless powders get a bit "hotter" as temperatures increase, but cordite was more sensitive to temperature changes than our modern powders. In the old days, hunters often found their doubles "crossfiring" at relatively close range when they used cordite ammunition in Africa's equatorial heat. In some cases, "tropical" loads were offered with a slightly lower powder charge designed for use at higher temperatures. Later on, it was common for large-caliber doubles to be specifically regulated for use in warm climates.

In his *Notes on Sporting Rifles*, Sir Gerald Burrard advises: "This crossing of the shots is a very common fault in very hot climates. . . . The only plan to advise is. . . to have the rifle regulated in England so that the two barrels shoot a little away from each other at 100 yards. . . As a general guide it may be taken that the barrels of double cordite rifles of round about .470 bore should be made to shoot from 4 to 6 inches apart at 100 yards in England. It will then be found that in the hot climate they will shoot so close together that it will be impossible to distinguish their groups under practical sporting conditions."

The flats of the barrel will tell you what bullet weight and charge of powder your rifle was regulated for, but the inscription won't tell you whether it was regulated for the tropics or for England. In other words, you've got a bit of a grab bag on your hands. Chances are your rifle will regulate with original Kynoch, but the ammunition is getting a bit old to trust in the field.

If you're luckier still, your rifle may regulate with B.E.L.L., A-Square, or the new Federal. Actually, the odds aren't all that bad, since all of these loads are designed to duplicate Kynoch velocities. My own English doubles have shot very well with B.E.L.L. ammunition, though never quite so well as with Kynoch. Most newer guns, of course, have been regulated with B.E.L.L., making life much simpler. I *wish* my Andrews rifle would shoot

A-Square's excellent Monolothic Solid factory load, but it won't—something about that load is too hot for my particular rifle, making the gun very hard to open.

Handloading is an option, and if your rifle has trouble regulating with modern factory loads, it's the only option available to you. Unfortunately, it isn't the joyful handloading you can do for a bolt-action, finding the very best load and the very best bullet for the job at hand—whether that job is punching the tiniest groups possible or dropping cleanly the largest of the world's game. Handloading for a double requires the same trial-and-error test firing, the same up-a-half-grain, down-a-half-grain tedium. But it has a fixed goal—to find the one load that achieves regulation. Once you find it, never lose the formula!

In practice, it isn't as bad as all that; most doubles regulate more or less readily with a handload of the approximate original bullet weight and a powder charge that yields something close to original velocities. But there won't be a lot of combinations that work, and it can take a good deal of hit-and-miss to find the right one.

The cases are very large, needed for the bulky cordite. But with modern powders, the case capacity is far more than needed. For this reason it's important to use extremely bulky, slow-burning powders. The older references suggested IMR 3031, and it will work. However, in some rifles I have had better luck with IMR 4831, a bulkier powder that uses much more of the case.

Even then, sometimes it's necessary to use a bit of polyester fiber on top of the powder. With the larger cases, I have experienced erratic ignition without a bit of filler. Jack Lott, one of America's foremost authorities on doubles, prefers to use a light cork overpowder wad. I've used Jack's wads—he showed me how to make them—but I've found it easier to put a half-grain of polyester pillow stuffing over the powder. Be advised, though, that *nothing* is noncritical with these cartridges, and the rifles that fire them will not handle extra pressure with the ease of a bolt-action. Once I got a little carried away—or a little careless—with the pillow stuffing, and pressures went up alarmingly.

You won't find much loading data available for Nitro-Express cartridges, but it can be ferreted out. Don't do a lot of freelance experimentation, and proceed to full loads very cautiously. If such care is taken, you really can't get into trouble—but once you find a load your rifle will regulate with, you're all finished experimenting.

Some doubles are extremely forgiving. George Caswell has been doing a lot of experimenting with his new .450 No. 2—a strong gun with the strongest of all the Nitro-Express cases. With it, he has achieved something rarely thought possible with a double rifle—the ability to use a variety of bullet weights.

Using 350-, 400-, and 500-grain bullets, all at essentially the same 2,150 to 2,200 feet per second, he has gotten his rifles to shoot all of them into a single ragged group, an amazing accomplishment. If it were a bolt-action, however, those lighter bullets could be pushed a great deal faster. As it is, their primary advantage would be a reduction in recoil—and just perhaps the lighter bullets would offer much more rapid expansion on cats.

The double rifle is not for the accuracy freak, and certainly not, generally, for the handloading experimenter. There's lots of experimentation to be done in finding a good load, but once it's found, that's all. On the other hand, relatively few hunters are serious ballistic tinkerers. All the double asks is that she be fed a diet she likes, and it isn't really all that difficult to comply these days.

Accuracy, well, you aren't going to make a long-range rig out of a big double. But the double's inaccuracy is generally exaggerated out of all proportion. No doubles can offer consistent minute-of-angle accuracy—but they're all minute of buffalo or elephant. They have the capability to put those big bullets where they're needed, when they're needed. And they're also a joy to own and shoot. Yes, a good double is a viable choice for today's African hunting. Africa is a feeling as much as a place, and a big double takes you back in time to the Africa you've read and dreamed about all your life. That's an equally good reason to use one.

# Chapter 15

# The Bolt-action Hunting Rifle— A Historical Perspective

In 1890, Oliver Winchester's lever-actions were the best-known and most-respected repeaters in the world. By the time the Spanish-American and Boer Wars had ended, about 1902, the bolt-action had taken over—perhaps not in America, but in Africa and the rest of the world.

The first turnbolt rifles were blackpowder guns, the classic form being the Model 71 Mauser firing the 11mm (.43-caliber) Mauser cartridge. But smokeless cartridges were right around the corner, and the first turnbolts to catch the eyes of sportsmen fired small-bore cartridges—the 6.5x53R Mannlicher-Steyr and later the 6.5x54 Mannlicher-Schoenauer; the Mausers in 7x57 and 8x57J; Britain's Lee-Metford .303. Hunters had seen the blackpowder expresses fail miserably on large game, but now the long, heavy-for-caliber, fully jacketed bullets for these military cartridges gave the penetration that, heretofore, it took an 8-bore cannon to achieve.

The rifles were also incredibly cheap, especially to English sportsmen accustomed to paying for individually crafted arms. In 1892, when Austria's Steyr began selling their 6.5x53R Mannlicher on the civilian market, the cost was about 80 shillings, or $16. An Englishman could purchase a used Martini-Henry for a bit less than that—but not much else! Although this passage has been oft quoted, the great sheep hunter, St. George Littledale, summed things up nicely in a letter written in the 1920s:

"In 1895 Sir Edmund Loder gave me a Mannlicher rifle, bayonet and all, complete on the eve of starting for Tibet. Had only time to have sighting altered. On my protesting that I had a room full of rifles and did not want any more, all he said was, 'Try the Mannlicher,' and like Lily Langtry and the soap, I have used no other since."

From today's perspective, it seems amazing that turn-of-the-century British hunters were so quick to adopt the small-bore bolt-action. It was a radical shift, especially for the staid Englishmen. However, the Englishmen who went out to Africa weren't the stodgy noblemen from smoke-filled club rooms. They were rebels, reckless and often resentful—and many of them had little to lose. If titled, they were often the second and third sons, and more than a few left scandals and unpaid bills behind them. Others were gentlemen of the highest order, but driven by a thirst for adventure that set them apart from their fellows in old England. It was people like these who built one of the world's great empires from a tiny island nation, and it shouldn't be surprising that they would try something new—especially if fits their budgets!

Whether the bolt-action happened to be a 6.5, a 7mm, a .303, an 8mm, or even an American Springfield or Krag, to understand its rapid, complete, and euphoric acceptance you must understand the arena it came into. Velocities were low; bullets were soft lead or, at best, hardened lead; small bores began at .40 caliber and ran to .577. The bullet performance and penetration we take for granted was unknown; the only way to reliably and consistently drop really large game was to flatten them with raw power—which also flattened the shooter. The writings of even the hairiest-chested of the early hunters are filled with references to the sometimes disastrous effects of recoil.

Smokeless powder had existed in experimental form for some time, but until now it had been impractical as a propellant for bullets; the blackpowder expresses were already at the upper limits of velocity that the existing projectiles would stand. Smokeless cartridges simply could not exist without a bullet hard enough to be driven at such unprecedented velocities. Which came first, the chicken or the egg? Who knows? But it's a fact that the first practical smokeless cartridges came out about the same time as the first jacketed bullets, the late 1880s. A Major Rubin of the Swiss army is credited with inventing the jacketed bullet, initially a lead core sheathed in an alloy of copper and nickel ("cupro-nickel"). Just a few years later, that lead core was sheathed in steel, then gilded with nickel—essentially the same formula for the "steel-jacketed solids" we use to this day.

The year 1888 saw the introduction not only of the 8mm Mauser ("J" bore, technically a 7.9mm), but also the .303 British. The .303, with a wonderful 215-grain roundnose jacketed bullet, was introduced as a blackpowder cartridge, using a compressed "express-type" load to push that bullet at 1,850 fps. When the switch to smokeless was made in 1892, the velocity was increased by only 120 fps.

The Mauser and Mannlicher cartridges all developed somewhat higher velocities, and the European rifles were stronger than the British Lee-Metford. Even so, with their jacketed bullets *all* of these new small-bore military rifles offered a whole new world of penetration, accuracy, and flatness of trajectory. And more; the rifles were wonderfully light, especially the little Mannlicher 6.5s. Recoil was nonexistent, and the great clouds of smoke were no more. The early military rifles were all designed to handle charging or "stripper" clips, so not only were they repeaters, but the firepower they offered was awesome.

Each of these small-bore bolt-actions had its fans, and in truth all of them, given good bullets, were probably just about equal. The 6.5mm, firing those pencil-like 160-grain bullets, may well have given the very best penetration of the whole lot, although the 7x57 with its original 173-grain bullet is hardly a slouch. But the .311-caliber .303 British with 215-grain bullet was and is a real killer; likewise the 8mm Mauser, with its original 226-grain bullet. H.C. Maydon swore by his "7.9" Mauser; Stigand, Tarlton, and many others swore by the 6.5, or .256; and Bell loved his .275 Rigby. But the soldiers, hunters, and adventurers who relied on the Lee-Metford .303 can't be forgotten. They were admired by the likes of Selous and Frederick Burnham, and it was a .303 that Lieutenant Colonel J.H. Patterson used to clean out the Tsavo man-eaters.

Perhaps the most anemic of the early smokeless military cartridges was the rimmed 8mm Lebel adopted by France. According to Tony Sanchez, it was the favorite of French ivory hunter Theodore Lefebvre, who is believed to have shot 700 elephant with his Lebel, never finding it lacking!

The first really successful smokeless-powder bolt-action was the German Model 88, variously called a Mannlicher and a Mauser, but actually the product of neither designer but rather an amalgamation of the ideas of both. Although chambered for the still-excellent 8x57 (technically 7.9mm with the earlier .318-inch bullet), this wasn't the rifle that caught the world's eye—possibly because, like many military rifles, it wasn't available on the civilian market.

One of its variations, manufactured by the Steyr works in Austria, was. This was the Model 1892 (and 1893) Romanian military rifle, using the same basic action but chambered for the 6.5x53R cartridge. Called the Mannlicher or Mannlicher-Steyr, this was the first of the 6.5s to see use on African game. By today's standards, the action is a bit weird. The bolt head is a separate piece from the bolt body, although the forward opposing locking lugs at the front of the bolt body are pure Mauser. The extractor, affixed to the bolt head, appears to be weak and is very small—but I've never heard of extraction complaints with this rifle.

The cartridges were loaded in clips, similar to the charging or "stripper" clips which would continue in vogue for many years. However, with the Model 88 and its derivatives, including the 6.5mm Mannlicher-Steyr, the clip *and* its cartridges were inserted into the magazine box from the top. The clip remained in place while the spring-loaded follower fed the cartridges up one at a time. As long as there were cartridges in the clip, it remained in place; when the last cartridge was fed into the chamber, the clip would drop out through an opening in the bottom of the magazine.

The clip-loading feature was obviously very fast, but if a sportsman didn't have any clips or if he lost them, the rifle became a single-shot. Other than the apparently weak extractor, it was a sound and strong action—but it had no facility to vent gases away from the shooter in the event of a ruptured case head or other catastrophic failure.

The later Mannlicher-Schoenauer rifle was developed at Steyr in 1900. Adopted as the Greek military rifle in 1903, chambered for the rimless 6.5x54 Mannlicher-Schoenauer, the rifle was introduced to the sporting marketplace at about the same time. Ballistics were essentially identical to those of the 6.5x53R Mannlicher-Steyr, which became known as the "old" 6.5. The action, too, was very similar, in that the bolt assembly is the same, including the detachable bolt head and small extractor. However, the Mannlicher-Schoenauer did away with the Steyr clips, using instead the rotary-spool magazine which would become the Mannlicher-Schoenauer hallmark from then on.

The top of the receiver was slotted to receive charging clips, essential on a military bolt-action, but the clips weren't required for operation and could be discarded. The spool magazine was and is a very fine system; it allowed for unbeatably smooth feeding, and the spool held the cartridges firmly in place and prevented softpoints from deforming in the magazine. Over the years, a great many sporting rifles were made around this action, and in its original 6.5 chambering it was a favorite among Africa's early small-bore fanatics.

The British Lee-Metford is in many ways a strange action. Never particularly strong (though plenty strong enough for the mild .303 British), its locking lugs are located about halfway down the bolt body. The Metford designation refers to the shallow, segmental Metford rifling—which was found to wear much too quickly with smokeless loads. In 1895, the deeper-grooved Enfield rifling was adopted, and from then forward the rifle was known as the Lee-Enfield. The basic action was the creation of American designer James Paris Lee, and for a time Remington offered "Remington-Lee" sporting rifles around an earlier version.

Although rarely available in any chambering other than .303, the Lee-Metfords and later Lee-Enfields saw wide use throughout Africa. The 10-shot magazine capacity was extremely desirable—if not to the hunter, certainly to the soldiers who carried it through two world wars and hundreds of colonial skirmishes. In few aspects is it the equal of the Mauser action that followed it by just a few years—but it was a fixture throughout the British Empire for generations, and Lee-Enfields are still seen all across Africa to this day.

Peter Paul Mauser, who must rank with John Moses Browning as one of the greatest of firearms designers, had been working for years to improve his Model 71 blackpowder bolt action. Between 1888 and 1896, every year saw a new Mauser action designed for rimless, smokeless cartridges—and each one was adopted by one country or another—the 1889 Belgian, 1890 Turkish, 1891 Argentine, 1892 Spanish (introducing the 7x57 cartridge to the world), 1894 Swedish, 1895 Chilean, and 1896 Swedish (again). Then, in 1898, Mauser's bolt-action reached what is considered its ultimate design in the Model 98 German Mauser.

The basics of the action are a one-piece bolt body with two massive, forward, opposing locking lugs and a third safety lug farther back. The famed long Mauser extractor of spring steel is attached to the bolt by a collar, and the fixed ejector is on the left side of the receiver. When the cartridge feeds up out of the magazine, it is held securely by the extractor until the bolt is moved to the rear. The ejector then passes through a slot in the right locking lug and bolt face until it contacts the case head and flips it to the right and out.

The military Model 98 action is slotted for charging clips, and the left side of the receiver has a semicircular cutout, the thumb slot, to facilitate clip loading. The bolt has openings to direct escaping gas in the event of a ruptured case, making it a safer action than most designs which preceded it.

Over the years, with numerous modifications—many simply cosmetic—the Mauser-type action, characterized by dual opposing locking lugs, long extractor, and fixed ejector, would dominate the sporting-rifle world as well as the military. Both the Springfield and Pattern 14 (or 1917 U.S.) Enfield were basically modified Mauser actions. So was the pre-'64 Winchester Model 70.

Dozens of firms have made commercial Mauser actions, in America as well as all over Europe. Initially only the standard-length 8.75-inch action was made, but by 1902 "magnum" Mauser actions, 9.25 inches in length, capable of handling larger cartridges, were available. Initially, too, the rifles were commonly available only in their military chamberings, which accounts for the almost instant success of the 7x57 and 8x57.

The days of the small bores were numbered, however. By the time George Grey was killed while using a .280 Ross, in 1911, the demand for more powerful bolt-actions had already begun. John Rigby, Mauser's British agent, chambered magnum Mausers modified with slant-box magazines to .400/.350 Nitro-Express as early as 1902, and a few Mausers in .500-3" Nitro-Express were also made. In 1908, unable to obtain magnum actions, Westley Richards introduced their revolutionary short-cased .425. By 1912, when Rigby's magnum Mauser monopoly ended, the .404 Jeffery, .416 Rigby, and .375 Holland & Holland were available.

Now for the first time, hunters who preferred magazine rifles—or who couldn't afford a double—didn't have to rely on a small bore. The British, of course, weren't alone. In Europe, the 9x56 and 9.5x57 Mannlicher-Schoenauer; 9x57, 9.3x57, 9.3x62, and 10.75x63 Mauser; and the 9.3x64 Brenneke were all available well before World War I.

Many of Africa's greatest hunters came to rely exclusively on bolt-actions—Bell, Harry Manners, Pete Pearson, David Blunt, and more. Others, like John Taylor, remained staunch double-rifle men. However, most hunters who preferred doubles, including Taylor himself, also used the cheaper, lighter bolt-action rifles extensively—often saving the doubles and their much more expensive ammunition strictly for close-cover work.

The advantages of the bolt-action rifle were readily apparent at the turn of the century, and they're the same advantages the turnbolt offers today. I've recited the litany of cost, weight, and repeat firepower—but, in truth, other repeating-action types could compete in all these areas. However, no other repeating-action to this day has been effective with the powerful, high-intensity cartridges readily available in bolt-actions.

Thus, one of the turnbolt's great advantages is *strength.* Yes, a bolt gun can be blown up—but every other action type known to man will give up long before a turnbolt does. Part of that strength, too, is in the great camming power the bolt exerts during primary extraction. In the tropics, stuck cases were an age-old problem in single-shots, doubles, and even the few lever-actions that found their way to Africa. In the very worst of situations, you may have to beat on the bolt handle to get the action open, but it takes more than hot weather to put a bolt gun out of service.

It was obvious, too, that the rigid bolt-action offered accuracy previously available only in single-shot rifles—and it offered this accuracy with flat-shooting cartridges such as the world had never seen. Some traditionalists clung to their doubles, but by World War I, you'd be hard pressed to find an African hunter who didn't appreciate the bolt-action's virtues.

Because so many bolt-actions began life as military arms, the tradition of customizing them started early. Theodore Roosevelt himself had a modified Springfield on the 1909 safari, custom-stocked to his specifications and undoubtedly one of the first Springfields so modified. At first, such "sporterizing" had the very simple goal of reducing the weight and perhaps the length of the military rifle. Later, as scope sights came into vogue, bolt handles would require modification to allow scope mounting. And of course, from the very start, discriminating sportsmen wanted wood and metalwork far superior to that which was suitable for a military arm.

In America, the New York firm of Griffin & Howe, still turning out fine work today, was one of the pioneers in custom bolt-action work. Hoffman Arms was another, as were Charles Newton's rifles, made by three successive companies in Buffalo, New York, until the Depression finished them forever.

The availability of Continental bolt-action rifles took a downhill turn during and just after World War I, but recovered rapidly. During World War II, however, the devastation was almost complete, and from 1939 onward the true commercial Mauser action would become ever more scarce. It's most unfortunate, because some of those commercial Mauser actions are the finest sporting-rifle actions the world has ever seen. Among the most prized are double square-bridge actions, wherein both receiver rings are flat on top, ideal for a variety of detachable and non-detachable scope mounts. Also seen are single square-bridge actions, wherein only the rear receiver ring is flat. And of course, there are dozens of standard actions of all variations from many makers.

To the average American, the loss of the Mauser action was not so severe. Starting in 1936, the Winchester Model 70 was available in .375 H&H, and for many years American interest in any other large-bore cartridge languished. After all, America's most popular rifle was chambered for Africa's most popular general-purpose cartridge, and what else mattered?

After the war, the great Oberndorf Mauser was no more, and in fact any Mauser action was in short supply. A few F.N. actions (Fabrique Nationale, Belgium) were available, including Browning's fine line of bolt-action rifles based on this action. A very few French-made Brevex magnum actions trickled in after 1955, and copies of Mauser actions were made in such diverse places as Japan and Spain. But the great days of the Mauser action were over, and the postwar "modern" bolt-actions would begin to take over.

# Chapter 16

# Bolt-actions Today

The Mauser action remains very much with us today, and even seems to be enjoying a resurgence in popularity. The Yugoslavian Mark X Mauser actions—available both in action-only form and as complete rifles, including the attractive Whitworth, have been around for some time.

There are also new "Model 70-type" modified Mauser actions from Kimber and Dakota on the American market, as well as very expensive custom actions from 'smiths like David Gentry and Fred Wells. Starting in 1990, U.S. Repeating Arms has begun producing a limited run of pre-1964 Winchester Model 70 actions. I have one of the prototypes, and it's a faithful Mauser-type controlled-round feeding action.

In Europe, Henri Dumoulin is producing a big, new magnum Mauser action, a very expensive proposition, while the Czechoslovakian BRNO Mauser-type action continues to be available at modest prices. As it comes from the factory, the BRNO action is rough, but it's a wonderfully sound design that makes into a lovely rifle with a bit of work. The prestigious firm of Rigby itself, now managed by Paul Roberts, uses BRNO actions for their own .416 Rigby rifles.

All that is well and good; all the actions mentioned, plus the basic Model 1898 Mauser—of which many thousands are still in use—are very fine. However, the majority of turnbolt sporting rifles in use today are neither Mausers nor Mauser derivatives. Mind you, there were always non-Mauser actions: Enfields, Mannlichers, Krags. But the first modern non-Mauser actions began making their appearance just after World War II. One of the first to become really popular was the Remington Model 721, a rifle that, with few changes, became the Remington Model 700—one of the world's most popular sporting rifles.

The Remington action does use the massive Mauser dual opposing locking lugs, but its extraction/ejection is totally different. For one thing, the bolt face is an unbroken circle of steel surrounding the case head. Now, that's clearly a good idea, and it's a concept found on virtually every commercial American action today. It's safer and stronger, and in these product-liability-conscious days, that must be the manufacturers' primary concern. However, Mauser controlled-round feeding is no longer possible; the extractor is a thin, C-shaped spring clip fitting into the rim of the bolt face, and the ejector is a spring-loaded plunger on the opposite side. (For a full discussion of controlled-round feeding, see Chapter 17.)

As the postwar decades rolled by, this and similar concepts gradually dominated the bolt-action world. The Sako, for instance, has an anti-bind device on the bolt that *looks* like a long Mauser extractor, but is not; the

Sako extractor is a sturdy hook, inletted into one side of the bolt face. It works, but it is not a Mauser extractor.

When the Winchester Model 70 action was radically altered in 1964, the Mauser extraction and feeding were dropped in favor of a case head surrounded by steel and the newer type of extractor/ejector.

Bill Ruger, a firearms genius of the first order, achieved a compromise with his 1968-vintage Ruger M77. He does have a classic long Mauser extractor on his rifle, but the ejector is the plunger type on the bolt face, and the cartridge head is encased by steel. When feeding, the cartridge is pushed ahead of the Ruger bolt, not gripped by it; the extractor is beveled to snap over the case head as the round chambers and the bolt goes home.

All of these, plus many other modern actions, use the Mauser dual opposing locking lugs. A different concept is the current Weatherby Mark V, using a large-diameter bolt with nine locking lugs machined from the forward portion of the bolt. Extraction/ejection are the modern type. All of these modern actions will stand up to incredible abuse, but the Weatherby is one of the strongest.

There have always been a few rear-locking bolt-actions around; in recent years, the Remington Model 788 was a good American rear-locking bolt-action. Austria's Steyr-Mannlicher SL series is a fine European rear-locking bolt-action. Extremely smooth and reliable, the SL locks up with six lugs just ahead of the bolt handle. This rifle is a modern descendant of the Mannlicher-Schoenauer, and it retains the butterknife handle that always set the Mannlichers apart. Unfortunately, the M-S rotary magazine has, in recent years, been replaced with a detachable plastic rotary magazine. It works, and with its modern space-age materials is darn near indestructible. But I've never understood what place a detachable magazine has on a hunting rifle.

Another unusual European bolt-action is the Sauer, imported into the U.S. some years ago as the Colt-Sauer and again imported in the late 1980s, this time by Sigarms as the Sig Sauer. This one is a very complex action achieving lockup via retracting lugs in the bolt body. It is one of the smoothest of all bolt-actions, but the bolt has some 30 parts—three times more than the 98 Mauser. That isn't in itself a drawback, but it does make it expensive and complex to manufacture.

There are, of course, a great many more bolt-action rifles from a great many more makers. But few of them differ from those mentioned in any significant way. More important to this discussion is how today's (and, for that matter, yesterday's) bolt-action rifle fits in as a safari rifle.

The advantages of the bolt-action have been covered—strength, accuracy, and relatively low cost. Of equal significance is the bolt-action's ability to be chambered for almost anything. The limitations are the length of the magazine box and the diameter of the bolt face, but in practical terms these restrictions are minor. For instance, every standard-length Remington Model 700 ever made is long enough to accommodate a .375 H&H. And that means it will handle the new .416 Remington or any of the .458-caliber wildcats based on the .375 case necked up and blown out.

The standard Ruger Model 77, unfortunately, will not accept .375-length cartridges. By the time these lines see the light of day, Ruger's new long action should be a reality. But the current Ruger and nearly all other .30-06 length actions will accept the short magnums—.338, .458 Winchester Magnum, and short wildcats like the .416 Taylor.

This versatility is important because it means an entire battery can be constructed around one action, with identical functioning and safety position. Or, for the price of a new barrel, an existing bolt-action with which you're completely familiar can be turned into a rifle capable of handling any African game. For instance, an Africa-bound acquaintance of mine rebarreled a pet .300 Winchester Magnum to .458; he thought he'd be better off with a familiar rifle of long-accustomed stock dimensions, and he certainly wasn't wrong in his thinking.

Although virtually any action type, including the double, offers adequate accuracy for most field shooting, the bolt-action, with its stable one-piece stock and rigid lockup, is easily the most accurate action type we have today. (I'm not forgetting single-shots, which can be exceptionally accurate but are more limited in their uses; single-shot rifles will be discussed in Chapter 18.) In some African hunting situations, every bit of accuracy you can get your hands on is to the good. Whether it's the mountains of Ethiopia or South Africa's Eastern Cape, the deserts of Botswana and Namibia, or the short-grass plains of Tanzania, the average shots can be well over 200 yards. Animals such as greater kudu, oryx, mountain nyala, and zebra might present a very large vital zone to shoot at. But animals such as springbok, bushbuck, Vaal rhebok, and mountain reedbuck certainly do not. The hunter needs not only the accuracy of a bolt-action rifle, but also the flat-shooting cartridges that the bolt-action handles best.

When setting up a bolt-action for African hunting, the first consideration is likely to be choice of cartridge. I can't disagree with that, but we've covered cartridges thoroughly in the first part of this book, and later on we'll discuss specific cartridge choices for various types of game. Here we're talking about the basic rifle. And indeed the bolt-action rifle can be chambered so it will serve as a light rifle, a medium, or even a heavy. And with a careful choice of both cartridge and bullet, it might well be the *only* action type that can adequately serve as a complete, all-round safari rifle.

Regardless of the intended use of the bolt-action, there are some basic considerations. Personally, I prefer the traditional non-detachable box magazine. Detachable magazines do have some advantages, one being that the rifle can be completely unloaded and completely loaded very rapidly. However, I've found a detachable magazine just one thing more to worry about—and if it becomes lost, you've got a single-shot. But to each his own; some of the world's best and most accurate bolt-action rifles today are cursed (or blessed, if you happen to like them) with detachable magazines.

I personally prefer the traditional Mauser-type box magazine that must be fed from the top. Should you run the magazine dry while shooting at game (I'll admit it; I have on a few occasions!), it's very fast to single-load through the top with such a rifle. Many of the detachable-magazine rifles have partially enclosed ejection ports that simply weren't designed for top-loading, and inserting the one cartridge that you desperately need might be a real struggle.

A couple of my favorite rifles have blind magazine boxes—no floorplate. This setup has the wonderful advantage of absolute reliability; there is simply no chance of a floorplate dropping open at the wrong time, because it doesn't exist. However, I don't generally prefer this arrangement for two reasons. First, with a floorplate that can drop open, you can quickly unload the rifle without running the cartridges through the chamber. That's a very minor advantage, but more significant is that you can easily access the magazine box for cleaning. In swamp country or during the rains, it's common to get the rifle absolutely soaked, and in the plains and desert you get it full of fine dust and sand. I've found it by far the best to be able to get into the magazine box and really clean it out after a day's hunt.

Whatever magazine system your bolt-action has, it is extremely important for it to be 100 percent reliable. Cartridges *must* feed from the magazine into the chamber each and every time you work the bolt, and well before taking the rifle hunting you must investigate each and every potential problem area.

At its best, the bolt-action is a marvelously reliable tool. It would be nice if every bolt-action came from its maker in such a state—but the realities are different. Most of today's rifles are mass-produced, and sometimes they have problems. Unfortunately, all too many hunters place childlike faith in their rifles without checking out all the potential trouble spots.

It's a traditional pre-hunt ritual to sight in the rifles—but all too many of us do that sighting-in by single-loading into the chamber. That's the first "no-no." Do your sighting-in with a full magazine and you'll be surprised what you might learn. Over the years, I've taken delivery on three large-caliber bolt-action rifles that wouldn't feed from the magazine. Mind you, these were rifles I might use against dangerous game, and they might well have gotten me killed.

Such failures generally have simple causes. It could be a follower spring that's too weak to push the cartridges up, or one that's too strong and makes the cartridge literally jump out of the magazine. It could be feed rails that are too narrow or too wide, or shaped slightly incorrectly for the cartridge. Failure to chamber smoothly can be simply caused by a rough spot at the chamber mouth, or a problem with the rails. Lord, I've had them all!

A feeding problem, time permitting, can be turned over to the service department of the rifle's maker, who will undoubtedly make it right. Generally, though, this is nickel-dime stuff that I've turned over to a local gunsmith. Such things are so commonplace that they're almost part of the breaking-in ritual of a new rifle—but if you don't catch them until the first day of a safari, shame on you!

Another common trouble is a detachable magazine detaching, or a floorplate dropping open under recoil. This is another problem that you generally won't discover unless you do your practice shooting with a full magazine; it often takes tension on the follower spring to create the conditions that make this happen. All too many professional hunters can tell you about clients whose cartridges went "bombs away" on the first shot at a buffalo. It's serious, shockingly common, and it's absolutely ridiculous that it wasn't caught on the range back home.

I had one rifle that was prone to do this, a very expensive European rifle. The maker was happy to fix it, and it never happened again. Usually the cure is a stronger catch spring, but in extreme cases a beefier catch is needed. If that takes more engineering than is financially sensible, then the answer is simply to weld the magazine box shut!

Of course, the bolt-action rifle must not only feed each and every time, but it must also extract the fired case from the chamber and eject it *clear* of the action when the bolt is pulled to the rear. Problems in these areas are rare, but they do happen. I mentioned that I had a Westley Richards .318 Mauser for some time. When I first took it to the range, I discovered that it wouldn't eject consistently; about half the time the fired cartridge just lay in the raceway when the bolt was pulled back. The culprit was a worn ejector, and fortunately my good friend Jack Lott had a spare Mauser ejector. It took two minutes to slip it into place, and the rifle never gave me another problem. On older rifles, worn extractors are also a potential problem. Again, none of this is serious—if you catch it *before* you go hunting.

Yet another problem area for bolt actions, especially those chambered for the powerful cartridges often taken on safari, is in the reinforcement given to prevent splitting under recoil. The forces of recoil may be tough on one's shoulder, but they're pure murder on a rifle stock, particularly in the fragile areas around the action inletting and the slim pistol grip. Again, it would be nice if you could purchase a rifle over the counter and never have to question its reliability. But you can't, especially not with rifles in the .375 and .458 class.

Optimally, a powerful bolt-action rifle will have a recoil lug on the barrel and will have the stock reinforced with crossbolts, generally ahead of and behind the magazine box. The stock must be slightly stress-relieved at the tang; the thin pistol grip simply must not be allowed to accept the full forces of recoil. Unfortunately, many manufacturers, including some of the majors, understand completely how to build accurate, reliable, functional rifles—but they don't understand how to build heavy rifles. All too often, the recoil reinforcement on heavy-recoil rifles is either inadequate or just plain wrong.

Several years ago, a well-respected manufacturer started offering a safari-type rifle with all the bells and whistles—classic English lines, quarter rib with express sights, the works. It was a beautiful rifle, but the bedding was a nightmare. The recoil lug on the barrel wasn't bedded tightly into the stock, thus did no good. The crossbolts were properly placed, but were D-shaped; the flat side of the D should have been placed facing rearward to offer a flat area to bed against and accept the force of recoil. They had been installed *backwards* so the recoil came against the rounded side of the bolt. I don't know if the stock would have split; we never gave it a chance.

It was a simple matter to reverse the bolts and bed both them and the lugs in tightly with fiberglass bedding compound. Yes, the factory should have done that—but don't leave it to chance. The first order of business, on purchasing a bolt-action rifle that has a fair measure of recoil (let's say, from the .300 magnums upward), should be to pull the action out of the stock and check the recoil reinforcement. If you don't know what you're looking at, take it to somebody who does.

If you don't check it out, you're inviting disaster. If you're lucky, the stock will split on the range in the first few test firings. More likely, though, it will split in the field after varying conditions of wet and dry have swollen and shrunk the stock and changed slightly the way the action fits it. On my own rifles, I always check and, if it seems called for, I rebed it. But in my job as a magazine editor, I often test various manufacturers' rifles. On a couple of occasions, we've sent them back with split stocks and a note of apology. One of the great attractions of synthetic stocks is, of course, insurance against swelling, shrinking, warping, resultant shifts in bedding, and the possibility of breakage. Good synthetic stocks (which are discussed in Chapter 20) are stable and virtually indestructible.

In later chapters we'll discuss scopes and sights in more detail, but here it should be said that the bolt-action rifle is the ideal vehicle for telescopic sights. The action rings provide ideal platforms for scope mounts, and the scope can be mounted low over the receiver without interfering in loading, firing, and cycling in any way. A heavy rifle may be preferred with iron sights; that's a matter of personal preference. But most bolt-actions are simply incomplete without a good, well-mounted scope—and that, too, is one of the bolt-action rifle's great advantages. In at least 99 percent of all hunting situations, a scope sight allows the shooter to see better and hit better. The stock of a bolt-action, if properly shaped, will be conducive to fast, accurate shooting with a scope.

The last two items to be discussed regarding bolt-action rifles are triggers and safeties, and to some extent they interrelate. Unlike other action types, the bolt-action rifle is well-suited to an adjustable trigger that can be fine-tuned to the shooter's preference. When it comes to very precise shooting, nothing is quite as critical as a crisp, clean, relatively light trigger pull—so this is yet another advantage of the bolt-action.

In today's atmosphere of product-liability paranoia, this advantage has been largely lost; most bolt-actions come from the factory with horrible trigger pulls of five and even six pounds—about what you'd expect on a double rifle or a lever-action. Fortunately, most bolt-action triggers can be adjusted. However, this is not a job for you and me. The problem is that, the lighter the trigger pull, the closer you are to an accidental discharge. Most bolt-action triggers can, in complete safety, be adjusted to pull of 3 to $3\frac{1}{2}$ pounds, about right for a hunting rifle. The job should be done by a competent gunsmith.

Safeties and triggers interrelate because most bolt-actions today have trigger-blocking safeties. Personally, I don't like them and refuse to trust them. The old Mauser-type flag safety was, to my mind, much more positive; it had nothing to do with the trigger, but instead positively locked the striker. The old three-position Model 70 safety, still in use on today's Model 70, is of this type. Many other bolt-actions can be modified by the installation of this type of safety, and I have done so on several rifles.

However, it must be remembered that any safety is a mechanical device, and therefore I refuse to fully trust any safety. In most of my hunting, I never carry a cartridge in the chamber unless I'm anticipating a shot momentarily. And it should go without saying that a firearm carried in a vehicle should never have a cartridge in the chamber. However, walking about in the African bush is a bit different; you just never know what you might encounter. Under many circumstances over there, it could almost be foolish to *not* have a cartridge in the chamber. A close-quarters charge by a buffalo carrying a grudge along with a poacher's musket ball isn't unlikely, nor is it unlikely to step around a bush and come face to face with the lion of your dreams. But if a rifle is to be carried with a round in the chamber, some reliance *must* be placed in the safety.

There are several considerations here. First, the safety must *work*. On the range, you should test it thoroughly, making certain the rifle does not fire with the safety engaged. With the rifle unloaded but cocked, it's a good idea to bounce the rifle around a bit, dropping it on its recoil pad. If the striker falls with the safety engaged, you have a very serious problem that must be corrected. Just recently, a hunting partner and I chanced across a fine lion. He had never shot one and wanted it badly. When he slipped his safety the rifle fired, fortunately into the ground. Just as fortunately, the lion—just 30 yards away—went the other direction. No harm done that time, but a rare opportunity lost.

You should check the safety's position; it must be accessible to the thumb, so you can slip it readily while you're bringing the rifle up. However, it must engage positively and be in such a position that it's protected from brush and twigs while you're carrying the rifle, whether in your hands or slung over one shoulder.

I had a prototype of a left-handed .375 one time. It was a lovely rifle, and in its right-handed version the sliding thumb safety was on the right side just behind and well-protected by the bolt handle. In the left-handed version they obviously switched the bolt to the left side, but left the safety on the right. Now it was unprotected, and when I slung the rifle over my left shoulder (as lefties are most likely to do), the action of walking rubbed the safety against my side. After a dozen steps, that rifle would be off safe every time.

Now, I don't believe a slung rifle should ever have a cartridge in the chamber; if you're carrying a loaded rifle, you must have the direction of the muzzle under complete control at all times—and you can't when it's slung over the shoulder. So this is just an example of a design problem in safety placement. The point is to pay attention to the mechanical safety, and if the way you carry a rifle tends to expose the safety's catch, you'd better think about a different safety or a different rifle. And that's yet another wonderful advantage to a bolt-action rifle; if you want a Mauser or Model 70-type safety, it's generally simple and inexpensive to so modify your rifle.

Perhaps, when it comes right down to it, of all the bolt-action's advantages, its greatest is that it can so readily be adjusted, fussed with, and modified to exactly suit its owner's tastes and its intended purpose. Double rifles are made from scratch, largely by hand. But no action is altered, improved, and customized as much as a turnbolt. From a simple sporterizing of a military rifle to a full-out custom job costing as much as any double rifle—and sometimes more—individually crafted bolt-actions run the full gamut. The custom gun business was never better, with the best craftsmen commanding top prices and staying booked up months and even years ahead.

The last rifle in Safari Club International's specially commissioned Big Five Series was a bolt-action built by David Miller. Its auctioned price of over $200,000 set an all-time record for the first sale of a new firearm. The bolt-action rifle, initially a cheap alternative to England's costly doubles and single-shots, has come a long way!

# Chapter 17

# A Question of Extractors

The factory-made bolt-action rifle is a sound, dependable, downright *cheap* piece of equipment. If the owner wants to, he can invest a great deal of money in select walnut, engraving, and other embellishment; he can also spend a lot of money for a custom-made or custom-modified action, a select barrel, and the services of a "name" custom gunsmith in putting it all together. The result will be a pleasing piece that may suit its owner's tastes much better than any factory rifle. It may even function a bit more smoothly than an out-of-the-box production gun, and it just might shoot a bit better. But the dollars spent for a full-out custom bolt-action as opposed to the cost of a production rifle of identical caliber and utility quickly reach diminishing returns in terms of increased performance. Today's factory bolt-actions are just plain *good* rifles.

Yes, as mentioned in the previous chapter, you may want to spend a little bit of time and money in bedding, trigger adjustment (or a replacement trigger like the Timney or Canjar), and even smoothing of the action and adjustment of the follower, follower spring, and feed rails. But that's all nickel-dime stuff compared to genuine custom work.

None of this is to say there's anything wrong with a custom rifle. I have several factory rifles that have been extensively customized, perhaps enough to qualify as custom rifles, and I have a couple of full-out custom jobs. One is an absolutely gorgeous 7mm Remington Magnum made by David Miller, one of the best; another is an equally gorgeous .458 Lott made by several fine craftsmen. David Miller did the barrel work; Pete Grisel did the action work and quarter rib; and Bishop's did the stockwork. I love both rifles, and I have a lot of confidence in them. However, that 7mm doesn't shoot any more accurately than a factory 7mm magnum I have which set me back something like 10 percent the cost of the Miller rifle. Nor will the .458 Lott stop a charge any better than a .416 Hoffman Randy Brooks put together for me by simply screwing a barrel so chambered onto a 7mm action.

All four of these rifles are worth some discussion, since all four of them were built around Remington Model 700 actions. I'm leaving for a buffalo hunt tomorrow, and the rifle I'm taking is a Weatherby Mark V in .416 Weatherby Magnum. Now, since I'm a lefty it shouldn't be surprising that I so often choose Remington 700 actions, or for that matter the Mark V; both actions are among the few that are available in left-hand versions. However, an awful lot of right-handers choose these actions, plus the current Model 70, the Sako, the Ruger 77, and, well, the list goes on.

What all these actions have in common is that none of them offers controlled-round feeding. This, plus the long extractor, was one of the great strengths of the Mauser design. It carried over into the Springfield, 1917 Enfield, pre-1964 Model 70 Winchester, and a few other actions. And much is made over this feature today—especially with regard to rifles for African hunting. To hear some writers tell it, you're absolutely taking your life in your hands if you hunt dangerous game with anything but a controlled-round-feeding action; which means a Mauser or its derivatives, nothing else.

First let's define controlled-round feeding. When a cartridge is fed from the magazine of a Mauser action, its rim is pushed up between the bolt face and the extractor, where it is held firmly and "controlled" as the bolt *carries—not pushes*—it forward into the chamber. It is able to accomplish this because the bottom portion of the bolt face is not encircled by steel; it's open, and as the cartridge comes up out of the magazine, its rim slides into place and is held by the long spring-steel extractor.

There are tremendous advantages to this system. The Mauser-type action, for instance, will feed reliably upside down, sideways, any which way. If your bolt movement is interrupted partway, the cartridge remains held in place until you resume; it cannot and will not be jarred out of place.

In contrast, the more modern action types, with the Remington 700 as a prime example, push the cartridge ahead of the bolt and into the chamber. The cartridge actually lies there loose and is held by nothing; the bolt merely shoves it forward, and as it chambers fully, the extractor snaps over the case rim.

There are disadvantages to this system. For one thing, a rifle of this type will not feed upside down or sideways; it must have the force of gravity in a favorable up-and-down position. It seems to me that this handicap may be much more significant in a military rifle than a sporting rifle, but many writers and professional hunters dismiss out of hand any action that lacks controlled-round feeding.

What the newer type of action gives you is *strength* and, in the event of a case failure, *safety*. The bolt face is encircled by a ring of solid steel, which encircles the case head when a cartridge is chambered. Controlled-round feeding, to exist, must leave part of the case head exposed.

Rarely is there a clearcut disadvantage or advantage to either system, but it must be recognized that modern actions are stronger than any Mauser— and if an action is going to blow, a Mauser, Springfield, Enfield, or even pre-'64 Winchester will blow long before a Remington 700, Weatherby Mark V, Savage 110, or similar modern action. And the older action will probably blow with much more disastrous results for the shooter.

Such catastrophic failures are incredibly rare, and with safe handling procedures that avoid barrel obstructions, and sane reloading procedures that eliminate overloads of wrong powders, they're almost impossible—but the very real safety margin of the more modern designs must still be accepted. On the other hand, the Mauser action has been adequately strong for generations; its inherent weakness must be considered just as theoretical a disadvantage as its ability to feed upside down an advantage.

The controlled-round feeding does have another disadvantage. Single-loaded cartridges must be fed down into the magazine; if simply pushed into the chamber, the extractor may not snap over the head and allow the bolt to close. A worn extractor or one that has been beveled to allow it to snap over will work. But you'd better know what you're dealing with; on a true Mauser, a single-loaded cartridge must be fed all the way down into the magazine. With the modern action designs, a single cartridge can simply be dropped into the raceway and the bolt slammed home. And if you've fired your last shell and you need one more shot, you're likely to be grateful for every millisecond you save!

The long Mauser extractor is yet another much-touted advantage of Mauser-type actions. It is important to note that this long extractor doesn't necessarily mean controlled-round feeding. The Ruger M77, for instance, does have the long extractor but does not have controlled-round feeding; the extractor is beveled so it will snap over the case head as the bolt goes home, but it does not control the cartridge until that moment. I do like the strength of the Mauser-type extractor and the great purchase it has on the cartridge rim; I've even had a couple of Model 700 actions modified with Ruger M77 extractors.

Once again, however, the advantages or disadvantages seem more theoretical than practical. I have, for example, fired many thousands of rounds through several dozen Model 700s, Weatherby Mark Vs, Sakos, you name it. I have had a couple of failures to feed, discovered on the range and easily fixed by a little work on the rails or magazine box. I have yet to have a failure to extract, either on the range or in the field—and with all the load development I've done, there have been more than a few loads that were a bit too hot.

On the other hand, the only genuine extraction-related failure I've ever seen was on a very nice FN Mauser .375. The rifle is mine, but my stepson, Paul Stockwell, was using it on a Botswana buffalo one day. He was still white as a sheet when he sheepishly handed me the now-useless rifle.

He and his professional hunter, Mark Tout, had found a nice buffalo bull and Paul had shot it badly. They followed it up and found it lying in high grass, facing away. Paul shot again, trying to break its neck, but missed the bone. By now the buffalo had had enough; he launched into a full charge from close range, and Paul worked the bolt.

Paul is a big, strong guy—half again my size, and a serious weightlifter. He was also terrified, as anyone would have been. All I can figure is that he worked the bolt with an incredibly powerful jerk. The long, foolproof Mauser extractor separated from the bolt collar, jamming the rifle completely and hopelessly with a fired cartridge in the chamber. The odd thing is that there was nothing structurally wrong with the rifle or any of its parts, but it certainly failed. And, Murphy being the optimist he is, when something goes wrong it goes wrong at the worst possible moment.

Well, that example isn't to imply that Mauser actions are prone to failure. Of course they aren't—but neither are the more modern actions. What type of bolt-action, then, is really the most reliable and the most desirable for African hunting?

All things being equal, I'd have to give the nod to controlled-round feeding, especially with the wonderful new actions available from Dakota, Kimber, Heym, McMillan, and so many others. But I wouldn't pick them by a significant margin.

Just because I'm a lefty, a great majority of my bolt actions will continue to be Model 700s, Mark Vs, and Sakos. And if I were a right-hander who was comfortable with any of these actions, plus the Model 77 Ruger and a whole bunch more, I wouldn't consider making a switch. Provided the rifle has been properly and carefully checked for all phases of feeding, firing, extracting, and ejecting, there's no reason for a sound rifle of any action type to fail in the field. And if one does, well, it can happen to true Mauser, one of its copies, or any other action with just about equal odds.

# Chapter 18

# Single-shots and Others

It would be easy to get the impression that only bolt-actions and double rifles are suited for African hunting. The bolt is the most common action in use in Africa—and the double rifle is perhaps the most classic. But it would be both misleading and unfair to exclude the other action types: single-shot, lever-action, slide-action, and semiautomatic. All of them are perfectly suitable, and African hunting, with the exceptions of her largest game, isn't significantly different from any hunting anywhere else. Let's take a look at the other action types and see where they might fit in.

## Single-Shots

The last half of the 19th century was the golden age of the single-shot rifle. In the Africa of a century ago, the .577/.450 Martini-Henry was the most common rifle, and it performed far beyond its apparent ballistic capabilities. It was the Martini-Henry that won the day at Rorkes Drift—and lost it at Isandhlwana—and it was the Martini-Henry that the early settler-hunter was most likely to carry. In America, the trapdoor Springfield in the somewhat less powerful .45-70 was the most common rifle of the day, so popular that it retains a following to this day.

In both Europe and America, however, there were a number of fine single-shot breechloaders that were far superior to these simple military actions. In America, the powerful blackpowder single-shot was the buffalo hunter's choice. The Sharps was the most famous, but there were many others. Some made it into the smokeless era: the Remington rolling block, and the Winchester Hi-Wall (now offered in modern form by Browning). The British and Europeans had a number of fine actions, the most famous of which was the Farquharson.

The action was the creation of Scottish gamekeeper John Farquharson, but the rifles were initially made by Bristol gunmaker George Gibbs. A Metford-rifled Gibbs single-shot, blackpowder, caliber .461, Farquharson action, was to be Frederick Courteney Selous's favorite rifle well into the smokeless era.

In the latter part of the 19th century, Gibbs had the exclusive on the "Farky" action, but in 1895, just when smokeless powder was coming into its own, the original patent expired and several top British gunmakers began building rifles on Farquharson-type actions.

The rifles did not do well in the smokeless era. They were much less expensive than double rifles, but unfortunately they were more expensive than European-made bolt-actions. They also lacked the bolt-action's camming power for primary extraction, and for that matter had less extraction power than a double, wherein several pounds of barrels act as the opening lever. In the earliest days of smokeless, when weak blackpowder cases were being used, the Farquharsons acquired a reputation for failure to extract, and it was a reputation they never recovered from.

The Farquharson action is one of the strongest in the world, and with modern cases there's no reason to fear extraction problems. Today, the few rifles still in circulation are highly prized, nearly as valuable as double rifles. Although relatively few were made, they were chambered for virtually any Nitro-Express cartridge you can think of. The most common are probably .450/.400-3¼" and .450-3¼", but you'll see them all the way up to .600 Nitro-Express.

In recent years, a few modern Farquharson actions have been built. Australian John Saunders of Century Arms/London Guns in Melbourne built a matched pair of .600 Farquharsons, and a few more have been built on a custom basis in England and Europe. The Farquharson falling block was also the basis for the most popular single-shot of all time, the wonderful Ruger Number One.

When Bill Ruger introduced the Number One, the world thought he was crazy. If he was, he was crazy like a fox; the Number One has been among the great firearms success stories in the postwar era.

With some modifications, the Ruger action is a Farquharson falling block; the underlever cocks the internal hammer and drops the massive breechblock to expose the loading port. It's a very safe, very simple action—and one of the strongest the world has ever known. It's available in several variations and almost every conceivable modern chambering up to .458 Winchester Magnum.

Two other very fine modern American single-shots are readily available, the interchangeable-barrel break-action Thompson/Center, and the Browning Model 1885, but only the Ruger is available with chamberings for large-caliber African cartridges. There are also several excellent modern European single-shots, mostly break-open designs.

The single-shot action has a lot of appeal. It's simple, reliable, and accurate; and the one-shot concept is attractive to sportsmen. I've used Rugers in various calibers for quite a variety of hunting, both in North America and Africa, and I like them. Professional hunter John van der Meulen has a Ruger No. One rebarreled to .470, and that's something I'd like to see Ruger offer on a regular basis. As is, the rifle has a near-perfect extraction/ejection system that works like a charm on rimless cases, but the action is also a natural for the big Nitro-Expresses. I've always wanted a Farquharson in .450/.400, and since I can't seem to find one I might well have one built on a Ruger action.

Fine though a single-shot may be, it does present problems, especially for hunting dangerous game. The attractive and sporting one-shot concept is a concept that can get you killed when the chips are down—or, at best, make your professional hunter join in when perhaps he wouldn't have needed to.

A good, practiced hand with a single-shot can get off a second shot very quickly. The routine is to carry extra cartridges between the fingers of your non-shooting hand, just as you would with a double. Fire, drop the lever, insert a cartridge. It can be done in less than three seconds, without looking at the action. Usually that second shot can be fast enough to prevent the escape of a wounded animal. Usually. In the case of a charge, unless it's launched from an unusual distance, forget it. One shot is all you have.

Most of the time, that one shot is enough, but when you need a follow-up it won't be there. Now, that does tend to make you very careful about your shot placement, which is certainly to the good. Unfortunately, with the largest of game it doesn't wash. With carefully placed brain shots, one-shot kills on elephant are common—but if the brain is missed, albeit only by a hair, follow-up body shots must be taken instantly or it's a lost animal.

My own experience with buffalo has resulted in dismally few one-shot kills, perhaps 30 percent excluding neck shots. It isn't that the first shot isn't fatal—eventually. Rather, it's that the buffalo is such a strong animal. Most of the time he's going to run, and I'm not willing to bet a dangerous tracking job on the exact placement of that first shot—and the performance of the bullet. With a double or bolt gun, the first shot can be backed up immediately, even if it's only insurance. With a single-shot, your professional hunter has a decision to make just as the bull reaches cover. If I were that professional hunter, I'd shoot if my client couldn't.

On cats, well, it depends; I'd certainly use a single-shot for baited lion, but I don't think I'd want one on a tracking hunt or when following up a wounded animal. For baited leopard, no problem. The one shot is all there is, and an accurate single-shot would be just the ticket. My own African use of the single-shot has been confined to a variety of plains game, and for such hunting there's absolutely no reason not to use a single-shot.

There is one further characteristic of the single-shot that needs to be taken into account, however. Like a double, a single-shot is either fully loaded or fully unloaded. If you're carrying it in a vehicle or on horseback, you have no choice—the rifle must be empty. That's not a huge problem, but it does mean you must have cartridges *very* readily accessible. Cartridge loops on a shirt work well, but many experienced Ruger fans carry a couple of cartridges in a Velcro carrier on the wrist of the nonshooting arm. Now that's *fast*. In the field, again, the rifle is either loaded or unloaded. Most of the time it will be loaded, but if you're climbing in tough country, for safety's sake you'll have to unload it.

For the reasons stated, I see the single-shot primarily as a light rifle or, at most, a medium. But it sure would be fun to take a single-shot .450/.400 after buffalo.

## Lever-Actions

The lever-action seems to be almost exclusively an American passion; Sako's shortlived Finnwolf is one of very few European lever guns. In America, the lever action remains a traditional choice. Tubular-magazine lever-action rifles from Winchester and Marlin define "deer rifle" for a great many hunters, and the rotary-magazine Savage 99 is another American classic. In recent years, Winchester didn't do well with the nontraditional but extremely sound Model 88. The most recent lever gun, Browning's BLR, doesn't set the world on fire, but it's a fine rifle and has its following.

The lever-action, despite its popularity, has some problems. The first is strength. Traditional rear-locking lever guns like the Winchesters are more than strong enough for the woods cartridges for which they're chambered, but they simply won't handle high-intensity modern cartridges. The Winchester 88, Browning, and Savage will—but they're restricted to short-cased cartridges. The .308 family or short, fat cartridges like the rebated-rim .284 Winchester are at the practical limit in both pressure and size.

The tubular-magazine rifles must of necessity fire flat-pointed bullets; since the cartridges rest nose to primer in the magazine, detonation can and has occurred with sharp-pointed bullets. The flatpoints are extremely effective on game, but trajectories suffer. The Winchester 88, Finnwolf, and Browning use staggered-box magazines, while the Savage has either the traditional rotary magazine or a detachable box. All of these will function perfectly with aerodynamic spitzer bullets.

Another problem is inherent with the lever, though, and that's weakness of primary extraction. The camming power of the bolt-action simply isn't there. The Browning is the strongest of the bunch, but it just isn't smart to use heavy loads in any lever-action. Factory loads are fine, of course, but you must exercise restraint with handloads.

The only catastrophic failure I've ever had in the hunting field was with a Savage 99 in .308 Winchester. I hit a blesbok a bit too far back, and the rifle seized up tight as a drum. I couldn't open it, not even by beating on the lever with a rock in my frustration. Eventually, we got the animal, but only after I ran a mile back to the truck for another rifle.

The only lever-action that achieved some measure of greatness in Africa was the Winchester Model 1895. Its chamberings included the .405 and .35 Winchester, both loaded for some time by Kynoch, plus the .30-40 Krag and .30-06. The rifle was apparently not very satisfactory in .30-06; sticky extraction wasn't uncommon. However, for many years it was the most powerful American production rifle in its .405 WCF chambering. This was Teddy Roosevelt's "lion medicine," and it was also a favorite of Stewart Edward White and Charles Cottar.

Cottar, the first American professional hunter, used it throughout his long career in Africa. He died with it in 1940 after failing to stop a charging rhino.

The lever-action's history in Africa pretty much ends with Charles Cottar. I have seen a few Winchester 94s in use as "camp rifles," and a very few Americans have occasionally taken a lever-action on safari. As mentioned earlier, James Mellon had a .358 lever-action in East Africa, and fellow left-hander Colonel Charles Askins used a then-new Winchester Model 88 in .243 in Kenya in the late 1950s. I had high hopes for that ill-fated Savage 99, but shot little game with it before it jammed and was out for the count for the rest of the trip.

In spite of little recent history, there's no reason not to choose a lever-action in a suitable caliber as a light safari rifle—and a Savage 99, Browning, or Winchester 88 (if you can find one!) would make a marvelous general-purpose thornbush rifle in .358. The lever gun isn't particularly accurate, generally, but it's certainly accurate enough for most field shooting—and the odd rifle is a real tack-driver.

There is faint hope of using a lever-action for larger game. One option would be to find a Model 95 in .405—and by our standards today you'd have barely enough gun. A more sensible course would be to concoct some .45-70 handloads for the strong Marlin Model 1895 so chambered. You can't quite duplicate .458 performance, but I suspect you could come close enough that the average buffalo would never know the difference. If you could find one, the same observation would apply to a Winchester Model 71 rebarreled to the wildcat .450 Alaskan.

The lever-action is very fast, a bit faster than a bolt gun. The problem is that the occasion when speed really counts (though still not as much as accuracy!) is the moment when you need to stop charging nasties, and the lever-action just doesn't carry the freight.

Still, there are possibilities. In 1988, when professional hunter Ronnie MacFarlane got slightly nailed by a lion, I was scheduled to hunt with him on one of those crazy tracking leopard hunts in the Kalahari. We were going to do it on foot; I'd been running for months, getting ready. The idea was that I would carry a rifle and Ronnie would carry a shotgun—the real kicker is that most of those hunts end in charges. I had pretty much settled on a light, fiberglass-stocked .416 Hoffman bolt-action. A double rifle would perhaps be best, but I knew I couldn't run 20 miles with an 11-pound double. Well, when Ronnie got hurt by a lion, the hunt fell through and we haven't yet been able to put it back together. But if we do, I've reconsidered my choice of arms; I think I'd carry either a lever-action Marlin .45-70 with 400-grain flatpoints at about 1,800 fps or my Model 71 .450/.348 lever rifle with the same bullet 250 fps faster. Either should get a cat's undivided attention!

## Slide-Actions

The slide-action is yet another American exclusive. Years ago, there were pump rifles from a variety of makers, but today Remington has this small market cornered.

The slide-action's chief field of use, to my mind, is among occasional deer hunters who prefer slide-action shotguns. It makes sense, of course, to use the action you're most familiar with. Traditionally, slide-actions have been close-cover whitetail rifles. They can certainly be accurate, and the Remington rifles are chambered for wonderful general-purpose cartridges such as the .270, .280, .30-06, and .35 Whelen.

I'm not a fan of the slide-action, but hunters who use them swear by them. I've seen a couple in Africa, and there's certainly no reason not to use one. They are very fast, and the Remingtons are very reliable. If they have a drawback, it's simply that they are not available in serious African cartridges. But for a light rifle, if that's what you happen to shoot best—or handle most comfortably—stick with it!

## Semiautomatics

In general, the same things that were said about slide-actions apply to semiautomatics. Today's semiautos are extremely reliable, and jams are very rare. Most of the sporting semiautos have been chambered in .308, .270, .30-06, and so forth. The Browning BAR is also offered in belted magnums up to .338, which makes it a pretty serious contender as a medium rifle. Jack Lott once rebarreled a Browning to .458, and it worked like a charm. Accurate, too.

The semiauto does have a couple of serious drawbacks. First, the semiautomatic is not authorized for sporting use in all African countries, so the legalities must be checked out. Second, the semiauto will be most reliable with factory ammo; it isn't a rifle for the serious handloader. Finally, though, there's a functional problem. The semiauto cannot be babied; to make certain the first round is chambered and the bolt is fully seated, that bolt must be released and snapped forward, not "ridden" home. That's noisy.

Therefore, like the single-shot and double, the semiauto is either fully loaded or fairly useless. Personally, I wouldn't have one in Africa, but I'm a bit old-fashioned. No appropriate semiautos are available for hunting dangerous game, that custom experimental Browning being the one exception I'm aware of. But for a light rifle, or even a medium, if it's legal and that's what you shoot best, there's really no reason not to take it along.

# Chapter 19

# Double or Magazine?

The question isn't new—and certainly it's been addressed, and addressed well, by more experienced hands than mine. But the question remains: Given that the double rifle is such an African classic, is it really preferable to a bolt-action repeater?

In preceding chapters, we've looked at the strengths of the double rifle—reliability, balance and quick-pointing nature, and instant availability of the second shot. We've also acknowledged its weaknesses—high cost, relative inaccuracy, limitation of sighting equipment, and weight. We've examined the bolt-action in the same manner. Its strong points are strength, reliability, accuracy, and its ability to be adapted to any situation in terms of load and sighting equipment. In truth, the bolt-action has few weaknesses, but it generally doesn't come up as quickly as a double, and certainly isn't as fast for the second shot. Or are these claims valid? It's time to look for a verdict if such can be found. Which is better for African hunting—double or magazine?

Although the question has been answered many times over the years, it's really a ridiculous question because there can be no definitive and objective answer. The double-rifle fanciers will always be in the minority, though extremely self-righteous. The bolt-action fans will be in the majority—but secretly, in their heart-of-hearts, a significant number of this group will covet doubles and wish they could afford them. Neither group is right or wrong; whatever rifle a person happens to shoot best and be most comfortable with *is* the right choice, provided only that its caliber is at least reasonably suitable for the intended game. On the other hand, however true that may be, the preceding statement is of no earthly use to the hunter who is trying to assemble a safari battery. If he's a beginning hunter, it's a bewildering situation. And if he's an experienced hunter in, say, North America, it's even more bewildering. After all, African game has such a legendary reputation for toughness. And it's in vogue among some writers to portray the African bush as being chock full of things waiting to bite, gore, trample, and eat you.

It would be easy to get the idea that the garden-variety whitetail, elk, or sheep rifle is useless in Africa, and that a whole battery of doubles is called for. That's ridiculous. Africa does have thick-skinned, dangerous game, obviously absent in North America, and thus there are some peculiar requirements for firearms. But an entire new battery is rarely called for—and while a double may be desired, it's hardly a requirement.

In a later section of the book we'll look at specific rifles and rifle types for various classes of African game, and we'll also look at sensible batteries for various types of safaris. In many cases, a double rifle may be a part of such a battery. But, under any circumstances, is a double actually *better* than a magazine rifle?

First we have to go back to our classifications of African rifles: light, medium, heavy, and so forth. The *classic* double is a heavy rifle. However, a great number of fine doubles have been built as light rifles. I recently saw a lovely Marcel Thys .22 LR side-by-side, and they've been built in .22 Hornet, .22 Savage Hi-Power, .240 Flanged Nitro-Express, .246 Purdey, .275 Flanged Magnum, 7x57R, 7x65R, Super .30 Magnum Flanged, .303 British, .30-40 Krag, and God knows what else.

There's no reason not to use a double as a light rifle. However, there are plenty of reasons why it's not the *ideal* light rifle—certainly not as good a choice as a bolt action in similar caliber. We're talking rifles of relatively low recoil, so the added gun weight of a double offers no advantage. We're also talking about a rifle that will generally be used at a variety of ranges, sometimes at small targets. So the accuracy limitations of a double are a real disadvantage. The light rifle will also be used on a wide variety of game, at a minimum from duiker up to possibly kudu. Because the double's barrels are regulated for a specific load, the flexibility of using different bullet weights and styles for different game is lost.

Finally, unless a double was originally built with claw-mount fixtures for attaching a scope (and very few have been so built), it will be inordinately difficult, expensive, and may ruin the collector value of a double to scope it. A light rifle without a scope is extremely limited.

The rapid second shot of a double is an advantage in *any* hunting, it's true—but with lighter game, often shot at longer distances, it's not as significant. The truth is that, as a light rifle, a double is at best a curiosity, at worst an eccentricity. It will do the job, of course, but not as well as an accurate bolt-action of similar caliber.

There are also a great many fine doubles in medium calibers, both my "light medium" classification that runs between .30 and .375 caliber, and the .375 itself. Although the .318 Westley Richards is a rimless cartridge, a number of doubles were so chambered. Obviously, most of these were built by WR, but Jack Lott had a wonderful Holland Royal so chambered, and he used it extensively on several African trips. There were also doubles for such excellent cartridges as .333 Flanged, .350 No. 2, .400/.350, .360 No. 2, and the European 9.3x74R. All of these cartridges are relatively similar in that they fire long, heavy-for-caliber bullets at fairly moderate velocities (in the case of the .400/.350, as low as 2,000 fps; for the .318 and .333, up to 2,400). Slightly more powerful is the .369 Purdey, and most powerful of this group is the .375 Flanged Magnum (simply the rimmed version of the .375 H&H). Today, with better ejection/extraction systems for rimless or belted rimless cases, a new "medium" double is almost certain to be either .375 H&H (belted) or 9.3x74R.

This group of cartridges actually represents a wide selection of good double rifles to be used as African mediums. The older cartridges, especially the .333 Flanged, .350 No. 2, and .360 No. 2, are quite good, can be reloaded, and can generally be had relatively inexpensively in vintage doubles. The 9.3x74R is probably the most common, and can be had in both older "working" doubles and new guns at modest prices—as such things go. For all practical purposes, the .369 Purdey (firing a .375 bullet), .375 Flanged, and .375 H&H are close enough ballistically that there's little to pick from.

This means that, whether your tastes in a medium run toward the .35 Whelen-.338 group or toward the .375 H&H, equivalent doubles are available. The question is, do they make sense?

To some extent, it depends on the intended purpose of a medium rifle. The limitations are the same; no double-rifle cartridge offers the flat trajectory of a .338 Winchester Magnum, .340 Weatherby, 8mm Remington, or .378 Weatherby. Nor, in any caliber, does a double offer either the accuracy or bullet-weight flexibility of an equivalent bolt-action. Often, however, the medium rifle isn't expected to reach out as far as the light rifle. In my view, a medium should surely be scoped, so an iron-sighted medium double is just as much an eccentricity as a light double. But if scoped, and especially for use in thornbush or forest, a very strong case could be made for a medium double.

Such a gun would usually be heavier than a like bolt-action, but not unbearably so. It would not be as accurate or as flexible—but it would offer that ultra-fast second shot, and it would be used against larger, tougher game where that fast second shot is ever more critical.

I can imagine few all-round lion guns better than a scoped double .375; likewise for eland. In the former case, no shot over 150 yards will be taken, probably half that, so the double's relative inaccuracy isn't a concern. In the latter case, with eland, a somewhat longer shot might be taken, but the vital area is huge so, again, accuracy isn't a major concern. In both cases, however, that instant second shot is important.

If a medium is to be used on buffalo (and in most countries today only the .375 would be legal), the double's instant second shot is needed. However, on buffalo I would submit that pinpoint shot placement is absolutely essential—so only a scope-sighted, accurate double would be acceptable.

As I've said, in heavy thornbush and forest, or specifically for hunting lion and eland, a scoped medium-caliber double would be extremely useful, possibly every bit as good as a bolt-action. However, the classic medium rifle is *not* a double; it's an accurate, scoped magazine rifle—probably in .375 H&H. There are good reasons for this; under most conditions, the medium rifle may be used for antelopes large and small, and while it may be called upon for a snap shot at close range, it could also be asked to reach out and touch a record kudu at 300 yards and more.

I think a medium-caliber double would be a lot of fun on safari, and in specific instances might well be the best thing going. The very fact that it is a somewhat special-purpose rifle, however, is the strongest argument against a medium double. On safari, the medium bore is the jack-of-all-trades, the most general-purpose rifle in the battery. In spite of its virtues, even a scoped medium double is not as versatile as its bolt-action brethren. It won't be as accurate, cannot reach out as far, and will not have the flexibility of multiple bullet weights.

I doubt if many readers will argue with the foregoing; light and even medium doubles are somewhat unusual. I correspond with an American diplomat-hunter who shoots a .360 No. 2, and I've encountered a smattering of 9.3x74R doubles (mostly over/unders) plus one or two .375s. That's about it. Most of the double rifles being made today, and most of the older guns still in use (possibly with the exception of the ubiquitous 9.3) are large-caliber rifles. The classic form of the double has evolved into a heavy rifle, a charge-stopping big bore designed specifically for the largest and most dangerous game in the world.

Such a rifle is chambered for a variety of cartridges ranging from .450/.400 through .600 Nitro-Express. It will be heavy; some $9\frac{1}{2}$ pounds at a bare-bones minimum up to as much as 18 pounds for a .600. A very occasional big double will be fitted for claw scope mounts, but the typical arrangement is open express sights: a wide standing V rear with or without additional folding leaves, usually on a quarter rib; and a bold ivory or gold ramp-mounted bead front with or without a hood.

As the big double evolved, so did the big magazine rifle—first in high-velocity mediums like the .425 Westley Richards, .404 Jeffery, and .416 Rigby; and then in ultra-powerful rifles like the .505 Gibbs and .500 Jeffery. Ultimately, economics would virtually kill the double, and the inexpensive American-made .458 Winchester Magnum would dominate. But the controversy has never died: Which is the best stopping rifle for dangerous game, double or magazine?

Even though so little dangerous game hunting exists today, this is hardly a silly controversy. After all, if you fail to stop it, *one* serious charge in a lifetime is one too many! If one or the other type were indeed a clearcut better choice, then it would be foolish not to have the very best in your hands when the chips are down.

When speaking of heavy rifles, we're talking about serious charge-stopping rifles—rifles you would prefer to have when going after a wounded lion, and rifles that will both open and close the ballgame with elephant, rhino, and buffalo no matter what happens.

It could be argued that the .375 is the minimum, and of course it's available in both action types. Personally, I would argue that the .450/.400 is the minimum in a double, while the .404 Jeffery *and* the current loading of the .458 Winchester Magnum are the minimums in bolt-actions. But whatever arbitrary minimum you set, there's absolutely no question that adequate cartridges—nay, *more than adequate* cartridges—are available in each action type. So, given that both doubles and magazines have the power needed, let's examine again the advantages and disadvantages of each, and see if any conclusions can be drawn.

A great advantage to the bolt-action is said to be its low cost, while the double's high cost is always listed as its first disadvantage. For this discussion, I think we need to throw that one out. After all, here we're talking about the most specialized rifle of all—the one you will rely on to save your tail. Cost should not be an object when one's life is at stake. Also, it should be mentioned that at the top end bolt-actions aren't necessarily less expensive. My Dumoulin .416 Rigby, really just a plain working bolt gun, cost a good deal more than my .470 double. And certainly a custom bolt-action from a name maker will rival many custom-made doubles in price. Yes, perfectly serviceable and reliable bolt-actions can be had for a great deal less than any serviceable double. But let's not consider here whether the rifle is affordable or not; let's decide which is *best*.

Yet another "failing" of the double rifle is said to be its extreme weight, and I would like to throw that one away as well. Yes, a double has weight; $10\frac{1}{2}$ pounds is a good average for rifles between .450 and .500. The .577s and .600s we'll leave out of this; they are indeed too heavy to carry all day! The average heavy-caliber bolt-action might weigh a pound less than a comparable double, and obviously magazine rifles can be built much lighter; I have a .416 Hoffman in a fiberglass stock that hardly weighs $6\frac{1}{2}$ pounds. It's a joy to carry, but Lord does it kick! And that's the point—the price paid in light weight is recoil, and so long as gun weight isn't unreasonable, the extra ounces will make the rifle steadier in tired hands and make the second shot quicker after recoil recovery.

One of the most-cited inadequacies of the double is accuracy, or rather its lack thereof. No, by bolt-action standards the double is not accurate. However, we're not talking about popping woodchucks at 400 yards. We're talking about getting a bullet into the vital zone of an unwounded elephant, buffalo, or rhino at some distance under 100 yards—and about *stopping* a charging animal at some distance between the muzzle and, say, 20 yards. When it comes to light and medium rifles, I'd be the first to say that the double rifle's level of accuracy creates a serious handicap. But for a heavy rifle, don't be absurd!

A well-made double in reasonable condition, with a good load that's at least close to the regulation load, should be able to put two shots from each barrel into a grapefruit at 100 yards. Tom Siatos, of *Guns & Ammo* magazine, had a Rigby .450-3$\frac{1}{4}$" that was an honest-to-God minute-of-angle rifle for four shots, but that's not only rare—it's expecting too much. And after all, what difference does it make? Minute-of-grapefruit is more than good enough, and the double can offer that.

However, sighting equipment is the most significant factor in actual accuracy. Sighting equipment can be the same for the two types, but generally is not. The bolt-action, especially a light heavyweight like the .416 (Rigby, Remington, Weatherby, Hoffman, *et al.*) is likely to be scoped. A .458 may be scoped. A double in any caliber is almost never scoped.

Quick handling abilities are said to be a great strength of the double. Now, any rifle taken after dangerous game should fit the shooter; an ill-fitting heavy rifle of any type is lunacy. A well-fitting bolt gun that comes up to the shoulder smoothly with the sights aligned can be very fast. However, I submit that no bolt-action, regardless of fit, will be as fast as an equally well-fitting double. The double comes up like a fine quail gun; it's short, but has a perfect center of balance and puts a lot of weight between the hands. It also has the heavy barrels forward and the broad sighting plane.

In the last moments of a determined charge, you are shooting your rifle as if it were a shotgun—and indeed you'd better be. In that extreme circumstance, nothing is like a big double that fits properly. The sights are there, but only the subconscious is aware of them; the rifle acts as an extension of the eye and hands, and if you take time to concentrate on the sight picture you'll be overrun before the shot is fired.

On the other hand, at any significant distance beyond bayonet range, even during the initial moments of a charge, it's critical that the sight picture be proper and the sights centered on the right place. *If you need to use your sights at all,* any optical sight, whether aperture or scope, is faster than any open sight. Period.

To understand this radical statement, it's essential that you understand how the eye works. With an open sight, you have three objects in three planes: the rear sight, the front sight, and the target. The eye cannot focus on all three, so it shifts back and forth. The target must obviously be clear, and younger shooters may be able to keep the front sight almost in focus as well. The rear sight will be blurry for everyone, and as eyes age and become less flexible, the situation worsens. Aperture sights operate in just two planes; the rear ring is supposed to be ignored while the eye automatically centers the bead. A scope operates in just one plane; all that's necessary is to concentrate on the target and superimpose the reticle on the point you wish to hit. Like it or not, optical sights are faster than an iron sight can possibly be at any distance at which you need to use sights.

Finn Aagaard is one of the few African professionals I know who really believes this; he went to a scoped .375 many years ago in Kenya, and found that even at very close range he was much faster and more efficient than he'd been with iron sights. Here in the States, he set out to prove his theory. He set up a range with life-size animal silhouettes at various distances, and virtually every visitor to the ranch took part in the testing. With a stopwatch, starting from a "Go!" with the rifle at port arms and ending with the shot, Finn timed a number of shooters with open sights, scopes, and apertures at various distances. Although I took part in his experiment, I don't have his data. I wouldn't quote it if I did, since I suspect (and hope!) he has his own book to write one of these days. Suffice it to say that nobody, close or far, was as fast *or* as accurate with iron as they were with a scope, especially a low-powered scope with a broad field of view.

As I recall, though, the one thing he didn't test was *short* range, last-chance-to-stop-him range. We're talking a matter of feet, just a few feet. Sights are superfluous and gun fit is everything. A well-fitting bolt gun would do it, but here, and perhaps only here, the handling abilities of a double could save the day.

What am I saying? If a double were scoped, everything would even up. But few doubles are scoped, while bolt-actions can be scoped with ease. The potential accuracy of either type is adequate for dangerous game at all distances at which they should be shot, but a scoped bolt-action will stand most hunters in better stead in all circumstances except a close-range charge. In that one circumstance, a bolt gun will of course do the job—but the handling abilities of a well-fitting double will do it better.

The double's fast second shot is indeed an advantage that can't be questioned. In the elephant-culling operations that are still done in a few places—and historically, when elephant cropping was common—magazine rifles have been the most common tools. Professional hunter Barrie Duckworth, who is just a few years older than I, shot very close to 1,000 elephant on control operations with the then-Rhodesian game department. He used a pair of Mannlicher .458s and had a loader behind him carrying the second rifle. Many hunters with the largest total bags (and remember, culling means eliminating entire herds, not selective shooting) used pairs of magazine rifles. For shooting numbers of elephant, there's little question that a pair of four- or five-shot magazine rifles offered more firepower than a pair of doubles.

However, the selective ivory hunter or the professional hunter backing up a client isn't concerned about large bags, nor is today's sportsman. He's concerned about anchoring his chosen animal. Here the fast second shot of a double can come in handy. The double's third shot will be slow, while in a magazine rifle it's ready and waiting. Take your pick. In a bad moment, I'd prefer a second shot instantly available to a third shot more or less available.

Of course, the second shot in a double is *instantly* available, with no movement whatever. The proper operation of a bolt-action keeps the rifle at the shoulder while the bolt is being worked, but there must obviously be movement—and the more rapidly the second shot is needed, the more violent that movement must be. A double must be taken from the shoulder to reload for the third and fourth shot, while the magazine rifle can stay in position until it's empty. The double can be loaded very quickly, of course, but if more than two shots are required, the nod has to go to the bolt-action.

Almost as much has been made of the reliability of the double's second shot as its speed. I have trouble with that; I've used bolt-actions all my life, and I have yet to "short-stroke" one and fail to pick up the cartridge from the magazine. Yes, mechanical failures can happen, as happened with my stepson during a buffalo charge. And yes, bolt-actions can fail to feed, and the magazine boxes can drop open, and the sky can fall. But all of that should be taken care of long before the rifle goes to the field. New double rifles, too, can have breaking-in pangs. And old double rifles can suffer broken springs and broken firing pins.

One significant advantage of the double is that few mechanical failures short of something really catastrophic will affect *both* barrels and both locks. I would rate a good, modern bolt-action as being every bit as reliable as any double ever built—but either can fail, and if a double fails you're generally left with at least a single shot. A bolt-action will usually be easier to fix, but until it's fixed you're left with a club.

A more important facet of reliability may well be maintainability, and here the simple bolt-action rifle has a significant edge over most doubles. With a single screwdriver it's easy to pull a bolt-action out of the stock, and without tools most bolts can be stripped for cleaning and lubrication. In wet weather, a double gets just as soaked as any bolt-action, but it's a lot harder to do something about it. If the double is one of relatively few "best" guns, with hand-detachable sidelocks or Westley Richards' hand-detachable boxlocks, you can at least take care of the all-important locks. With non-detachable locks, you have to pray a little, and with any of them, removing the buttstock is a chore. Now, it does take a lot to put a double out of action. But just last year I carried my .470 through several driving rainstorms in the Selous, and I cried a lot inside as I watched rivers of rain sluice down over the action.

Silence of operation is a definite advantage of the double—but these days I'm not sure how significant it really is. The ivory hunters who used doubles often used them without ejectors, and then not only was the second shot available with no noise—so was the third, fourth, or however many were possible. The theory was that the clatter of a bolt-action (and the "ping" of a double's ejectors) did more to pinpoint the hunter than the report of the rifle. With a double's silent operation, some of the oldtimers felt larger bags were possible.

These days, that seems a very obscure point. I do like a double's instant and silent second shot, and I like having it with no motion. I have, I'll admit, blown my first shot at an animal and had him stand for a second. That instantaneous, silent second shot with a double can save the day, and it just might make a difference. But not enough difference to make a great deal out of.

One of the most significant advantages of a double rifle, as far as I'm concerned, is one that is rarely mentioned: instant choice of bullet type. It's pretty much the same deal as a double-triggered two-barreled shotgun, with instant choice of choke and shot size, except that with a rifle the choice is either solid bullet or soft, one in each barrel.

Professional hunter Gordon Cormack, in a story written for South Africa's *Man/Magnum* magazine about backup rifles for professional hunters, does mention this as an advantage, but suggests this was primarily "useful for right and left on lion and elephant!" Well, Gordon's a good hand, and this was a marvelous article—he was good enough to send me an initial draft, and we're in agreement on most things. (Good thing, since he has at least 50 times my experience!) But I suspect he doesn't see that to be a real advantage, and I do. On elephant, no, it's not an advantage; you'll be loaded with solids only. Likewise on rhino. And if you're hunting specifically for lion, you'll be loaded with softs. But for buffalo, or for just kicking around in the bush, I like to load a double with one of each.

Of course, as I've mentioned earlier, that's because I prefer softs for the first shot on buffalo. Those who don't, fail to see any advantage, and well they shouldn't since it doesn't exist for them. For me, I *know* I can kill a broadside buffalo more quickly with a softpoint—and in a herd, if I put the bullet on the shoulder it isn't likely to go clear through.

That's the nifty thing about a double; if the angle isn't quite what I like for a softpoint, that solid is right there in the next barrel with no movement whatever. I can remember a couple of buffalo that presented nothing but a bad angle at the end of tough tracking jobs, and the solid did the job when the softpoint wouldn't have. Which, I suppose, is a good argument for sticking with solids altogether on buffalo. But a softpoint in the ribcage just works so well that I hate to give up on them—so long as I can hedge my bets with a solid next door!

In a kind of reverse situation, just last year I was buffalo hunting with a .416 Rigby bolt-action when we bumped head-on into a nice lion. The first shell, my softpoint, misfired. Now, that's a rare occurrence, but it can happen with anything. Had I been carrying a double, I suppose I still would have had to shoot the lion with a solid, since the one softpoint was the one that misfired. But Lord, how I wished for my .470 while I was oh, so slowly working the bolt to get rid of the bum cartridge!

A last comparison, rarely made but important, regards safety. As I mentioned in an earlier chapter, a double shares an inherent safety problem with the single-shot in that it's either fully loaded or unloaded. I don't know about most hunters, but with a bolt-action I habitually empty the chamber when I'm negotiating tough country, carrying the rifle slung, or just in general when I feel action isn't imminent. It's just as easy to do that with a double, but now you've got a completely empty and thus completely useless rifle—and I fear, in Africa, the common solution is to leave it loaded.

Now, if the chamber is loaded, a bolt-action is no different from a double—only two things stand in the way of disaster: safe gun handling procedures and, as a backup only, a mechanical safety. Safeties on doubles are pretty good, I guess. I don't trust any mechanical safety, but the ones I trust the most are the striker-blocking types found on Mausers, Springfields, and such. The best solution is to keep the chamber empty unless it really needs to be loaded (meaning that the bolt-action, with its loaded magazine in reserve, is a better option) and, of course and always, to keep the rifle pointed in a safe direction.

One of the big problems with doubles—which are normally carried loaded—is the so-called "African carry." It's a neat way to carry a rifle, especially a double. Barrels are grasped in one hand or the other, and the flat of the action just ahead of the trigger guard is nicely balanced on the shoulder. It's comfortable, and it goes back to the days when the tracker/gunbearer would walk *ahead* with the rifle so carried; then all the hunter need do is reach forward to grasp a ready rifle. Problem is it's *too* comfortable, and everybody started doing it. When the guy carrying a rifle in that fashion isn't first in line, the rifle winds up pointed at the man in front of him.

A professional hunter friend of mine had a double .500/.465 go off when carried in that manner. The bullet went through the legs of both trackers in front of him. One was injured just slightly, but the femoral artery of the other was severed and he bled to death. My friend and he, incidentally, had grown up together, and though their colors were different they were lifelong friends and hunting companions. It will be a tough thing to live with.

Obviously, something snagged the trigger, but was the safety also knocked off somehow or did it fail? Who knows? It wouldn't have happened had the barrels been pointed in a safe direction, but the "African carry" is a way of life, and it's a bad habit that doubles seem to promote. I carry them that way myself—but never if the bush is too thick to offset myself from the guy in front of me and thus get the barrels pointed well to one side! Safety rules simply must not be ignored. It seems to me that, in terms of safety, the double may not be well-suited to the inexperienced or extremely nervous hunter. But of course no rifle of sound design is inherently unsafe, and I'm certainly not suggesting the double is.

Can a bottom line be found? All things being equal, the average sportsman on the average safari will get the best service from a scoped bolt-action. He can hit better with it, plain and simple; and hunting *is* a game of shot placement first and foremost. On the other hand, the man who chooses the bolt gun will not have the instant second shot, nor, in my opinion, will he have quite as reliable a last-instant shot.

Now, anyone can benefit from a quick second shot—but anyone is also better off with a perfectly placed first shot. And, since nobody wants to get trampled, gored, tossed, or mauled, anybody can benefit from a better last-instant chance. However, let's face the facts. From the hunting client's viewpoint, if things go sour, chances are it's the professional hunter who will clean up the mess. Not only is it his job, technically and legally, but he's also better prepared to handle it—or should be. So it would seem that the man who could best benefit from using a heavy double is the guy who can probably afford one the least—the professional hunter in the field.

Sounds logical, but there's a fly in the ointment here. If things get really bad, the professional hunter may have to shoot a nasty from off the end of his gunbarrel. But before things reach that point, generally there's been another opportunity to settle things, and that's *before* the animal gets into the thick stuff in the first place. Perhaps, just perhaps, it's more important for the professional hunter to be able to place his bullets in an *outbound* wounded buffalo at 100 yards or a fast-vanishing lion at 150. It's food for thought.

Which do I think is better? The jury is still out; I think, all things considered, a scoped bolt-action is the most *practical*, except for elephant in close cover. For that game, *nothing* beats a big double. But even if a scoped bolt-action is a better all-round choice for a heavy rifle, the tremendous pleasure I get from carrying and shooting a classic big double more than outweighs any slight impracticality. They're a joy, and while I have passed mine off to the tracker in favor of a scoped bolt gun on several occasions, in very close cover there's never been any question about which gun to carry. Maybe that's the answer; the rifle types are so different that each has its place. Or perhaps, as they've said since about 1910, it really does come down to personal preference.

# Chapter 20

# Stocks, Related Gear, and Recoil Reducers

The purpose of a gunstock is twofold: first, to provide a platform on which the working parts of the rifle perform their functions; and second, to fit the rifle to the man who will shoot it and assist him in hitting what he shoots at. Some stocks are incredibly beautiful, while others are, well, something less than that. But if a stock performs those basic functions, cosmetics really don't matter in any practical way.

Of the many dimensions that go into making a stock fit properly, the two most critical seem to me to be length of pull and height of comb. Length of pull is basically the straight-line distance between trigger and butt, and this dimension determines proper positioning of the rifle on both shoulder and cheek. Something between $13\frac{3}{4}$ inches and $14\frac{1}{4}$ inches is about right for most adult shooters. This is also the easiest dimension to correct, since a stock that's too long can easily be shortened, while a stock that's too short can generally be lengthened by a thicker recoil pad and, in extreme cases, by a wooden shim between butt and pad.

The desired height of comb depends largely on personal preference, shooting style, and sighting equipment. Americans, for instance, are usually taught to shoot with the cheek (about midway between jaw and cheekbone) firmly welded to the rifle's comb. Europeans, on the other hand, tend to shoot with head more erect and contact much closer to the jawbone. The typical European stock therefore has a much lower comb than most American stocks.

A stock designed for use with iron sights will have a substantially lower comb than if intended for scope use since most scopes are mounted about $1\frac{1}{2}$ inches above center of bore, while iron sights are less than half that distance above.

Neither the American nor the European style of shooting is right or wrong, but it's very difficult for an American to modify his shooting style to comfortably handle a European-style stock—and vice versa. And although many detachable scope mounts work extremely well, it is virtually impossible to design a stock that is really right for both scope and iron sights. Almost invariably, a decision must be made regarding which is the primary sight and which the auxiliary.

My fiberglass-stocked .416 Hoffman had wonderful iron sights and detachable scope mounts. The height of comb was perfect for a 3X scope in those mounts; it came up on target like a dream. However, when I took the scope off, I couldn't see the iron sights at all—no matter how hard I scrunched my cheek into the stock, it was just too high. Eventually I decided I might well want to use irons with the rifle, so Chet Brown switched stocks for me, installing one with a lower comb. With walnut, of course, it's usually no great trick to lower a comb and refinish the wood. It's much more difficult to raise a comb without hurting a rifle's looks, but it can be done.

Drop at heel is the distance the heel, or uppermost portion of the butt, lies below centerline of bore. Depending on the relationship between heel and comb, this dimension also determines the sighting equipment and shooting style for which the rifle is best suited. More importantly, drop at heel will give a good clue how the rifle handles recoil. A lot of drop—take the old Model 1895 Winchester as the worst example—and you're sure to have a horribly kicking rifle, especially if the butt is narrow and, worse, has an old-fashioned crescent shape.

The American classic style of stock has very little drop at heel and a straight comb, with or without cheekpiece. This stock style handles felt recoil extremely well, especially if the comb is gently rounded and the butt is broad and flat to spread out the kick. The concept behind this style of stock is to bring recoil back in a straight line, and the butt will ride high on the shoulder. The face will slide along the stock. (If you don't believe that, shoot a rifle with a fiberglass stock of classic configuration that has lots of recoil and a very rough krinkle-paint finish. I guarantee you'll lose some skin on your cheek and then reach for the sandpaper to smooth the stock where the face makes contact.)

I personally like a classic stock; the clean lines appeal to me, and I like the way such a stock comes into my shoulder. However, various degrees of Monte Carlo comb are also quite popular. With the Monte Carlo style, the comb is fairly high and slants forward while the heel drops away from the comb and thus rests lower on the shoulder. This is a concept long promoted by Roy Weatherby—and he is absolutely correct. During recoil, the forward-slanting comb slides *away* from the face. Recently I did a lot of shooting with the new .416 Weatherby, a rifle of very heavy recoil. It was borne home to me once again that the Weatherby stock style unquestionably gets the recoil away from your face.

Of course, recoil is recoil. In my experience, classic-stocked rifles kick the face a bit harder and the shoulder a bit softer; Monte Carlo stocks are the other way around. Take your pick, based on what feels best to you.

Cheekpieces, as far as I'm concerned, are just a few ounces of ornamental wood. Rollover cheekpieces are *several* ounces of ornamental wood. A well-designed cheekpiece looks good and feels good, but so does a well-shaped comb *sans* cheekpiece. Again, take your pick. Thumbhole stocks aren't for me; I'm a lefty and I've seen so few I could use that I have no feeling for them. They *are* very steady for offhand shooting, and they do take a fair amount of recoil into the shooting hand. My only problem with them is, to be honest, I abhor their looks and I find them too slow to get into action. But one man's meat is another's poison.

The classic gunstock material is walnut, and the relative merits of American, English, French, Bastogne, Circassion, etc., could be discussed endlessly. The problem with *pretty* stocks is that the lovely figure denotes weak places in the wood. The ideal stock for a rifle that will see hard use (and especially a heavy-recoiling rifle) will be straight-grained through the action area and the pistol grip, the weakest part of any stock. A little figure in the butt is nice, of course, but with a hunting rifle go for strength first.

I've had several (yes, by now, *several*) gunstocks broken during transit on airlines; several more have cracked and been repairable, and I've seen a couple just snap off when the Land Rover hit a bump. It's disconcerting, and also a good argument against a one-rifle battery. Generally, a careful inspection will reveal hairline cracks before the damage becomes catastrophic, and that should be part of any pre-hunt ritual. Cracked stocks can often be filled and strengthened with epoxy and bedding compound, and even drilling and pinning can make a stock stronger than it ever was. I have three favorite guns that were repaired by pinning with dowel rods seated in epoxy: A Remington Model 700 .30-06, the stock of which snapped off at the wrist; my pet left-hand-converted pre-'64 Model 70 .375, which developed a serious horizontal crack in the butt; and a favorite Model 12 skeet gun that had the toe of the stock broken clear off. All repairs are virtually invisible, and all are stronger than they ever were.

Unfortunately, repairs are tough or impossible to make in the field. A little baling wire and a lot of duct tape may make a temporary fix, but it's far wiser to inspect rifle stocks carefully before going afield! Most (not all) catastrophic stock failures give a little warning.

With bolt-actions, recoil reinforcement needs to be given special attention. Much as I hate to say it, don't trust any manufacturer to have it right; nothing will split a stock faster than an improperly bedded recoil lug or a tang that isn't stress-relieved.

Pistol grips are very much a matter of personal preference. I like them thick enough to offer some strength, but not so thick that you can't wrap your hand comfortably. The classic style is for the grip to be "laid back," curving back gently so the knuckle of your second finger is well away from the triggerguard.

Fore-ends, too, are a matter of personal preference. I prefer them rounded and not too thick, while others prefer a beavertail. That's all inconsequential. More important is that the forward sling-swivel stud on a heavy-recoiling rifle (let's say above .375) *must* be barrel-mounted ahead of the fore-end. My right index finger (remember, I'm a lefty) has the scars from a stock-mounted swivel to prove this! Another option, of course, is a flush-mounted stud arrangement.

Incidentally, the sling and its swivels are a much-ignored piece of equipment that I find of critical importance. Whatever style of swivels and studs you choose, they must be properly and firmly installed—and checked religiously. When a sling swivel lets go (or a sling breaks), the rifle is sure to careen off your shoulder backwards and land on the scope or sights.

A word about synthetic stocks must be included. I used to think they were the ugliest things in the world, but they're so darned practical that I've almost grown to like their looks. The various synthetics (fiberglass, Kevlar, Rynite, etc.) will never rival a lovely piece of walnut for sheer appeal. However, they're sturdy (perhaps, in many cases, stronger than wood), durable, and *stable*. They won't warp in wet weather or crack in dry. They won't change point of impact, and they won't turn white after a rainstorm. They also reduce weight substantially. Now, that's good news if you're *carrying* the rifle and very bad news if you're *shooting* it. Light rifles do kick more. The foam-injected construction of some synthetic stocks does have a tendency to soak up a bit of the extra recoil, but to one degree or another a light rifle will kick much more than heavy rifle. At 10 pounds, a .416 is reasonably bearable; at 6½ pounds it's an unmanageable beast. And even at 10 pounds, it could be more than most shooters are willing to accept.

Lastly, let's discuss briefly the various means to attenuate felt recoil. First, recoil is simply an instance of Newton's law of equal and opposite reaction. Its force depends primarily on weight and speed of projectile and gun weight. And everybody has his or her own level of recoil tolerance. A nine-pound .375 H&H developing something like 45 foot-pounds recoil energy might be too much for some folks, while others (damn few others!) can handle the 100-plus foot-pounds of a .460 Weatherby Magnum or .577 Nitro-Express with no problems.

Gun weight is very significant, and can go far toward reducing recoil energy and thus felt recoil. Stock style is just as important, perhaps more so. A broad comb and a broad butt really make a difference, not in recoil energy but how it affects you by spreading it out over a larger area. Art Alphin's A-Square "Coil-Chek" stock is perhaps the ultimate in recoil-attenuating design. Very heavy, almost clubby, his rifles are indeed the softest-recoiling big guns I've ever seen. He achieves this by building them heavy, with a broad comb, massive butt, and almost a target-style pistol grip that brings some of the recoil into the shooting hand and wrist.

These days, there are also a number of excellent add-on devices that really help. Pachmayr's Decelerator recoil pads are one example of modern polymer recoil pads that soak up one heck of a lot more kick than traditional rubber. Just forget those handsome checkered-steel buttplates on hard-recoiling rifles; they look great but increase recoil and, worse, tend to slip off the shoulder at the worst moment.

Other options are muzzle brakes and muzzle-venting systems, of which many are available today. Best-known of the venting systems is Larry Kelley's Mag-Na-Port venting. It greatly reduces muzzle jump, keeping the rifle off your face and thus reducing significantly felt recoil. Of the muzzle brakes, the one I'm most familiar with is K.D.F.'s Recoil Arrestor, a screw-on brake that works like gangbusters. I've used it on several rifles now, and it simply must reduce felt recoil by 40 percent.

One of the disadvantages of any muzzle brake or, to a somewhat lesser degree, barrel-venting system, is a tremendous increase in muzzle blast. The redirected noise is bad enough that, in African hunting, where a tracker is likely to be forward and to the side when a shot is fired, I have a real concern about breaking someone's eardrum—or distracting a professional hunter's attention to the point where he might be ineffective as a backup on dangerous game.

Since hearing protection is impractical in the African bush (but must always be used on the range), I like the muzzle brakes that can be removed for hunting and replaced with a blued metal thread protector—and this system I recommend most emphatically if you have a rifle with problem recoil. Kick is something you must come to grips with, difficult though it is. None of us like to admit that our guns hurt us. I've finally accepted it on a couple of rifles—and with brakes or vents installed, I find I can shoot them a whole lot better than I could when I was afraid of them!

# Chapter 21

# Iron Sights

The open express sight is the classic African sight. Unfortunately, there are two problems associated with such a sight. First, an open sight is optically the least efficient kind there is; and, second, both making and using good iron sights are nearly lost arts today.

Since the eye cannot focus sharply on front sight, rear sight, and target all at once, something will be out of focus. If the sight is used correctly, it will be the rear sight that "fuzzes out," and the degree to which it's blurry depends on the age of the shooter, his visual acuity, and the spacing of the rear and front sights on the rifle.

All open sights function essentially the same way, although there are nearly-endless variations. The classic American rear sight is a buckhorn or semi-buckhorn rear, and sights with U-shaped notches are also common. The "express" rear sight is a broad, relatively shallow V, used in conjunction with a large front bead—the object being to get on target with instinctive speed. Front sights are most commonly beads, but post front sights aren't all that unusual. In any case, the object is for the eye to position the top of the front sight in the bottom of the rear sight, and then, maintaining this sight alignment, place the front sight on the desired aiming point.

To those of us who grew up with scopes, this is a complex operation. To those who grew up knowing nothing but iron sights, this is simply the way to shoot—and shooters accustomed to iron sights can indeed work wonders with them. The problem is that iron sights take serious practice to master, and there are some pitfalls. For one thing, consistently good shooting with iron sights depends heavily on stock fit; if the gun is cheeked ever so slightly differently from one shot to another, the sights may not align in the same way.

In poor light, iron sights are hard to see and the tendency is to see too much bead or post and shoot high. Likewise, if you shoot in haste it's very easy to fail to get the bead all the way down into its notch or V. Iron sights work on the principle of the eye being able to center the front sight properly in the rear sight. Strong light from either side confuses this issue, shadowing one side of the front sight and creating a false center. This will throw the shot to one side or the other—and it takes very little aiming error to place the shot off by a matter of feet. A sight hood reduces this problem, but in very poor light may make the front sight more difficult to see.

In spite of the difficulties involved, open sights have provided good service for many generations, and still do today. Although my first shooting was with U-notch open sights on a .22, I pretty much grew up with scopes.

Only in recent years have I spent a lot of time really working with iron sights—and it's amazing what you can do with them.

My Westley Richards .318 had the 1920s version of precision long-range sights. The rear sight was one standing leaf and four folding leaves marked, somewhat optimistically I suspect, for distances out to 500 yards. The front sight, protected by a Westley Richards patented folding sight protector, was a tiny silver bead. I had trouble seeing it in *good* light, let alone bad.

This is another pitfall of the iron sight; as the front sight gets smaller, the aiming point becomes more precise and less of the target is obscured, but aiming becomes slower. I never had the nerve (or the eyesight) to try the 500-yard leaf on that rifle, but I did shoot targets and game out to 250 yards. It was difficult, but possible.

Even so, for most of us the iron sight is a short-range proposition. And the classic African express sight, with its broad, shallow V rear and bold bead up front, is not well-suited to precision work (which, for open sights, we'll define as anything beyond 100 yards). Even for shooting large game at relatively close range, open sights take practice to master. And here's yet another pitfall—all too many hunters, like me, are accustomed to hunting almost exclusively with scopes. When we get ready to go to Africa, we put together iron-sighted heavy rifles and go charging off without understanding the capabilities of the sights—and our capabilities with them.

Practice is really the key, plus an understanding that it doesn't take much aiming error for a shot to go incredibly wild. I've personally missed whole *buffalo* inside of 75 yards by not hauling the front bead of my .470 down into its notch. With a well-fitting rifle that comes up with sights aligned and on target, for snap-shooting at very short range the open express sight is almost as fast as a low-powered scope. When precise aiming is required, it is unquestionably slower.

However, the open sight does have its advantages. Properly built, it's extremely sturdy—almost damage-proof. In very close cover, where buffalo and elephant are often hunted, the low, snag-proof profile is a blessing, while a vine-snarling scope is a dangerous curse. And in the final instant of a determined charge, when the rifle must be pointed like a shotgun rather than aimed, a scope is just a nuisance.

Yet another benefit of open sights—in fact, for general use perhaps their greatest benefit—is that they're totally weatherproof. Modern scopes from reputable manufacturers almost never fog; it's a possible danger but very remote. On the other hand, surprisingly few raindrops on either lens of a scope will obscure vision sufficiently to make the scope useless until it's wiped clean. Scope caps of some type are a quick fix, but they take time to remove. Even peep sights, of which we'll speak in a bit, can be rendered useless by water droplets that gather in the aperture. They can be blown clear in an instant, but any time lost at all can be serious when the trophy of a lifetime presents a quick glimpse—not to mention the consequences of a waterlogged sight with dangerous game at close quarters. The open sight may be the least precise and most limited in range, but it's always ready.

A little-discussed problem with iron sights today is that very few are any damn good. It's a scope world, and iron sights—particularly on American production rifles—seem to be present strictly as ornamentation. I've had a couple of American iron sights and one European iron sight fall off a rifle during recoil. If an iron sight is to be used, it must be absolutely sturdy and reliable. It should be bump-proof, knock-proof, and it *must not* have a folding leaf as the *primary* sight.

Additional folding leaves of greater height for greater distances are all right, I suppose; for most of us, they're an anachronistic ornament. But the primary iron sight simply must be a standing, solid affair. I find the British shallow V the simplest and fastest type of rear sight, though perhaps not the most precise. But whatever type you prefer, it should have some device to make it fast and easy to center the bead in the bottom of the V or notch. A silver, platinum, or gold centerline is traditional with English sights, and it works. My Dumoulin .416 Rigby has a gold triangle, apex pointing up, at the bottom of the V. I've found it extremely fast; the front sight is a gold bead, and the eye naturally nestles the bead against the apex of the triangle.

The best placement for the rear sight is a fair distance down the barrel. This somewhat reduces the problem the eye has focusing on rear sight, front sight, and target; the closer the rear sight is to the receiver, the more pronounced this problem is and the longer it will take to achieve proper sight alignment.

Most barrel-mounted iron sights are in a good position, perhaps five to six inches forward of the receiver. Eight inches would be better still, especially for shooters with older eyes. There is, of course, a trade off here; the less distance between front and rear sight, the greater discrepancy on target any slight aiming error will cause. However, an open sight simply must be fast, so the eye's limited ability to focus in different planes needs all the help it can get.

Quarter ribs are, in concept, sound bases for rear sights. They provide a flat, nonglare sighting plane (and of course, they look great on a rifle!). However, beware of quarter ribs that are primarily cosmetic. The best are milled along with the barrel blank, and they're tremendously expensive. The worst are poorly soldered or brazed onto the barrel—and may not be nearly as stable as they look. Quarter ribs that are there for looks may also be very short, placing the rear sight just three or four inches ahead of the receiver. That's great for a shooter in his twenties, but could be a serious handicap for a shooter in his fifties.

To my mind, the very best open sight is the simplest one of all. A solid (or solidly-attached) quarter rib is great, but so is a standing leaf dovetailed into place and peened slightly to keep it there. Rear-sight bases that are screwed into the barrel are fine, too, but the more pieces must be attached to other pieces, the weaker the sight is. I prefer a rear sight to be non-adjustable—installed with a very shallow V, then filed to the desired zero by shooting, filing, and shooting.

Front sights, too, should be carefully scrutinized before being considered for serious use. All too many are fragile affairs, and some are impossible to see in poor light. The classic English sight is an ivory bead, but a brass bead works just as well for me, especially if it's filed just a bit so that it slants forward to avoid reflection. Sight hoods are certainly desirable; they guard against light distortion, and, just as importantly, protect the rather fragile front sight. However, I have seen few that would stay on during heavy recoil. A little quick gunsmithing can fix that, of course. Generally, to be honest, I've just taken them off and thrown them away. But if you use a naked front sight, you must pay attention to it—and after any possible knock, take a hard look at it and make sure it's straight!

Although it's an iron sight, the aperture or peep sight is a vastly different animal from the traditional open sight. Technically, it's actually an optical sight in that the eye *automatically* centers the tip of the front sight in the center of the rear opening or aperture—where the light is the strongest. There is no focusing problem, so the aperture sight is both faster and more precise than the open sight. With a big opening (like, for instance, the opening that's left when the eyepiece of a typical aperture is removed and thrown away) and a bold front sight, the aperture sight is possibly the fastest close-range sight of all.

If there's a problem with peep sights, it's that they're so rare today. In years gone by, flip-up peep sights were often affixed the rear bridge of a bolt-action, or even to the cocking piece of a Springfield or Mauser. A few custom makers (Joe Balickie for one) will fit an auxiliary peep sight to the rear bridge of one of their rifles.

The peep sight removes most of the potential pitfalls of the open sight; it's much less likely to fail to center the front sight properly, and it's certainly faster. However, iron sights—even good ones—are often used as auxiliary sights on a scope-sighted rifle. Failing a custom arrangement of some type, this is almost impossible with a peep sight.

On over-the-counter rifles, peep sights are extremely unusual today. Lyman still makes some good ones; I've installed several on lever-action rifles. In fact, such a sight seems to me to be not only the most traditional but the most natural sight for a lever-action, and I've had no trouble shooting game with such rigs up to about 200 yards. I've used aperture-sighted military rifles enough to know that precision shooting is possible at very considerable distances; I've qualified for Marine Corps "Expert" for 17 years now, shooting at ranges up to 500 meters. However, I can't say that a commercial aperture sight is any more rugged than today's scopes, which makes it questionable why one would pick an aperture over a low-powered scope.

Whether it's an aperture or open sight, though, the real weakness is quickly seen—or *not* seen—in poor light. The best English guns (and a few modern custom rifles) have a second fold-up sight bead, a huge ivory bead referred to as a "night sight," designed for short-range use in fading light. Such a device is some help, but not much. Long before it's too dark to shoot with a decent scope, front sights just disappear. And long before that, the sight picture becomes vague, and serious aiming errors are likely.

Iron sights have their place—in thick cover, for the largest of game, and during the rainy season. And Lord knows they should be present in case something goes wrong with a scope. Not only present, but sturdy and sighted in. But for general hunting use, they don't hold a candle to a scope. So let's turn next to scopes and mounts for African hunting.

219

# Chapter 22

# Scopes and Mounts

Telescopic sights have been with us for much more than a century, but as little as a generation ago scopes were a bit fragile and all too susceptible to fogging—and serious hunters avoided them like the plague. Those days are long since past; today's high-quality telescopic sight is rugged and reliable, virtually impervious to the elements, and as shock proof as a Timex watch.

American hunters have accepted this truth, and have almost universally embraced the scope sight. In the past ten years I can count on my fingers the open-sighted rifles I've seen in North American hunting camps. Most of them have been peep-sighted lever-actions that I've carried myself, but to those you can add a couple of lever-action .30-30 camp rifles, plus a couple of iron-sighted .338s and .375s carried as backup by Alaskan guides. And that's about it.

Yet, in the same period, I've seen a host of iron-sighted rifles in Africa. Most were in heavy calibers, and many were carried by hunting clients, not by professional hunters. If a scope sight has been accepted as the best possible sight for North American hunting, I fail to see why so many hunters turn to iron sights when they head for Africa. Except for shooting in a driving rainstorm, I can think of almost no instance when an open sight is preferable to a scope. Finn Aagaard, mentioned earlier as one of the few professional hunters I know who is a dyed-in-the-lens scope user, summed it up nicely: "In order to achieve shot placement, I preferred clients to use a scope-sighted .375 H&H for dangerous game. Scopes should be not over 4X, and $2\frac{1}{2}$X is fine."

Within rather broad parameters, the caliber used is never as important as the placement of the shot. Shot placement with a scope will be more precise than shot placement with iron sights. End of discussion. You can't shoot better than you can see, and with a scope you just plain see better.

I will admit I *like* iron sights on a heavy rifle; it's a quirk of my nature. But I don't shoot better with them, nor do I shoot faster. I just happen to like them for certain limited applications. And I would be the first to tell you that, as a hunting client, iron sights will get you into trouble more quickly than anything I know of.

For one thing, they are extremely limited in range. It would be nice if all buffalo could be shot at 40 yards, but you'd be surprised how often a 75- to 100-yard shot is called for. Many of us just can't handle such a shot with open sights—and if we can, our shot placement will not be as precise as with a scope.

The scope's tremendous ability to gather light is another significant advantage. For use on lion or leopard, an open-sighted rifle is not only hopeless—it's downright dangerous. Leopard are almost always taken at last light; the target is small and shot placement must be perfect. Baited lions are usually taken at dawn, and a good, light-gathering scope will give the best odds. If the lion is tracked up, once again a scoped rifle is the best choice. When you close with the lion, you will often need to make out tawny hide against golden grass, or a piece of shoulder through heavy thorn. The scope sight will give you the best chance for a good, undisturbed shot before you get *too* close.

If you're after a wounded cat, it's a toss-up. In the case of a charge, a perfectly-balanced open-sighted rifle might be the best equipment—but only if the shooter is perfectly comfortable with iron sights. And if we're honest with ourselves, few of us are. The thing to remember is that charges only happen when somebody screws up. The chances for such a screw-up are greatly reduced with a good scope sight—and that's a fact. Even during the follow-up of a wounded animal, a charge is fairly unlikely provided everyone goes very carefully and takes full advantage of any opportunity for a shot *before* a charge occurs. Those opportunities may be fleeting, almost always in shadowed cover, and are invariably best exploited with a scope-sighted rifle.

In addition to the optical factors that make a scope so much easier for the human eye to use, there's another aspect of scope use—a rarely mentioned aspect—and it might be the most important of all the scope's advantages. So much African hunting is conducted in thornbush of varying density—and brush eats up a bullet like you can't believe. With a scope, you have a much better opportunity for picking a clear path for your bullet.

There was a time when I wouldn't have believed unseen sticks and vines would turn a bullet, but it's happened too often to question. The first time it happened I was hunting buffalo along Zimbabwe's Bubye River. We closed in to about 60 yards in thick thorn, and I let drive with a 500-grain .470 solid at a buffalo's shoulder. The animal dropped as if pole-axed, and although I was delighted, I recognized that such a reaction to a shoulder shot was most unusual.

The thing is, it *wasn't* a shoulder shot. The bullet centered on the neck, about three feet to the left of my aiming point. And it entered *sideways*, leaving the exact profile of a .470 solid. We found a freshly bullet-clipped sapling about halfway between the dead buffalo and where I'd knelt to fire. I would have sworn the path was clear—but it was a good thing the bullet didn't deflect in the opposite direction.

Just last fall Paddy Curtis and I closed in on a big buffalo herd in Tanzania's Selous Reserve. We picked out a decent bull, nothing monstrous, and when he turned broadside I fired a very careful shot from my .470. The herd ran, of course, but there was no sound of the bullet hitting, no reaction, and, on inspection, no blood. I asked Paddy what happened and he shrugged. "I dunno. I saw a leaf fall."

We walked the ground, and there was a pencil-like vine neatly severed by a bullet just a third of the way toward the buffalo from where I'd fired. It doesn't take much. Later during that same trip I had a 400-grain .416 Rigby softpoint fail to make it through light brush that screened a zebra. That time it was obvious; a branch fell, but before it hit the ground the bullet had raised a huge cloud of dust at the stallion's feet.

Now, that zebra was partially obscured and I knew it; I might have gotten a bullet through and I might not have, but I doubt that a scope would have helped. With both of those buffalo, though, a low-powered scope would have helped me pick a more clear path. I was lucky; neither time did I have a wounded buffalo to chase. But it could have happened, and that isn't my idea of fun.

The choice of scopes for African hunting is really quite simple; any low-powered scope of good quality will do the trick. For use on a light or medium rifle in open country, a fixed 4X or, at the most a fixed 6X might be considered. Hunters who prefer variables won't get any argument from me; I've done some wonderful shooting with 2-7X and 3-9X variables, and my David Miller 7mm magnum wears a Leupold 3.5-10X. Once in a great while, for a longish shot on a small antelope, the highest power setting is nice to have. However, it is extremely important to remember to leave the scope on a moderate setting—no more than 4X in close cover, no more than 6X in open country.

On a .375 (or a .416 intended for general purpose) I prefer a low-range variable—1¾-5X, 1-4X, perhaps a 1.5-6X. My own .375 wears a Bausch & Lomb in the latter magnification, and it's a wonderful scope. But if a .375 or larger caliber is intended for specific use on large, dangerous game, then a fixed 2½X or 3X might make the most sense.

Much more important than magnification is the need for absolute reliability in both the scope and its mounts. I have my favorites, but I won't pick favorites here. I've heard of, or seen, failures by any scope you can think of—including my favorites. I will say you get what you pay for, and your chances of failure are less with a top-quality scope.

The best course is to look at several brands and buy the scope that seems to suit you best. One thing you must pay special attention to is *eye relief*. This is the distance your eye must be from the scope to achieve a proper sight picture. It becomes very critical on rifles above, say, .270 Winchester in recoil levels: too little eye relief, and your scope will hit you between the eyes every time you pull the trigger. It's painful, messy, and the fastest way I know to develop a flinch.

Very few scopes, including some of the most expensive ones, offer enough eye relief for rifles with heavy recoil. In American scopes, Leupolds are pretty good, as are Bausch & Lombs. Although optically magnificent, many European scopes lack enough eye relief for safe use on hard-kicking rifles.

It doesn't make much sense for me to tell you how much eye relief you need; it depends on your shooting style and the amount of recoil you're contending with. But I suggest you try to buy a scope that appears to have a clear picture at least three inches from your eye. Then mount it as far forward as you can get it and still achieve that clear picture. Finally, no matter how much it hurts, get the rifle out to the range and shoot the hell out of it from all positions. If your scope is a "lemon," that fact will generally make itself known during the first 50 shots. If the scope hits you once, it's possible you aren't holding it properly. Wipe off the blood, grit your teeth, and try it again. If it hits you again, get rid of the scope and get one with more eye relief.

I have a bad habit of "crawling" the stock, and I often get nailed right between the eyes by riflescopes. That's my fault, and I always feel stupid when it happens. But twice I've had scopes that simply didn't have enough eye relief. One was a on .300 magnum; no matter that I did everything right, I simply couldn't get away from the scope. It's a magnificently accurate rifle, and its only problem is a badly designed scope. But that rifle cut me so badly—and so repeatedly—on a 1983 safari that I haven't taken it out of the safe since I got back from that trip. My other horror story involves a .340 Weatherby that, because I was short on time, I didn't sight in for myself (for shame!). This one had a scope with a neoprene ring around the "cutting edges." As Bob Milek says, "It doesn't cut you—it just bludgeons you to death." This one did. Every time I squeezed the trigger, the scope cracked me squarely between the eyes. I had it on a moose hunt, and it was cold—Lord, did that hurt. Again, it wasn't the rifle's fault—but I got rid of the whole works as soon as I got back.

It should be obvious that such ridiculous problems are easily avoided by spending time on the range before the hunt. If the scope touches you at all, there's something wrong. It could be in your shooting style, but it's just as likely to be lack of eye relief. Whichever it is, it must be taken care of before your safari.

Scope mounts are a subject of much debate, and the question most often asked is whether they should be of the detachable type. Personally, I like to have iron sights on scoped rifles, especially rifles of medium bore and larger. However, I view those iron sights as auxiliary sights, to be used only in the event of scope failure. I do have detachable mounts on several rifles—but I have never, ever detached a scope in favor of iron sights.

Although detachable mounts are great in theory, I don't really trust them, especially on rifles with very heavy recoil. My ultra-light .416 Hoffman, for instance, has destroyed a whole shoebox full of good scope mounts—and a couple of good scopes as well. I finally gave up on detachable mounts for that beast, settling finally on Tasco's "World Class" mount with the steel stud running between base and ring.

This underlever Army & Navy 8-bore is classic of the stopping rifles of the blackpowder era. In energy, the 8-bore is, probably not coincidentally, identical to the .450-3 1/4'' and its brethren—but that huge bullet undoubtedly hit with tremendous punch.

The 8-bore is not really unpleasant to shoot; the rifles are very heavy, and the low velocity makes it a healthy shove rather than a violent kick.

George Caswell of Champlin Arms in a corner of his gunroom. The shooter seriously looking at investing in a double rifle is well-advised to take a trip to Enid, Oklahoma—nowhere can one look at more good doubles in one place.

This is a Holland Grade 2, a back-action sidelock. As in all the better guns, the locking lugs are "chopper lump"—integral forgings with the barrels, then brazed together.

My Winchester Model 71, rebarreled to the wildcat .450/.348 Ackley, lags only slightly behind the .458; it would do the trick for cats and even buffalo—but somehow a lever-action seems out of place in an African setting.

The Farquharson single-shot action was widely copied by many of England's top gunmakers after the patent expired. This Westley Richards .360 is typical of the many fine English single-shots; they were made in virtually all calibers up to .600.

Here's a closeup of a classic Farquharson falling-block action. That the Ruger No. One owes much to the Farquharson design is obvious.

These five guns are by five different makers in five different calibers. Included in the lineup are "name" guns, but the bottom four all have Webley actions, made in Birmingham and bought by the various riflemakers. The top gun is a new Champlin-Famars using a newly manufactured Webley-type action.

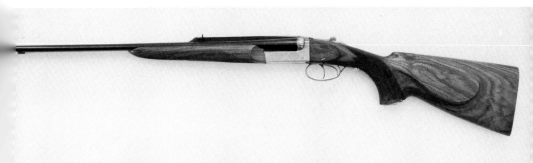

The French-made Chapuis double was imported into the U.S. for several years. This one is in 9.3x74R, a good, sound working side-by-side.

Here's the classic underlever Jeffery .600 Nitro Express, a lovely rifle—but few hunters chose to carry 18 pounds or so on foot safaris.

Best-known of the current double rifles is the Heym 88B, a sound, good-handling, surprisingly light double. This one is in .470.

# RIGBY MAGAZINE RIFLES

In the Rigby Magazine Sporting Rifle the Breech Loading System with its flush double column Magazine, powerful breech closing and strong yet simple and light construction, holds the foremost position for shooting purposes. It was first introduced by John Rigby & Co. in connection with the .275 (7 m/m).

To meet the requirements presented by heavier game the .350R Special was designed using a 310 grain bullet. This cartridge

has now been superseded by a redesigned cartridge caliber known as the .350 "Magnum" using a 225 grain and acknowledged to be ideal for medium game in all the world.

The third Proprietary cartridge of Rigby is known as bore big game gun, specially built at the request of b hunters and recommended for killing all classes of big

## MODEL NO. 2
### High Velocity, Cal. .275

Price in London....
Price in U.S.A.....

Weight of Bullet........140 Grs.
M. Velocity ........2750 Ft. Sec.
M. Energy ........2400 Ft. Lbs.

This rifle shoots the new High Velocity Ammunition which gives a very flat trajectory, and is therefore an ideal weapon for Deer-Stalking. One sight only is required for any distance under 300 yards, and for running shots the forward allowance is small.

Bore—275-inch (7 m/m). Stock—Half Pistol Hand, 8
Length of barrel—23½ inches. Weight—About 7½ pounds
Sighting—Standard sight, 100 yards, and Folding Leaves, 300, 40
Foresight Ivory Tipped Bead, Spare Foresight supplied.

## MODEL NO. 4
### .350 Magnum

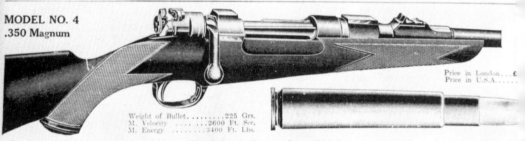

Price in London...£
Price in U.S.A......

Weight of Bullet.........225 Grs.
M. Velocity .........2600 Ft. Sec.
M. Energy .........3400 Ft. Lbs.

The improved Model of the already well-known .350-inch bore is the ideal all-around magazine sporting rifle. The cartridge is a powerful one with very flat trajectory and great striking energy and this action has been designed for it.

Bore—.350-inch. Stock—Pistol Hand, Spe
Length of Barrel—24 inches Weight—8¾ pounds.
Sighting—Standard sight, 100 yards, and Folding Leaves, 300, 40
Foresight Ivory Tipped Bead. Spare Foresight supplied.

## MODEL NO. 5
### .416" Bore "Big Game"

Here's a page from a Rigby catalog, this one advertising their .275 (identical to the 7x57) and .350 Rigby Magnum. As loaded, the .350 Rigby was very similar to the .35 Whelen, although it had the case capacity to be a good deal hotter with modern powders.

This buffalo from Zimbabwe came to join a group of hunters for lunch! It walked to within 10 yards of the lunch party. It was shot by various rifles simultaneously. This hunter holds his .450 3 1/4", one of the guns that killed the buffalo.

Here's a closeup of the Dan'l Fraser .470's action. It's an ejector gun, and displays embellishment that was most unusual in boxlock guns made a generation ago.

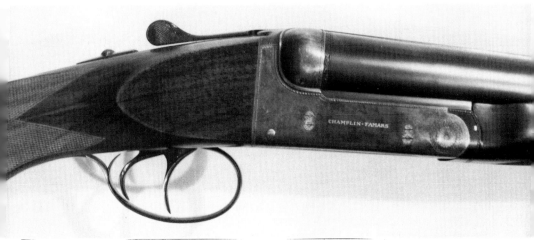

The Champlin-Famars rifle on a Webley action is being offered not only in .470, but also in .450 No. 2—a fine, stout-cased Nitro Express cartridge that's been forgotten for generations.

Heym resurrected another fine cartridge in the .500-3″ Nitro Express. It offers a bit better bullet weight with larger frontal area than the .470 class of cartridge, while its straight case also develops slightly lower pressure.

The bolt in most modern actions, like this Remington on my .458 Lott, doesn't control the round but pushes it into the chamber. Such actions won't feed upside down, but I've personally never had one fail or seen one fail in the field.

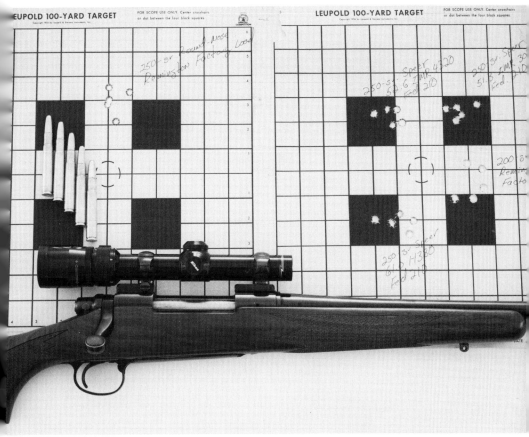

Today's factory bolt-actions are incredibly accurate and reliable right out of the box. This is a .35 Whelen, a cartridge for which I see real use in Africa.

Sako was one of the first to offer a "Safari Grade" as a factory upgrade. Theirs is an extremely attractive rifle, with a quarter rib and a good express sight as well as nice wood.

The Whitworth Express, on a Yugoslavian Mauser action is an excellent, inexpensive rifle available in good safari calibers. Dave Hetzler has had excellent results with his in .375.

Drop magazines offering added capacity are an increasingly common feature on limited-production rifles. This is a Dakota, holding a whole fistful of .375 cartridges.

Henri Dumoulin's Imperial Magnum, available in .505 Gibbs as well as this .416 Rigby (this is my lefthand rifle), is an excellent limited-production rifle built around a monstrous Mauser action.

The Steyr-Mannlicher rifles have changed a lot since the days of the 6.5 Mannlicher, but they're still very fine rifles. I used this one in 7x57 quite a lot, and got very fine service from it.

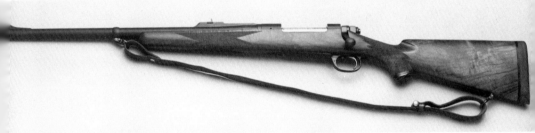

I had this .458 Lott built around a left-hand Remington action, my idea of what a bolt-action stopping rifle should look like. The stock is by Bishop, the action work by Pete Grisel, and the barrel work by David Miller.

The Dakota is another limited-production rifle with a controlled-round feeding action. Without question, many hunters are prejudiced against the more modern action types that lack this feature.

This Westley Richards .318 "Accelerated Express" is very typical of the British bolt-rifles built around Mauser actions from early in the century until World War II. Classic features include optimistically multi-leaved folding sights, a very long barrel, and buffalo-horn fore-end tip.

A new entry into the big-bore bolt-action market is Heym's new Express on a Mauser-type controlled-round feeding action. They expect the .416 Rigby to be the most popular, but they're making a few for the .500-3" Nitro Express with a slant-box magazine.

The U.S. Repeating Arms Winchester Model 70 Super Grade is a factory upgrade offering an entirely different action from the standard Model 70—a controlled-round feeding action that is actually a modernized version of the old pre-1964 action abandoned a quarter-century ago.

Here's a view of the Dumoulin from the top, showing the long Mauser-type claw extractor.

The Weatherby Mark V, with its distinctive styling and nine-lug bolt with short uplift, is a classic modern bolt action. This excellent nyala was taken with a .340 Weatherby Magnum, a powerful and versatile cartridge.

KDF built their reputation around accuracy, and this .411 was no exception.

One of many period illustrations of Theodore Roosevelt's epic 1909 safari, this one clearly shows T.R., pith helmet and all, stopping a leopard charge with his Winchester Model 95 .405. The .405 developed a significant following in Africa prior to World War I.

This is a real rarity, one of Charles Newton's original rifles, essentially a modified Mauser action. Far ahead of his time, Newton's cartridges were nonbelted magnums. This rifle, in .30 Newton, can be loaded to equal the .300 Winchester Magnum.

Here's a classic double-versus-magazine confrontation. Which is best, my .470 or Ronnie MacFarlane's .416 Rigby? The answer, of course, is neither—or both. It depends on which action type you prefer.

U.S.R.A.C.'s return to the controlled-round feeding action on their Super Grade Model 70 is a clear statement that the preference for it exists in many shooters' minds. At bottom is a Super Grade bolt, at top a pre-'64. As in all Mauser-type actions, the extractor holds the cartridge and controls it through the feeding cycle.

This 100-pounder was taken on the Gwane River in Zaire in 1973. The rifles are a Charles Osborn .577 and a Dumoulin .458. The double did the work—but the magazine rifle could have. (Photo by Owen Rutherford)

A good place for a double rifle could have been right here, should the big bull's askari have charged instead of waiting for his picture to be taken. This was in Kenya's Northern Frontier District; the tusker dropped to a brain shot from a .400 Jeffery, and the second barrel was ready. (Photo by Owen Rutherford)

Much controversy still exists concerning ejector and extractor doubles. The ejectors are fast, but many early hunters objected to the "ping" when the cases flew, believing it allowed game to pinpoint them. Some hunters prefer extractors only.

I prefer extractors, myself. A flip of the wrist—which must be practiced—and the empties are out just as quickly. Since I'm not after a large bag, the noise of ejectors isn't important—but I don't have to scrabble around the bush looking for empties!

Rapid reloading needs to be practiced with a double. Those big cartridges between the fingers look neat, but it takes practice to keep from fumbling the reload.

Muzzle brakes and barrel venting are effective means of reducing felt recoil. At left is a KDF Recoil Arrestor; at right is the Mag-Na-Port barrel venting. Both work well, but there is a price in increased muzzle blast.

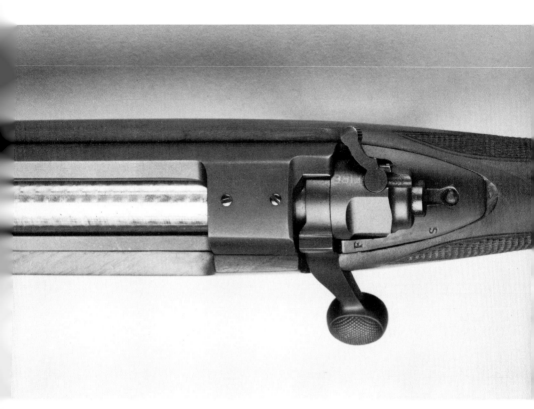

Safeties are more or less taken for granted, but are actually important items to consider—and take with a grain of salt. They must work, but should never be trusted. My personal preference is a flag safety of some type on the cocking piece.

Sometimes the bush is so thick that a scope is ridiculous, as well as a twig-snaring nuisance. The problem is that, just when it seems open sights are all that make sense, the bush opens up and you're handicapped without a scope.

Much more sensible than folding leaves is a single standing leaf, very solid with a gold or platinum centerline to aid in quick alignment. In this case the sight is mounted on a quarter rib, a nice touch but not essential.

Folding leaves are attractive, perhaps because they're traditional. Their real utility, however, is extremely questionable—especially if the iron sights are auxiliary to a scope.

A low-range variable like this 1 3/4-5X is an excellent choice for most African hunting, especially when mounted on a medium bore like a .375.

The open-sighted heavy rifle is a wonderfully romantic notion, and I love such rifles dearly. But a great many shots simply won't be attempted, let alone made, if a scoped rifle isn't available. This is especially true for small animals such as this bush duiker.

The simplest approach I've found for a detachable scope mount is this little Pilkington lever. For just a few dollars it turns a Redfield-type mounting system into a detachable scope—and it works!

The very best detachable mount, of course, is the European claw mount—but the expense is tremendous.

The bulge of West Africa offers a tremendous variety of forest duiker, usually taken in the thickest cover, often by calling. This outstanding Peters duiker, above, and bay duiker, below, were taken in southern Cameroon. A shotgun with coarse shot is unquestionably the best medicine.

As in North America, the average shot on African game in most areas is something under 100 yards. I've had a lot of fun playing with open-sighted rifles, and you can do all right with them—but especially for smaller, open-country plains game, this is hardly a suitable rifle.

There's no wingshooting action to compare with a mixed bag of doves and sand grouse over an African water hole.

The .375 H&H is about the largest rifle that can seriously be considered for lighter plains game, but if you know the rifle well and it has a decent scope, there's no reason not to use it.

Finn Aagaard ran stop-watch tests of aimed shots with a wide variety of actions. The double is fast—but not as much faster as you might think when timed against proficient bolt-action men.

I shot this wildebeest at about 225 yards, using the second leaf on my .318. With a scope it would have been an easy shot; without one, I was at the absolute limit and perhaps a bit beyond it.

Snap caps are an excellent $15 investment with any double; these guns shouldn't be stored with the action cocked, nor should they be snapped on empty chambers.

This Number One Tropical Rifle is a .375, also available in .458. An interesting concept, though, is to use that ultra-strong action and rebore it to one of the Nitro Expresses. The Ruger action coupled with the added case capacity would make for some very interesting loads.

A fairly new wrinkle in American gunmaking is the semi-custom, or limited-production, rifle—not a true custom rifle but offered with a wide range of individual specifications. This is A-Square's Hannibal, designed as a workhorse rifle with a stock that goes a long way toward eating up recoil.

The wonderful balance and reasonably heavy nature of a big double makes it surprisingly comfortable to shoot. It's important to learn to really grip the barrels just ahead of the splinter fore-end or they'll kick out of your hand.

# New ·375-Bore, Holland-"Velopex" Magazine Sporting Rifle

As a Sporting Magazine Rifle, this weapon is the latest development of our well-known ·375 bore, and is constructed to carry our NEW PATENT "VELOPEX" CARTRIDGE, giving a muzzle velocity of 2,500 feet per second, and striking energy of 2,583 foot lbs., with hollow point or solid bullets. It is a light, handy and well balanced rifle, carrying five cartridges without projecting magazine.

---

### SOME OF ITS LEADING FEATURES.

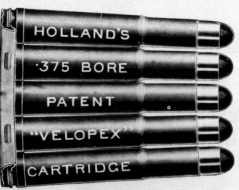

Clip of five Cartridges (full size)

VERY HIGH VELOCITY (2,500 f.s.).

FLAT TRAJECTORY.

GREAT STRIKING ENERGY (2,583 ft. lbs.).

A PERFECTLY BALANCED WEAPON.

LIGHT AND HANDY.

THE PERFECTION OF A MAGAZINE RIFLE.

IMPROVED SYSTEM OF DETACHABLE BARREL.

MAY, WITH ITS AMMUNITION, BE IMPORTED INTO INDIA.

EQUALLY SERVICEABLE IN THE JUNGLE OR ON THE HILLS.

FOR ELK, MOOSE AND OTHER SOFT-SKINNED ANIMALS.

---

PRICE ... ... ... 25 Guineas

Extra quality and finish, with selected Stock, Cheek Piece, Box for Spare Sights in hand of Stock, &c., 30 Guineas. Improved pattern Detachable Telescope Sight, including Fitting, 12 Guineas. Peep Sights, from 31/6

**Winners of all "The Field" Rifle Trials, London.**

Forerunner of the .375 H&H, and one of the first belted cartridges, was Holland's .375 Velopex. It fired a bullet too light for its caliber and was not very successful—but it did lead to the development of the .375 H&H.

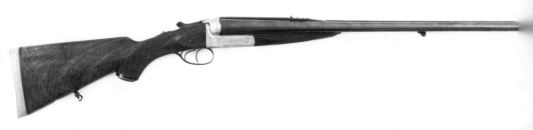

My own .470 is a typical "working gun," a boxlock by an unknown maker named C.W. Andrews. Its lines are classic English, and it probably dates to the 1920s.

This brand-new Beretta over/under is a beautiful, well-made rifle. This one is in .30-06, but calibers up to .458 are available. Beretta has also started making top-of-the-line side-by-sides in large calibers.

This is another 9.3, a sidelock by Francotte of Belgium. This firm has made a small number of fine side-by-sides for many years, including a few in the large Nitro Express calibers.

If recoil is at normal levels, there are a number of good detachable mounts. Strongest, of course, is the European claw mount, which is absolutely rigid but fantastically expensive. The same could be said for the many one-of-a-kind detachable mounts made by a number of American custom gunmakers. At an affordable price, the most attractive option is Kimber's Leonard Brownell double-lever mounts. Slightly stronger, in my view, are the German EAW and Bock mounts. The simplest solution of all is a little lever made by Pilkington that converts any Redfield-type mount into a single-lever swing-off detachable mount. I've had one on my .375 for a couple of years, and it hasn't shifted a bit.

I don't know if it would hold up at higher recoil levels. Darn few detachable mounts will. It isn't important to me; if I scope a rifle, then I commit myself to scope use. This business of taking scopes off and putting them back on willy-nilly is, as far as I'm concerned, an invitation to disaster. If a mount is detachable, that's nice—but the scope is going to come off only if it has a problem. If the mount isn't detachable, then I make sure my kit contains whatever screwdrivers are needed to remove the scope. I place a premium on rigidity and reliability. Detachability isn't nearly as important. For moderate recoil levels, the Redfield system works extremely well. At higher levels, I prefer Conetrol, Buehler, or the Tasco mounts already mentioned. More important than the mount itself is that it be properly installed—tight screws Loc-Tited into place, and surfaces that fit properly (with additional work if needed).

Iron sights are a perfectly viable alternative if something goes wrong with a scope—but perhaps a better hedge against disaster is a spare scope, already set in rings and, if possible, more or less sighted in. Hunters accustomed to scopes will find iron sights a damned poor substitute if something happens to their one and only scope.

I usually have auxiliary iron sights on a rifle, and I almost always carry a spare scope. The likelihood of using such fallback substitutions is extremely remote. I have had scopes "crap out," it's true. It's an eventuality worth planning against, since the lack of sights renders a rifle useless and a safari hopeless. On the other hand, if you've had the rifle on the range and it's holding its zero, your chances of scope trouble are extremely remote.

Scope reticles are largely a matter of personal preference. The "plex"-type crosshairs, with thick outer wires and a thin center, are the most popular today. This type is my favorite as well; I find it very fast in low light, yet the thin inner wires allow precision when you need it. In close cover or on moving game, a bold dot with crosswires is nice, but for general use I prefer the "plex." For a specialized leopard rifle, the relatively new illuminated reticles are wonderful at last light, but I prefer to keep scopes as simple as possible—especially on heavy calibers with lots of recoil.

All too often, you see hunters carrying lovely expensive rifles mounted with inexpensive, needlessly powerful variable scopes in poorly chosen mounts. As there are many good rifles on the market, so are there many good scopes and sturdy, well-designed mounts. Shop for your scope and mount it with as much care as when you shop for your rifle. If you do, that scope, like your rifle, is perfectly capable of providing your grandchildren with the same good service it gave to you.

# Chapter 23

# Shotguns on Safari

**B**ob Brister, longtime shooting editor of *Field & Stream*, is one of America's greatest authorities on shotgunning. He's also the finest wingshot I've ever seen in action. Several years ago, on a sort of bet, he killed a Cape buffalo very dead with one Brenneke slug from his Perazzi bird gun. No, a 12-gauge isn't an ideal buffalo gun—but the lethality of the shotgun cannot be argued.

A good thing that is, too, because in a couple of out-of-the-way African countries, firearms importation restrictions are such that hunting is "shotgun-only." This is the case in Liberia, an English-speaking West African country known for its incredible variety of forest duikers. In the dense forest, the primary hunting technique is to call the duikers, much as we would call foxes or coyotes. Under such conditions, the borrowed buckshot-loaded shotguns with which hunters are supplied are nearly ideal. However, Liberia also holds a few bongo and some dwarf forest buffalo. I'm told that carefully smuggled Brenneke slugs will do the trick, though I'm not certain I want to see for myself!

Slug-loaded shotguns are used to harvest hundreds of thousands of whitetail deer annually—and not a few black bears and wild hogs. In brushy country, a well-sighted slug gun would be absolutely deadly for most African game. Except for special situations such as Liberia, though, I can't see any reason to use a shotgun for the general run of African game. On the other hand, the shotgun has several very real uses on the average safari.

The most obvious is for bird shooting. We'll discuss that in a bit. The other traditional use for a shotgun is as the backup gun on wounded leopard. The old formula was a double-barreled shotgun loaded with SSG, the English equivalent of 00 buck. A few hunters prefer that combination even for wounded lion. Wally Johnson, Sr., has been quoted as saying that a hunter with a buckshot-loaded shotgun is as safe from a charging lion "as a baby in its crib."

The key to buckshot use is that the animal must be ever so close. At 25 yards, where a charge might originate, a full load of buckshot may or may not do much damage. From the muzzles to 10 yards, the results will be certain and devastating.

A double-triggered, double-barreled 12-gauge, relatively short in the barrels and with open chokes, would be my choice for this kind of work. If possible, I'd want it in three-inch magnum—every bit of shot you can get into the shell is to the good. I would personally not care to trust an automatic; I shoot birds with them, but birds don't have sharp teeth and long claws, and I have yet to see an automatic that never jammed.

Professional hunter Russ Broom does use an automatic for backup on leopard—and his is probably the ultimate charge-stopper. It's a 20-inch-barreled Ithaca Mag 10 Roadblocker, the police version of their now-discontinued 10-gauge automatic. Using 3½-inch shells stuffed with 000 buckshot (.36-caliber pellets), Russ has stopped enough leopards to have total confidence in the gun. As for me, I just don't have that kind of faith in an automatic.

If I were to use a repeating shotgun, I would opt for a slide-action. In experienced hands, the pump is just as fast as an automatic (actually faster!) and I have more faith in its reliability. There is also a subtle aiming advantage. When the slide is worked to chamber the second and subsequent round, the final action *pushes* the slide forward to close the breech on a fresh shell. That pushing action is toward the target, and I believe this motion of the supporting arm creates a natural pointing action that does not occur with any other action type.

Given my druthers, I'd use a double-trigger side-by-side—but a close second choice would be a well-broken-in Winchester Model 12. Ronnie MacFarlane has a Remington 870 three-inch magnum with a couple of interchangeable barrels—a vent-rib choke barrel for birds and a 20-inch slug barrel with iron sights. Now that's a sensible, versatile African shotgun!

Whatever shotgun is chosen, it simply must fit well and point naturally. A charging cat must be *hit*, and hit squarely, to be stopped. At the close ranges you're dealing with—feet, not yards—there's very little pattern spread, and no margin for error. In fact, you're actually delivering a ball of shot, at most a few inches across. In terms of pattern, at such distances the shot charge from a shotgun offers little advantage over a single rifle bullet. That isn't the reason the shotgun is preferred.

Rather, it's because the shotgun's fast-handling abilities and lack of sights are better-suited to the instinctive shooting essential to stopping a close-range charge. And because the combined impact and instantaneous energy transfer of nine or a dozen soft lead pellets does more damage to a soft-skinned animal like a cat than a single rifle bullet possibly can. But only if it's *close*. The greatest danger in stopping a charge is to fire too quickly, and that's especially true with buckshot. Most leopard charges are launched at very short range, so this isn't as big a problem as with lion. However, if buckshot is to be used on a lion charge, the shot simply must be held until the very last second or it will not have the needed effect.

Incidentally, said effect of close-range buckshot is quite unbelievable. A friend of mine had a client wound a leopard recently, and he followed it up with SSG. The cat came from very close in, and my buddy hammered it right off the muzzle. His client was most upset over the condition of the pelt, while my buddy was much more relieved over the intact condition of his own hide. It's actually quite a simple matter to avoid pelt damage from buckshot—just don't wound a cat in the first place!

260

Aside from stopping things that bite and claw, a shotgun is also nearly ideal for the very small antelopes in close cover. It would be useless for game such as steinbok, Vaal rhebok, and klipspringer; you'd never get close enough. But for hunting forest duikers and, in most thornbush, dik dik and grysbok, a shotgun makes sense. In heavy brush, hunting such tiny animals differs little from hunting cottontails or jackrabbits, and a shotgun gives a slight edge. It will also do far less damage than a high-velocity centerfire rifle. Personally, though, I'd stay away from the larger buckshot for such things, instead using No. 4 buck or BB.

I'm terrified of snakes—especially some of the snakes to be found in Africa. In the bush, the best thing to do with snakes is leave them alone, but in camp a shotgun seems to me the best means for dealing with the odd mamba or cobra that comes calling.

Although all these special purposes are interesting, bird shooting either for sport or for the pot is far and away the most common use for the shotgun on safari—and in the right place at the right time, African bird hunting is unequaled. Several species of dove and wild pigeon abound, as do the snipe-like sand grouse. Tasty francolin come in several varieties, ranging from quail-size to nearly as large as a hen pheasant. And then there are the guinea fowl, both crested and vulturine—strong runners, fast flyers, and a great addition to camp tablefare. Waterfowl, too, are abundant in some areas—spurwing and Egyptian geese, and a wide variety of ducks.

In some areas at certain times of the year, game birds are few and far between. But in most safari areas it's no great trick to have an afternoon of fine bird shooting any time you feel like it. The problem is always *time*, and that's why I'm ambivalent about taking a shotgun on safari. The bird shooting is there—but I don't go to Africa to hunt birds. The use you will get out of a shotgun in exchange for the hassle of dragging it 20,000 miles really depends on you—on how serious a bird hunter you are, and how serious and difficult the primary objectives of your safari may be.

I have taken a shotgun on several safaris—and hardly had time to use it. On the other hand, I've *not* taken one on other trips and wished desperately that I had one with me. Such was the case in Masailand last year; I didn't take a shotgun, and I was in the most wonderful game bird paradise I've ever seen. Francolin of three different species were running everywhere, and both crested and vulturine guinea fowl were abundant. The way the hunt went, I would have had time to really enjoy some bird shooting. As is usual, there was a shotgun in camp—but only a double handful of shells. We shot some guineas for the pot a couple of times, but shells were too scarce to squander on francolin.

That's usually the case, by the way; somewhere within reach, in most hunting camps, is a well-worn shotgun of some persuasion, but shells are likely to be scarce. Here's the way I recommend you play the shotgun angle: Evaluate your interests and desires. If you're a serious bird hunter, and if you're willing to sacrifice some hunting time to some shotgunning, by all means take your favorite bird gun along to Africa. I would especially recommend this for longer safaris and for one-hunter/one-professional-hunter arrangements, where time tends to be less critical. After a major animal is taken, it's nice to rest for a day, and there's no better way to rest than by a waterhole with a shotgun in hand!

But, if you don't much care about bird shooting one way or the other, don't bother dragging a shotgun all the way to Africa. You won't use it unless you make yourself use it. I do recommend, however, that anyone going on safari take at least one box of shotgun shells, if not two. Make them 12-gauge, 2¾-inch, high-base No. 6 shot. This versatile load will do for almost anything. And if you're leopard hunting, whether you take a shotgun or not make sure you stuff at least one five-round packet of *fresh* buckshot loads in your kit. You'll hope nobody needs them, but just in case.

Now, if you plan on doing some serious bird shooting, you can't possibly bring along enough shells. So you'll need to arrange beforehand for your outfitter to have a supply on hand. In South Africa, you won't have any problem finding shotgun shells, but elsewhere in Africa expect them to be magnificently expensive and probably damn hard to come by. And if you don't make very specific arrangements ahead of time, expect them to be nonexistent.

In all the time I've spent in Africa, I must confess that I've done relatively little bird shooting. It always seems more important to spend one last evening looking for a buffalo, kudu, or whatever. But that's a very personal choice, and for hunters who really want to enjoy Africa, a bit of bird shooting adds memorable spice to any safari.

# Part III

# Guns for Game

# Chapter 24

# Light to Medium Plains Game

We have discussed in some detail a great many cartridges well-suited to African hunting and have taken a hard look at rifles chambered for these cartridges. Now it should be possible to match these tools more specifically with their appropriate jobs by examining the rifles and their cartridges that are best suited for hunting various types of game.

It's important to understand there are no absolutes in this discussion, and what works extremely well for one person may be a disaster for someone else. The best rifle is the one that gives its user the most confidence and maximizes his shooting ability. By definition, if the hunter gets his game without wounding, with no horror shows, then the rifle and its cartridge were adequate—at least in that person's hands. But if the hunter does not get his game, was it the fault of the rifle or the shooter?

There is a broad range of rifle/cartridge suitability for any type of African game. An unusually skilled marksman may use a cartridge much smaller than the generally accepted parameters—and he might do very well. Someone who is a very good hunter, and thus is able to consistently close on his game, may use a cartridge much larger and more limited in range than is common for a given type of game. I would never question an experienced hunter's choice. On the other hand, few of us are widely experienced with African game. For that matter, considering today's short seasons and low bag limits, few of us are particularly experienced in shooting game of any type.

Genuine experts may read this book, and I hope they enjoy it. I also hope they don't find grievous fault with its ideas and opinions on African rifles and cartridges. But whether they agree or not, they've already made up their minds—and so long as their choices work, they're dead right. On the other hand, the hunter contemplating a first or second safari, or even the old hand planning a trip to an unfamiliar part of Africa, may find some real value in this discussion—while bearing in mind that the suggestions are general guidelines, not absolutes. Nor, I hasten to add, are these guidelines mine alone. To a degree they're based on the experience of 20 African hunts. But to a larger degree they're based on correspondence and campfire discussion with a great many professional hunters—the real experts. These ideas are not new, nor should they be; at this writing, smokeless cartridges have been used for over a century in Africa. Today's hunter is not only well-served by paying attention to that century of experience—he's foolish if he ignores it.

Let's begin with what I call "light to medium" plains game. This is the huge class of antelope and wild swine that run the gamut from 10-pound dik diks up to 400-pound hartebeest and waterbuck. It's a huge group, and so diverse that it would be ridiculous to lump them together as a single category that can be perfectly matched to a single small selection of rifles and cartridges. However, as many as a dozen of these animals might be hunted on the same safari—and opposite ends of the spectrum might be hunted on the same day. In Masailand or Ethiopia, for instance, you might scour dense cover for lesser kudu in the mornings and evenings—and spend the midday hours out on the plains looking for an exceptional gazelle. In the Okavango Delta or the Bangweulu Swamp, you might comb the reeds for sitatunga—but wind up taking a 400-yard shot at a lechwe. In South Africa, you might hunt bushbuck in dense cover in the morning and springbok on open plains in the evening.

Even if we exclude the really large plains species and *all* the dangerous game from this discussion, the game within this "light to medium" group varies so much in size, habit, and preferred habitat that it would be almost impossible to come up with one rifle/cartridge combination that would be truly suitable. And yet that is what we must try to do, for it is almost never practical to have on safari more than one rifle that will be used for this type of game.

Now, from safari to safari, that single rifle may not be the same one; the plains-game rifle chosen for the Kalahari or Masailand may not be the best choice for the thornbush of Zambia or Zimbabwe. But on *one* safari, regardless of how many areas are to be visited, any single rifle must cover a very broad range of game that will be taken under widely varying conditions.

It would be a lot of fun to come up with the ideal rifle/cartridge combination for each specific African species. For instance, for Vaal rhebok, spooky little antelope that inhabit South Africa's highest mountains, the lightest, fastest, flattest-shooting, most accurate rig I could come up with would be perfect. A light-barreled .22-250 firing bullets of about 60 grains would be nice, and I'd probably top it with a 10X varmint scope.

And then there are springbok and the gazelles. Power isn't important but, depending on the terrain, you want plenty of reach. Something ranging from .243 or 6mm up to .240 Weatherby, .25-06, or .257 Weatherby would be close to ideal. You'd want plenty of scope, but not too much since mirage and heat waves could be a problem. A variable with a powerful upper end would be good, perhaps a 3.5-10X or 4-12X.

Bushbuck are one of my favorite antelope to hunt, and I've been fortunate to hunt a half-dozen different varieties. All are found in heavy cover, and the purest and most enjoyable form of hunting them is still-hunting. They're tough, for so small an antelope—and they can be downright dangerous. Great fighters, they've ripped open many a hunter who approached too quickly. I can't imagine a better bushbuck rifle than a lever-action in .35 Remington, .358 Winchester, or even .444 Marlin, topped with a bright, quick, low-powered scope.

The same sort of rifle would be ideal for bushpig, but if dogs were being used you might want to leave the scope off. The warthog, on the other hand, is more often seen at a greater distance—and he must be hit hard and anchored lest he make it down a burrow before expiring. (Considering the crawly things that might also inhabit pig holes, you wouldn't catch *me* digging around in one!) Something fast, flat, and hard-hitting is good warthog medicine; you could make a good case for a .270.

Then there are the heavyweights of this group—the hartebeest, water-buck, and lechwe. All of these are likely to be shot in open country at very long range; a scoped .300 magnum would be hard to beat. And yet, in the same size category, you have the cover-loving nyala. I can't imagine anything better than my .35 Whelen.

Since you can't take a half-dozen rifles on safari—and even if you could, chances are you'd have the wrong one in your hands most of the time—the name of the game must be versatility. And to obtain that versatility some compromises must be made. Your plains-game rifle will almost certainly be needlessly powerful for the smaller antelopes, and its sighting equipment probably won't be perfect for everything. However, it must be powerful enough for the largest game you will use it on, and it must shoot flat enough to handle any terrain you think you *might* encounter.

Later on, we'll discuss building specific African batteries. Here, though, it's important to understand that the less broad your spectrum of game and/or terrain, the more you can indulge in specialized rifles. For instance, if you're planning a typical hunt in Southwest Africa, you know all your hunting will be in relatively open thornbush, desert, or mountains. In other words, your shots will be long. Under most circumstances in that country, you will not be hunting any dangerous game, so your battery need not include charge-stoppers. For such a hunt, it would be wonderful to take an accurate, scope-sighted .243, 6mm, or .257 Roberts. A rifle like that would be great fun to use for springbok, impala, duiker, and blesbok. But such a rifle would not be adequate for the full spectrum of plains game; you would still need a rifle that could handle hartebeest, plus kudu, gemsbok, zebra, and perhaps eland. The rifle suited for such game would duplicate the .243 in that it would also have to be accurate, flat-shooting, and scope-sighted. But obviously it would be much more powerful, perhaps a .300 Winchester or Weatherby, 8mm Remington Magnum, or .338.

There's no harm in such duplication—but in safari batteries that *must* contain specialized rifles for the dangerous game you generally can't afford the luxury. Dangerous game rifles, by their nature, must be somewhat specialized—while the plains-game rifle must be highly versatile, covering the broadest spectrum of game possible.

The rifle chosen for this work might be asked to punch a bushpig at 10 yards, or a tiny steinbok at 100, or a hartebeest at 300. The first chore requires little more than some measure of raw power, but the second dictates accuracy, while the third calls for flat-shooting capabilities.

Depending on the cover, a lever-action in .308 or .284 might be a good choice. Certainly there's no reason why a modern single-shot wouldn't do the job. For my money, though, I'll take a bolt-action for this kind of work. The accuracy is there, plus the bolt-action's reliability and strength. And of course, it's available in a host of suitable chamberings.

Choice of caliber is important, and there are several good ones. But choice of scope is perhaps just as important. Again, versatility is the key. This is a rifle that might be asked to reach out a long way—but it also might need to handle a point-blank chance encounter in heavy cover. A skilled marksman will do just fine with a garden-variety fixed 4X scope. This rifle really screams for a top-quality variable, though. Power ranges like 2-7X, 3-9X, and 3.5-10X are just right; the power ring should be kept low, no higher than 4X, *most* of the time—but if you need to make a longish shot at a smallish antelope, that magnification is there when you want it. And it helps.

I just flipped an old notebook open to 1977, the year I hunted Kenya. On that trip, I used two rifles. The larger, a .375, was to be used for lion, buffalo, and eland. The light rifle was used for everything else, and there was a tremendous variety of everything else. With that light rifle, my notebook tells me I shot a running warthog at 10 yards; a dik dik at 100 yards; a steinbok at 200 yards; a waterbuck at 275 yards; a gerenuk at 300 yards; a duiker at 40 yards; a bushbuck at 60; a hartebeest at 400; and so forth.

The rifle was topped with a 3-9X Redfield scope, and you can bet it was cranked up all the way on the longer shots—and on the smaller antelopes. The rifle was a plain out-of-the-box Ruger Model 77, but it seemed to be a magic wand; if I waved it in the general direction of an animal, he fell over dead. The cartridge was hardly anything unusual or hot-rock—the good old .30-06, with handloaded 180-grain Nosler Partition bullets.

The .30-06 has not been my only choice for a light safari rifle, but it has remained my most consistent. It isn't the flattest-shooting cartridge, but it offers the wonderful intangible of near-perfect bullet performance.

In consistently open country, a good light rifle could be a .264 Winchester Magnum or a .270 (either Winchester or Weatherby Magnum). In mixed country or thornbush, I prefer a bit more bullet weight. There I would suggest almost any of the 7mms, from the 7x57 up through the 7mm magnums; or a .308 or .30-06. The .300 magnums, in my view, form the upper end of the light-rifle arena. They are, all of them, wonderfully versatile and tremendously effective; with proper bullets, they will go well beyond what I think of as light to medium plains game. Unfortunately, it's a sad fact that darn few people shoot the .300s really well—and a .300 magnum is not a substitute for good marksmanship.

If you shoot a .300 well, then it will serve you well. If you don't, and there are all too many of us who don't, forget it. You'll do much better with a .270, .30-06, or 7mm of some persuasion. My father-in-law, a fine pistol shot, took up big-game hunting in his retirement. He doesn't like recoil and has no lifelong habit of dealing with it—but, like most of us, is reluctant to admit it. His main battery consisted of an old Springfield that he'd lovingly customized, and which he shot well; and a very accurate Model 70 .375 which he would shoot only when he had to. The groups from the Springfield began to deteriorate alarmingly, and shortly before a Zimbabwe safari we realized the barrel was shot out. Paul did the sensible thing; rather than rely on the .375, he got a Ruger Ultra-Light .270 for the trip. With it he made one-shot kills not only on warthog, impala, and waterbuck—but also on sable and kudu.

That's a problem with my "light to medium" classification; African plains game doesn't stop with the waterbuck-size animals. It keeps on going, up through tough game such as oryx, sable, and roan to 500-pound kudu and 800-pound zebra, all the way to three-quarter-ton eland. Properly chosen, the light rifle can handle some of these chores, just like Paul's .270 did—but it can't handle them all. So let's turn now to rifles and cartridges for the largest plains game.

# Chapter 25

# Large Plains Game

**D**angerous game gets, if you'll pardon the pun, the lion's share of the glory and the press. And, as I've said, the smaller plains species comprise the greatest percentage of the bag. Nevertheless, the large plains species are serious business. A few animals in this group—specifically sable, roan, and oryx—can be dangerous when wounded, but only if the hunter makes a foolish and too-hasty approach. The seriousness isn't from potential danger, as it is with the Big Five. Instead, it comes from two other considerations.

First, this group contains some of Africa's most desirable and most difficult-to-obtain prizes. Included are the ultra-rarities like bongo, Derby eland, and mountain nyala—each of which may be, properly, the sole objective of a lengthy and expensive safari. Also included are prizes less rare, but every bit as desirable for their sheer beauty and majesty: greater kudu, sable, roan, eland, oryx. Members of this latter group may or may not be a safari's single goal, but in areas where they occur they will invariably be very high on the list.

These animals vary considerably in toughness; pound for pound, members of the oryx clan are amazing for their ability to take punishment, while the larger kudu are relatively soft for their size. But all are big enough to be most unforgiving of poor shot placement or unsatisfactory bullet performance—and all are uncommon enough and/or sufficiently difficult to hunt that multiple opportunities on one safari are rare. In other words, you can expect just one opportunity at a really good trophy of any member of this group; both you and your rifle and cartridge must be up to the task.

Also included in this group are some animals that, while hardly rarities, are some of Africa's toughest, which is a second important consideration in selecting appropriate rifles and cartridges. I'm thinking particularly of wildebeest and zebra, but it occurs to me that giraffe should properly be included as well. The toughness of the wildebeest is legendary; it seems they have a slow nervous system, and while they're hardly bulletproof, they do seem impervious to shock. Zebra are often underrated both as a game animal and in terms of difficulty to put down—except by those who have experience with them, of course. Professional hunters seem to lament over running gun battles with wounded zebras more than with any other species. Why this should be I'm not altogether certain; the zebra is big, strong, and very tough, and that's a partial answer. I think there's also something in the natural camouflage of the stripes that confuses the aiming point. In any case, shot placement and bullet performance must be near-perfect on Africa's striped horses.

I have never seen a giraffe shot, nor do I care to. However, these huge creatures do become overpopulous and must be harvested in some areas. Though it's hardly a hunting trophy, the very size of the giraffe makes it a wonderful meat source that should be utilized. Few sport hunters take them, but occasionally there's a sensible reason. On such a huge beast, it goes without saying that shot placement is critical; I understand that attempting to cleanly drop one of these seemingly gentle giants with a body shot is quite a trick!

We can leave the giraffe out of the normal safari mixed bag, but zebra and wildebeest will often be included. Unlike hunting the more glamorous of the large plains species, it's usually not terribly difficult to get a shot at an acceptable specimen of either wildebeest or zebra. But when you get that shot, you'd best do it right or you may wind up with a long, drawn-out mess on your hands. Remember that wounded animals will almost always be counted on your license, and even if they aren't you're obligated to follow as long as any chance remains for recovery. I lost nearly two days of hunting one time when a partner wounded a wildebeest. We eventually got the animal, but timing on a safari can be critical. Perhaps the time spent on that wildebeest is what prevented me from getting a leopard that trip—or my partner from getting a roan. Perhaps not, but it would have been much simpler if the shot on that wildebeest had been placed just slightly better.

So far, you'll note that I've been speaking of bullet placement and performance rather than caliber. There is such a thing as an inadequate caliber, to be sure. But regardless of caliber, the bullet simply must be properly aimed so as to reach the vitals—and it must be constructed well enough so it can reach those vitals.

We are fortunate to have wonderful bullets available to us today. The over-the-counter stuff is damned good, as are component bullets from major manufacturers. Better still, even downright amazing, are the semi-custom bullets from makers such as Lee Reid (Swift) and Jack Carter (Trophy Bonded). Another even newer "wonder bullet" is Randy Brooks's (Barnes) "X-bullet." If you're bound and determined to use relatively light rifles on animals in this "large plains game" class, you *need* the kind of bullets these folks make. They are so good they can, in effect, take a cartridge a step up into another power class.

Even with the best bullets in the world, there are limits; the various 6mms and .25s simply should not be used on the likes of wildebeest, zebra, oryx, and sable. But with carefully selected bullets and a cool marksman willing to wait for a good shot, cartridges such as the .270 Winchester, any of the 7mms, and the non-belted .30s can do a great job. I've made one-shot kills with the .30-06 on zebra, wildebeest, oryx, and sable with no problems whatever; likewise with the 7mm Remington Magnum. And I've had the same species require multiple hits from a .375. No two animals are alike in their reaction to receiving a bullet—but if that bullet is properly directed and makes its way to the vitals, the eventual outcome is certain.

Still and all, when we get into this class of very large and/or very tough plains game, I prefer a bit more power than the .30-06/7mm magnum and lighter cartridges can deliver. I should say, too, that I'm not overly sensitive to recoil, and I'm a trophy hunter. I believe in shot placement, but proper shot placement can come from any angle *if* the cartridge, the shooter, and the bullet are up to the task. If I have an opportunity to take a very fine specimen of the animal I'm hunting, I want to be able to take the shot even if the angle is bad.

Back in 1985, I was hunting kudu along the Limpopo River, and we got onto a wonderful bull, seen clearly for just an instant before he bolted. I'm not very lucky with big kudu, and he was better than anything I've seen before or since. We were specifically hunting kudu, and I'd been carrying my .375. But that day I decided, for some forgotten reason, to carry my .30-06. We tracked him and we jumped him, and then we tracked him some more until we jumped him again. We were in riverine growth, and although we jumped him several times, all we could see were flashes of gray and his splayed, deep-cut running tracks.

I got a shot just once. We caught him at the near edge of a small clearing, not a dozen yards across. He waited until we were nearly on him before he bolted, and when he went he headed straight across that small clearing. I can still see his corkscrew horns laid back along his flanks, and the white tail so much like that of our Virginia deer. With the .375, he was a dead kudu. But it was late in the day, too late, and with the .30-06 there was no shot at all. I put the crosshairs square on his rear and hoped he would give me a hint of ribs to shoot at. But he covered those dozen yards without the slightest swerve, and we never saw him again.

The various .300 magnums are excellent tools for the larger antelopes—especially with 200-grain spitzer bullets in open country and 220-grain bullets in heavier cover. The old .300 H&H is probably still the most popular .300 magnum in Africa, but both the Winchester and Weatherby will do just as well or better with good bullets. The last time I took my .300 Weatherby to Africa, I loaded 200-grain Nosler semi-spitzers as fast as I could push them, and it was an absolutely devastating rifle. And yet, even with a rifle of unquestioned adequacy, you never know for sure what's going to happen when you squeeze the trigger.

I got a chance shot at a roan in the hills far above the Luangwa Valley. A herd crossed in front of us, running hard, then stopped on a burned-off slope 200 yards away. We picked out the bull, and I dropped into a sitting position and fired as quickly as I could. Absolutely nothing happened. The animal had been quartering away, and now he took one small step and quartered to me. I shot again with the same hold, and he broke into a heart-shot death run, folding up within 60 yards. Funny thing is, the wound channels from the two 200-grain Noslers crisscrossed in the heart.

In spite of that roan's refusal to succumb to the inevitable, the .300 magnums with good, reasonably heavy-for-caliber bullets (180 grains at a minimum) are magnificent choices for the large plains game—especially in open country. Nobody could argue rationally against their use, except possibly on eland.

Personally, though, I prefer to go up another step to the .338 Winchester/.340 Weatherby/8mm Remington/8x68S/.350 Rigby/.358 Norma class of cartridge. The flat-shooting capabilities are so close to the .300s as to be indistinguishable, depending on the bullets chosen, and yet the added frontal area and greater bullet weight combine to offer a very real advantage in killing power—if not in energy on paper.

For the American hunter, I think the .338 and .340 Weatherby are the most sensible choices, since the bullet selection is easily the best. But all of the cartridges mentioned, plus several others of their ilk, will perform perfectly on African game—and offer a marvelous level of versatility that a lighter rifle cannot deliver.

My longest shot on African game—a mountain reedbuck at well over 400 yards—was made with a .338 Winchester Magnum. There was a bit of luck involved there; bad luck for the reedbuck and good luck for me. Six years later, in the same mountain range with a different rifle also chambered to .338, I made what I think was my best shot on African game—a single well-considered shot at a tiny Vaal rhebok at something over 300 yards. Neither of those animals, obviously, is part of our "large plains game" group. But on the two trips where those shots were made, the same .338s accounted for wildebeest, gemsbok, sable, zebra, and kudu. And another hunter borrowed one of the .338s to use on a lion—which it handled very nicely.

I have personally never shot an eland with a .338, but I have seen them shot very satisfactorily with that caliber. In a pinch, there is no question that the .338—and the other cartridges of its class—could do the trick nicely on buffalo. However, eland (and giraffe) are technically "large plains game." Buffalo and lion are not. And in several African countries, the .375 H&H is the minimum allowed by law for all these diverse species.

As much as I love the .338, it would be difficult to pick one over the .375. The .375 is the cartridge I have used to shoot all of my eland, and additionally many zebra and wildebeest, kudu and oryx, my best sable—and a whole host of lesser animals. Not to mention buffalo, lion and such.

It will not shoot as flat as the .338s, certainly not as flat as the .300s and the likes of the 7mm magnums. But it will shoot adequately flat for almost all African hunting—and, as it has since 1912, it will absolutely flatten game. And it has wonderful bullets available.

On a South African hunt in 1987, I decided it was finally time to collect some of the oddities. One fine day we drove to a farm way out in the Karoo to hunt white springbok and bontebok. For some reason, despite their reputation, these bontebok were spooky as hell; shooting was very long on both animals. The only scoped rifle I had was a .375, but it grouped well with Trophy Bonded 240-grain spitzer Bearclaws, a screamer of a little bullet that really flattens out the .375. It wasn't easy, but we got the job done. Earlier in that trip I used the same bullet on a marvelous Cape kudu that appeared high on a ridge.

Years before, with a single-shot Ruger .375, my old friend Ben Nolte and I sat on an overhanging rock in Namibia's Orongo Mountains. Below us, straight down nearly 100 yards, was a herd of Hartmann's mountain zebra. On that day the bullet I was using was at the other end of the .375 spectrum—a 350-grain Barnes ultra-heavyweight. Finally the stallion identified himself by his antics, and I shot him from the top of one shoulder to the bottom of the opposite one. Without hitting spine, zebra are almost impossible to put down, but this one was driven down onto the rocks by the impact—and he never moved.

A rifle for large plains game need not be a tackdriver; animals in this group present a large vital zone. However, the rifle cannot be inaccurate, since several of these animals are commonly taken at very long range. It absolutely must be scoped, not only for taking gemsbok across an open pan, but also for picking out an aiming point on a black sable in black shadow. Again, though, we're dealing with large animals. A simple, rugged fixed 4X scope is a fine choice, possibly the very best. Other good options include variables in the 1.5-6X or 1.75-5X range.

The most logical action choice for such a rifle is the bolt-action, with its caliber determined somewhat by the terrain and the *upper end* of game size and toughness. For instance, in very open country with almost no chance of using the rifle on dangerous game, a .300 Weatherby might be a good choice. But if eland is a primary quarry *and* the rifle might be employed against buffalo or lion, then one of the .375 bores (H&H or Weatherby) might be a better choice.

The Ruger single-shot is available in several chamberings that fit nicely into our "large plains game" arena, and this might be the natural habitat of a single-shot African rifle, rather than for use on dangerous game. In somewhat thicker cover, a very good case could be made for a scoped double, a .375, 9.3, or perhaps an old-timer like the .360 No. 2. However, if the same rifle is to be used on smaller plains game, as is often the case, then the accuracy of a bolt-action or single-shot might be called for.

The various .416s available today all shoot plenty flat enough to be considered for use on large plains game, and with its great velocity the .416 Weatherby could legitimately be considered a long-range cartridge. The over-.40s would indeed be effective on eland, and when I hunt for Derby eland I will probably choose a .416 in some persuasion. There is, however, no real reason to look beyond the .375 for use even on the largest of plains game. And under many, perhaps most, circumstances, the hunter will be better served by a lighter, faster caliber.

# Chapter 26

# Leopard

The leopard is part of Africa's Big Five of dangerous game, and dangerous he is, indeed. However, he is hardly *big*—in the sense that a rhino, elephant, buffalo, or even lion is. When selecting rifles, cartridges, and especially bullets for leopard, it's important to keep in mind that, although he is a deadly efficient predator, the leopard is a very small animal.

A big male will weigh 150 pounds, about the same as a large impala ram. I suspect most leopards taken by hunters weigh a third less, say 90 to 110 pounds. An occasional monster leopard is taken, of course. My hunting partner, Ron Norman, shot a very big male leopard late one evening on the Sabi River in Rhodesia. They couldn't find it before it grew dark, so had no choice but to look in the morning.

The cat was still alive when they found it, but very sick, and it had bled tremendously. On hunter/rancher Roger Whittall's grain scale, the cat weighed some 225 pounds, one of the heaviest *verified* leopards I know of. A leopard like that is a virtual freak of nature, a huge specimen—and is still a good deal smaller than a big Rocky Mountain mule deer or an average black bear. And it's clearly much smaller than even a modest lion, let alone a Cape buffalo.

Now, I'm not sure there's such a thing as being over-gunned, especially on animals that can hurt you, your tracker, or the next local who happens along. But with leopard it's easy to be over-bulleted; a tough bullet, designed for animals several times larger, may just burn through a leopard, doing little damage. That's fine if the hit is perfect; a leopard succumbs rapidly to a well-placed heart or lung shot (what doesn't?). But if the hit is off by just a bit, he'll show some of the nine lives cats are famous for.

I'm not very proud of it, and I'm not sure I've ever written about it before, but here's as good a place as any. I lost a leopard about a dozen years ago. Barrie Duckworth and I had put up a *machan* for a cattle-killing cat, and in the full moonlight a magnificent leopard sauntered into the clearing. I could see him well against the short brown grass, and the .375 absolutely flattened him. We slapped each other on the back, then waited a few moments. Nothing.

We were halfway out of the machan when the cat woke up, and before I could climb back up and bring my rifle to bear he was gone. Needless to say, we never found him. The blood petered out in 200 yards, and the brush was thick. We even tried the old trick of driving cattle through the area; they'll spook at the scent of wounded leopard every time. But that leopard had kept on going.

It's obvious that I could have, and should have, made a better shot. But, all things considered, it's also obvious that the big .375 bullet burned through without opening up, passing close enough to the spine to momentarily knock the cat down and out.

I'm not altogether certain what bullet I was using. I do know that American Airlines threw a fit over the amount of ammunition (and reloading components) in my bags, most of it for the beleaguered Rhodesians. Almost all of my own ammunition was left sitting at the ticket counter at LAX, and I managed to buy a box of RWS .375s in Bulawayo, loaded with the hard TUG bullet. I also scrounged a handful of .375s from professional hunter Hilton Nichol. My own .375 ammo had been loaded with 270-grain Hornady roundnose bullets, pre-Interlock. That bullet would have opened. The TUG bullet, ideal for very large game, would not have.

The .375 H&H is a great leopard rifle, to be sure, and it's probably used by more hunting clients to take more leopards than any other single cartridge. There are reasons for its widespread use, some good and some not so good. In some countries it's the minimum caliber allowed by law for use on dangerous game—and that's a very good reason to use it. Another reason is less logical: The leopard is a dangerous animal, and the .375 fires a big bullet that should do a bang-up job of scotching the potential danger. That doesn't wash very well. Consider that an impala or gazelle shot with a .375 is likely to have two small, neat holes, little interior damage, and will probably carry on for some distance before falling over. A leopard is essentially the same size, and provides the same resistance to the bullet.

If the .375 is the minimum caliber allowed by law, by all means it should be used. But not with a tough, controlled-expansion bullet of the sort you would want for lion, buffalo, or eland. Instead, consider taking a handful of handloaded 235-grain Speers or 240-grain Bearclaws, or 270-grain A-Square Lion Loads. These will expand, even in a leopard. At the very least, plan on using a relatively fast 270-grain bullet like Remington's Core-Lokt roundnose or Winchester's Power Point—*not* the slower 300-grain bullets.

If the local game laws don't obligate you to use a .375 or larger, consider using your light or medium rifle. I submit that a .30-06, 7mm magnum, or .300 magnum with a good expanding bullet will typically expend more energy inside a leopard-size animal than a larger caliber, and with similar bullet placement will dispatch the animal more quickly. Forgetting for just a moment that screwing up on a leopard can be extremely hazardous to your health, there is no question over the adequacy of a 165- or 180-grain .30-caliber bullet, a 160- or 175-grain 7mm bullet, or even a 130- or 150-grain .270 bullet on a 150-pound animal.

I shot a nice leopard on the point of the right shoulder with a 210-grain Nosler from a .338 Winchester Magnum. The bullet exited the left hip, and the cat dropped without any further movement. In general, I quit using the light bullets in the .338, but based on that performance I'd go back to it in a heartbeat for leopard.

When it comes down to it, though, any discussion of adequate cartridges for a 150-pound animal is ridiculous; the .243 would do a wonderful job. It's really a question of bullet placement, and since most leopards are taken over bait, that bullet must often be placed by making your shot in the poorest light imaginable. A good scope is thus almost more important than the caliber of rifle.

Ranges are generally very short; 50 yards is about average, and 100 yards would be an unusually long distance from blind to bait. The leopard may come at four in the afternoon, and on rare occasions he may turn out to be a morning feeder. But most of the time, if he comes in the daylight at all, he will come in the very last twilight. A proper bait arrangement will silhouette the feeding cat against the sky to maximize whatever light remains—but the cats have a way of not cooperating. The best insurance for leopard is the brightest scope that can be had.

Magnification isn't important. In fact, considering the short range, it isn't particularly desirable—and low-powered scopes tend to gather more light than those with higher magnification. Although they're very large and clumsy, the German scopes with 56mm objectives, made for shooting boar at night, are the ultimate for leopard hunting. I must admit I don't like them; they must be mounted so high that I find them most uncomfortable to shoot with. But they sure do gather light.

Good compromise scopes are the 4x40 and 4x42 scopes readily available in the U.S. today. And of course, make sure you pick a highly visible reticle with a clear aiming point that can't be confused in dim light. As I've said, I prefer the plex-type reticle; the post-and-crosshair and German reticles are confusing to me. A bold dot with crosshairs would work just fine, but thin crosshairs alone should be avoided.

The illuminated crosshairs, as marketed by Bushnell and others, might be a good way to go; I've used them on black bear in very bad light, and there's nothing worse than a dark animal at last light. The projected-light aiming devices, like Tasco's Pro-Point and the Swedish Aimpoint, could be very good options for leopard, but they're a bit tricky for my taste. I think I'd just as soon stick with a low-powered scope that gathers a lot of light—and hope the cat comes in while you can still see.

In some areas, it is legal and widely accepted to shoot leopards after dark with an artificial light. If it's legal, I don't have any problem with the practice, but it does change the shooting situation markedly. Lack of light isn't a problem, but when the torch comes on, the shot must be taken very quickly—and of course it has to be in the right place. Again, a low-powered scope with a highly visible reticle is the way to go.

Botswana, in many ways my favorite African hunting ground, has some funny game laws. One of them prohibits baiting, apparently because of concerns over meat utilization and waste. It's unfortunate, because Botswana is marvelous leopard country. Out in the Kalahari, where Bushman trackers can follow anything, several safari companies conduct highly successful tracking leopard hunts. Typically, such a hunt starts when reasonably fresh leopard tracks of an appropriate size are found. The trackers run on the spoor in relays while the hunter follows close behind in a vehicle. Eventually, the leopard is jumped, sometimes two or three times before a shot is possible. And then he charges.

Now, it should be said that this hunting method is also technically illegal, since it involves use of the vehicle. It might be possible to do it without a vehicle, but only if the hunter were prepared to run 20 miles in soft sand and *then* stop a charge. Legalities aside, the use of the vehicle, if anything, makes the hunt *more* dangerous. It gives the leopard a highly concentrated and visible target, and if the leopard gets into the truck with you (which has happened more than once) it's almost impossible to shoot.

Exactly that happened to video cameraman Chip Payne, a good friend of mine and fortunately a cool hand. Somehow he was able to exchange his camera for a .375 and shoot the leopard, but not before the young man sharing the back of the truck with him was seriously mauled.

Something that handles very fast and hits very hard would be ideal for such a hunt; another friend of mine, John Hutcheson, went on such a hunt and, as happens about 90 percent of the time, got a charge. He used a big double, I think a .470, and stopped the cat cold. A big double is enticing for such a hunt, but there are three problems: First, the bullets might be too hard to do any real damage. Second, if a vehicle is used I don't relish bouncing around in a truck with a fully loaded double. Third, if a vehicle is *not* used, nobody could carry a heavy double on such a hunt.

A shotgun would be ideal *if* you got a charge. But, if you're fast enough, there's a very good chance of a stationary shot at 40 or 50 yards—*before* the charge. I think this is a good place for something on the order of a .458 or .458 Lott specially sighted-in with handloaded 350- or 400-grain bullets (or Federal's 350-grain factory load). A Marlin in .45-70 or even an old Winchester 71 in .450 Alaskan, loaded with similar bullets, flat-pointed and pushed as fast as possible, would be another ideal choice.

Whether to use a scope or open sights on a deal like that is, I think, up to the individual. Whichever you shoot fastest and best with would be the right choice. I would personally use a very low-powered scope; I know I shoot more quickly and much more accurately with one, and I shoot a scope with both eyes open—a most important consideration for stopping a charge with a scoped rifle.

When it comes to following up a wounded leopard, there's little argument—a shotgun loaded with coarse buckshot is the way to go. Whether you accompany the professional hunter is entirely up to him; if he says no, don't take it personally. Properly, it's his job—and it's generally a one-man job. He simply can't be worrying about anything except the leopard, or somebody is more likely to get hurt. If he asks you to go with him, take it as a compliment and by all means go—but mind you don't shoot anyone in the melee. That's the real danger of following a wounded leopard.

The best course of all is to make absolutely certain the shot is placed well the first time. If it's placed right, it really doesn't much matter what rifle you used—and there won't be any argument over who carries the shotgun for a follow-up. Instead, you can all gather around and admire one of Africa's most magnificent creatures.

# Chapter 27

# Lion

For me, the lion is the ultimate African trophy. Of the entire Big Five, he's the only one that I'm unashamedly terrified of. With all the rest, I'm more than willing to concede a healthy measure of caution and respect. But the lion makes my palms sweat and my chest go cold.

I'm not altogether sure why this should be; quite possibly it has nothing to do with the animal at all, but something deep in my own psyche. All children have nightmares, and in some kids' bad dreams they're chased by monsters, spiders, the neighbor's dog, you name it. As a child, John Wootters had bad dreams of elephants. He doesn't know why, but he knows he grew up with a pathological horror of pachyderms. He finally cured it when, as a middle-aged man, he shot a fine tusker. I'm not conscious of a deep-seated childhood fear of lions—but I do know that I'm inordinately afraid of them today.

Over the course of several safaris, I hunted lion for 105 days before I shot my first one. In the course of those hunts I had plenty of time to think about my fear, and I had a number of close encounters with lionesses and maneless males. Since then, I've shot several more—certainly more than my share, and enough that I don't care if I shoot another. The fear has never gone away, and I've decided it's not a bad thing. It doesn't seem to prevent me from getting the job done—and the heightened sensations when I'm in close contact with the great cats are a palpable thing.

On the other hand, it isn't necessary to be as frightened of lions as I am. It's merely damned important to treat them with plenty of respect. A lion is most unlikely to weigh 500 pounds outside of a zoo; a mature wild male lion is more likely to weigh 350 to 400 pounds—which is still a lot of cat. He may or may not be the King of Beasts, but he is the king of African predators, with no enemies save man. Sometimes timid by day, he is bold by night and twilight, and he may or may not have learned to fear human-kind; if he just came from a park, he may hold people in contempt rather than fear.

The lion is amazingly fast, and as unpredictable as a housecat. Often he seems cowardly, but if he's hurt and he knows what hurt him, he may decide to do something about it. If he comes, only death will stop him. The leopard, even if badly wounded, has a tendency to leap from one to another of a hunting party. He usually will inflict horribly painful but somewhat super-ficial wounds on several people, eventually giving someone an opening to finish the job. The lion will finish what he starts, and he's armed with the equipment to make very short work of a puny man.

Lions are generally taken in one of three ways: over bait, by tracking, and during chance encounters. In the first instance—and sometimes during chance encounters—the lion is generally undisturbed and unaware, and may be taken very successfully with a relatively light rifle. A .300 with a 200-grain bullet, a .30-06 with a good 180-grainer, a 7mm with a 175-grain bullet, even a .270 with a 150-grain bullet, will without question do a number on a lion. But in most countries, the legal minimum for hunting lion is .375—and there are lots of good reasons.

Although raw power will not make up for poor shot placement, there are varying degrees of *good* shot placement. A light rifle leaves no margin for error, even on an undisturbed cat. And a cat with his adrenalin up must not be merely killed; he must be *stopped*.

In spite of minimum-caliber laws, a number of lions are taken annually during chance encounters while the hunters are carrying light rifles. A lion asleep on an anthill or strolling across the veld is no real problem to knock over, and as hard as good lions are to come by, few professional hunters would sacrifice a golden opportunity because of a few thousandths of an inch in bore diameter. Most of the time, if a decent stalk is possible and the client shoots reasonably well, there's no problem.

Should a problem arise, however, the light rifle isn't enough gun to keep you out of trouble. It wasn't for George Grey nearly 80 years ago, and it isn't today. Truth is, I'm not altogether certain the great .375 is enough gun if things go completely to hell—but it's a giant step in the right direction.

The .375 H&H is *the* classic lion gun. It's available with wonderful bullets, and it's perfectly at home with a low-powered scope for early morning shooting. However, I should say that, except for brain shots, I have yet to see a one-shot kill on a lion with a .375. I have seen one-shot kills with .416s and .458s.

Even so, the .375 (and I'll include the near-identical 9.3x64 as well as the .375 and .378 Weatherby) is the traditional choice for lion hunting—and it's a good one. Accurate, easy to shoot, and plenty adequate in power, the .375 is just plain hard to beat for the big cats.

A rifle for a baited lion should without question wear a scope. The vast majority of baited lions are shot just as dawn breaks, after the pride has fed most of the night and is lounging around with full bellies. Shortly after dawn—or, with hunter-wise lions, before—the lions will steal into heavy cover to sleep off their meal. The idea is to shoot the lion on the bait, undisturbed. A scope that gathers in plenty of light is an absolute must.

We had a pride feeding on a hippo along the Luangwa River. Before dawn we stalked carefully into a wall of grass about 30 yards short of the hippo carcass. When we arrived, it was still too dark to see, but the lions were there—we could tell because the hyenas were standing off a little way making a tremendous outcry.

Finally, it started to gray up just a little. Professional hunter Bill Illing-worth removed a plug of grass and took a careful look, and on his signal I did the same. Directly in front of the bait, just 25 yards from us, lay a lion and lioness—both just dimly seen forms. It was still too dark, but shooting light was just minutes away. I waited, and when the light changed almost imperceptibly I slowly moved the .375 into position. But it was already too late; the lioness remained where she had been, motionless—but the lion was gone. Sometimes, as then, getting a lion or not getting a lion is a matter of being able to see to shoot just a few seconds earlier. In a baited situation, it's possible that a heavier rifle might flatten a cat with more authority than a .375—but there's really no reason for a larger rifle, especially since few hunters shoot larger rifles well enough to have any business tackling lion with them. In a chance encounter, all the recommendations in the world are useless; fate alone dictates what rifle you're carrying. That's why, if lion is on the menu, I never get very far from a .375. It will do everything a safari rifle needs to do on the various plains species—and if you happen to run into a good cat, it will handle that as well.

A tracking lion hunt is a different situation. Sometimes you can follow the tracks to the pride's lying-up place, find the male, and get into shooting position without the lions being the wiser. All too often, though, the lions become aware they're being followed before you're able to close the deal. Then it starts getting dangerous because lions don't like to be pushed around.

In Botswana, where tracking lion hunts are the norm, a couple of hunters seem to get hammered every year. Elsewhere, a hunter being mauled is a much rarer occurrence. I've heard it said that "Botswana lions are especially cheeky," but I don't buy that; a lion is a lion. Rather, I think it's the danger inherent in tracking.

A scoped .375 is a perfectly acceptable rifle for a tracking hunt. A scoped .416 might be a better choice yet. Just last year, I bumped into a wonderful lion while buffalo hunting with a .416 Rigby. Quarters were awfully close, and I was happy I wasn't carrying a lesser rifle. But if I were to undertake a serious tracking lion hunt, I think I'd carry a big double loaded with softpoints I knew I could rely on. In the thick cover lions generally lie up in, chances of a shot beyond 75 yards are remote—and the chances of a shot at a third that distance are very good. A scope would be a definite aid in picking out a tawny form in yellow grass, but when things happen with lions they happen very fast. The fast second shot from a double could be important. Let's put it this way—the next time I walk into lions at 15 yards I want my .470 in my hands!

Pretty much the same goes for following wounded lions. With a scoped rifle, there might be a better chance of picking out a hidden lion and getting off a shot before he charges or moves on. But in the event of a charge, you want all the raw power you can muster. I would choose a double, since I have one and I'm comfortable with it, but a big-bore bolt-action in experienced hands is every bit as effective.

Choice of bullets for lion merits a short discussion. It should, obviously, be a softpoint. A solid will deliver the penetration you want, but the lack of shock and tissue damage can get you dead. The lion is not a huge animal, so the softpoint need not be as heavily constructed as it should be for buffalo. However, the lion's shoulder bones are relatively stout, and they can eat up a bullet that's too soft, is pushed too fast, or malfunctions. And it happens.

*Hunting* magazine's Publisher, Ken Elliott, had a factory .375 softpoint blow up on a lion's shoulder some years ago. I haven't exactly had a bullet fail, but I had a funny thing happen several years ago. I shot a lion in the head at extremely close range with a .375, and of course it killed him very dead. Good thing it was a head shot, though; the bullet vaporized in the skull—no exit, and it didn't penetrate beyond the back of the head.

Bullets I like are Winchester Power Points and Remington Core-Lokt in factory .375, and there's no reason why Federal's loadings won't be excellent as well. With component bullets, it's hard to make a mistake. The Swift A-Frame bullet and the Trophy Bonded Bearclaw are magnificent, and Nosler's .375 will be, too. And there aren't any flies on the .375s from Hornady, Sierra, and Speer.

Choice is more limited in .416 and larger, but the bullets are generally very fine. If I were using a big bolt-action, I'd perhaps pick a lighter-than-normal bullet of good construction. Jack Carter makes a 400-grain solid-shank Bearclaw in .458 that just might be the finest lion bullet made in that caliber, and Speer's 400-grain flat-point would do a real job as well. In a double, of course, you're pretty much obligated to use the bullet the rifle is regulated for. As mentioned earlier, though, George Caswell has been shooting the light .458 bullets in his new .450 No. 2 rifles. Now that has potential as a lion gun!

Day in and day out, though, you can't go wrong by hunting lion with a good .375 that you shoot well. But I do believe the .416s are a bit more effective. If you shoot a bigger gun well, there's absolutely no reason not to use it. I've already stated how I feel about messing around with lions!

# Chapter 28

# Buffalo

In the Swahili of East Africa they call him *m'bogo*. In most of southern Africa he's known as *inyati*. Hunters generally just call him "buffalo," but they're usually referring to the southern Cape buffalo, largest of the four African buffalo. This is the one that is hunted throughout southern and eastern Africa. Somewhere in the Sudan, a subtle transition begins; the buffalo begin to get smaller in both body and horn, and an occasional animal is red rather than black. Hunting them is the same, but we call these animals "Nile buffalo" rather than Cape.

Farther west yet, across the savanna zone that separates the Sahara from the forests of West and Central Africa, is found what is called the north-western buffalo. Smaller yet, evenly divided between red and black, these animals are a true transition from the familiar Cape buffalo to the largely unfamiliar dwarf forest buffalo. Found strictly in that forest zone from West Africa south to Angola and across Zaire into the southern forests of the C.A.R., the dwarf, or red forest, buffalo is fully a third smaller than a southern Cape buffalo; a big forest bull might weigh 1,000 pounds, while a Cape buffalo bull will weigh 1,500 pounds or more.

Few hunters know the forest buffalo; I certainly do not. It's said that what they lack in size they make up for in short temper. Short their temper may or may not be—but in the dense forests they inhabit the ranges they're shot from will be very short indeed. In spite of the difference in size, I would rate the caliber requirements for buffalo the same across the board, since the average cover becomes more dense as the buffalo grow smaller.

Hunters with far more experience than mine have rated the buffalo as the most dangerous of Africa's big game. All of the Big Five are certainly very dangerous; which of them is the most hazardous to hunt is a very subjective ranking dependent mostly on one's own experience. I am most frightened of lions, but in the close cover where today's poacher-harried elephant are hunted, I think they must be considered the most dangerous. As much as I respect the buffalo and enjoy hunting him, my own limited experience doesn't show him to be nearly as dangerous as lion or elephant.

Though I have now shot several dozen buffalo, I have not had a major problem with one. Yet it happens; my stepson caught a dead-serious charge on his first buffalo, and only through luck was serious injury avoided. Just a couple of weeks ago, in the Chobe area of Botswana, a group of citizen hunters followed us on the spoor of a buffalo herd, proceeding on after we had taken two bulls. A couple of hours later, they carried their leader into our camp, seriously and almost fatally gored just under the heart. In my stepson's case, he hit his bull badly with a .375—adequate rifle, poor shot placement. The local hunter just mentioned hit a buffalo somewhere with a .30-06 softpoint, then got hammered on the follow-up. Poor shot placement, undoubtedly—*and* an inadequate rifle.

I have never shot a buffalo with a caliber smaller than the .375 H&H. In most cases, it would be illegal, but if it were legal I would have no real qualms about shooting undisturbed buffalo in open country with anything from a 7x57 on up—provided, on a light rifle, that the bullet was a very reliable solid or extremely tough controlled-expansion softpoint and I could be absolutely certain of shot placement.

Actually, it can be singularly uneventful to kill an undisturbed, unwounded buffalo. And that's the way it's supposed to be. All too much is written—and these days, shown on video—of buffalo charges and derring-do. Some first-time clients, believing all that bunk, are downright disappointed if they don't get charged at least once. Keep in mind, first, that charges rarely happen unless somebody screws up badly; and second, that it's the professional hunter's job to keep things like that from happening!

Yet, with buffalo, there is that special spice of potential danger—and it's very real. Once you open the ballgame with a Cape buffalo, somebody is going finish it—you or him. In my view, the idea is to open and close the game neatly and efficiently, with minimum mess and fuss. That requires calm, deliberate shooting and careful shot placement, nothing more and nothing less. And make no mistake—if you screw it up, things will get very exciting in short order, and they can get extremely messy besides.

Undisturbed, a buffalo will succumb to a heart or lung shot from a .375 (or a .30-06, for that matter) just like any other very large animal. Typically he will receive the bullet and run like hell—until he runs out of blood. The problem comes if that first bullet fails to either wreck the heart or thoroughly perforate *both* lungs. Then, with adrenalin pumping, that placid, grazing beast becomes another animal altogether. In fact, from my limited experience, he becomes the toughest animal on earth, pound for pound, to bring down.

In my view, that's why it's wisest to use a totally adequate rifle for the first shot on buffalo. After all, if that first shot doesn't do what needs to be done, the next half-dozen might not, either. The literature of Africana is full of tales of buffalo that took a dozen .375s, .416s, .458s, .470s, and such to bring down. It happens, there's no question about it. But it cannot happen if the first bullet does its work. And that's why, regardless of the cartridge chosen, it must be remembered that shot placement remains the critical issue on buffalo—as much as on anything else, and perhaps more so.

At this point I must admit that I'm ambivalent regarding choice of rifles for buffalo. I have hunted them with a wide assortment of rifles, ranging in caliber from .375 to .500 Nitro-Express, and in foot-pounds from the .375 up to the .460 Weatherby. There is a big difference between hitting a buffalo with a .375 and hitting one with a .416; the animal won't go as far when hit well with the .416. And there's an equally big difference between a .416

and a .470, .500, .458 Lott, or .460 Weatherby—*provided the shot placement is equally good.*

There's the rub; the strength of a buffalo is unbelievable, and a poor shot with even the largest of sporting rifles is just as big a disaster as with a popgun. Given a good hit, the more powerful rifles will achieve quicker results, but without good shot placement, raw power counts for nothing.

For general use, the buffalo rifle should be scoped. Shots at 50 yards in heavy thorn are average, but shots at 100 to 125 yards across openings aren't unusual. And even in the thick stuff, you're trying to pick out an aiming point on a black animal in black shadow. The scope will help. The heavy rifle is often unscoped, and whether it is or not, the average guy just plain shoots better with a scoped .375 than with a bigger rifle—like it or not.

If I'm serious about buffalo hunting, I like to carry an open-sighted heavy rifle myself, but I'll ask one of the trackers to carry a scope-sighted .375, all set to go with a softpoint on top and solids underneath. Quite often, we've caught a herd in an open glade, and it's been farther than I cared to try with open sights. If you're hunting lone bulls, or a small bachelor herd, it often isn't a problem to close in, so long as the wind is steady. But in big herds it can be almost impossible to get as close as you like—and even if you do, the bull you want is apt to be on the far side of the herd.

That's when it's nice to be able to hand off the big gun for an accurate scoped .375 (or, where legal, even a smaller rifle). You take a good rest, wait until the bull stands broadside, make sure there isn't another buffalo behind (this, too, is easier with the scope), and place the shot just so.

"Just so" is one of three places. If you're a gambler, you'll go for the neck shot. I won't; if it's far enough that I feel better with the scope, it's too damn far to try a neck shot. The second shot, the one that's recommended most often, is square on the center of the shoulder, about a third of a body width up. That shot will penetrate, and usually break, the shoulder and go on into the heart. A solid bullet will keep on going through the other shoulder, while a softpoint will usually lodge in the off shoulder. If the shot is placed ideally, a solid will break both shoulders and drop the bull. However, I personally prefer a softpoint; the larger wound channel seems to take effect more quickly, while with a solid the shoulder bones are penetrated rather than smashed. On a shoulder shot there's little likelihood that a softpoint will overpenetrate and hit an unseen animal on the far side.

That shoulder shot is extremely effective, but it is a bit tricky. The heart is a relatively small target, and it doesn't take much error for the bullet to slide over, under, or to either side. In any case, the wound is terrible and, except for a brisket shot too far forward, eventually fatal. But I suspect many of the horror stories of buffalo charging and requiring multiple hits to finish originate from a slight error on a shoulder shot. And it may not be the shooter's fault; the bullet could become misdirected slightly after impacting the heavy shoulder bone.

The third option is one I've been using a lot the past few years, and so far I've found it 100 percent deadly. That's the simple, garden-variety lung shot that you might use on a much smaller animal. It is not as spectacular as a perfectly placed shoulder shot where everything goes right; there is no chance that the animal will drop to the shot. However, it offers the largest target area, the greatest margin for error, and is absolutely fatal—just as it is on a whitetail deer. The aiming point is just behind the shoulder, halfway up the body. There's no heavy bone to worry about, but you do need to worry about what lies behind—a .375 softpoint *may* exit, but a .416 or larger almost surely will.

A good lung shot actually seems to take effect more quickly on buffalo than a heart shot. Why this should be I can't say, but the last three buffalo bulls I've shot in this fashion—one with a .375 Swift softpoint, one with a .470 Kynoch softpoint, and one with a .416 Swift softpoint—all died within a matter of a very few yards, between 25 and 60. I've had properly heart-shot buffalo go much farther.

Wherever you choose to shoot your buffalo, it's critical that you hit him right. I've traded a big open-sighted rifle for a smaller scoped rifle too often to recommend the former without serious reservations. The .375 is, I think, a very sensible minimum—and a bigger gun, if you can handle it, will provide more impressive results. But if you choose a bigger gun, it, too, should wear a scope. The 100-yard shot, or the shot in heavy shadow, is just too common to overlook—and an open-sighted rifle is a poor choice for such shooting. And of course, there's also the problem of picking a path through brush with open sights. As I mentioned in a previous chapter, no matter how big the bullet may be, it doesn't take much brush to deflect it.

Of course, if a wounded buffalo charges—coming straight at you—a lung or shoulder shot is out of the question and of no use anyway. Since the massive boss shields a large portion of the buffalo's skull and there isn't much facial area (nor will the withers present a useful target), the normal thing to do is send a bullet straight up the beast's nose. Sometimes another option—but only for a fast, extremely adept rifleman with cool nerves—is to fade to one side a bit and hold just under the curve of the horn.

I've had wonderful fun hunting buffalo with various big doubles; as Ian MacFarlane told me one day, "You just feel good about shooting something with a rifle like that." But if I had to pick a perfect rifle for hunting buffalo, it would be that rarity—a double from .450/.400 up that wore a claw-mounted scope.

I would not choose a single-shot for buffalo; even with the very best shot placement, only through blind luck will a buffalo go down on receiving a single bullet. Instead, he'll typically turn tail and head for heavy cover. Often, in a herd, there will be no chance for a second shot—but there might be. And unless you're willing to bank on the placement of that first shot *and* the performance of the bullet, it's time to shoot again.

A second choice, after the almost mythical scoped double, would be a scope-sighted magazine rifle in one of the .416s. But if you're even slightly recoil-sensitive, stick with a .375. On buffalo, the biggest bullet in the world won't do you a damn bit of good if you can't put it in the right place.

# Chapter 29

# The Heavyweights

In days gone by, it might have made sense to discuss varying rifle/cartridge requirements for hunting rhino, elephant in open country, and elephant in the forest. After all, there is quite a variation in size among Africa's largest game animals. The black rhino, for instance, generally weighs about 3,000 pounds, while a big white rhino may weigh 6,000. Elephant, too, vary greatly in size. The elephant of southern and southwestern Africa—Zimbabwe, Botswana, Angola—are believed to weigh as much as 14,000 pounds. I have hunted Zimbabwe elephant, and they're huge. Immense, too, are the elephant I hunted in northwestern Mozambique—as large as or larger than Zimbabwe elephant. Entirely different are the elephant of the eastern coastal regions; the elephant I hunted in Tanzania's Selous Reserve are little more than half the size of the Zimbabwe elephant—certainly no more than four to $4\frac{1}{2}$ tons for a big bull. I'm told that the forest elephant of central Africa, too, are small in the body.

Elephant and rhino are considered part of the Big Five (although many will argue that this applies only to the black rhino, not the larger but more docile white rhino), while the hippo is not. For the record, a big bull hippo not only weighs about the same as a white rhino—three tons or more—but also must be considered extremely dangerous when encountered on land. Hippos probably kill more Africans than all the Big Five combined, simply because they feed far out into grasslands at night, then return to water at dawn, a habit in direct conflict with the rural African's habit of going to water at dawn and thus occasionally committing the suicidal error of getting between a hippo and his aquatic sanctuary.

In the water, the hippo is hardly a game animal at all; he is most susceptible to a brain shot from a very light rifle, and his chief value is for use as a huge lion bait. On land, however, the hippo can be a most dangerous and extremely exciting animal to hunt. I bring him into this discussion because, in today's Africa, the opportunity to hunt thick-skinned game is shrinking rapidly.

The last legal black rhino hunting was conducted in Zambia's Luangwa Valley and in Tanzania nearly a decade ago. The Zambezi Valley still sustains a huntable population, and the enormous trophy fees that a handful of black rhino permits could command would go a long way towards financing effective anti-poaching efforts. But it seems the political climate no longer exists for such a rational solution, and in spite of long-range projections, I seriously doubt if another black rhino will be legally hunted in my lifetime. If one is, I know the trophy fee will be many times what I or any other normal person can afford.

When South Africa was able to re-open white rhino hunting in the 1970s that was big news—and certainly it was a major victory for both conservation and sensible wildlife utilization. The tremendous value of this animal to sport hunters has aided enormously in restocking efforts; what game rancher wouldn't like to be able to sell even *one* white rhino bull per year? When I first hunted South Africa, the white rhino had just become legal game, and it was not yet possible to import a trophy into the U.S. At that time (hindsight being a wonderful thing), I could have shot an excellent white rhino for much less than the trophy fee for leopard.

Eventually, I did get around to shooting a white rhino. It was a good hunt, a search for a specific rhino bull that was roaming a large area with no regard for fences, and I shot him for a very good price: a trophy fee of $5,000. Today, just a few years later, the average trophy fee for a white rhino is approaching $30,000. I understand it's a question of supply and demand, but that's *crazy*. What all this means is that a wealthy sportsman who really wants to collect the Big Five may shoot *one* rhino. I did, though I wasn't wealthy, and I enjoyed the experience tremendously. But I will certainly never shoot another, nor is anyone else likely to become an expert on rhino shooting.

Elephant hunting, too, is closing down very rapidly. It seems there is no stopping the poaching; in the span of just a few years, the endless herds of the Luangwa Valley were all but eradicated—and that's just a microcosm of what has happened all over Africa. Pockets remain, and some of them are hunted. Zimbabwe has a marvelous elephant program that, so far, is working. South Africa's few elephant are on the increase, and although poaching is a problem, Mozambique has much promise. The greatest concentration in Africa, the 60,000-plus elephant in northeastern Botswana, are badly overpopulated and must be reduced—but in an odd turn of reverse politics, at this writing it appears they may starve before they're hunted.

There are a small number of elephant-hunting experts left in the world. Some of Zimbabwe's game rangers have culled elephant into the thousand, and a very few of the oldtime ivory hunters still live—Wally Johnson and Harry Manners, to name just two. Although he started amazingly late, Tony Sanchez has shot over 800 elephant—most of them good tuskers. These guys *know* what works for elephant, and fortunately many of them have written of their exploits—I say fortunately because a sport hunter starting his career today has no chance to become an expert on elephant hunting or elephant shooting. If he's extremely lucky, he may take one or two reasonable bulls—"reasonable" today being half the ivory weight it was 20 years ago.

I believe African hunting will last for a good many years to come. The safari industry brings too much money into starved African economies for it to end. But I do not believe elephant hunting will be a part of the African safari of a decade from now. Just like the black rhino's horn, the value of the ivory is so high that no risk is too great for the poachers. Legal utilization of the surplus, including sport hunting as in Zimbabwe today, makes perfect sense—but I doubt that the bleeding hearts of the world will allow it to continue much longer. In any event, it's hardly sport hunting that's hurting the elephant. Unless the world market for illegal ivory can be killed, the African elephant has no chance except in small enclaves where total protection is possible.

Since it seems likely for this book to outlast elephant hunting by a tremendous margin, I think it's best to discuss rifles and cartridges for the heavyweights as a group—including rhino, elephant, and even the ugly-duckling hippo. Beautiful he may not be, and his tusks are a pitifully small trophy for so large an animal. However, the hippo remains common throughout much of Africa. Hunters who wish the experience of stalking in close to a truly dangerous and unquestionably huge animal may be left with only the hippo in the not-too-distant future. And, indeed, they can get all the thrills they want. It's very possible that I've shot my last elephant—but I wouldn't mind stalking in on another hippo or two.

Although he tends to lie up in heavy thornbush, the white rhino is a grazing animal, so he can occasionally be tracked up (or glassed) and shot in relatively open country. However, his eyesight is poor enough that, if the wind is favorable, there's hardly a need for a scope sight.

In years gone by, elephant could be hunted in quite open country. Along the upper reaches of the Nile in Uganda was one such place, as were the famed Tsavo and Galana River regions of Kenya. I will never forget the 70- and 80-pound tuskers I saw standing in open grasslands along the Tsavo Park boundary south of Voi. I don't really know where the last savanna elephant hunting took place, but I do know it's over and done with now. When elephant could be hunted in open country, you could make a case for a scope-sighted rifle backed up by a heavy double; pinpoint shot placement at 100 yards would be easy with a scoped .375 or .416.

I shot my first elephant with a .416 Hoffman topped with a 3X scope. We caught a herd of bulls in relatively open mopane and stalked within 30 yards. A brain shot was absolutely child's play—but it wouldn't have been significantly more difficult with open sights. And if it had been, a heart shot would have been even easier. That country was unusually open; most modern elephant hunting is done in the thickest cover imaginable, where it's more usual to have elephant at arm's length—in stuff so thick you *still* can't judge the ivory! And yet, you never know; after days and untold miles of tracking in dense cover, I shot my Mozambique tusker in the reedbeds on the shores of Lake Cabora Bassa. That time I used the safe, certain shoulder shot with a double .500.

A scope is simply not necessary, and any appendage added to a rifle's profile is just a menace to snag on vines and branches. If Botswana ever re-opens, there will be elephant taken in relatively open thorn, but even there the better bulls will be in the thickest mopane they can find—and probably in dense riverine growth.

295

All things considered, I can't see any reason for a scoped rifle for hunting today's elephant—provided the shooter is capable of some small degree of precision with open sights because, as huge as an elephant is, it still requires precise shooting.

A word about shot placement is in order. All of us have read far too much W.D.M. Bell. He was the master of bullet placement, undoubtedly one of the finest field marksmen who ever lived. He believed absolutely in the brain shot—and in his ability to find the brain from any angle. Remember several things. First, Bell was an extraordinary man with extraordinary talents and experience. Second, he hunted elephant in open country to which they will never return. Third, he recommended *against* novices (which we all are, in comparison with a Bell or Sutherland or Rushby) taking brain shots.

I have killed elephant with a brain shot (once) and with body shots. The results of a brain shot are spectacular, and making such a shot is rendered quite easy by the use of a low-powered scope. However, I personally recommend against brain shots, and I think most professional hunters would join me in that suggestion.

Just as Bell, Taylor, and all the other greats have written, there's a lot of elephant skull and not a lot of brain. If the brain is narrowly missed with a very large rifle, the elephant may be knocked down long enough to allow a finisher. But the common .458 isn't enough gun, and anything under a .577 *probably* isn't. If the brain is missed and the elephant isn't knocked down, a follow-up body shot must be taken instantly. The problem is that the muzzle blast of the client's shot may disturb the professional's aim. Or he may be waiting for the client to back up his own shot. Or the target elephant's movement—or that of another in the herd—may be so rapid as to preclude a follow-up.

I have heard of just two sport-hunted elephant being lost recently. Both were very fine bulls, and in both cases the client insisted on brain shots in spite of the professional hunters' strong admonitions. In the first case, the client not only insisted on a brain shot, but insisted further that he not be backed up. He missed the brain with a double .465, failed to fire a second shot, and his bull was never found—and quite probably is still walking around. The other one was very recent, in Mozambique a couple of safaris before I went in. Again, a hunter insisted on a brain shot, but took it from the very tricky quartering-away angle. At the shot, the bull was instantly in motion and all follow-up shots were in thick brush at the worst possible angle. The bull eventually outdistanced his pursuers, and the track was lost among other elephant tracks.

The one elephant I killed with a brain shot was indeed an amazing spectacle; the bull fell out from under my recoiling rifle. However, it was something my professional hunter, Peter Johnstone, and I had discussed long beforehand. I wanted very much to try the brain shot; as I said, I'd read too much Bell. But I agreed to try it only if Peter gave me the go-ahead—

which meant that he was absolutely certain he could back me up. In the actual circumstance, I was prepared to make a heart shot. Then the bull took several steps, coming completely clear of another bull that partially shielded him and thus could have prevented a back-up. When he came clear, true to his word Peter touched his own forehead in signal, and I made the brain shot. But if I'd muffed it, I'd have been most grateful for all the back-up available. Nobody wants a lost elephant. And in very heavy cover, I would be most reluctant to attempt such a shot.

Not nearly so spectacular, but much surer, are the heart shot (centered on the foreleg, low) and the lung shot. Both will kill an elephant very dead within 200 yards—usually much, much sooner. Both offer a much larger target area, and all will take effect with or without a back-up—which may not be possible in the heavy cover where most elephant are hunted today.

A solid bullet is the only sensible choice, and a good solid at that. And unlike the choice of arms for leopard, buffalo, and lion, the best rifle to use is the very largest you can possibly handle. The finesse of open-country elephant hunting is gone, and the .375 for elephant should have gone with it. Yes, shot placement is essential. But understand that the stuff you're hunting in is *thick*, thick beyond most hunters' imaginations. An elephant at a dozen yards may be invisible—and while you *must* (or not shoot at all) be able to line up on an elephant's shoulder, you cannot be as precise as you would like to be. This is one of the few places in all hunting where raw power counts for something.

In today's elephant hunting, I would rate the .375 H&H as barely marginal, and the .458 Winchester Magnum with factory loads as not much better. In the last chapter of this book we'll look at a survey I sent out to several hundred professional hunters. The .458 Winchester was by far the most popular caliber for thick-skinned game, followed by the .375. That's appropriate, since availability is most of the battle in Africa. However, a surprising number of professionals specified that the .458 should be used only with handloaded ammunition—*not* factory loads.

Any of the .416s will offer more reliable penetration as well as more energy, and powerful wildcats like the .458 Lott are marvelously effective. My hunting partner in Tanzania, Bill Baker, used a .458 Lott to body-shoot an elephant on our 1988 safari. Those are small-bodied elephant but, even so, the .458 Lott, with a 500-grain bullet at about 2,350 fps, darn near knocked the bull off its feet with a quartering-away behind-the-shoulder heart shot. Then it recovered and went 20 yards before piling up.

Even better, in my view, are big doubles from .450 to .500. The bigger guns—.577 and .600—are just as effective now as they were 75 years ago, but elephant hunting today means miles and miles of tracking, often in extreme heat. Nobody wants to carry a 15-pound rifle, but a 10-pound double balances nicely for carrying—and that quick one-two punch that only a double offers is incredibly comforting in thick cover—and most effective.

Several years ago, gunmaker David Miller decided on a .404 for his first hunt into the C.A.R. Elephant were still open then, and he took a marvelous bull. But he emptied the rifle, first with a reasonably well-aimed shot considering the dense forest—and then at a shadowed retreating form. David still believes in bolt-actions rather than doubles, but after that experience he's been recommending the .458 Lott to his clients instead of the .404 and .416s.

Personally, I'll stick with a double for the limited elephant hunting I have yet to do, but I certainly wouldn't argue with anyone's choice of a .458 Lott, .460 Weatherby, or one of the big bores like the .500 Jeffery, .505 Gibbs, .510 Wells, or .500 A-Square. After all, the elephant is the largest land animal in the world, and it's common sense to hit him with the biggest thing you can handle. As a *caveat* to that, I will say that elephant, in spite of their size, may be easier to kill than wounded buffalo—and, in the charge, are easier to turn aside.

There's little point in discussing black rhino, but it should be mentioned that white rhino (like, I'm told, black rhino) are quite impervious to bullet shock, and although relatively docile by nature are known for going tremendous distances after receiving fatal hits. Considering the circumstances under which white rhino are often hunted today—i.e., game-ranch situations—I don't suppose it makes much difference what they're hunted with, so long as a .375 or something bigger is used with a solid bullet. But again, this is a good place for a double rifle; that instantaneous double punch unquestionably speeds things along. My own rhino was hit with one .470 solid on the shoulder, a second behind, and a third at the base of the tail that actually did little damage, since it missed the spine. The bull went about 50 yards and piled up in mid-flight, and that's a very short run for a rhino.

The hippo will never be regarded as the grand game animal that the elephant is and the black rhino was. But if you can catch one resting in thornbush in daylight, you can have a wonderful adventure stalking in close and carefully shooting him in the chest rather than the brain. This monstrous creature soaks up bullets like the fatty sponge he is, and it's pretty much a matter of luck as to which direction he may head when you shoot him. If your bull heads your way, you should know exactly where the soft spot in the forehead lies—and be able to hit it. An enraged hippo will carry his charge all the way in, and at its conclusion he'll gleefully bite you in half. If he heads the other way, you'll see how fast you can work a bolt or reload a double—and you'll get some idea of what your bullets are or are not doing.

In today's Africa, no sport hunter can gain extensive experience with rhino or elephant; the resource is no longer there to support it, and the cost is beyond mere extravagance. Perhaps, as a hunter of modest means, that's why I love the Cape buffalo so much; I can still hunt him without guilt. The hippo is much the same if you can hunt him the right way, on the ground.

I wish the prognosis were better for Africa's heavyweights, but facts are facts. We're seeing the last of it, and I wish there were some means of stemming the tide.

# Chapter 30

# Rifles for Bush and Savanna

**H**unters who have not yet been to Africa tend to envision either Tarzan's jungle or the endless cinematic plains of Robert Redford. Africa doesn't have true jungle, but it does have vast forests, denser than anything Johnny Weissmuller encountered in his Tarzan movies. And it does have broad short-grass plains and vast deserts. However, the reality is that most African hunting—the normal safari for a varied bag—is conducted in neither extreme.

Savanna woodland is a term for plains interspersed with hardwood cover and thornbush. The more open hunting areas are likely to be this kind of country—Masailand, northern C.A.R., the region surrounding the Okavango Delta, as examples. Other areas, such as most of Zimbabwe and Zambia, may be primarily mopane woodland—relatively open hardwood forest with a varying understory of thornbush.

In some areas the woodlands—thornbush, if you will—extend for miles without a break. More frequently, though, the sea of brush is broken by waterways with even denser riverine growth *or* ridiculously open floodplains. There are natural clearings, too. Sometimes they're huge, sometimes very small. In the early season, they're choked with high grass, but later the grass will be burned and the game will flock to the new green. The terrain may be very flat, but more often it's broken by the typical African kopjes, rocky hills that make such good vantage points—and sometimes these hills are full-fledged mountains with their own microcosms of habitat.

Even the deserts are less open than you might imagine; most of the Kalahari, for instance, is a sea of low brush. Perhaps the most open country I've seen in Africa is the wind-swept Karoo of South Africa's Cape Province—and even here you will find low brush and the occasional hill mass.

Whether in a typical general-bag area in Ethiopia, Tanzania, northern C.A.R., Zambia, Zimbabwe, Botswana, South Africa, or you name it, the vegetation varies from relatively thick cover to fairly open and back again. And while it could be constant either one way or the other, it's also likely to change back and forth in the space of a few kilometers.

Take the Selous Reserve of southern Tanzania, for instance. Much of it is relatively open *miombo* forest, with little understory and good visibility. But, seeming to follow almost imperceptible shifts in elevation, the Selous is cut by monstrous belts of near-impenetrable thicket, where visibility quickly dwindles to zero. And there are also vast open areas, too big to be called clearings and almost big enough to be called plains. In the course of a day, you could switch from terrain that calls for long-range shooting to terrain that calls for "average" shooting, and then into the thickets where any shot at all would leave powder burns.

It's the thornbush, woodland, plain, and even desert regions of Africa that hold the continent's great variety of game. The forests, swamps, and mountains are interesting—but the hunting is mostly very specialized and the species limited. In the thornbush and savanna, it's the subtle and constant variation of vegetation and terrain that has created habitat for the fascinating mixture of diverse species.

Country like this is not particularly hard on a rifle. Although unseasonal rain is a remote possibility, most safaris are conducted in the long dry season. Rust will form, but it will be from perspiration, not precipitation. Dust is a constant problem, fine red dust and fine white sand that will filter into a rifle's action. Normal daily maintenance will keep a rifle working— but without it, the grit could keep an action from closing when you need it most.

But if such areas demand only minimal maintenance, they demand the utmost in performance. In the morning, you may shoot an impala for leopard bait at 75 yards. In the afternoon, you may chance across a wonderful sable standing on the far side of a broad *dambo*—and the only shot you have is 300 yards. In between, you may chance across buffalo, steinbok, lion, duiker, eland, reedbuck, warthog, zebra, and more. The distances may be from a few yards to as far as you are comfortable shooting; the game may be placidly grazing or heading for the thick stuff as fast as it can get there.

Versatility is the key; within reason, the rifle you're carrying should be able to handle almost anything the area you're hunting can throw at it. One rifle doesn't have to do everything; there's always a place for that ultimate specialist, the dangerous-game rifle. The problem with such thinking is that your heavy rifle could be miles away in the Land Rover when you need it most.

If dangerous game is on the menu, the rifle you *regularly* carry when you leave the vehicle should be able to handle it in a pinch. That doesn't mean you won't find uses for the ultra-accurate flat-shooting small bore; but just like the heavy rifle, the small bore is specialized. The heavy rifle won't reach across an opening—and a very light rifle won't stop a buffalo. In thornbush and savanna, the most important rifle—the one you'll carry most and, on a typical safari, harvest the most game with—must be versatile.

Its caliber depends on you and the kind of game you're spending the most time hunting. It might be a .375, what I call the ultimate compromise cartridge. If it is, you are ready for anything. It might be something on the order of a .338, arguably not quite as versatile as a .375, but more or less able to handle anything that comes along. At an absolute minimum it could be a .270, 7x57, 7mm magnum, or .30-06. If it is, and you're an extraordinarily good shot, and you pick your bullets with the utmost care, you *may* be able to handle anything that comes along. Many hunters have. But you might also give serious thought to having a tracker carry a heavier rifle just as a matter of course.

A lighter rifle, such as a 6mm, a .25, or a hot .22 centerfire, may well have its place—but it will not do as the only rifle available to you, whether you're in the hunting vehicle or on foot. Nor, incidentally, should an open-sighted heavy rifle be the only rifle available to you—unless, in either case, you have decided to make that particular outing a specialized quest for the type of game either rifle is suited for. Today, few safaris are lengthy enough to allow that kind of luxury.

My very best lion was taken during a chance encounter. I had a lion on license, but I wasn't really hunting lion and didn't expect to shoot one. Fortunately, the lightest rifle I had was a .375, and when this magnificent lion appeared I was ready. Had I been carrying a light rifle, there *might* have been time enough to switch guns. Or, had I shot him with a light rifle, I *might* have gotten away with it.

By the same token, I've shot a great many springbok, warthogs, impala, and other game with rifles far larger than necessary. Overkill isn't the worst thing that can happen, so long as the rifle you carry has both the accuracy and flatness of trajectory to make careful shot placement practical over the full spectrum of hunting ranges your area might offer. And, quite obviously, you must be able to *shoot* your chosen rifle. If its recoil is too much for you to handle, whatever capabilities it might have are useless.

It goes without saying that the typical rifle for bush and savanna will be scoped, and it will probably be a magazine rifle. It *could* be a single-shot, and it could even be an unusually accurate double—but it will probably be a bolt-action, neither too large nor too small in caliber.

Such a rifle will be the basic gun in your battery for a general-bag safari. It may be backed up by a heavier rifle or a lighter rifle, or both; we'll discuss safari batteries in more detail later. First, though, let's take a look at rifles for more specialized hunting.

# Chapter 31

# Rifles for Forest, Swamp, and Mountain

A hunt in Africa's thornbush and savanna could well be a specialized quest; *any* serious cat hunt is specialized, and a veteran hunter may return to a specific area to concentrate on big kudu, an extra-special buffalo, or some other animal found locally in exceptional quality. But most safaris to general-bag areas are just that: hunts intended for a general bag, with some priorities usually established as to what animals should occupy the bulk of the time.

In contrast, safaris to Africa's forests, swamps, and mountains are usually very specialized, single-purpose hunts, with one or two unique species of game as the only objects. Hunts like that may be very long—a month's safari to the forests of southern C.A.R. strictly for bongo, for instance. Or they may be very short, perhaps conducted as a side trip to another safari. The three-day hunts up the slopes of Mount Kilimanjaro for Abbott's duiker and Chanler's mountain reedbuck would be a good example—a highly specialized endeavor, but usually conducted as part of a general-bag safari.

A number of these very specialized hunting situations exist from one end of Africa to another. Some of these include mountain nyala hunting in the forests and heather of Ethiopia's high country; sitatunga hunting in any one of a dozen African swamps and river systems; duiker hunting in Liberia. Even hunting the elusive little Vaal rhebok in the mountains of South Africa can be a highly specialized undertaking. Any bongo hunt is extremely specialized, and on today's market any elephant hunt, whether in forest or thornbush, is perhaps the most demanding and specialized of all.

Most areas where such hunting is done are very hard on both people and equipment. The mountains can be constantly wet and are usually cold. The forests are often wet and extremely hot, and biting insects are much more of a problem than on the average safari. The swamps are not only wet, but add leeches and the threat of bilharzia. Yet the animals found in such inhospitable regions are among Africa's greatest prizes, and generations of hunters have found them worth whatever travails their hunting requires.

Such quests test both stamina and psyche—and can literally eat up a good rifle. Serious rust can be an overnight problem, and in swamps and many forests you can forget about a stock's lovely finish. After a few days it will be a uniform scaly gray.

Safari life isn't the luxury vacation a general-bag hunt often is. The country is more remote, the supplies scanty and harder to replenish. Food might be plain terrible, and not overly plentiful. The hunting will most likely be on foot, and some nights may be spent on a track. Daily maintenance takes on new dimensions: maintenance of aching muscles and feet raw from immersion; ritual inspections for leeches and insect bites; and lubrication, cleaning, and thorough inspection of the rifle so it will be ready when you finally get a shot.

A hunter might leave these last chores to his professional hunter—who will undoubtedly delegate them to his tracker. Perhaps that's all right; considering the cost of most specialized African hunts, it's unreasonable to expect the client to sit up late punching the bore of his rifle. But he'd damn well better inspect his rifle and his ammunition carefully each and every day. The more specialized the hunt and the more elusive the animal, the fewer and farther between are the opportunities. It's always important that a hunter be absolutely certain his rifle will function, especially on dangerous game. But these specialized hunts can be murder on a rifle, and failure to clean and lightly lubricate each day and inspect your ammunition could result in a failure when your one and only chance comes. Sometimes it's hard to do, when you stumble into camp late. But you might have been drenched with rain or half-submerged in flooded plain all day—and by the morning you can have a serious and lasting rust problem on your hands. If your rifle fails you when you need it, it's nobody's fault but your own.

Sometimes a little casual inspection reveals some interesting things. My good friend Jack Lott was hunting gaur in southeast Asia. One day he discovered wasps busily building a nest in the muzzle of his .458—possibly turning it into a pipe bomb.

Although the maintenance requirements become more stringent as the hunting becomes more specialized, the choice of rifle should get easier. Quite simply, the rifle chosen should be whatever rifle is best for you for hunting your primary quarry. "Best for you" implies some caliber suitability, of course, but also a comfort level. The rifle chosen for a specialized hunt must be adequate for the main prize—but it must also be a rifle you are thoroughly familiar with and have total confidence in. Chances are you'll need both the confidence and the familiarity when your chance comes.

The concept of a safari battery still applies, of course; the rifle you choose for your main quarry may not be the only one you have with you. But it is likely to be the only one readily available at any one time. Remember, chances are your hunting will be on foot. You could have a tracker carry a second rifle—but there's little point. You won't be doing any random shooting until you have taken the main prize, whatever it is. And if you run into something so spectacular that you have to deviate from your game plan, it's unlikely there will be lots of time to change guns.

I mentioned earlier that gunmaker David Miller chose an open-sighted .404 for his first C.A.R. safari. Elephant was the main quarry—but very early in the hunt, while tracking elephant, he shot a spectacular bongo. Clearly that was a trophy worth being sidetracked for. His open-sighted

.404 might not have been ideal; the way he described the shot to me, a low-powered scope would have made life easier. But he managed.

Another friend of mine, Bruno Scherrer, shot a fine bongo with his .300 Weatherby. A yellowback duiker jumped up and he shot it as well, giving him two great forest prizes within a few yards of each other. A flat-shooting, high-velocity cartridge like the .300 Weatherby might not be the classic choice for either animal—but his battered .300 is a rifle Bruno has hunted the world with. He can shoot it well, and since it's easily within the bounds of adequacy, what else matters?

We have already discussed rifles for various classes of game, but it should be noted here that rifles for forest hunting, optimally, should be heavier in caliber than the game might seem to indicate. In the good old days—just a few years ago, actually—almost all forest hunts were for elephant as well as bongo, always with the possibility of encountering giant forest hog, yellowback duiker, and so forth. Under those circumstances, many bongo were taken with elephant-class cartridges—and that's just fine.

Today, a bongo hunt is more likely to be just that, but it seems a mistake to bring the average caliber down a great deal below the elephant-capable category. Bongo are big and strong-boned, it's true. More importantly, the country is very tough, and a perfectly clear shot is most unusual. No bullet has a really good chance of getting through brush undeflected, but a big bullet of high sectional density has as good a chance as a small bullet—and even if deflected slightly, it will do a whole lot more damage when it arrives.

Elephant or no elephant, I would personally choose no less than a .375, and probably one of the .416s, for a forest rifle. If elephant were to be hunted, as mentioned earlier I would prefer a big double. If elephant were not on the list, I would choose a large-caliber magazine rifle topped with a low-powered scope.

In swamp country, my caliber requirements would be about the same. Regardless of the game being hunted, all African swamps have one thing in common: hippos. The closest call I have had was when a hippo decided to come into a dugout canoe with me. I will never step into an African swamp again without a rifle big enough to handle such an uninvited guest.

Much as I love double rifles, I would not take one into the swamps; there's too much damage that can remain hidden if you submerge the action. And you're likely to, jumping in and out of canoes, wading channels—and sometimes even swimming a bit.

I would also not take a double on a mountain hunt. Mountains are often rainy, and even if they're forested the relief can mean very long shooting. That's not the double's strong suit. Depending on the game, a mountain rifle might be a .375, a .340 Weatherby, or one of the .300s. If really large game is possible, then the .416 Weatherby might be a sound choice; it will shoot flatter than a .30-06, and up close could stop anything.

Under all of these conditions, it's very likely that your bullet's path won't be perfectly clear. There is no predicting what will happen when a bullet meets an obstruction, but there are some probabilities. First, the nearer the screen of brush to the target, the better your chances are. Second, long bullets that are heavy-for-caliber tend to hold their course best, even through obstructions. These may not be the bullets that offer the flattest trajectory, but they are the bullets that have the best chance of reaching the target if there's brush in the way. The best way to shoot through brush is to find a hole so that you don't have to. A scope always helps. If there is no hole to shoot through and no other choice, try it if you must—but understand that the risks are great.

Some of these specialized hunts are in ideal habitat for today's synthetic stocks and rustproof metal finishes. Both have come a long way in recent years. A few years ago there was just a smattering of fiberglass stocks. Today there's fiberglass, Kevlar, Rynite, Cycolac—and Lord knows what. There are also matte finishes, Parkerized finishes, Teflon-coated finishes, and even rifles of stainless steel and, just around the corner, titanium. Let's look at synthetic stocks first.

I was slow to embrace these things; they just don't have the warmth of a fine piece of walnut. However, I've ruined a lot of good pieces of wood on tough hunts. I've also seen wood stocks swell and warp in wet weather— and then shrink, warp, and split in dry weather. Regardless of how you feel about looks, synthetic stocks are *stable*. They can't shift zero on you, and these days they're stronger than wood.

In 1984 I had no synthetic-stocked rifles. Today I have five: a .280, a 7mm Remington Magnum, a .338, a .35 Whelen, and a .416 Hoffman. All of them are on Remington Model 700 actions (remember that I'm left-handed, which limits my choices). Today, most of the major manufacturers offer over-the-counter fiberglass-stocked guns, and the custom and semi-custom makers are doing a booming business. Some of my rifles were put together with North American hunting in mind, but the .416 is my for-est/swamp African rifle. And the .338 is my mountain rifle for hunting large game—wherever that game is found.

The fiberglass stocks offer another advantage, and it's important—they shave gun weight. At about 6½ pounds, that .416 Hoffman of mine is a beast to shoot—but it is very pleasant to carry all day. A K.D.F. recoil arrestor has tamed it quite a bit. I can shoot it, and I sure enjoy carrying it.

Rustproof metal finishes (and rustproof metals) have tremendous prom-ise for wet-climate hunting. No, they aren't nearly as attractive as old-time rust bluing. But under rough conditions you can watch the finest rust bluing turn to rust in hours. There are a number of finishes today that are actually self-lubricating as well as rust-resistant. The old Parkerized dull finish remains one of my favorites, but the technology is advancing so quickly that I would suggest discussing it with a good gunsmith. Keep one thing in mind—the best anything can offer is *resistance* to rust. Even stainless steel will rust in time; the only real *proof* against corrosion is care and cleaning.

# Part IV

# The African Battery

# Chapter 32

# The One-rifle Safari

There's a saying in the whitetail woods: "Beware the one-rifle hunter." The hunter who shoots just one rifle season after season will come to know that rifle like an extension of his body. If he hunts a good deal, or if he practices as much as a hunter should—or both—he will become exceedingly deadly with that one rifle. This is just as true in Africa as anywhere else; the hunter who relies on one rifle will become wonderfully familiar with and confident of that rifle. There will be no confusion over which rifle to reach for, and no confusion over ammunition.

It's a concept that makes sense, no doubt about it. The problem is that African game varies tremendously in size—and the hunting conditions can vary widely even within a limited geographic area. Limiting oneself to a single caliber simplifies many things—but it does severely limit one's choice of rifles and cartridges. And it means compromises must be made, for it's obvious that no one cartridge is particularly well-suited for the entire range of African game from dik dik to elephant.

It should be just as obvious, however, that if only one rifle is available, then that rifle *will* be used on the entire spectrum of game to be hunted, and the rifle and the cartridge it fires must be chosen with extreme care.

If the game to be hunted runs the full gamut from dik dik to elephant—or, to be more reasonable, from duiker to buffalo or impala to lion—then the choices are very limited. The rifle must be adequate for the largest game that will be hunted, especially if that largest game happens to be dangerous. Adequacy on the upper end must come first; but it would also be nice if the rifle were accurate enough for the smallest antelopes, flat-shooting enough for the longest likely shot, and portable enough to carry all day.

If dangerous game such as lion, buffalo, or elephant will be on license, you have to stretch your imagination to find more than one candidate—the 1912-vintage .375 H&H. The .375 isn't perfect for elephant, nor is it the best thing going for shots past 300 yards. But it will do it all, and while there are a few other choices for a one-rifle safari, there may not be any *better* choices.

Other possibilities are the other .375s, the old .375 Weatherby and its replacement, the .378. In more open country, either could be a more sensible choice than the .375 H&H—if the shooter finds the recoil acceptable. In denser cover, the extra velocity may adversely affect bullet performance.

The European 9.3x64 could certainly be an alternative to the .375, but for a full range of game I can't envision any smaller cartridge being chosen. I can envision a larger cartridge for a one-rifle safari, especially if the cover tends to be thick and dangerous game is high on the hunter's want list. All of the mid-.40 cartridges, from wildcats like the .4ll K.D.F., .416 Taylor, and .416 Hoffman through the newer factory cartridges, the .416 Remington and .416 Weatherby, and even the old .416 Rigby, are all perfectly capable of handling almost any shooting chore. More powerful by far than the .375, and thus better suited for the largest game, the .416 class of cartridges will shoot almost as flat as the best .375 loads. And of course the .416 Weatherby will shoot flatter.

It goes without saying that such cartridges are needlessly powerful for anything *but* the dangerous game—but as I've said before, there are worse things than overkill (if overkill even exists). I can't see using a cartridge larger in bore diameter than a .416 as a one-rifle battery, unless of course the hunt is strictly for elephant. But a scoped .416 could do everything, and do it well.

On a recent trip, the only rifle I took was a .416 Weatherby. It performed admirably, but I should say that it was a short hunt with limited objectives— mainly buffalo and a couple of head of plains game. Still, that .416 was all that was needed, and as short as the hunt was, another rifle would have been nothing but excess baggage.

The last chapter of this book is devoted to a survey I sent out to several hundred licensed African professional hunters. That survey could well be the most valuable part of the book, since the professionals not only know what works for them—but their lives depend on their clients' choice of arms and their skill in employing them.

Fully 75 percent of the professional hunters surveyed listed the .375 H&H as their own personal "all-round" choice—and 65 percent suggested it as the rifle they would recommend to their clients as a one-rifle battery. Aside from the .375, there were a few votes each for the .416 (unspecified as to which one), .300 H&H Magnum, and .30-06 for all-round use. In the section under recommendations to clients, the .30-06 and .300 magnums got about the same number of votes for a one-rifle battery. The 8x68S, 9.3x64, .338, and .416 Hoffman were among the other cartridges specifically mentioned.

In connection with cartridges less than .375 being recommended to clients for a one-rifle safari, one has to ask a couple of questions. First, will dangerous game be a part of the bag? And if so, is the client expected to use his own relatively light rifle, or borrow one from the professional? Let's explore both angles.

It should be recognized that not all safari agendas include members of the Big Five. If they don't, there's absolutely no reason for a rifle of .40 caliber or larger; and if eland is not on the list, there's no real need for a .375. A .375 would be fine for the average plains-game safari, of course. But a lighter, easier-to-shoot .300, .30-06, or 7mm magnum might better serve most hunters.

All too many hunters seem to drag along a .375 or heavier rifle "just in case." Believe me, in today's Africa if you haven't specifically booked a hunt for lion, buffalo, or elephant, the chances of just "running across" such animals *and* being able to legally capitalize on the opportunity are extremely slim if not nonexistent.

There is some small possibility of leopard on most African hunts; even if they're on quota, the spotted cats are hard enough to come by that the quota may be unfilled. But, as we've seen, a big gun isn't necessarily the best choice for leopard anyway. If you feel better about having a big gun along, more like you're really in Africa, by all means take it—but understand that if you haven't specifically booked a hunt that includes dangerous game, you probably won't use it. And you'll shoot better and more consistently with a lighter rifle that you're more familiar with.

That rifle must still be adequate for the full range of game, but your favorite elk rifle—if not deer rifle—will be up to the task. And you'll probably shoot it well, just as you do at home.

What about taking along your favorite rifle and planning to borrow a "heavy" if needed? There are good points and bad points to such a plan. In my experience, professional hunters may or may not have the best equipment available. Rifles and ammunition are hard to come by in Africa, and a professional hunter might have very fine rifles or, he might have tired old relics. I wouldn't take it on blind faith that a professional hunter will have a spare .375 or larger available. On the other hand, if he says he has an adequate rifle, I'd bank on it—he's banking his life on its proper functioning.

The obvious disadvantage to borrowing a heavy rifle is that you'll be using an unfamiliar rifle. However, if you aren't taking your own heavy rifle, it's likely you either don't have one or you don't have one that you're totally familiar with. I suggest that you are better off borrowing a heavy rifle from your hunter than purchasing one especially for your safari—unless, of course, you are willing to spend the time and energy to become totally familiar with your new heavy, and to shoot it enough to work any potential bugs out of it.

As I've mentioned, "over-the-counter" heavy rifles are notorious for feeding problems and splitting stocks. A "camp" rifle may not be pretty, but odds are good that the bugs were worked out years before. If you plan on borrowing a rifle for the two or three shots you might fire at dangerous game, then your one rifle can be whatever rifle you shoot best.

My hunting partner on a safari about 10 years ago brought just one rifle—a slide-action Remington .30-06. For his lion he borrowed my .338 in favor of a .375 offered by our outfitter, but for everything else he used his Remington pump—and he shot extremely well. He knew it was an odd choice, but damn it, it was *his* gun. And it was the right choice *for him.*

Incidentally, if you do plan on using a professional hunter's rifle for *anything,* find out what the caliber is and bring along at least a couple of boxes of ammunition. This will ensure that you have enough ammo and that it's fresh—and insist on burning up some of that ammo sighting in your borrowed gun and becoming familiar with it.

Since most gun cases are built for two long arms, taking only one rifle makes it extremely convenient to pack along a shotgun. If things break right, there might be time for some spectacular bird shooting. Or you might have to make time—or you might not use the shotgun at all. Chances are, though, that it will be a handy thing to have, if only to shoot a few guinea fowl for the pot. On the trip just mentioned, I threw in a 12-gauge over/under and two boxes of shells in addition to the .416. We didn't have time for serious bird shooting, but we did wind up with some most welcome guinea fowl, francolin, and even a few doves for the pot. If you really aren't a bird shooter, but some birds to eat sound good, consider filling the other half of your gun case with a .22 Magnum or .22 Hornet.

An interesting option for a one-rifle safari is an interchangeable-barrel rifle. There aren't a lot of them, but there are some very good ones. Professional hunter Russ Broom, for instance, has a Lebeau-Corally double with barrels in both .375 and .458. A somewhat less expensive option might be a break-open single-shot with barrels in different calibers. Thompson/Center's American-made single offers interchangeable barrels, though none in powerful chamberings. A number of European single-shots can be had with interchangeable barrels. Such a rig might not be the best for dangerous game, but with one barrel in .375 and another in a very flat-shooting chambering, you'd have a pretty versatile setup.

Bolt-actions, too, have been made with interchangeable barrels. The Sauer Model 90 is a factory-made setup, and a number of semi-custom shops build such rigs. Generally speaking, the cartridges chosen must have the same head diameter, and usually overall length can't vary too much. The Bighorn rifle, made up in Utah for a time, was a lovely switch-barrel bolt-action. I messed around with one that was set up with one barrel in 8mm Remington Magnum and another in .375 H&H. It worked, and was a lot of fun to play with.

I finally decided, for me, that a switch-barrel rifle wasn't the answer, not even a double that allows the switching of barrels in seconds. The problem is that no matter how you slice it, only one barrel and one caliber will be available for use at any one time. At least some of the time, it's not going to be the one you want. But if both barrels had reasonably broad applications, such as that 8mm/.375 rifle, the problem wouldn't be all that significant. If such a setup is chosen, do make certain each barrel has its own sighting equipment. A single-shot or double, for instance, if scoped, should have a sighted-in scope on each barrel. With a bolt-action, where the scope is on the receiver, the scope mounts should be detachable, and there should be a sighted-in scope in rings available for each barrel. The last thing you want is to have to sight in the rifle every time you switch barrels.

An inherent problem with using one rifle for all of your big game, aside from the compromises involved, is that there is no back-up whatever. Your professional hunter will have some kind of rifle, should yours fail—but you can't rely on the presence of an extra rifle, let alone its reliability. Instead, if you decide on just one rifle you must bank on your chosen arm being able to get you through the entire trip.

You'll want to go over it with a fine-tooth comb, carefully examining the stock for signs of minute cracks. You'll want to disassemble it completely and examine all the springs and parts—and if you aren't sure what you're looking at, ask a good gunsmith to do so. The sighting equipment requires special attention; the scope mount and scope-ring screws need to be checked over and Loc-tited into place, and there simply must be auxiliary sighting equipment. Optimally, you'll have iron sights on the rifle *and* an extra scope already set in rings. And of course, you'll have the full range of ammunition, both solids and softs.

If you're very lucky, you might have a rifle that throws different bullet weights to the same point of impact. If you do, you can work out some interesting combinations. My battered old .375, for instance, will group handloaded 300-grain softpoints and solids together. With a specific powder charge, it will also shoot 240-grain Bearclaws, about 300 fps faster, exactly one inch higher and on line. That's a pretty neat setup for a one-rifle safari—but such a combination is most unusual, and it's pure luck. Unless the groupings are very, very close, it's usually a very unsound practice to mix up bullet weights. You will want both solids and softs, however. The solids are useful not only for the largest game, but also for the smallest—*if* you know exactly where they shoot.

The one-rifle safari has merit, and I would never argue against it. It's simplicity itself—but it does require serious compromise. I'm too much of a rifle nut to limit myself to just one. So let's look next at two-rifle batteries.

# Chapter 33

# The Two-rifle Battery

I have never been comfortable with just a single rifle on a hunting trip a long way from home. The chance of a gun becoming inoperable or a stock breaking beyond field-expedient repair is remote, but such things do happen. And, as I said, I'm a dyed-in-the-nitrocellulose rifle nut. Part of the fun of any safari, at least for me, is in the anticipation and preparation—a large portion of which involves planning the perfect rifles and loading the perfect ammunition for the game I intend to hunt.

Admittedly, I've gone much too far on several occasions; at least twice I've taken four rifles to Africa, and more than once I've taken three rifles and a shotgun. If a non-hunting companion is traveling with the hunter, it's no problem to haul two gun cases. However, it's important to point out right now that traveling with more than three firearms is not only an incredible nuisance but might also be illegal. Unless you secure an export license, you cannot leave the United States with more than three firearms of any one type. That means up to three each of rifles, shotguns, and handguns—but not four rifles under any circumstances.

Seems like a strange law, but it does allow hunters to take plenty of guns. Whether or not you plan to take a shotgun, two rifles comprise a sensible battery for most hunting safaris. I have a couple of cases that will hold three firearms, but most hold just two. By using a large duffel bag and a two-gun hard case, it's generally possible and practical to go on safari with just the two pieces of luggage, plus a carry-on camera bag that will also hold a change of underwear and toilet kit. In this fashion, with just the two bags to check, overweight charges are usually avoided.

Under most circumstances, two rifles are also plenty to look after and use. Having two different rifles means each one can be slightly more specialized than the single rifle for a one-gun safari. However, part of the reason for carrying two rifles instead of one is so you'll have back-up available if either rifle develops an unsolvable problem.

One way to do this would be to pack two rifles of identical caliber. John Taylor suggested that an ideal battery, to him, would be two Westley Richards .425 rifles—one bolt-action and one double. This would give him a double, which he preferred for thick-cover work; and it would give him the accuracy of a bolt-action for hunting in more open country. Best of all, he would need to worry about just one caliber of ammunition.

It's a strange idea, at first glance—but perhaps not all that strange. One common caliber of ammunition would be nice, and it would be nice, too, to know that either rifle was perfectly capable of handling anything you came across. A pair of .425s (one of the few cartridges that were made in both double and magazine form) would be damned hard to come by today—but a double .375 backed up by a bolt-action would be, if expensive, very possible. For that matter, a matched pair of bolt-action rifles in .375 or one of the .416s wouldn't be a totally ridiculous choice, though the only purpose would be back-up in case of mechanical failure.

I suspect most hunters would opt for a two-rifle battery that included two substantially different calibers. This allows a bit more specialization, which means that one of the rifles will probably be better for smaller animals and/or longer ranges, while one of the rifles will be of heavier caliber for much larger game. One caution is to avoid *too much* specialization in a two-rifle battery. A better plan is to have some small degree of overlap, so each rifle could, in a pinch, take the place of the other—not only in case of a mechanical problem, but in case you happen to be carrying the wrong rifle at the right moment.

As an example, it seems to me that a .25-06 and a .458 make a damn poor battery, even if the .25-06 is a favorite rifle that you shoot extremely well. Both rifles are very specialized, and neither can adequately replace the other. The .25-06 cannot be used on a buffalo, while the .458 cannot reach out across an open pan and drop a springbok for the pot.

There are endless permutations of two-rifle batteries, and their choice can be greatly simplified by two hunting partners pooling their batteries. For instance, on a 2x1 safari where each hunter will be shooting buffalo, it might be advantageous to share a heavy rifle. On a Zambian safari, my own battery was comprised of a scoped .300 Weatherby and an open-sighted .460 Weatherby. But I knew my partner had a scoped .375, and I used it on several occasions. Obviously, if both parties have rifles they *want* to use, there's no reason to share—and mixing and matching is rarely practical if each client has his own professional.

It's easy to have too many rifles, but it's also possible not to have enough. When my father-in-law, my stepson, and I hunted on a 3x2 basis, they each had a light rifle and planned to share a .375 between them. I had a .318 Westley Richards bolt-action, a .470 double, and a scoped .375. First the stock of Paul Senior's .30-06 shattered. Then the extractor broke on their common .375—and they were nearly out of rifles. I gave them my .375, which worked just fine. But if I hadn't had three rifles, it might have been an awkward situation.

The choice of the two rifles depends very much on the game to be hunted; if there will be no dangerous game available, then things are simplified considerably. However, it seems to me that at least one of the two rifles should be very versatile, able to handle *all* the game to be hunted under *all* the conditions anticipated. For instance, let's go back to our pet .25-06. That's a fine flat-shooting cartridge, and it would be useful for a wide variety of plains game, especially in open country. But it would be very marginal for anything larger than waterbuck, and useless for dangerous game. If matched with an open-sighted .458, you'd have two specialized rifles—and absolutely nothing that would make sense for kudu, zebra, eland, sable, roan, wildebeest, and so much more. But if you matched up your .25-06 (or .243, .270, 7x57, .280, etc.) with a scope-sighted .375, you could get effective use out of both rifles.

On the other hand, you may have a heavy rifle that's a real prize, perhaps a vintage double or a customized bolt-action. So long as your safari includes one or more of the Big Five, there's no reason not to take your heavy. After all, that's what it's for, and if you can handle the recoil and place its bullets where they'll do some good, no lighter rifle will be as effective.

So take your big bore—but with the understanding that it's the most specialized of rifles, and you won't use it more than two or three times in the course of an average safari. And since you'll have limited use for the big bore, your other rifle will have to serve for everything else. That means the second rifle will have to be very versatile, but will also have to be on the heavy side. It must serve for the larger plains game, perhaps for lion and leopard, and for the smaller plains game as well, and that's a tall order.

A good match for an open-sighted double or big-bore bolt-action is obviously a .375, and there are few other choices. The .338 and .340 Weatherby are possibilities, and the .358 Norma Magnum is another good one. But an open-sighted big bore, though indispensable when you need it, is so limited that you are almost obligated to back it up with the most versatile of African calibers. And that's the good old .375 H&H.

In 1983, as I mentioned, I took the .300 and .460 Weatherby Magnums as a two-rifle battery. But I knew my partner would have a .375. I planned on borrowing her rifle, and I did several times. The next year I went back to Zambia, but I was hunting alone. Again I took just two rifles: an open-sighted .458 Lott bolt-action and a scoped .375 H&H. In terms of game bagged, that was one of my most successful safaris; I got my best lion, my best buffalo, my best sable, my best eland, my best reedbuck, and my best hartebeest. I also got a wonderful Kafue lechwe, shot at over 400 yards; and a good oribi, shot at 125 yards. In the course of the entire safari I carried the .458 Lott three times. The .375 did everything, and did it all well. I could just as easily have left the .458 at home—but I enjoyed carrying it, and I was glad I had it. A flatter-shooting light or light-medium rifle might have been more useful, but we did just fine with the .375.

When I went on my first safari, I didn't own a heavy rifle. I did own a good .375, a rifle I'd hunted with considerably in the Rockies. For a second rifle I took a .30-06, but I actually expected to use the .375 most of the time. It didn't happen that way. I carried the .375 when hunting lion, buffalo, and eland; the .30-06 was used for everything else with near-perfect results. I couldn't have done without the .375, and indeed, when we got into some heavy cover with a wounded buffalo, I wished for a much bigger gun. But if I'd shot the .375 a bit better when I had the chance, there would have been no need for anything larger.

On another safari I carried a .338 Winchester Magnum and a .416 Hoffman—both bolt-actions, both fiberglass-stocked, both scoped. This was an unusual hunt in that it started in the Okavango Delta, where I hunted leopard, buffalo, and sitatunga; thence to an elephant hunt in the Matetsi area; and finally to South Africa's eastern Cape, where I hunted (for the third time) and finally shot a Vaal rhebok. That hunt covered not only a disparity of terrain, but also a wide variety of game. The .416 was used only on buffalo and elephant—but it was most welcome. The .338 handled everything else with wonderful efficiency.

As much as I love the big boomers, I believe the most effective two-rifle battery will *not* include a rifle that's *too specialized*. The .338/.416 combination, or something along those lines, may well be one of the very best batteries available. It wouldn't have to be a .416 Hoffman, of course; it could be a Rigby, a Remington, or a Weatherby. Or it could be a .411 K.D.F., a .425 Express, or even a classic .404 Jeffery or .425 Westley Richards.

The lighter rifle wouldn't have to be a .338, but for the most versatility and efficiency it should shoot flatter than a .375 and be somewhat more powerful than a .30-06 or 7mm magnum. Other good choices would be belted magnums such as the .340 Weatherby, 8mm Remington, or .358 Norma. A .300 magnum would fill the bill, especially with well-constructed, heavy bullets. I would rather have a .338 any old day, but that's personal preference.

I wish I could say my survey of professional hunters agreed with me, but in truth it did not. Only my good friend Ray Millican, professional hunter in Zambia, stipulated the .338 and .416 for a two-rifle battery. I knew he would; we were chewing the fat at a convention a while back, and he stated that the .338 and .416 (at that time, either Hoffman or Rigby) made the most versatile and sensible two-gun battery. I replied that the only thing that might be better would be the .340 Weatherby in place of the .338, if one could handle the extra recoil. I guess Ray and I are a quorum of two; no other professional hunter who suggested specific two-caliber batteries mentioned the .338 and .416 together.

The results are interesting, even if they don't agree with my own thinking. (Perhaps more interesting because they don't—remember, these recommendations come from professional hunters in the field!) The .416s weren't ignored altogether; there were four votes for a .416 and a 7mm magnum, and two votes for a .416 and a .300 magnum.

Unlike the one-rifle recommendations, which overwhelmingly recommended the .375, the professional hunters differed widely on their two-gun suggestions. However, it is significant that nearly 75 percent recommended that one of the rifles be a .375. About 10 percent suggested a .458 or larger coupled with a much lighter rifle—and there were two recommendations for a .375 and a .450-plus. With the overwhelming majority recommending the .375 as the heavier of the two rifles, the difference of opinion was in

Wildebeest, though only a third the size of eland, are notoriously tough. A 7mm or .30 caliber will do the job, of course, but not nearly so reliably as something on the order of a .338 or .375.

Although not particularly difficult to hunt, the sable is another very strong antelope—and of course, bad-angle shots like this are hardly uncommon. As important as choice of caliber is to use well-constructed, heavy-for-caliber bullets that are sure to penetrate.

This Lichtensteins hartebeest was shot with a .30 caliber Nosler Partition bullet. Bullet construction is a vital consideration for the hartebeest clan.

A record-book sable antelope from the Matetsi region in Zimbabwe. A .300 Winchester with a 180-grain Nosler partition was used. An excellent choice for a tough animal like the sable.

Professional hunter Joof Lamprecht and I with a fine Namibian gemsbok taken with a .340 Weatherby Magnum. It's in open country on large, tough antelope such as this that the .338 and .340 really come into their own.

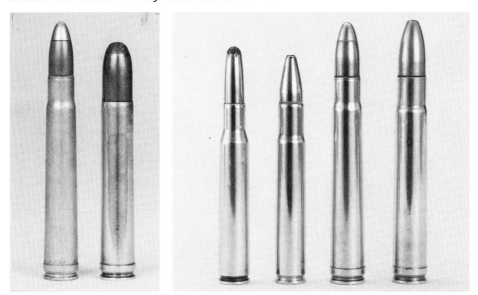

Above left: For everything from large plains game on up, the .375, left, was the overwhelming choice of today's professionals—except for thick-skinned game, where the .458 Winchester Magnum got the nod. The .375, too, was the most recommended rifle for clients to bring on safari.

Depending on the country and the range of game, here are four excellent candidates for hunting the largest of the plains game: left to right, .30-06, .35 Whelen, .375 H&H, and .416 Remington.

This Nyasaland wildebeest was shot with a .375 H&H. Wildebeest are among the toughest animals of Africa. When given a choice, the author prefers to use a large caliber on these animals.

While the kudu is not to be taken lightly, he is not as hardy as other African animals of his size. However, a greater kudu is a hard-won prize, and an exceptional bull may not stand around like this one did. I didn't shoot at the best kudu of my life because I was carrying a .30-06 instead of a bigger gun; it's a mistake I won't forget.

That day I was carrying a .416—and a good thing. Underneath the first cartridge were solids. Nobody wants to tackle a lion with solids, ever—but if you must, the bigger the better. This is a reasonable Masai lion, by the way.

I've shot all my eland, from this first one up to the present, with a .375, so I can't speak first-hand about using lighter cartridges. For darn sure the .375 is enough gun—but none too much.

Kim Adamson dropped this cat cleanly with one shot from her .30-06. Local laws may dictate a .375 as the minimum; but if they don't, I believe you're better off with a lighter, faster caliber on such a small animal.

It goes without saying that leopard hunting is a scope game, and the more light your scope can gather, the better off you are. You also want bold crosshairs so you can pick up an aiming point quickly in poor light.

I used a .338 with a 210-grain Nosler Partition on this leopard. I was, of course, overgunned, but the rifle wore a very good scope, and it was getting awfully dark when I shot him.

When there's true savanna grassland, where short-range encounters like this are most rare. In that kind of country your rifle must shoot flat and hit hard. This is where the flat-shooting magnums come into their own.

The sighting of fresh lion tracks is an exciting moment on any safari—but when you find them, it's amazing how much better you feel with a .375 in your hands rather than a .270 or '06.

Here's my .416 Rigby with a nice Selous Reserve bull. There is a very significant difference in hitting power between the .375 and the various .416s. The .375 will kill them, but the .416, as my buddy Jack Atcheson likes to say, will "numb" them.

Every professional hunter has his own preferences regarding solids versus softs, and I believe in following your PH's advice within reason. However, for buffalo I always load solids in the magazine with one good softpoint on top. With doubles, I load one of each.

This tsessebe was shot with a Remington 7mm magnum with 175-grain Core-Lokt bullet. That caliber with that load has become an African standard in the last quarter-century.

If dangerous game isn't on the menu, one of very few rifles I'd consider for a one-gun safari would be an accurate .338 (or .340 Weatherby) wearing a good scope. I used a .338 for this blesbok.

We found this bull resting at midmorning in some thornbush in the Selous. The brain shot is relatively easy on hippo, but if you go for a body shot you can have a lively time dumping cartridges in and out of a big double.

Here's the classic frontal brain shot, a sure shot to be certain, but very tricky. The brain lies more or less between the eyes, but buried very deep in the skull. Since you're shooting from below, you must shoot under and be-tween the eyes to reach the brain.

The white rhino is a huge beast, but hunting these usually docile monsters is a pale shadow of what hunting black rhino was. Still, their great bulk—up to three tons—demands big rifles firing good solids. I used a Heym .470 on this one.

Luke Samaras, left, and Bill Baker with a Selous Reserve tusker taken with Bill's .458 Lott. These are very small-bodied elephants; a single solid to the shoulder very nearly dropped this bull in his tracks.

Here's a genuine 100-pounder from Zaire. The hunter is Owen Rutherford, the rifle his double .577. Owen was one of few modern hunters to stick with the big gun; he used it on over 100 tuskers. (photo by Owen Rutherford)

I used a Heym double .500 on this Mozambique bull. My professional hunter, Roger Whittall, had his Holland Grade 2 .500/.465 for backup. It's extremely unusual today to see two doubles in the field at once.

This is a season's worth of ivory from the reopening of Mozambique in 1989, the work of many hunters. In the old days, this would be the bag of just one hunter, which is why the points of view of the oldtime hunters are so different and of limited application now. Today's hunters are in search of just one good animal, and may get just one opportunity.

Here's another 100-pounder taken on the Gwane River in the early '70s. As you can see, Rutherford was a big man and had no trouble with the .577—but it's too much gun for lesser mortals like me! (photo by Owen Rutherford)

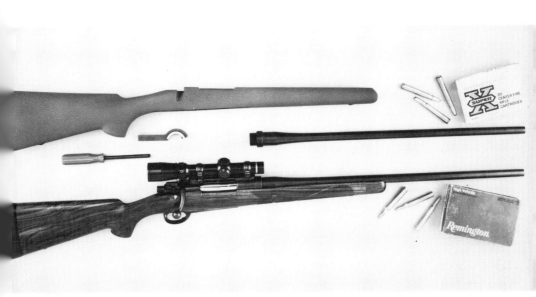

This Bighorn interchange-
able-barrel rifle has one
barrel in .375 and the
other in 8mm Remington
Magnum, plus a "beater"
stock as well as a pretty
one. It's a neat setup, to
be sure. The only problem
is, with my luck, I'd be
sure to have the 8mm
barrel in place when I
wanted the .375.

Here are two quick rights
and lefts on the same hippo, two quartering one
way and two the other.
All were solids, and
nothing exited.

Still, it seems I have my .375 in my hands an awful lot of the time. We were after kudu on this particular day in the Okavango Delta, but we might well have run into the buffalo of my dreams. Unless you're really specializing in your hunting, it makes sense to carry a rifle that will handle anything you might run into in the area you're hunting.

Nubian ibex are found in the Red Sea Hills of North West Africa. Anything that works on North American sheep, such as the .270 or the .30-06, is ideal for these mountain dwellers.

Ludo Wurfbain chose a Kevlar-stocked Remington 700 in .416 Remington for his hunt in the forests of Cameroon. He felt the rifle was perfect for game like this bongo, but barely adequate for elephant in such heavy cover.

This steenbok was taken with a .30-06, which is more gun than is needed for this small animal. However, it was the only gun available when this male was sighted. The 165 grain Nosler Partition bullet used did relatively little damage.

One of the ultimate swamp trophies is the sitatunga. Shots are often long, but the animal must be hit very hard and anchored. Tracking is almost impossible, and once these animals sink under the swamp foliage, finding them becomes very difficult. A .338 with spitzer bullets is a good choice.

A good swamp gun is a fiberglass-stocked job with a rustproofed metal finish. It will rust eventually, of course, but you're not likely to mind as much as you would if it were a lovely double!

A .375 H&H will serve for run-of-the-mill camp meat chores as well as other hunting.

I used a basic three-rifle battery in Tanzania, with my David Miller 7mm as the light. I was glad to have it, too—some of the shooting was long, difficult, and tricky, and I'm not sure I would have gotten this Chanler's mountain reedbuck with my .375.

This 33-inch lesser kudu is possibly my very best African trophy. It was a tough running shot, and that's where a light rifle that you shoot all the time in your deer woods back home can really pay dividends in African hunting.

Here's the problem with a one-rifle safari. If anything happens to that one rifle, you're in trouble. In this case it was the light rifle, my .30-06, that broke. My .375 became my one-gun battery, and of course it worked just fine.

Here's the bag from one camp in that Zambian hunt where I had just my .375 and my .458 Lott. The .375 was adequate for everything, but the big gun was a comfort when working buffalo herds in heavy cover.

Kudu have a reputation for not being hard to kill. However, they are often shot in dense brush and a gun such as my .375 H&H is very suitable for this animal under such circumstances.

This is my custom .458 Lott, shown with an average Zambian buffalo. Unlike most wildcat cartridges, the Lott can be used with .458 Winchester Magnum ammo, a real advantage.

Thornbush hunting often involves picking a vital zone to shoot at on a partially obscured animal. The scope isn't needed for distance, but rather for its pure ability to allow you to see better and pick a path for your bullet.

Frederick Courtenay Selous is every African hunter's hero, one of the greatest of the oldtime hunters and a true conservationist as well. He saw the transition from muzzleloader to breechloader to smokeless repeater. This photo shows a middle-aged Selous on safari with book, bustards, and one of his beloved single-shot Gibbs Farquharsons.

Although virtually
tuskless and thus taken
on a non-trophy permit,
this is one of the largest
elephant s I have ever
seen. He dropped to a
side-on brain shot from
my .416 Hoffman.

The .375 was the work-
horse of this safari, as it
usually is. The 7mm
would have worked on
this white-bearded gnu,
for instance, but I prefer a
bit more gun for such
tough animals.

For back-up work in Tanzania, Paddy Curtis relied on this rare Mannlicher rotary-magazine .458. Paddy was tossed by a buffalo while using this rifle, so I wonder if there's a big double in his future.

Professional hunter Russ Broom used a Winchester Model 70 Super Grade (pre-'64) .375 exclusively when this photo was taken. He's since made the shift to a big double in .458 for back up, with .375 barrels for general-purpose work.

The .30-06 was enough gun for Theodore Roosevelt during his 1909 African safari, and it is still an ideal gun for most plains game today. This Grants gazelle was shot with a 165-grain Nosler partition.

This lion was taken with Winchester's XTR-Express, the current version of their .375. I believe that rifle to be the most inexpensive .375 bolt-action around—and it's a very good one.

American John Speed, left, and Gary Hoops with the latter's .510 Wells. This rifle is a real thumper, and Gary swears by it. Considering the problems with ammo and components, it takes a serious commitment for an African pro to choose a wildcat cartridge.

Luke Samaras is a double rifle man; he's relied on his Army & Navy .470 for many years. In recent seasons, however, he's been leaving the double behind more and more in favor of a Rigby .416—perhaps because elephant hunting is playing an ever-decreasing role in his safaris.

Finding elephant in the open like this is rare these days. These three bulls offer a wide choice of shots, from shoulder to heart to lung to side-on and quartering brain shots. This is the kind of situation that Bell exploited using his accurate small bores, and indeed a scoped .375 or .416 would be ideal—but you don't find them like this much any more.

Here are three classic rifles from the good old days that show three altogether different schools of thought—the Westley Richards .318 for the small-bore fans, John Rigby's .416 for the big-bore magazine rifle boys, and a .470 for the big double boys.

California sportsman Dave Prizio used a .340 Weatherby to obtain his mountain nyala in the highlands of Ethiopia. The size of a small elk, mountain nyala are found in steep terrain and often long shots are required to obtain one. A .340 Weatherby is an ideal rifle for this kind of hunt.

Zebras are hard to kill. First-time safari hunters are often amazed at their toughness. This stallion had fought off a lion attack; the zebra had plenty of scars on its hind quarter to prove the encounter. Any animal that can successfully repel a lion attack is tough, yet one shot from a .30-06 killed it.

Professional hunter Nicky Blunt, currently guiding in Tanzania and the CAR, uses a custom built .416 Remington based on a pre-64 Winchester action. He prefers his rifles light; this one weighs in at just over 8 lbs.

George Angelides, a long-time Tanzania outfitter and professional hunter, prefers all the gun he can get his hands on. His backup rifle is a Rigby-built .460 Weatherby.

This topi, one of the various forms of hartebeest found in East Africa, was taken with a .30-06. All hartebeests are considered tough and well constructed bullets need to be used to hunt them.

Hippos are often shot in the water. The objective is to hit the brain. A well constructed 7mm or .30 caliber bullet is adequate for this job.

I used a Ruger No. One to shoot this Hartmanns zebra. I have had excellent results using this rifle on safari.

Dave Prizio used a .270 Weatherby with a 150 grain Nosler partition to shoot this leopard in Tanzania. The .270 Weatherby is excellent for this purpose.

the choice of a lighter rifle. The .300 magnum was the most common lighter rifle, with nearly 20 percent. However, the .30-06 and 7mm magnum were close behind with about 15 percent each. And then there was a non-specific group that recommended the .375 plus a ".270, .280, .30-06, or 7mm magnum."

I don't think there's a quantum leap in power as you progress from .270 to .280 to 7mm magnum to .30-06 to .300 magnum. Actually, I like all of those cartridges, though some better than others. If you consider these cartridges together, then fully 65 percent of the professional hunters suggested one of that group in combination with the .375 H&H for the optimum two-gun battery.

As I said, I think one of the .416s mated to an over-.30-caliber magnum makes a more flexible battery. But I can't argue with the experts; after all, a .30-06 paired with a .375 has been one of my favorite combinations, and it sure does work. Just as so many professional hunters say it will!

# Chapter 34

# The Three-rifle Battery

The classic African battery has traditionally consisted of three rifles—a light, a medium, and a heavy. This concept originated in a different world, when hunters traveled to Africa by slow-moving steamer and, once there, the average safari stretched into months. With trips of such duration, the amount of allowable baggage wasn't as critical as it is today—and certainly there was much more shooting to be done than there is these days.

For his 1894-1897 safari, covering on foot some 4,000 miles of Africa, Edouard Foa chose a blackpowder 8-bore double for his heavy rifle, a pair of .577 Express blackpowder doubles for the "medium," and a smokeless .303 Lee-Metford as a light rifle. All served him well.

Just a few years later, the new .450-class Nitro-Express cartridges would replace the big 8- and 10-bores; and even smaller smokeless cartridges would supplant the old blackpowder Expresses in the medium classification. The light rifle, well, as such it hardly existed before smokeless powder, unless you'd consider such as the .577/.450 Martini a small bore!

In 1909, Theodore Roosevelt's primary battery took the classic three-rifle form: his .30-06 Springfield as a light rifle; his Winchester Model 95 in .405 as a medium (his "lion medicine"); and his Holland & Holland double .500/.450 for the largest game.

Similarly, the great American hunter/author Stewart Edward White stayed with his Springfield .30-06, Winchester .405, and Holland double .465, not only in the years before World War I, but also on his last safari in 1925. Pioneer photographer Martin Johnson's battery, used from 1921 to 1935, was almost identical—a .30-06, a .405, and a .470 double by Thomas Bland.

Hemingway's 1935 battery was a departure; he had a 6.5mm Mannlicher, of course his .30-06 Springfield, and a big double—three rifles, but none of them a classic medium. In 1952, however, Ruark's battery was perhaps *the* classic three-rifle armament. He had a Remington .30-06, presumably a Model 721; a Winchester Model 70 .375; and a Westley Richards .470 double. He also took along a .220 Swift, but found it unsatisfactory and quickly gave up on it.

Ruark's first safari, so ably recorded in *Horn of the Hunter*, was typical of the day—a three-month free-wheeling safari that wound its way across much of Tanganyika. The bag included two lions, a great leopard, some marvelous buffalo, plus waterbuck, oryx, and the typical East African plains game. They did not hunt elephant, and were unlucky with both rhino and kudu. But all three rifles got substantial workouts.

About five years later, my uncle, Art Popham, made a 30-day safari into Tanganyika on a collecting expedition for the Kansas City Museum of Natural History. Although not as leisurely as the Ruark safari, his safari got down to business; he shot the usual two lions, buffalo, an 80-pound elephant, and the full range of plains game.

His battery consisted of two Winchester Model 70s, one in .300 Improved and the other in .375 Improved (respectively identical to .300 and .375 Weatherby); and a big double. Unfortunately, there was no ammunition for the double, and information on the big Nitro-Express cartridges was extremely sketchy in America in those days. It was a .450 of some type, but the .450 cartridges they had split badly. I suspect they were trying to shoot .450-3¼" cartridges in a .500/.450 or possibly .450 No. 2 chamber. Anyway, he took the rifle to Africa hoping to find ammunition in Nairobi or Arusha. No such luck, not even in 1957. The heavy rifle was thus useless, and the .375 served with perfect satisfaction on buffalo and elephant.

The three-rifle concept has great merit. On the one end you have a very specialized, short-range, charge-stopping big bore; on the other end you have an accurate, flat-shooting, low-recoiling light rifle. And in the middle you have a versatile medium bore, a rifle that will be perfect for lion and very large antelope, and in a pinch serve for both the largest and smallest of game.

The medium, the general-purpose rifle, is the mainstay of a three-rifle battery. The most logical choice is a .375, but if a lot of heavy game is to be encountered, a .416 or similar rifle could serve. Whatever the caliber, the rifle must be scope-sighted, and of course both solid and softpoint ammunition must be available.

The heavy rifle could be a double or a magazine rifle, whichever the hunter prefers. It should definitely be of .450 caliber or larger. Traditionally, such a rifle is open-sighted, but there's no reason why it shouldn't wear a low-powered scope and good reasons why it should. It is the rifle that will be used the least, but when it's used the stakes are highest—so it must be selected with care; it must fit the shooter perfectly, and it must be in perfect working order.

The light rifle could be anything from .243 up to .338, but its most likely and most sensible calibers lie between 6.5mm and .300. It will be scope-sighted, and it must be accurate and flat-shooting. It is probably the rifle that will be used the most, but depending on the range of game and the hunter's preferences, that honor could go to the medium. The light rifle will surely be used on a variety of game at a variety of distances, and it should be in a caliber as versatile as possible—and one with which the hunter is familiar and comfortable.

I have used Ruark's battery of a .30-06, .375, and double .470 on a couple of occasions, and that's a wonderful mix. I've also replaced the .30-06 with a 7mm magnum, and the .375 with a .416—with equally good results.

There are problems with a three-rifle battery, the main objection being that three rifles add up to a lot of weight to haul around. Most often, two gun cases will be required, so the hunter traveling solo is asking for a monstrous overweight baggage charge. Of course, if you will have two gun cases anyway, you might as well haul along a shotgun.

The three-rifle battery does have a place, and I've been grateful for all three on most occasions when I've opted to take that number. However, this is a lot of rifles to look after, and a lot of rifles to use on the average safari today. A three-rifle battery might make sense on a lengthy safari, but only if a large variety of game will be hunted—including two or more members of the Big Five.

On a shorter hunt, the opportunity to use three rifles will generally not present itself, and the last thing you want is confusion over which rifle to reach for. I have carried heavy rifles to Africa and never fired them once, using the medium instead when the opportunity occurred. By the same token, I've carried a light rifle all the way to Africa and never fired it, again using the medium instead—not because I needed to, but because it was the medium I was carrying when I might have used the lighter rifle.

The professional hunters I surveyed had a wide divergence of opinion about a three-rifle battery, but some 60 percent made specific recommendations. Darn few were alike. There were several votes for a .30-06, a .375, and a ".400-plus," and a couple more for a 7mm magnum, .375, and .458. Several suggested a .300 magnum plus a .375 and .458, and a couple more recommended the .243, .30-06, and .458. One recommended a .270, an 8x68S, and a .458.

Several recommendations didn't clearly differentiate between light, medium, and heavy. For instance, one professional recommended a 7x57, a .270, and a .375; another recommended a .270, 7mm magnum, and .375. Some of the recommendations were most interesting. Soren Lindstrom, for instance, declined to recommend a second *or* third rifle, saying that if the hunter had a .375 nothing else was necessary.

Mike Rowbotham, with 37 years in the field, personally uses a .275 Rigby, .300 H&H, .338, .375, and .470 double for the various types of game. He recommends to clients that, for a three-rifle battery, they bring a .275 (meaning, I assume, a 7x57), a .338, and a .458 *with handloaded ammunition.* Mike Carr-Hartley, another pro with vast experience, recommended a 7mm magnum, a .375, and a .458—but added that, if available, a double of .470 or similar caliber was preferable. S.A. Wahib, also with several decades of experience, declined to recommend specific calibers to hunters, but suggested that three rifles were only appropriate for lengthy, general-bag safaris.

Other comments by hunters who did not recommend three rifles are perhaps more telling. In the three-rifle block, George Hoffman wrote, "Too many—you never know which one to use! Better the third gun be a shotgun or .22." Cotton Gordon said simply, "Two is enough." Finn Aagaard said,

"Not necessary. .22 rimfire or varmint rifle if he likes." Franz Wengert wrote, "Anything more than two guns is a headache."

Franz is dead right. More than two rifles *is* a headache, and can lead to having the wrong equipment in your hands when a major opportunity arises. There are times when you might want three—on a very lengthy safari, or if you feel the need for a highly specialized rifle like a big double. And, after all, for rifle cranks like me, using different rifles in Africa is part of the enjoyment of the safari. But don't take three if you don't really need them; you'll find it more trouble than it's worth hauling them from airport to airport!

# Chapter 35

# The Professional's Choice in the Good Old Days

Writing this book has been quite a project, albeit an enjoyable one. From the start, I knew it would be presumptuous if all the ideas were my own—and such folly would negate any real benefit the book might have. Fortunately, the community of currently active professional hunters were most generous with their opinions on African rifles, and in the next chapter we'll look at both the rifles they use personally and their recommendations to clients. Here, I thought it would be interesting to take a historical look at the batteries that served sportsmen in the early days.

Some of the oldtimers were ivory hunters, so their choices ran to the heavier rifles. Others were sportsmen and women, adventurers, naturalists or soldiers. But all had considerable experience shooting game in an Africa that will never be seen again.

The people we will look at here hunted Africa from the earliest days through World War II. Very few of these hunters, if any, are alive today. Fortunately, many of them left behind written records, part of the impressive body of African literature that still stirs our imagination. Usually the old timers tell us what rifles they used.

There's another marvelous reference, long out of print, by S.R. Truesdell: *The Rifle—Its Development for Big Game Hunting* (now available in new edition from Safari Press). In it, Lieutenant Colonel Truesdell takes oldtime gunwriter Ned Crossman's advice to heart: "After all, the digest of the experience of a hundred men—picked men, not chaps who once killed a buck in the Adirondacks and know all about game rifles, is the best way to reach an intelligent decision."

Truesdell gathered up the experiences and choices of arms of more than a hundred—170, to be precise—extremely experienced hunters, many of whom were still alive at that time. The 170 included American buffalo hunters, early African explorers, ivory hunters, colonial administrators, missionaries, the great turn-of-the-century sheep hunters, and even more familiar names such as Jack O'Connor and Elmer Keith. In the text, he discusses the rifles and cartridges as well as the experiences of those who used them, and he provides fascinating tables that list the names, hunting experiences and locales, and batteries of his chosen experts.

The way Truesdell saw it, between the beginning of the 19th century (when rifled arms came into widespread use) and World War II, the use of hunting rifles could be divided into four eras: from about 1834 to 1874, the time of the large bores; from 1875 to 1892 (coinciding with the British Express rifles), the era of the medium bores; from 1893 to 1905 (the infancy of smokeless powder), which he reckons as the time of the small bores; and from 1906 to 1946, when the *high-velocity* small bores held sway. It's a most interesting premise and a fascinating book; I hope someone resurrects and reprints it for today's hunters. I'd also like to know what Truesdell would make of the *last* 40 years of sporting rifles!

In any case, this excellent reference provides a marvelous thumbnail sketch of the rifles used and preferred by widely experienced hunters the world over. Most of this material is, of course, to be found in books written by the individuals themselves (which means that, to obtain the same information, one must face the enjoyable but time-consuming task of reading 170 volumes, as Truesdell undoubtedly did).

Truesdell's African experts start at the beginning, with Captain William Cornwallis Harris, whose 1835-36 South African expedition was perhaps the first safari in the modern sense. Harris relied primarily upon a double-barrel, muzzleloading 8-bore, and he had trouble with the largest animals— as did all the hunters until the advent of the reliable penetration afforded by jacketed bullets. William Cotton Oswell followed hard on the heels of Harris, and he hunted from 1837 to 1852. His favorite rifle was a smooth-bore double 10-bore by Purdey, of course a muzzleloader, and a rifled 12-bore by Westley Richards.

The wild Scotsman, Roualeyn Gordon-Cumming, wandered and hunted in southern Africa from 1843 to 1848. His favorite arm was a muzzleloading 12-bore double by Purdey, but he also used a huge 4-bore single-shot along with several other big muzzleloaders. This passage, from his *Five Years Hunting Adventures in Africa,* is not atypical of the lengths the early hunters had to go to kill the largest African animals: "Having fired thirty-five rounds with my two-grooved rifle. . . I opened fire upon him with the Dutch six-pounder. . . and when forty bullets had perforated his hide he began for the first time to evince signs of a dilapidated constitution."

Earlier we referred to Sir Samuel Baker's "Baby," a 2-bore that fired a half-pound explosive shell. He actually used the cannon very little, however, relying mostly on 8- and 10-bore muzzleloading doubles. Later on, he was one of the first of the famed African explorers to rely on a breechloader, a .577 blackpowder double made by Holland & Holland. However, he believed strongly that a .577 was a light rifle, only for thin-skinned game. He died in 1893, still maintaining that a double 8-bore was the only medicine for the largest game.

William Finaughty, hunting from 1864 to 1875, was another hunter whose career saw muzzleloaders replaced by breechloaders; he eventually gave up on his 4-bore single-shot muzzleloader in favor of a breechloading 12-bore double. Arthur Neumann, one of the great ivory hunters, had an unusually long career; he hunted ivory from 1868 to 1906, thus seeing the transition not only from muzzle-to breechloading, but also from blackpowder to smokeless. He finished his career using a double .450-3¼" by Rigby and a .256 Mannlicher as a light rifle. However, unlike so many hunters who swore by the 6.5mm or .256, Neumann never used it for elephant.

Perhaps that was because, back in 1896, he was almost killed by an elephant after his .303 Lee-Metford failed him. His .450 was one of the first to see service in Africa, and he swore by it.

Frederick Courteney Selous hunted for ivory in his earlier days, using a beast of a muzzleloading 4-bore single-shot that he came to hate. Later on, it's fair to say that he was more of an explorer, writer, and naturalist than an ivory hunter—but he was always hunting, often for the British Museum. He saw the changes that Neumann saw, and he was also quick to adopt the new smokeless cartridges. In the middle years of his career, his favorite rifle was a Gibbs-Farquharson .461; he preferred its accuracy to the brute force of the big bores—and he still preferred it after the Nitro-Expresses came into being.

Around the turn of the century, he had Holland build him a single-shot .303, virtually identical to his old .461, and this also became a much-used rifle. Like virtually all the turn-of-the-century hunters, Selous also used a .256 Mannlicher extensively. For his last East African hunting, just before World War I, Selous used a .375 Holland & Holland—a rifle worlds removed from the single-shot 4-bores he started with. Of these newfangled little guns Selous said, "Had I only one of these rifles in my early days, I would have shot thrice the number of elephants I did."

In the 1890s, the most common batteries were a mixture of blackpowder and smokeless arms. Edouard Foa's heavy 8-bore, medium .577 Express, and light .303 formed a very normal mixed battery—at least until confidence in the new, fast-moving smokeless cartridges grew. Lieutenant Colonel H. G. C. Swayne, who hunted in Somaliland between 1884 and 1897 (and is immortalized by the Swayne's hartebeest subspecies) used 8- and 12-bore Paradox guns, the ever-present .577/.450 Martini, and later a .303—but his primary arm was a blackpowder .577 by Holland. The .577 was perhaps the only caliber that was revered in both blackpowder and smokeless form. As a blackpowder cartridge, it had enough bullet weight and caliber to get the job done, albeit with little to spare. When it was transformed to a smokeless cartridge, it became hell on wheels!

On his earlier trips, Edward North Buxton used a blackpowder double .500 Express almost exclusively, but by 1893—very early in the smokeless game—he had added a .256 Mannlicher, unquestionably the 6.5x53R Mannlicher-Steyr, to his battery. This very quickly became his only rifle.

Sir Edmund Loder (the Loder's gazelle of North Africa bears his name) started his career in India and Sumatra with 8- and 12-bore doubles by Reilly. Later he gave up on the big guns in favor of a .450 Express, but by the early 1890s he was sold on the .256 Mannlicher; it was the only rifle he used on his 1906-1907 East African safari.

Around the turn of the century, the smokeless era had well and truly taken hold, and blackpowder rifles were vanishing from the scene. Major C.S. Cumberland started his hunting career in Asia with a 12-bore double, but when he hunted East Africa in 1911 he used a double .500 by Henry, a smokeless gun, and a .303 Lee-Metford.

The Reverend William Rainsford, an American Episcopalian clergyman from New York, was quite a hunter. On his earlier trips to the western United States, he used a .50-110 single-shot and a double 8-bore by Rigby. He preceded Roosevelt to East Africa, not once but twice between 1906 and 1909. His battery, like Roosevelt's, was the classic three-rifle arrangement: a .450-3¼", probably by Rigby, as a heavy; a .350 Rigby Magnum as a medium; and a .256 Mannlicher as a light. Like many hunters before and since, he got the most use from his medium and was lavish in his praise of it.

Richard J. Cunninghame and Leslie Tarlton were contemporaries in the Kenya Colony; Cunninghame settled there in 1889 and hunted until 1924, Tarlton from 1891 to 1926. Both were early settlers, sport hunters, commercial hunters, and professional hunters. Both undoubtedly started with blackpowder arms, but both eventually became fans of Holland's .500/.465 and, a seeming contradiction for English colonists, the American .30-06. Tarlton, one of the greatest of all lion hunters, also favored .275 and .350 magnums by Rigby.

Although Truesdell ascribes the period from 1893 to 1905 to the new smokeless small bores, hunters who used the little 6.5, 7x57, .303, and so on *exclusively* were somewhat rare. On the other hand, such rifles were used extensively on a tremendous variety of African game. Often the light rifle's use was accidental, in that it was the rifle the hunter customarily carried, while a tracker carried the heavy rifle. When an opportunity for a shot arose, it was sometimes more expedient to shoot than to switch guns—and it was discovered that the light rifles, with long, heavy-for-caliber solid bullets, performed surprisingly well. But very few of the serious professionals actually relied on the small bores; Bell was a notable and outspoken exception.

Sir Alfred Pease hunted in North Africa in the early 1890s, then in East Africa between 1896 and 1924. His .256 Mannlicher was indeed his most-used rifle, but he also used Jeffery rifles in both .333 and .404, a .350 Rigby, and a 10-bore Paradox. Naturalist John G. Millais, on the other hand, used only his .256 Mannlicher on his many expeditions between 1893 and 1924.

Major P.H.G. Powell-Cotton was another who used a Paradox gun—they were actually very popular. But for light game, he relied on his .256 Mannlicher. He wasn't necessarily a small-bore addict, however; for his Central African hunting between 1902 and 1904, he used a double .450/.400 on most of his heavy game—and a tracker carried a double .600 by Jeffery for use in tight spots.

Denis D. Lyell, who hunted in Africa and wrote about it extensively between 1897 and 1920, was a vociferous small-bore advocate. He used a

.404 Jeffery, but on the whole much preferred a 7.9mm Mauser, .275 (7x57), or .256 Mannlicher.

Lyell was much more experienced with the largest game than most hunters of today, but he didn't have anything like the experience of a James Sutherland. Sutherland, as we've seen earlier, used the .318 and also the 10.75 Mauser, but for elephant he relied on a pair of double .577s—and with them he had one of the longest careers of any of the serious ivory hunters, from 1896 to 1932.

The American naturalist Carl Akeley hunted and collected throughout East and Central Africa between 1896 and 1926; he died of fever and was buried in the Belgian Congo. On his earlier trips, he carried a .256 Mannlicher as a light rifle, a 9mm Mauser as a medium, and a double .470 for his heavy. Later he seems to have given up on a medium, using mostly a Jeffery double .475 No. 2—but also carrying three light rifles: a .275 Hoffman, a 7.9mm Mauser, and a .30-06. Major C.H. Stigand, killed in action in the Sudan in 1919, was a courageous and well-liked officer who served primarily in Africa from 1899 until his death. He was definitely a small-bore man, preferring his .256 Mannlicher although he did have a double .450 available for back-up. A. Blayney Percival, author of *A Game Ranger's Notebook* was another .256 man. He also had a double .360 and a double .450, but he wrote, "I shot most of my lions, say forty with the .256. I do not remember exactly, but I feel sure that two-thirds of the lions did not need a second shot; if one did, it usually meant several more. When hunting alone I seldom fired till I had a lion just how I wanted him, and I shot to put him out of business. Soft-nosed bullets I gave up long ago except for small stuff or in heavy rifles."

Colonel J. Stevenson Hamilton, a contemporary of Percival, shot an enormous number of lions—perhaps more than even Tarlton. He apparently used a .303 Lee-Metford for much of his lion shooting, which definitely qualifies him as a small-bore man. However, he also used a .350 Rigby Magnum, and for larger game both a .416 Rigby and a double .577.

Marcus Daly, hunting between 1897 and 1936, was a magazine-rifle man. He much preferred them to doubles, doing most of his later hunting with a 10.75 Mauser and .416 Rigby. He did not believe in the small bores for elephant, feeling that they were adequate for brain shots on undisturbed game, but not for use in thick cover.

The Hungarian Kalman Kittenberger, author of *Big Game Hunting And Collecting In East Africa, 1903-1926* used Mannlichers in 6.5, 8, and 9mm; and Mausers in 7x57 and 8x57. He seems to have preferred the 8mm and 9mm magazine rifles, but he also relied on a Holland double .465 for the largest game.

American Charles Cottar, one of the most colorful of the early professional hunters, plied his trade in Kenya between 1902 and 1940. He never lost his love for the .405 Winchester, but he also had a double .470 by Rigby, a .35 Newton that he used extensively, and a .250 Savage for light game.

He also, it appears, used the incredibly anemic .32 Winchester Special to take virtually *all* species of African game when he first arrived.

Major H.C. Maydon, whose marvelous *Big Game Shooting in Africa* remains a valuable reference a half-century after publication, was primarily a small-bore man; he had a .470 double, which he used extensively on his first safari to Portuguese East Africa, but after he acquired a 7.9mm Mauser his .470 became a seldom-used back-up.

Captain A.H.E. Mosse, who hunted in Somaliland for five years, 1907 to 1912, had a three-gun battery: a 12-bore Paradox, a double .450/.400 by Watson, and a .318 Westley Richards magazine rifle. He did not hunt elephant, but, unlike his small-bore contemporaries, he relied on his .400 double for most of his lion hunting.

On their 1909 safari, Kermit Roosevelt's battery was similar to his father's. For a light rifle, he also had a .30-06; for a medium, another .405 Winchester; only his heavy differed in that he had a .450-3¼" by Rigby. Like his father, he used the big double but little, relying mainly on his .405 Winchester.

George Agnew Chamberlain, another visiting sportsman who hunted in Portuguese East Africa between 1909 and 1923, used a .450 double by Evans and a .470 by Churchill. He had a .256, but his favorite light rifle was a .318 Westley Richards.

American naturalist James L. Clark, best known for his *Great Arc of the Wild Sheep*, hunted and collected extensively in Africa. He used a number of rifles, but his Springfield .30-06 and William Evans .470 double remained his two mainstays. Another American author, Edison Marshall, also used a two-rifle battery on his 1929-1930 safari. Unlike most Americans, he eschewed the .30-06, using instead a 9.5mm Mannlicher and a .470 double.

Dr. Richard Sutton, surgeon and naturalist, hunted widely in both Africa and Indochina. His favorite rifle was a Holland double .465, which he used essentially as a medium rifle. His "heavy" was heavy indeed, a double .577, while as a light rifle he used a .30-06. Later on, he turned to a 9.3x62, but rarely used it in place of the .465.

After the death of her father, Vivienne de Watteville carried on with their joint expedition in East and Central Africa. A petite woman, she had no problems with her .416 Rigby, which she used extensively. Her light rifle was a .318 Westley Richards.

Captain E.T.L. Lewis, hunting in East Africa between 1924 and 1928, and later in India, is one of the few who used what we would consider today an ideal three-rifle battery; his heavy was a Holland double .465, his medium a .375 H&H Magnum, and his light a .303 Lee-Metford. Perhaps surprisingly, his favorite rifle was the big double—but he made no bones over being a double-rifle man.

Count Vasco da Gama wandered and hunted throughout French Equatorial Africa for nearly two years during the late 1920s. Apparently a man of some means, he tried out a variety of rifles, including doubles in both .577 and .600. He found them obviously effective, but too heavy to carry and with so much recoil that the second shot was too slow. Much better as a stopping rifle, he reckoned, was the Holland .465 that he settled on, but he was actually more of a small-bore magazine-rifle man, preferring to use a .275 Rigby Mauser, a 7.9mm Mauser, or a 9mm Mannlicher.

A list of this sort—the choices of the old hands—could go on almost forever. Such a study is fascinating, but its value to today's hunter is somewhat limited for two reasons. First, many of the rifles and cartridges used before World War II are no longer available, or available only with extreme difficulty. If they were better than modern counterparts, pursuing them would be worthwhile at all costs, but with the possible exception of some the big Nitro-Expresses, this is hardly the case. We have excellent modern cartridges chambered in modern rifles fully capable of handling any game that walks. Second, African hunting conditions aren't the same today as they were 50 years ago. Sad that is, but true.

It would be nice, even from purely historical interest, if some kind of consensus could be gleaned from the study of the rifles and cartridges chosen by the oldtimers. But even that seems impossible; they were as human as we are, and their choices, recommendations, and biases were based on what worked for them. Some of them favored small bores, some big bores; some used doubles while others preferred magazines. It will be always thus; as Mark Twain observed, "It is difference of opinion that makes horse races." Let's leave the past now and take a look at the rifles and cartridges of *today's* experts—the professional hunters still in the field.

# Chapter 36

# The Professional's Choice Today

There are African professionals who happen to be firearms enthusiasts and may experiment year in and year out with various guns and loads. In that profession, though, such a man is rare. More frequently, a professional hunter has neither the time, the budget, nor the inclination for such experimentation. He'll find what works for him—and stick with it.

On the other hand, the professional hunter sees it all in the long procession of clients' rifles that show up in his camps. He gets to see what works and what doesn't—to a degree unmatched in the hunting world. In 20 safaris I have shot and seen shot a great deal of African game, and I've done it and seen it done with a wide variety of rifles, cartridges, and bullets. But it would be extremely egotistical, foolish, and just plain wrong for me to presume to have anything like the hands-on experience of an African professional hunter.

That being the case, I felt it important to add the recommendations of this group to my own. Using the mailing lists for the International Professional Hunters Association (I.P.H.A.) and the Professional Hunters Association of South Africa (P.H.A.S.A.), I sent one-page questionnaires to several hundred active professional hunters, men who pursue their careers all across Africa.

Realizing that professional hunters are busy men—and most of them abhor correspondence—I kept it short, just a one-page fill-in-the-blanks. I asked how long they'd been in the field and what type of country they hunted: plains, desert, thornbush, forest, swamp, or a combination thereof. Then I asked which of the Big Five, if any, they hunted.

The next set of questions asked for the professional hunter's own choice of rifle for use on light plains game, medium plains game, large plains game, lion, leopard, thick-skinned game, and all-round use. Following that, I asked for specific recommendations to clients for a one-rifle safari, a two-rifle battery, and a three-rifle battery. Finally, I asked whether the client should bring a shotgun, and whether one is kept in camp.

There are other things I would have liked to find out, such as preferences in scope sights, choice of bullets (especially solids versus softs), and even barrel lengths. But I felt that the more details I pressed to obtain, the fewer the responses would be. As it happened, the responses totaled about 30 percent—which I understand is very good for such things. I also invited further comment, hoping that those who had more to say than allowed by the limited questions would take the time to do so. Many did, and some of these extra comments, for which I'm most grateful, may be the most valuable tidbits in this entire volume.

The responding professional hunters run the gamut of the industry. Perhaps the largest number operate in South Africa, which doesn't surprise me since that country hosts something like 50 percent of all of today's hunting safaris. Zimbabwe had the next highest number, also not surprising. The third largest geographic grouping, however, had Kenya postmarks. A few of these hunters are retired, while most currently hunt in Tanzania—but as a group, the old Kenya hands are extremely well-represented in this survey. There was also a scattering of responses from Central African hunters, but admittedly once you get away from East and Southern Africa, the language barriers begin to go up.

The senior professional hunters to respond—Tony Henley and Harry Selby—have 44 years each in the field; the junior man but two. Collectively, the respondents represent more than 1,800 years of African hunting, with an average of 16 years per man. That figure is humbling, for it clearly indicates *vast* experience with African game—far more, on the average, than I will ever live to attain, let alone have at this writing.

I've had a wonderful time writing this book, and I believe its ideas are sound. However, I am happy to conclude with the collective wisdom of today's professional hunters. If my own ideas seem to differ with them, I must recommend that you listen to these guys. On a daily basis, their reputations, livelihood, and very lives depend on sound choices in rifles and cartridges!

I have attempted to encapsulate much of the data in the accompanying charts, but I think it all requires comment. I expected most safaris to be conducted in thornbush, followed by plains, and this proved a good assessment. Interesting was the fact that desert, swamp, and forest habitat seem to be hunted about equally—and with half the frequency of thornbush and 40 percent less than plains.

Many respondents hunted more than one type of habitat, and most hunted one or more of the Big Five. I was amazed at the number of hunters who hunt lion, but even more surprised by the percentage who have experience with rhino and elephant.

## Personal Choices

It goes without saying that the rifle a professional hunter chooses for himself might not be one he would recommend to a client; like most of us, professional hunters are prone to use old favorites. And, since they live in Africa, they have occasion to use rifles that are perhaps more specialized than they might advise a client to bring. I asked for personal choices in seven areas.

**Light Plains Game:** Like all of the game categories that follow, this one was purposely vague. My idea of light plains game may or may not be the same as it would be for the professional hunters, and what really mattered to me was what they considered an adequate rifle for the light plains game of their own areas.

Of all the dozens and dozens of truly fine "deer-class" cartridges that would fill this need, only 19 cartridges were mentioned. They did run the gamut; French hunter Pierre Caravati, a professional of 32 years, uses his .460 Weatherby for everything—including light game. Campbell Smith, on the other hand, a 10-year professional in several southern countries, specifically limited "light plains game" to duiker, steinbok, and such—and stated his choice was a .22 Hornet.

In terms of numbers, the .243 Winchester was a surprising winner, with 32 specific mentions, followed by the .270 with 28, the 7mm magnum with 13, the .30-06 with 12, the .300 H&H with nine, the 7x57 with nine (Mike Rowbotham had the distinction of being the only respondent to call this cartridge the .275 Rigby!)—and on down from there. Lord knows there are no flies on the .243 or .270 Winchester for use on thin-skinned African game—but I was amazed to find them as popular as this.

Perhaps the most interesting choice, to my mind, came from my old friend Joof Lamprecht, who hunts in Namibia. In that open, arid country, where springbok are often taken at extreme range, his choice as a light rifle was the .264 Winchester Magnum. Although unusual in Africa and underrated in America, for him that's an excellent choice. And of course, one's choice of a personal rifle, whether .22 Hornet or .460 Weatherby, can hardly be wrong as long as it works.

**Medium Plains Game:** This category, though also vague, was perhaps clearer to the respondents than the previous one. It obviously stops short of eland, but could be taken to include animals well into the quarter-ton category. Just 15 cartridges were mentioned in this group, the largest being Pierre Caravati's .460 Weatherby again. The smallest was .243, but only three respondents still clung to such a light rifle.

The most common choice by far was the .30-06, with 33 mentions. The 7mm edged the .300 H&H by three, 25 mentions to 22, while the .270 came up a close fourth with 21. Notice that if you took the 16 .300 H&H entries and added eight votes for the .300 Weatherby and three for the .300 Winchester, you'd have an overwhelming amount of support for the .300 magnum for use on medium plains game.

As can be seen from the chart, there were a few scattered mentions of the .338 and 8x68S. I would have expected both to have come in a bit stronger, likewise the old 9.3x62, which had but one vote. Interesting to me was the fact that opinion was hardly divided at all in this category; to me, there is very little difference in effect on game between the .270, 7mm magnums, .30-06, and .300 magnums—and these cartridges, collectively, comprised about 75 percent of the responses in this category.

**Large Plains Game:** This category seemed very clearcut in that it would have to include eland, roan, sable, bongo, zebra, and such—whatever happens to be the largest in one's hunting territory.

I was therefore surprised to see three respondents hanging in with the .243 in this category. However, that doesn't mean those two hunters *hunt* eland; more likely, the largest plains game they personally hunt is greater kudu for meat—and the .243 is a favorite among South African kudu hunters willing to pick their shots.

Except for another lone respondent who stuck with his .270, most of the respondents made a shift here to heavier calibers. Fully 58 chose the .375, way up from just four for medium game; but the .300s stayed strong—an aggregate of 41.

The sudden strength of the .375 is telling; that's clearly the arm of choice among a majority of professional hunters for use on the largest plains game. Many of those who recommended the .300s, incidentally, specifically stated that they use 200- or 220-grain bullets.

**Lion:** It's important to keep in mind that this question concerned the rifle the professional uses himself, not the rifle he recommends for his client. Some professional hunters are or have been farmers, and have occasion to shoot lions—while others manage to fit in a private safari of their own between clients. So, in some cases, the rifle suggested is what would be used when hunting lion; in others, it would be a rifle used strictly for back-up, and thus might be heavier in caliber.

Some respondents specified one rifle for personal use and another for back-up; Gary Baldwin of Hippo Valley Safaris, Zimbabwe, for instance, uses a .375 on lion for his own hunting, but for back-up carries a double .470.

Surprisingly, 19 different calibers were mentioned for use on lion. With few exceptions, however, there were just a couple of votes per caliber. No surprise was that the .375 got about half of the total votes, 66. Next was the .458 with 15, followed by the .416 Rigby with 10. There was one vote for the .270, four for the .30-06, two for the 7mm magnum, and six for the .300 H&H. Everything else was up into the medium-bore class or larger.

Only three double-rifle cartridges were mentioned: the .500, the .470, and the .475 No. 2. More surprising, to me, was that four wildcat cartridges were mentioned: the .450 Ackley, .450 Watts, .416 Hoffman (three votes), and the .510 Wells.

It seems that a majority of professional hunters feel the .375 is enough gun for lion under most conditions, while a very few rely on picking their shots with smaller cartridges. Peter Johnstone, for instance, reported that he has shot 60 lions himself and another 50 to 60 with clients. He preferred a .30-06 for his own use, but admitted that the .375 was better. Still, some prefer bigger guns—all the way up to the .500s.

"Googee" Wahib, a Nairobi-based professional with over 20 years' experience, was one of few who listed a buckshot-loaded shotgun for wounded lion. Several hunters, however, did mention specific bullet designs. Most often mentioned were Noslers, Swift A-Frames, and Bearclaws. I find it fascinating that such relatively new designs as those last two have found such rapid acceptance in Africa.

**Leopard:** Only 11 rifle calibers were mentioned, but a number of hunters did list their choice as a buckshot-loaded shotgun. A couple of those specified the 3½-inch 10-gauge! Among the rifle calibers, the .375 again ruled the roost. However, several respondents made the notation that this was the minimum caliber required by law, thus perhaps not reflecting a true preference.

Interestingly, only five votes came in for cartridges larger than the .375—Caravati's ever-present .460, of course, plus a .416 Hoffman and three for the .458. Second in votes to the .375 was the .300 magnum, followed closely by the .30-06. A number of professionals specified low-powered scopes of high-quality—and the general message of the additional written comments was that accuracy and exact shot placement are far more important than caliber where leopard are concerned.

**Thick-Skinned Game:** Here, finally, the light rifles are all weeded out. No caliber under .375 H&H was mentioned, but 16 larger cartridges were. Most commonly used is the .458 Winchester Magnum, and that should be no surprise—it's the most available, and the rifles are the most economical. However, as I mentioned earlier, a good number of those relying on the .458 specified handloaded ammunition.

Second most popular was the .375 H&H, again no great surprise. The rest of the choices are a real grab bag. Fully nine of the old British cartridges were mentioned, including 18 .416 Rigbys and 15 .470s. There were also doubles in .450-3¼", .475 No. 2, .500/.465, .500, and .577—plus two .500 Jeffery bolt guns and three .404s. I was very surprised not to see a .505 Gibbs listed by anyone, but I must say there are a lot of classic old guns still in action. Many, of course, are in the hands of the old guard, like Tony Henley and his Holland Royal .465.

The big wildcats were almost as well represented, with two each using the .458 Lott, .450 Watts, and .450 Ackley; and three using the .416 Hoffman. Considering the difficulty of getting components for handloading in Africa—and the potential problems with non-standard ammunition—it's amazing more people don't rely on the inexpensive, available .458. Evidently, those who choose either the wildcats or the old British cartridges are extremely committed to their choices.

**All-Around Use:** This was a tough question, and a number of respondents said so. What, for instance, does "all-round use" mean? Was I asking for a useful rifle to be carried around in the truck just in case? Or did I really mean one rifle that would do it all? Was I including or excluding dangerous game?

As before, I wanted the respondents to take it any way they wanted to, but I also wanted just one rifle mentioned for whatever they considered "all-round" use. That really cut down on the number of cartridges; only 11 were suggested, and only five of these got more than one vote.

Most of the professionals must have had dangerous game in their general hunting category; the .375 was the overwhelming choice, with nothing else making even a close showing. In second place were seven mentions of the .416. However, several professionals specified one rifle for personal use and another for guiding. Rudy Lubin, longtime professional hunter in Central Africa, suggested a .375 for his own use, but a .416 Rigby when he was with a client. Thirty-two-year veteran Cotton Gordon, one of few Americans to do really well in African professional hunting, uses a 7mm magnum for his own hunting—but carries a .458 when he's with clients.

There were a couple of other interesting choices. German professional hunter Franz Wengert, for instance, uses a 9.3x64. And of course there were a couple of guys who carry their heavy rifles for everything. By and large, though, after all these years it seems that the .375 H&H is still hard to beat as that elusive, perhaps imaginary "all-round" rifle.

## Recommendations to Clients

Since, it's almost impossible for a hunting client to bring more than three firearms to Africa—and more than two can be most inconvenient—for this section I abandoned the game classifications and simply asked, "What rifles do you prefer your clients to bring on safari?" Then I asked for recommendations for one rifle, two rifles, or three rifles, with blank spaces left for each.

Some of the respondents made recommendations for one-, two-, and three-rifle batteries. Others made suggestions in one or two categories, but not all. A great many of the recommendations to clients differed from the hunter's personal choices.

**One Rifle:** Approximately 90 percent of the respondents suggested bringing just one rifle—not necessarily as the only or best option, but as a viable option for their clients. Only 10 cartridges were mentioned—and the only one with more than a handful of votes was, naturally, the .375 H&H. Most professional hunters added a comment such as, "Bring both solids and softs," or mentioned a specific bullet type. One man commented, "Anything they can shoot well from .270 to .416."

Several light cartridges were mentioned. In most of these cases, a close look at the survey revealed that this professional hunter had but limited hunting for dangerous game—perhaps only leopard. In other words, there wasn't a real need for a dangerous-game rifle. Other cartridges mentioned were the 8x68S (two votes), .416 Hoffman, .338, 9.3x64, and .416 Rigby. All of these are in the ballpark, with regard to energy, for all African game—although those below .375 may or may not be legal, in some countries. Several professional hunters commented on the manageability of the .375, in terms of recoil, and a few recommended *only* the one rifle.

Flinching was reported as a common problem; many professionals stated, in spite of specific recommendations for relatively heavy cartridges, that they would much rather see a client with a light rifle he could shoot than with a more powerful rifle that he feared.

**Two Rifles:** More recommendations were made here than in the other two categories—and several respondents left the other two blank. It's interesting to note that all of the cartridges recommended are commonly available—no obscure wildcats and nothing obsolete.

With just two exceptions, the recommended two-rifle batteries consisted of a reasonably heavy rifle and another of somewhat smaller caliber. The two exceptions are worth mentioning because, quite frankly, I don't understand them. One suggested a .270 and a .300; the other a .30-06 and a .300. In neither case did the professional hunter offer dangerous game, so the power level makes sense. But I really can't understand hauling two rifles of different caliber but such similar characteristics all the way to Africa. Better, in my view, would be to have two rifles of *identical* caliber, one strictly for a back-up but with ammunition much simplified.

The more common suggestion was to bring two rifles of different calibers intended for different purposes. The suggestions for a light rifle were extremely diverse—although mostly within the same basic power range. On the other hand, there were just three recommendations for a second, heavier rifle—.375, .458, and .416 in that order.

In combination with the .375, most respondents suggested a .270 Winchester, .30-06, 7mm magnum, or one of the .300s. Several didn't specify an exact cartridge, writing down instead something like ".270—.30-06—7mm + .375."

Finn Aagaard added the .280 Remington to that mix, but he was the only one who mentioned that particular cartridge. For some reason, this truly excellent cartridge has remained more or less an "American" round, while the very similar .270 has really established itself in Africa. I guess the same could be said of the wonderfully versatile .338; it did much better in the survey than the .280, but not nearly as well as I would have expected.

Aside from the .270-to-.300 range of cartridges, little else was recommended as a second rifle. Interestingly, there were three votes for the .243 in combination with the .375. I'd never considered such a battery, but that's not a bad combination at all: the pleasant-shooting little .243 for camp meat and lighter plains game, and the .375 for everything else. Two professionals, on the other hand, recommended the .338 in combination with the .375. This is another battery in which the utility eludes me. The two cartridges are both superb, but so close in trajectory, energy, and penetrating powers that, again, I'd prefer two rifles in either chambering to both of them.

Most suggestions for a second rifle in concert with a .416 or .458 followed right along; in other words, something between a 7mm and a .300. In this case, there were no votes for a .270, so it appears that those who like heavier rifles on the upper end like heavier rifles on the bottom end as well. There were a few more recommendations for a .338 in combination with either a .416 or .458. Although only a handful of professional hunters recommended this battery, I'll stick with it as my personal recommendation, especially for the .338/.340 together with one of the .416s.

**Three Rifles:** Oh, boy! This one turned out to be a real can of worms, with very little consensus, and some 30 different recommendations to sort through. As I reported in my own chapter on three-rifle batteries, mixed in with the recommendations for three rifles were a number of strident comments against a three-rifle battery.

Many of these hunters stated flatly that three guns are too many to look after and use, or that it's too confusing deciding which to use. As I mentioned, Franz Wengert called three rifles a "headache." Gerry Gore, who hunts in both South Africa and Botswana, said of three-rifle batteries, "God preserve me."

I agree most emphatically that three rifles is a lot. Considering my interests and vocation, I'll admit that I've taken as many as four rifles to Africa on more than one occasion. Honest, guys, I'll never do it again! Under most circumstances, two is plenty and three's a crowd—but I'll stand on what I said earlier; for longish safaris involving a wide variety of game, three rifles can be useful. And many of my respondents made carefully considered recommendations for the classic, if not altogether practical, three-rifle battery.

When two rifles were all that would be available, the .375 was the overwhelming choice as the heavier rifle. However, when three rifles could be chosen, a much larger percentage—in fact, a decided majority—recommended that one of them be over .400 in caliber. Several wrote it just that way, suggesting that the third rifle be "any .400-plus," or words to that effect. A number specifically suggested one of the .416s or the .458. And for the first time in recommendations to clients, suggestions of double rifles began to appear. There were four recommendations for the .470, and a couple wrote in the .458, then added "if available, a double over .450 is preferable."

The .375 was the most common choice for a medium bore—but not by as great a margin as you might think. A surprising number of hunters suggested that the medium should be a .300, .338, or 8x68S. In these cases, the lighter rifle was often much lighter, a 7x57, .270, or .243, while the heavy rifle could be a .416, .458, or .375. The light rifles ran the gamut from .22 Long Rifle to .300 magnum.

My idea of the "classic" three-rifle battery, comprised of something in the .270 to .300 class, the .375, and a big gun, was certainly present in the survey. Although the results were so varied as to be bewildering, this was probably the most common recommendation. The second most common variation, however, listed the .243 as the light rifle. And, often enough to take into serious consideration, the .375 was either listed as the heaviest rifle or ignored altogether, in which case a .300, .338, 7mm, or .30-06 was listed as the medium rifle.

A number of hunters suggested that the third firearm be a shotgun. This brings us to the final questions of the survey, which asked if a client should bring a shotgun, and if one was kept in camp. The answer to the former was about six to one in favor of clients bringing shotguns, while only three respondents didn't keep a shotgun in camp, and several added that they also kept a .22.

## Additional Comments

A great many respondents took the time to add comments on their own choices of rifles and observations on what has worked best for their clients. This unsolicited information sometimes ran into several pages; it was generally valuable, and always fascinating. Space precludes quoting every comment by every professional hunter, but what follows, in no particular order, is some of the most interesting information and opinion from professional hunters all over Africa.

Kenyan *Mike Carr-Hartley* has hunted Tanzania, the Sudan, Kenya, and Zambia since 1962. He was one of the hunters who suggested that the heavy rifle should be, "if available to client a double of .470 or such caliber." He also suggested that if the heavy rifle is a .458, the ammo "should be handloaded and beefed up as factory loads lack punch."

*Andre De Jager*, of South Africa's Nyari Safaris, hunts the entire Big Five. He made no specific recommendations for a client's battery, but made a checkmark alongside the box for one rifle, stating: "It is better for the client to use one rifle so that he can get used to it in a strange country and different environment instead of changing rifles every time we hunt a different animal. He can bring both softpoint and solid bullets for one caliber."

An American who has become a legend in Africa, former Colorado outfitter *Cotton Gordon* has 32 years in the business. He specifically recommended that his clients bring a 7mm or .300 magnum plus a .375, and then stated that "two [rifles] is enough!" He also wrote in that he keeps a shotgun in camp because he prefers "that clients not have to bring three firearms."

Hunting in Botswana and South Africa, *Gerry Gore* hunts all of the Big Five except elephant. He's a big fan of the 7mm Remington Magnum for light and medium plains game and the .416—either Hoffman or Rigby (and now, one would presume, Remington or Weatherby) for lion and thick-skinned game. He wrote, "I hate the .375 H&H." I hope our paths meet someday and I get to ask him about that. I'm sure there's a story there.

Here's an unsigned report (not intentional, I'm sure; sometimes the envelopes with return addresses became separated from the surveys) from a professional who's a fan of the .338 and .375, and for his own use has a wildcat .450 Ackley. Under recommendations for a three-rifle battery he suggests ".338, .375, and a large caliber of your choice—preferably not .458 for elephant."

*Alex McDonald,* now retired after 25 years experience, suggested that "a .22 rimfire is good for practice, gamebirds, and curing a flinch." He went on to say, "Bullet placement is the main criterion. Clients should practice a lot before a safari and know their rifles intimately. Bullet construction (and not so much caliber) is the second most important factor. No caliber ever went out there and killed an animal; it's the bullet that does this and it must be good—but it cannot do its job if placed incorrectly. Practice is essential." Amen!

*Gary Baldwin* of Hippo Valley Safaris in Zimbabwe had the following excellent advice: "Positively only one weight of bullet for each rifle. Different weights only cause confusion. Take into account re-zeroing your rifle when assessing the amount of ammo to take on your hunt.

With 15 years as a professional hunter and another dozen years hunting on his own before that, *Farouk Qureshi,* an East African pro, prefers his .460 Weatherby Magnum for heavy game, stating: "I have also used the .30-06 on all plains game and the .458 on Big Five. I used to carry a .450 Straight double .450-3¼". The .450 was better than the .458, but I gave it up due to ammo problems. Now I use the .460 which was assembled by a friend on a Mauser action. I find it to be the best of all. The .30-06 is the best plains-game rifle. I have used a lot of different calibers during my hunting career, such as .275, 7x64, .470 DB, .500 DB, and .416 Rigby. I sold these last three due to expensive ammo."

A 10-year veteran hunter in Zimbabwe, *Clive Lennox* is another hunter who recommends handloaded .458 ammo rather than factory loads. He went on to say: "We find the .375 to be the most versatile of all calibers, however not all Americans like to shoot the .375 as it is considered to be slightly heavy for the average American game. We tell clients to bring the rifle they are comfortable with and most of all, familiar with."

My old friend *Joof Lamprecht,* hunting in Namibia, added the following: "Bullet weights should not be on the light side; rather on the heavy side. For example, a 180-grain bullet should be the minimum for a .300 Winchester Magnum."

*Stephen J. Smith's* outfit, Hunt Africa, is a new South African concern, but Steve has been involved in African hunting for 31 years, with a wide variety of experience. He writes: "I shot my first buffalo in 1954 and have been hunting ever since. I used a .30-06 and .470 double for years, then a 9.3 Mannlicher-Schoenauer and a .458. From experience with clients, I reckon that the .338 will handle everything from duiker to buffalo and from there up the .458 is ideal. It's best to have the least number of guns in your truck. So a shotgun (12-gauge) plus .338 plus .458 is what I have always recommended. A factor often overlooked is the availability of ammo! Both .338 and .458 can be purchased from Nairobi to Capetown. My favorite double is the .577, but where can you buy ammo—and the price!"

With 30 years' experience covering the full range of African species, *J.H. Swanepoel* uses light rifles .270 and .30-06 for most of his own hunting, but carries a .458 or .460 Weatherby when backing up clients. He had this to say regarding recommendations to clients: "Any rifle my client prefers. After all, it's his hunt; nine times out of ten it's not the caliber that counts but bullet placement. The client usually dreams of that hunt with *his* rifle, not the professional hunter's rifle."

*Ray Millican,* now hunting primarily in Zambia, offered this: "People may query why I use preferably .375 H&H for leopard. Well, when shooting a lighter caliber, if you don't hit a vital spot you could lose your cat. He may take off, and on average the light factor is diminishing rapidly. Quite possibly you'll have to continue the next day. Our friend the hyena comes across your leopard and all you end up with is pieces. I think the last time we had a chat, we were unanimous about the combination of .338 and a .416 as an unbeatable combination."

South African *Carl Labuschagne* of Wagendrift Safaris has experience with all of the Big Five, and he was the only man who personally used a rifle as big as the .577 double, which he wrote that he loads for and uses extensively. For a one-rifle client he recommended ".375 H&H Magnum with a quick-detachable scope (Kimber mounts)."

One of the all-time greats, *Tony Dyer* hunted professionally from 1947 to 1961, and since then has been keeping the lions properly thinned on his farm well up on the slopes of Mount Kenya. He shoots a pre-'64 Model 70 .300 H&H rechambered to .300 Weatherby for all plains game and leopard, a .416 Rigby for lion, and a .375 H&H for all-round use. He wrote: "The .458 used to be good, but not anymore. I will be rebarreling my .458 to .375 H&H. The .416 with all the new ammunition is superb."

A professional with 25 years' experience, *Paul Vimercati* says: "I have shot many lion and leopard with my .270." His personal choices were the .270, 8x68S, .375, and .458—but he carries a .450-3¼" double for back-up with clients. He mentioned specifically that he doesn't like Silvertip bullets in .375 caliber.

Under the heading of "one man's meat is another's poison" would be *Glen Devine's* comments. A professional hunter with 20 years experience as a game ranger, Glen uses the .300 H&H and .375 H&H for most of his hunting. He prefers Silvertip bullets for *everything* except thick-skinned game, for which he uses solids in his .375 or goes to a double .450.

A veteran of 37 years of African hunting with a personal bag exceeding 800 elephant, *Tony Sanchez-Ariño* is one of the most experienced of the modern-day hunters. For thick-skinned game, he personally uses a .416 Rigby, a .500 Jeffery (magazine rifle), and a double .465. However, like almost everyone else, he recommends the .375 for all-round use. Perhaps surprisingly, Tony's recommendation for clients is a two-rifle battery: "One in the .300 class plus the .375 H&H Magnum with a good scope."

Although relatively inexperienced as a professional hunter, *Ricky Walsh* hunted all over southern Africa on his own before obtaining his license. He writes: "I feel that caliber selection depends on a number of factors. These include the density of the vegetation, the topography (plains, desert, thorn-bush), the type of animal, the reason for the hunt (trophy or meat), the ability of the hunter to handle the rifle, and his skill in placing his shot. The last factor is arguably the most important of the lot! The 'caliber controversy' is argued around nearly every campfire where hunting is taking place, and probably will be for many years to come. But if the hunter is ill-prepared and/or the recoil is too much for him, he is still going to miss (or worse—wound)."

*George Hoffman,* who developed the .416 Hoffman and still swears by it, advises his clients to bring only two rifles, a 7mm magnum and a .375 or .416. Three rifles are "too many; you never know which one to use. Better the third gun be a shotgun or .22."

Among his many clients, 16-year veteran *Don Price* is pure gold. A Zimbabwean, he's been hunting in Zambia for several seasons and is now in Tanzania. For his own use he's a .470 and .416 Rigby fan, but he suggests a .375 for his clients—or a .30-06 and .375. He says he "still feels clients should stick to one rifle and get really good with it. Ideally the .375 H&H with solid ammunition."

My old friend *Finn Aagaard,* former Kenya professional hunter, had this to say:

"1. No cartridge has the power to flatten an animal in his tracks regardless of where hit. *Penetration* and *shot placement* are the two absolutely essential factors. If you achieve them then caliber, etc., aren't terribly important within reason.

"2. In order to achieve shot placement, I preferred clients to use scope-sighted .375 H&H for dangerous game, while I backed them up with .458.

"3. I believe the fad for bad-mouthing the .458 is mostly hot air and blaming cartridge/gun for own failures. Apart from some lots of bad ammo, I have never been able to detect any difference in the field, on game, between the .458 and .500/.450, .465, .470, or even the .500 N.E."

*Doug Kok,* a 13-year veteran, stated: "I prefer a client to bring a lighter rifle if he is scared of recoil. I would rather have a lighter rifle and a confident client than a heavy rifle and a flincher!"

And along those lines, another professional who asked not to be named said: "A client must be used to the rifle he brings out. Often he arrives with some superduper firearm that he flinches from after the second shot!"

*Campbell Smith,* with a decade of experience in southern Africa, uses a .450 Watts personally for heavy game. He excludes the .458, stating that he wants "something firing a 500-grain bullet with velocity more than 2,150 fps and not more than 2,300 fps." He mentions the .458 Lott, .450 Watts and Ackley, .460 G&A, and .470. He was also one of the few to specifically recommend bullets, suggesting Nosler, Swift, and Bearclaw for softpoints and Hornadys and Monolithics for solids.

*Rudy Lubin,* with 17 years of hunting the C.A.R., the Sudan, Gabon, and the Cameroons, hunts tough country almost exclusively on foot. He recommends: "No sophisticated rifle for African hunting. Better use well-known and widely used ammunition. In case you lose them, the PH can help you. There are very few gun shops in these countries." Rudy also recommended solids only for the very small antelopes, plus elephant, rhino, and hippo. He feels that all the rest, including buffalo, are better shot with softs.

Hunting several areas in southern Africa, *Francois Loubser* offers a wide assortment of game in a wide variety of terrain. He had a number of excellent comments, and I hope he'll forgive me for toning them down a bit for public consumption. "The reason I appear so adamant about the use of the 7mm magnum is the fact that everybody—man, woman, or child— can handle this caliber. It really doesn't matter whether you call it a Remington, a Weatherby, or a 7x61.

"The two major reasons for lost trophies are most definitely: (1) Too much gun—a gut shot with a .300 Winchester Magnum does not kill like a lung shot with a 7mm; (2) bad bullets—thank St. Hubertus for people like *Jack Carter* of Bear Claw fame and *Lee Reid,* who gave us Swift bullets. When you're shooting at a trophy that costs $$$$, why worry about a $2 bullet?

"I would like to add that I do not always understand the choice of scopes. If you have an $800 rifle with the latest junk scope, held together by junk mounts, you have in effect got a $40 rifle—but the cost of the safari is the same.

"The 9.3x64 is hell on wheels. If someone will make us some tough bullets, it will be my preference over the .375 H&H."

Another widely experienced professional hunter who did some magnum-bashing was *John Brelsford*, currently hunting South Africa and Zambia, formerly Gabon and Tanzania. He commented: "A client who can use any of the [fast] magnums consistently well is a rarity. I have personally never had one. Their shooting might start off well, but by the end of the safari it has generally deteriorated to a terrible extent, with the client developing a flinch. I think certain types of clients who are attracted to the super magnums are possibly inherent bad shots, hoping that the extra power will make up for accuracy, or rather lack of it."

To a large degree, *Harry Selby* is responsible for keeping the .416 Rigby alive. He didn't choose it for all-round use, citing the .375 instead, but he added: "Of all the big-bore cartridges available, I think that the .416 Rigby is totally outstanding. Great penetration and knockdown; with modern powders its performance is unique." While his peer, *Tony Henley*, is a double-rifle man, Harry prefers bolt guns because "doubles don't shoot straight enough."

Another living legend with 27 years in the field, *Robin Hurt's* personal heavy rifle is a double .500. For his clients, he recommends a .375 for one rifle, adding a 7mm Remington Magnum for two, and a ".450-plus" as a heavy rifle. He suggested that the heavy not be a .458: "Lacks penetration."

379

Robin also commented that most clients can't shoot well with calibers larger than .375.

*Ian Wilmot* of East Cape Trophy Safaris generally recommends the .270 Winchester and .300 Winchester Magnum, stating: "I have grown up in the Eastern Cape, which as you probably know has a wide variety of terrain with genuine long shots often taking place, hence the flatter-shooting calibers over the 7x57, .30-06, etc. In the bush I really advise these slower calibers, though. The lightest bullet in .300 must be 180 grains in my opinion. In the .270, 130- or 150-grain."

*Tony Tomkinson* has nine years' experience as a professional hunter, mainly in Zululand, and before that was a game ranger for 16 years. In the latter occupation he was involved in some large-scale culling operations, and had some extremely interesting observations:

"In my experiences both as a professional hunter and game ranger, where in the latter case I took more than 20,000 head of game during cropping operations, I have found that within reason it is very often not the caliber or rifle type which is of importance, but rather bullet weight and design.

"It is those badly angled shots where the whole bit of bullet performance comes to play and accordingly when advising my clients I also stress that preference should be given to bullet design that will hold up when hitting bones, etc. Here the Nosler Partition bullets and custom-made H-mantel bullets certainly have a bit of an advantage over the conventional types.

"During 1982 to 1984 I was involved with the annual removal of 150 hippo from the Lake St. Lucia Game Reserve where I was warden in charge. During this period I was able to evaluate bullet and rifle performance on thick-skinned game pretty thoroughly as most of these animals were shot on land at night in circumstances that forced us to use body shots.

"First, the rifles we used were .30-06, .375, .338, 9.3x64, .400/.350 Rigby, .450 No. 2 Nitro-Express, and .470 Nitro-Express. Second, none of the rifles used resulted in immediate kills unless spine or central nervous system was destroyed. In all cases, lung- and heart-shot animals covered between 75 and 200 yards before becoming immobilized.

"By virtue again of bad angles, we finally settled on calibers that would give us the best penetration. Accordingly we landed up using the .30-06 with 220-grain full-metal-jacket bullets for daytime shooting, i.e., head shots, and .375 full-metal-jacket bullets for night work. Our second choice on night work was the .458 Winchester Magnum.

"I'm sure you will probably raise an eyebrow on our non-selection of the British calibers; however, we only had Kynoch full-metal-jacket ammunition available and on a number of occasions these solids became misshapen or broke up completely on striking heavy bone.

"Based on the above experiences I personally now use a .458 Lott with solids for dangerous game and a .300 H&H Magnum with 220-grain full-metal-jacket bullets for back-up on plains-game hunts."

*Mark Tout,* an energetic young professional of nine years' experience in South Africa, Botswana, and Zambia, had this to say regarding bullet performance:

"In my experience as a PH I reckon there is not such a big problem of clients using inappropriate rifles but rather having unsuitable ammunition and even more a lack of capability in using the rifle they bring—especially in offhand shooting conditions."

Another old friend, *Peter Johnstone,* long-time proprietor of Rosslyn Safaris in the Matetsi region of Zimbabwe, sent me a very long letter with his questionnaire. I'll never forget the beautifully battered pre-'64 Model 70 he carried when he backed me up on my first elephant, and apparently that rifle is just Peter's style. According to him, "using one rifle has a great advantage in that the hunter becomes very familiar with it, shooting the ordinary animals, and therefore when he comes under emergency conditions he can handle and shoot his rifle without any problems."

Discussing personal favorites, he says: "In the late 1950s I had a team of hunters shooting zebra, wildebeest, giraffe, kudu, and eland, using the 9.3x62 with 286-grain solids. This provided penetration at all angles and plenty knock-down power. We also shot some elephant, mainly cows and young bulls.

"My next-favorite rifle is the 7x57mm. The one I had was deadly accurate; I could brain-shoot antelope out to 100 yards, and buffalo bulls at a few yards were great fun. I preferred the long roundnose solid bullet. When I see a client with a 7mm magnum, I shudder; it's all noise and blast and deflected bullets!

"The .30-06 is an exceedingly good rifle which has done me very well over the years. With my .30-06 I've shot many lion, leopard, antelope, also some buffalo bulls, giraffe, a moose, a grizzly, Dall sheep, caribou, ibex, red deer. . . .

"The .375 is the greatest rifle and that's really the only one necessary for a client to bring for big-game savanna hunting. To be responsible for the care, safety, and shooting of one rifle is really enough for a client/hunter in Africa."

*John Reeve Moller,* currently hunting in Tanzania but with experience in the Sudan, Zaire, and Ethiopia, in part had this to say: "This may sound odd to you, but I have never had much time for the .375. I do not advise clients to bring one on safari as I have never been very happy with the results of the factory ammo. My medium-calibre rifle is a .338 Winchester Magnum. I have had it for years and the results have been very good indeed. I have used it on elephant and buffalo on control work and have never had any problems. I always take it to a lion blind in case of a runner at a distance. However, I also have the .460 with me for anything that needs a bleeding nose at close quarters. For wounded leopard I use a 10-gauge AYA with OO or No. 4 buck. On wounded lion I always use the .460 Weatherby, and of course on other dangerous game. . ." Always outspoken—and most astute—veteran hunter *Gordon Cormack* sent volumes of information, all of it helpful. Among his comments were several that should be passed along: "The trouble with this sort of questionnaire is that circumstances can differ, e.g., a long shot at a lion (150 metres) would be better taken with a .375, 300-grain soft, utilizing a scope sight, than with a .450-3¼" Nitro-Express using open sights. By the same token, I would rather use a double .450 with open sights and a 480-grain softnose at close quarters in thick bush.

"As one rifle I would take a bolt-action .416 Remington. A client, who does not do as much shooting, would be better off with one weapon as a .375 H&H.

"Bullet weights are important, and the heavier the better, especially with grass and bush in the way."

Finally, I was most honored to receive a nine-page letter from *Ian Henderson*, a 28-year veteran who, as Henderson and Marsh Safaris, together with Brian Marsh, was one of the pioneering outfitters in what is now Zimbabwe. I wish I could reproduce his comments in total; not only is he more experienced than I, but he's a fine writer. Here are some of his comments:

"In *general* I would recommend the *heaviest* weight of bullet for the caliber in question, viz. 220 grains for .300 H&H and 300 grains for .375 H&H. This gives the best sectional density, which is of vital importance for penetration. That is why the solid in both cases is only available in the heaviest bullet weight.

"Also in general, one must use the heaviest bullet and caliber with which one can shoot *with accuracy*. Put another way, a small caliber in the right place is far better than a large caliber in the wrong place. . . . Flinch is an insidious fault and far more prevalent than realized, a subject deserving of far more attention than it receives at the moment."

Ian chose the .375 H&H for large plains game, stating: "Probably the most popular weapon in this category. I have, however, found it somehow is lacking knockdown effect. I would actually prefer to use a .416 or .404, which I cannot fault, but because of the availability of ammunition becoming more difficult (and expensive) the .375 remains the obvious choice."

For lion, he chose the .470: "Once again, I would prefer to use a .404 or .416, but as lion are often hunted in thick bush, and may be wounded, the .470 double is the obvious choice, especially as I already have the rifle and it fits me. Any other heavy double is as suitable."

Ian goes on to discuss, at length and with great clarity, the perennial problem of velocity versus bullet performance. Like most African professionals of vast experience, he isn't overawed by velocity but demands penetration above all else. He'll willingly accept velocity, mind you—but only if he can also get penetration.

Finally, he concluded with his "dream battery": "Over the years one builds up a particular respect for certain calibers; though not spectacular in any sense, they perform consistently, and just do what they are supposed to do. No doubt I am also influenced by the store I place in sectional density, thus if I had to change and put together a battery that I find appealing to me I would choose:

1. 6.5mm firing a 160-grain bullet (soft- and hardnose).
2. .333 Jeffery.
3. .505 Gibbs.

"What a combination! No finer could I imagine."

After all these years, with all of our brave new cartridges, perhaps we haven't progressed much beyond the infancy of smokeless powder. Or, to put it another way, in the last 80-odd years we haven't come up with a better solution than to use a long, heavy bullet at moderate velocity. Or have we? There may never be a consensus on calibers, but the professionals agree on this: Whatever rifles and cartridges work best for you, give you confidence, and perform consistently because you shoot them well—those are the ones to use on Africa's game.

# PROFESSIONAL HUNTER SURVEY

## GENERAL DATA

| | |
|---|---|
| TOTAL NUMBER OF RESPONDENTS: | 113 |
| MOST YEARS IN THE FIELD: | 44 |
| LEAST YEARS IN THE FIELD: | 2 |
| AVERAGE YEARS IN THE FIELD: | 16 |

**TYPE OF TERRAIN HUNTED:**

| | |
|---|---|
| THORNBUSH | 101 RESPONDENTS |
| PLAINS | 91 RESPONDENTS |
| SWAMP | 47 RESPONDENTS |
| FOREST | 46 RESPONDENTS |
| DESERT | 45 RESPONDENTS |

**DANGEROUS GAME HUNTED:**

| | |
|---|---|
| BUFFALO | 95 RESPONDENTS |
| LION | 95 RESPONDENTS |
| LEOPARD | 94 RESPONDENTS |
| RHINO | 67 RESPONDENTS |
| ELEPHANT | 64 RESPONDENTS |

# PROFESSIONAL HUNTERS' PERSONAL CHOICES

| LIGHT PLAINS GAME | | MEDIUM PLAINS GAME | | LION | | LARGE PLAINS GAME | | LEOPARD | | THICK-SKINNED GAME | | ALL-AROUND | |
|---|---|---|---|---|---|---|---|---|---|---|---|---|---|
| CALIBER | # | CALIBER | # | CALIBER | # | CALIBER | # | CALIBER | # | CALIBER | # | CALIBER | # |
| .243 | 32 | .30-06 | 33 | .375 H&H | 66 | .375 H&H | 58 | .375 H&H | 50 | .458 | 48 | .375 H&H | 81 |
| .270 | 28 | 7mm Mag. | 25 | .458 | 15 | .300 H&H | 31 | .300 Mag* | 22 | .375 H&H | 33 | .416* | 7 |
| 7MM Mag. | 13 | .300 H&H | 22 | .416 Rigby | 10 | .338 Mag | 11 | .30-06 | 19 | .416 Rigby | 18 | .30-06 | 6 |
| .30-06 | 12 | .270 | 21 | .300 H&H | 6 | .30-06 | 10 | 7mm Mag | 12 | .470 NE | 15 | .300 Mag* | 5 |
| .300 H&H | 9 | .300 Wby Mag | 8 | .470 NE | 5 | 7mm Mag | 9 | shotgun | 9 | .460 Wby Mag | 3 | .338 Mag | 3 |
| 7x57 | 9 | .338 Mag | 7 | .338 Mag | 4 | .300 Win Mag | 6 | .338 Mag | 8 | .450-3 1/2" NE | 3 | .270 | 2 |
| .308 | 8 | 8x68S | 5 | .30-06 | 4 | 8x68S | 4 | .270 | 6 | .416 Hoffman | 3 | .243 | 2 |
| .300 Wby Mag | 3 | .300 Win Mag | 5 | 8x68S | 3 | .300 Wby Mag | 4 | 8x68S | 3 | .404 Jeffrey | 3 | .460 Wby Mag | 1 |
| .338 Mag | 3 | .375 H&H | 4 | .416 Hoffman | 3 | .243 | 3 | .458 | 3 | .450 Ackley | 3 | .450 Watts | 1 |
| .223 | 3 | 7x57 | 3 | .460 Wby Mag | 2 | .416 Rigby | 2 | .460 Wby Mag | 1 | .475 No. 2 NE | 3 | 9.3x64 | 1 |
| .375 H&H | 2 | .308 | 3 | 7mm Mag | 2 | .340 Wby Mag | 2 | .416 Hoffman | 1 | .500 NE | 3 | 7mm Mag | 1 |
| .460 Wby Mag | 1 | .243 | 3 | .510 Wells | 2 | .460 Wby Mag | 1 | .280 Rem | 1 | .500 Jeffrey | 2 | .458 | 1 |
| 8x68S | 1 | .460 Wby Mag | 1 | .500 NE | 1 | .270 | 1 | .243 | 1 | .458 Lott | 2 | | |
| .280 Rem | 1 | 9.3x62 | 1 | .450 Ackley | 1 | | | | | .450 Watts | 2 | | |
| .264 Win Mag | 1 | .280 Rem | 1 | .475 No. 2 | 1 | | | | | .500/.465 NE | 2 | | |
| 7x64 | 1 | | | .500/.465 | 1 | | | | | .510 Wells | 2 | | |
| .25-06 | 1 | | | .450 Watts | 1 | | | | | .577 NE | 1 | | |
| 6mm Rem | 1 | | | .404 Jeffrey | 1 | | | | | | | | |
| .22 Hornet | 1 | | | .270 | 1 | | | | | | | | |

*Denotes exact cartridge of that caliber unspecified. Note: In almost all cases, the 7mm magnum cartridge specified was 7mm Remington Magnum. No other 7mm magnum cartridge was specified by name.

# RECOMMENDATIONS TO CLIENTS

## ONE RIFLE

| CALIBER | #MENTIONS |
|---|---|
| .375 H&H | 70 |
| .30-06 | 8 |
| .300 Mag* | 5 |
| 8x68S | 4 |
| .270 | 3 |
| .338 Mag | 2 |
| 7mm Mag | 2 |
| 9.3x64 | 1 |
| .416 Hoffman | 1 |
| .416 Rigby | 1 |

## TWO RIFLES

| CALIBER | CALIBER | #MENTIONS |
|---|---|---|
| 7mm Mag | .375 H&H | 19 |
| .300 Mag* | .375 H&H | 18 |
| .30-06 | .375 H&H | 13 |
| .270/.280/.308/7x57 | .375 H&H | 15 |
| .300 Mag* | .458 | 6 |
| .243 | .375 H&H | 5 |
| .30-06 | .458 | 4 |
| .338 Mag | .375 H&H | 3 |
| .375 H&H | .458/.460 | 3 |
| 7mm Mag | .416* | 3 |
| .338 Mag | .458 | 2 |
| .270 | .300 Mag* | 2 |
| 7mm Mag | .416* | 2 |
| .300 Mag* | .416* | 2 |
| .338 Mag | .416* | 1 |
| .30-06 | .416* | 1 |
| 7mm Mag | .458 | 1 |
| .30-06 | .300 Mag* | 1 |

## THREE RIFLES

| CALIBER | CALIBER | CALIBER | #MENTIONS |
|---|---|---|---|
| .243 | .30-06 | .375 H&H | 7 |
| .22 LR | 7mm Mag | .375 H&H | 6 |
| .30-06 | .375 H&H | .400+ | 5 |
| .300 Mag* | .375 H&H | .458+ | 4 |
| 7mm Mag | .300 Mag | .416* | 3 |
| 7mm Mag | .375 H&H | .458 | 3 |
| .338 Mag | .375 H&H | .458+ | 3 |
| .243 | .300 Mag* | .375 H&H | 3 |
| .243 | .30-06 | .416 Rigby | 2 |
| .30-06 | .375 H&H | shotgun | 2 |
| .270 | 8x68S | .458 | 2 |
| .270 | .300 Wby Mag | .458 | 2 |
| .243 | .30-06 | .458 | 2 |
| .300 Mag* | .375 H&H | .470 NE | 2 |
| 7x57 | .300 Mag* | .416+ | 2 |
| .270 | .375 H&H | .458 | 2 |
| .243 | .300 Mag* | .458 | 1 |
| 7x57 | .338 Mag | .458 | 1 |
| .30-06 | .300 Mag* | .375+ | 1 |
| .30-06 | .300 Mag* | .416 | 1 |
| .243 | .338 Mag | .375 H&H | 1 |
| .223 | .300 Mag* | .375 H&H | 1 |
| .270 | .30-06 | .375 H&H | 1 |
| 6.5mm* | .375 H&H | .450+ | 1 |
| .270 | .30-06 | .416 | 1 |
| .308 | .300 Mag* | .375 H&H | 1 |
| .223 | .30-06 | .375 H&H | 1 |
| .270 | .30-06 | .375 H&H | 1 |
| .22 Mag | 7mm Mag | .416+ | 1 |
| .222 | .270 | .375 H&H | 1 |
| .270 | .300 Mag* | .458 | 1 |
| .243 | .270 | .458 | 1 |
| .270 | 7mm Mag | .375 H&H | 1 |
| 7x57 | .270 | .375 H&H | 1 |

*Denotes exact cartridge of that caliber unspecified

+Indicated respondents gave minimum caliber for third rifle.

Note: In almost all cases, the 7mm magnum cartridge specified was the 7mm Remington Magnum. No other 7mm magnum cartridge was specified.

386

# Part V

# Appendices

# APPENDIX 1

## Current and Historic Makers of Double Rifles

At this writing, smokeless powder has held sway for over 100 years, and in that time countless small gunmakers in the British Isles and western Europe have turned out unknown numbers of double-barreled rifles. Two world wars and a great depression have combined with the typically poor records of skilled but highly individualistic makers to leave us with a very incomplete picture of who actually made double guns, let alone how many of the guns have been made. The following is an extremely incomplete picture which includes all of the principal makers of doubles, both current and past, but falls far short of including every name one may occasionally see engraved on the barrel of a double. Such an undertaking may or may not be totally possible, and although an attempt would be worthwhile, it's beyond the scope of this work. The following list is a rundown of the most common makers.

### Asprey's,

Albermarle Street, London, England. Current maker of double rifles by special order.

### Atkin, Grant and Lang,

6 Lincolns Inn Fields, London WC2, England. Under different ownerships this firm has been in business since the last century. Most doubles from this firm have been good, solid boxlocks. Doubles still made to order, though no longer on the premises in England.

### Beretta U.S.A. Corp.,

17601 Beretta Dr., Accokeek, MD 20607. Importer of Beretta over/under rifles available in calibers up to 9.3x74R, .375 H&H, and .458 Win. Mag.; and Beretta's side-by-side double available in a variety of chamberings including .416 Rigby, .470, and .500 Nitro-Express.

### D. McKay Brown,

32 Hamilton Road, Bothwell, Glasgow, Scotland. Current maker of double rifles to order.

### Champlin Firearms, Inc.,

Box 3191, Enid, OK 73702. Importer of the Champlin-Famars side-by-side doubles up to .450 No. 2.

### Cogswell and Harrison,*

London, England. A prolific maker of both doubles and magazine rifles, primarily "working" guns. It is believed the .475 Nitro-Express was developed by this company.

## John Dickson,

Edinburgh, Scotland. Made relatively few double rifles, but this firm's unique round-barred action is highly prized.

## Ernest Dumoulin-Deleye,

Belgium. American importer is Midwest Gun Sport, 1108 Herbert Dr., Zebulon, NC 27597. Excellent maker of top-quality doubles in the English pattern, with calibers up to .470 available.

## Ego Armas "Azor" S.A.,

Victor Sarasqueta 1, Apartado, 76, 20600 Eibar (Guizpuzcoa) Spain. Maker of side-by-side double rifles in calibers up to 9.3x74R and .375 H&H.

## Elko Arms,

28 Rue Ecole Moderne, 5-7400 Soignies, Belgium. Maker of over/under and side-by-side doubles for their proprietary .459 and .376 Elsa-K Magnums.

## William Evans,

67A St. James Street, London SWI, England. Historically, a good maker of excellent doubles, mostly boxlock guns on trade or Webley & Scott actions. No longer builds on premises, but will build doubles to order.

## Ferlach, Austria,

Genossenschaft Der Buchsenmachermeister. This association of master gunmakers in Ferlach, Austria, represents generations of fine gunmaking. Collectively or individually, the Ferlach makers will produce virtually anything in the way of a fine firearm. Current members of the Ferlach, Austria, trade association are:

Ludwig Borovnik, Dollichgasse 14, A-9170, Ferlach.

Johann Fanzoj, Griesgasse 1, A-9170, Ferlach.

Wilfried Glanznig, Werstrasse 9, A-9170, Ferlach.

Josef Hambrusch, Gartengasse 2, A-9170, Ferlach.

Karl Hauptmann, Bahnhofstrasse 5, A-9170, Ferlach.

Gottfried Juch, Pfarrhofgasse 2, A-9170, Ferlach.

Josef Just, Hauptplatz 18, A-9170, Ferlach.

Jakob Koschat, 12-November-Strasse 3, A-9170, Ferlach.

Johann Michelitsch, 12-November-Strasse 3, A-9170, Ferlach.

Walter Outschar, Josef-Ogris-Gasse 23, A-9170, Ferlach.

Herbert Scheiring, Klagenfurter Strasse 19, A-9170, Ferlach.

Herbert Urbas, Sparkassenplatz 2, A-9170, Ferlach.

Benedikt Winkler, Postgasse 1, A-9170, Ferlach.

Josef Winkler, Neubaugasse 1, A-9170, Ferlach.

## Auguste Francotte & Cie, S.A.,

Rue de Trois Juin 109, 4400 Herstal, Liege, Belgium. A fine maker of excellent doubles for many years. Francotte guns are highly regarded and may be encountered in virtually any Nitro-Express caliber. This firm still makes an occasional double on special order.

## Dan'l Fraser & Co.,

Peddieston, Cromarty, Ross-shire, Scotland, United Kingdom. Maker of side-by-side doubles and falling-block single-shots from .22 Hornet to .600 N.E.

## George Gibbs,

Amalgamated with I.M. Crudgington Ltd., 37 Broad Street, Bath BA1 5LT, England. Best known for the .505 Gibbs, this firm produced a good number of doubles for most of the big Nitro-Express cartridges. Will still build doubles to order.

## W.W. Greener,*

Birmingham and London, England. Few large-caliber Greener doubles are seen today, but this was another good, sound maker.

## Friedrich Wilhelm Heym GmbH & Co.,

KG., Postfach 160, Coburger Strasse 8, D-8732 Munnerstadt, West Germany. American importer is Heym America, Inc., 1426 East Tillman Rd., Fort Wayne, IN 46816. Maker of large-bore magazine rifles, over/unders, and side-by-side double rifles (and drillings). Possibly the largest current maker of double rifles, including side-by-sides in 9.3x74R, .375 H&H, .458, .470, and .500 N.E.

## Holland and Holland Limited,

33 Bruton St., London W1X 8JS, England. One of very few historic makers continuing to offer double rifles. Today's Hollands are all fine guns, but historically this firm made double rifles in all grades—all of which are highly prized today. Although Holland made doubles to order in virtually every Nitro-Express chambering, their own .500/.465 is the most common.

## W.J. Jeffery,*

London, England. In later days a subsidiary of Hollands, Jeffery produced a tremendous number of large-caliber doubles. The most common is probably their own .450/.400-3", but they also had their own loading for the .475 No. 2, and are believed to have produced more .600 doubles than anyone else.

## Charles Lancaster,

P.O. Box 6, Brewood, Stafforshire, England. Credited with developing the .470 Nitro-Express, Charles Lancaster built many double rifles, including some of the best-appointed of all box-lock guns. Will still build doubles to order.

## London Guns,

P.O. Box 89, 303 Whitehorse Road, Balwyn, Victoria 3103, Australia. Dealer in used double rifles.

## William Larkin Moore & Co.,

31360 Via Colinas, Suite. 109, Westlake Village, CA 91360. Importer of Perugini Visini, Leabeau-Corally, and other current European doubles.

## P.V. Nelson,

Folly Meadow, Hammersley Lane, Penn, Buckinghamshire, England. Current maker of double rifles by special order.

## James Purdey & Sons,

Audley House, 57-58 South Audley Street, London, England. Best known for their shotguns, Purdey nevertheless produced a fair number of double rifles, mostly very fine guns that are extremely valuable today. Still produces double rifles by special order.

## John Rigby & Co.,

66 Great Suffolk St., London SE1 OBU, England. In recent years, Rigby has made a decided comeback into the big-bore rifle arena with their .416 Rigby bolt-actions, and this firm will still build sidelock best-quality doubles to order. Starting with their .450-3 1/4" in 1898, Rigby was long a leader in big-bore doubles, and used Rigby doubles—both sidelock and boxlock guns—are highly prized today.

## Guy Ripamonti France Ltd.,

16, Rue Alfred-Colombet, 42000 Saint-Etienne, France. Maker of over/under and side-by-side double rifles up to 9.3x74R.

## Thad Scott,

P.O. Box 412, Hwy. 82 West, Indianola, MS 38751. Importer of current Continental doubles, dealer in used doubles.

## Don L. Shrum's Cape Outfitters,

412 South King's Hwy., Cape Girardeau, MO 63701. Importer of Marcel Thys double rifles ranging from .22 L.R. to .600 Nitro-Express; dealer in used doubles.

## Franz Sodia Jagdgewehrfrabrik,

Schulhausgasse 14, A-9170 Ferlach, Austria. Maker of primarily over/under double rifles, calibers up to .458

## Perugini Visini & Co. s.r.l.,

Via Camprelle, 126, 25080 Nuvolera (Bs.), Italy. Maker of over/under and side-by-side doubles up to .470.

## Webley and Scott,

Birmingham, England. The vast majority of all boxlock doubles by all makers used Webley actions, but relatively few large-caliber doubles were produced under the firm's own name. Although still in business, this firm no longer offers double rifles.

## Westley Richards & Co., Ltd.,

40 Grange Road, Bournbrock, Birmingham 29, England. Like Rigby, Westley Richards is making a comeback with magazine rifles, and will build doubles to order. Their doubles, in Westley's own hand-detachable boxlock or other actions, are considered among the best—a "name" gun even in a plain working grade. The .476 Westley Richards was their own proprietary cartridge, and they even made a few doubles in the unlikely .425 W.R.—but calibers such as the .470 are much more common than either of these.

## John Wilkes,

79 Beak Street, Regent Street, London, England. Still under original family ownership, this old-line firm continues to build double rifles by special order.

## Zoli Antonio spa,

25063 Gardone Valtrompia Brescia Italia 39, Via Zanardelli-Caselle Postali 21-23, Brescia, Italy. Maker of over/under express rifles up to 9.3x74R.

*No longer making rifles.

# APPENDIX 2

## Current Makers of Big-bore Bolt-actions

It would be impossible to list every manufacturer or custom gunmaker currently offering large-caliber bolt-actions. This listing is intended to single out those who have been mentioned in the text for the reader's convenience—or, of equal importance, those who *specialize* in heavy-caliber magazine rifles.

### A-Square,

Rt. 4, Simmons Rd., Madison, IN 47250. Maker of the Caesar and Hannibal big-bore bolt-action rifles in calibers up to .500 A-Square.

### Blaser,

Autumn Sales, Inc., 1320 Lake St., Fort Worth, TX 76102. Importer of the Blaser R-84 interchangeable-barrel rifle.

### Brown Precision, Inc.,

P.O. Box 270, Los Molinos, CA 96055. Maker of the custom Pro-Hunter rifle in calibers up to .458; maker of the Brown Precision synthetic stock.

### Browning,

Rt. 1, Morgan, UT 84050. Manufacturer of the Browning A-Bolt rifle.

### Champlin Firearms, Inc.,

Box 3191, Enid, OK 73701. Maker of the Champlin custom rifle, dealer in fine used rifles.

### I.M. Crudgington Ltd./George Gibbs Ltd.,

37 Broad Street, Bath BA1 5LT, England. Originators of the famed .505 Gibbs, this traditional English firm continues to build big-bores up to the .505 as well as stalking rifles. Builds primarily bolt-actions and single-shots and will produce doubles to order.

### Dakota Arms, Inc.,

HC55, Box 326, Sturgis, SD 57785. Maker of the Dakota 76 limited-production rifle in calibers up to .416 Rigby, right- or left-hand bolt.

### Dubiel Arms Co.,

1724 Baker Rd., Sherman, TX 75090. Makers of the custom Dubiel rifle.

### Ernest Dumoulin-Deleye,

Midwest Gun Sport, 1108 Herbert Dr., Zebulon, NC 27597. Importer of Dumoulin big-bore magazine rifles up to .416 Rigby.

### Henri Dumoulin & Fils,

P.O. Box 30, Herstal-4400, Belgium. American importer is New England Arms, Kittery Point, ME 03905. Maker of Imperial Magnum big-bore magazine rifles up to .505 Gibbs, including .416 Rigby.

## Frank's Custom Rifles,

5832 East Speedway Blvd., Tucson, AZ 85712. Custom maker of big-bore magazine rifles up to .505 Gibbs.

## David Gentry,

314 North Hoffman, Belgrade, MT 59714. Custom rifles and Gentry's own double-square-bridge magnum Mauser action.

## Griffin & Howe,

36 West 44th St., Suite. 1011, New York, NY 10036. Custom-rifle maker and dealer in fine used firearms.

## Gun South,

P.O. Box 129, Morrow Ave., Trussville, AL 35173. Importer of Steyr-Mannlicher sporting rifles, representative of Ferlach, Austria, gunmakers.

## Friedrich Wilhelm Heym GmbH & Co. KG,

Postfach 160, Coburger Strasse 8, D-8732 Munnerstadt, West Germany. American importer is Heym America, Inc., 1426 East Tillman Rd., Fort Wayne, IN 46816. Maker of fine bolt-action rifles in calibers up to .416 Rigby and .500-3" N.E.

## Holland and Holland Ltd.,

33 Bruton St., London W1X 8JS, England. Maker of fine custom rifles in bolt-action, single-shot, and double-rifle form.

## Paul Jaeger, Inc.,

P.O. Box 449, 1 Madison Ave., Grand Junction, TN 38039. Custom gunmaker, representative of F.W. Heym.

## KDF, Inc.,

2485 Hwy. 46 North, Seguin, TX 78155. Maker of the KDF limited-production rifle in calibers up to .458, including the .411 KDF.

## Kimber of Oregon, Inc.,

9039 Southeast Jannsen Rd., Clackamas, OR 97015. Maker of the Kimber limited-production rifle in calibers up to .505 Gibbs.

## G. McMillan & Co., Inc.,

21438 North 7th Ave., Suite E, Phoenix, AZ 85027. Maker of the McMillan Signature limited-production rifle in calibers up to .416 Rigby, .375 H&H, and .458 Win. Mag., including stainless-steel and titanium rifles.

## David Miller Co.,

3131 East Greenlee Rd., Tucson, AZ 85716. Fine custom rifles to the customer's specifications.

## Pachmayr,

1875 South Mountain Ave., Monrovia, CA 91016. Custom gunmaker, dealer in new and used top-quality firearms.

### Parker-Hale,

Bisleyworks, Golden Hillock Rd., Sparbrook, Birmingham B11 2PZ, England. Maker of bolt-action sporting rifles in calibers up to .404 Jeffery.

### Remington Arms Co.,

1007 Market St., Wilmington, DE 19898. Maker of Remington Model 700 rifles in calibers up to .416 Remington Magnum and .458.

### John Rigby & Co., Ltd.,

66 Great Suffolk St., London Se1 OBU, England. Maker of the Rigby bolt-action rifle in calibers up to .416 Rigby and .458.

### Sako,

Stoeger, Inc., 55 Ruta Court, So. Hackensack, NJ 07606. Importer of Sako bolt-action rifles in calibers up to .375 H&H and .458 Win. Mag.

### Sturm, Ruger & Co.,

Southport, CT 06490. Maker of Ruger Model 77 bolt-actions and No. One single-shots in calibers up to .458, including .416 Rigby.

### U.S. Repeating Arms Co.,

P.O. Box 30-300, New Haven, CT 06511. Maker of Winchester Model 70 and Model 70 Super Grade rifles in calibers up to .458.

### Weatherby, Inc.,

2781 East Firestone Blvd., South Gate, CA 90280. Maker of Weatherby Mark V rifles in calibers up to .416 and .460 Weatherby Magnums.

### Fred Wells' Wells Sports Store,

110 North Summit St., Prescott, AZ 86301. Custom rifles up to .510 Wells.

# APPENDIX 3

# Sources of Ammunition and Components

Hunters who choose cartridges such as the .30-06, .375 H&H, and .458 Winchester Magnum have no problems with ammunition; any sporting-goods store almost anywhere in the world will carry an ample supply (which is one perfectly good reason to choose popular cartridges such as these).

Those of us who choose more obscure cartridges—whether because we like the performance of the cartridge itself or because we like a rifle so chambered—have more of a problem. The following list is far from comprehensive regarding commercial sources of ammo. It concentrates chiefly on sources of bullets, cases, and loaded ammo for unusual, obscure, or obsolete cartridges.

### A-Square,

Rt. 4, Simmons Rd., Madison, IN 47250. Monolithic, Dead Tough, and Lion Load bullets available in most large calibers. Loaded ammunition in a wide range of sporting cartridges, including many metrics and most Nitro-Express rounds up to .577 N.E.

### Barnes,

P.O. Box 215, American Fork, UT 84003. Homogenous-alloy solids, expanding X-bullets, and Barnes softpoint bullets available in virtually any sporting caliber, in stock or by special order.

### Custom Hunting Ammo & Arms, Inc.,

2950 Fisk Rd., Howell, MI 48843. Custom handloaded "Superior Ammunition" available in most cartridges from .22 Hornet to .600 N.E.

### Dynamit Nobel of America, Inc.,

105 Stonehurst Ct., Northvale, NJ 07647. Supplier of RWS ammunition, including a number of hard-to-find metric cartridges.

### Eldorado Custom Shop,

Box 308, Boulder City, NV 89005. A division of PMC, owner of Brass Extrusion Laboratories, Ltd., the Eldorado Custom Shop offers brass and loaded ammo for a wide variety of Nitro-Express numbers and other hard-to-find cartridges.

### Federal Cartridge Company,

900 Ehlen Dr., Anoka, MN 55303-7503. Federal's Premium Safari line includes .470 N.E. and .416 Rigby as well as .375 H&H and .458 Win. Mag. Importer of Norma ammunition, including many metrics.

### Jack First Distributors, Inc.,

44633 Sierra Hwy., Lancaster, CA 93534. Dealer in hard-to-find ammunition as well as used firearms.

### Huntington,

P.O. Box 991, 601 Oro Dam Blvd. Oroville, CA 95965. Distributors of reloading supplies and equipment, specializing in hard-to-find and custom-ordered dies and components for wildcats and obsolete cartridges.

### Nosler,

107 Southwest Columbia, Bend, OR 97702. Maker of Nosler Partition bullets in calibers up to .375 at this writing.

### Old Western Scrounger,

12924 Hwy. A-12, Montague, CA 96064. Dealer in hard-to-find ammunition; importer of Australian Woodleigh bullets. Carries Berdan primers for Kynoch cases and Berdan decapping/priming tools.

### Omark Industries,

P.O. Box 856, Lewiston, ID 83501. Maker of Speer bullets and R.C.B.S. loading dies. Speer's safari bullet line is in development at this writing, and R.C.B.S. is one of the best sources of loading dies for obsolete cartridges.

### Professional Hunter Supplies,

P.O. Box 608, Ferndale, CA 95536. Custom-made bonded bullets in a variety of calibers, including many for Nitro-Express cartridges.

### Trophy Bonded Bullets, Inc.,

P.O. Box 262348, Houston, TX 77207. Maker of the Sledgehammer Solid and Bearclaw softpoint bullets in a variety of safari calibers.

### Swift Bullet Co.,

Rt. 1, Quinter, KS 67752. Maker of A-Frame expanding bullets in calibers up to .416.

### Harald Wolf Mastergunworks,

Krinkelt 13, B-4761 Rocherath, Belgium. Maker of brass cases and ammunition loaded with Australian Woodleigh bullets in both solids and softs for a variety of Nitro-Express cartridges up to .600 N.E., including the scarce .500 Jeffery.

# APPENDIX 4
## Ballistics Tables
## A Selection Of Light Cartridges
### (current and obsolete)

| Cartridge | date introduced | bullet diameter (in.) | bullet weight (gr.) | VELOCITY (fps) | | | | ENERGY (ft-lbs) | | | |
|---|---|---|---|---|---|---|---|---|---|---|---|
| | | | | MUZZLE | 100 | 200 | 300 | MUZZLE | 100 | 200 | 300 |
| .22 WMR | 1959 | .224 | 40 | 1910 | 1326 | — | — | 324 | 156 | — | — |
| .22 Hornet | 192? | .224 | 45 | 2690 | 2042 | 1502 | 1126 | 723 | 417 | 225 | 127 |
| .22 Savage High-Power | 1912 | .228 | 68 | 2800 | 2453 | 2131 | 1833 | 1190 | 911 | 687 | 510 |
| .222 Remington | 1950 | .224 | 55 | 3020 | 2562 | 2147 | 1773 | 1114 | 801 | 563 | 384 |
| .223 Remington | 1957 | .224 | 55 | 3240 | 2747 | 2305 | 1906 | 1282 | 922 | 649 | 444 |
| 22-250 Remington | 1965* | .224 | 60 | 3600 | 3195 | 2825 | 2485 | 1727 | 1360 | 1064 | 823 |
| .220 Swift | 1935 | .224 | 60 | 3600 | 3199 | 2824 | 2474 | 1727 | 1364 | 1062 | 816 |
| .240 Belted Rimless Nitro-Express | 1923 | .245 | 100 | 2950 | 2770 | 2580 | 2400 | 1940 | 1710 | 1480 | 1280 |
| .242 Vickers | 1923 | .249 | 100 | 3000 | 2810 | 2610 | 2420 | 2000 | 1760 | 1520 | 1310 |
| .243 Winchester | 1955 | .243 | 100 | 2960 | 2697 | 2449 | 2215 | 1945 | 1615 | 1332 | 1089 |
| 6mm Remington | 1955 | .243 | 100 | 3100 | 2829 | 2573 | 2332 | 2133 | 1777 | 1470 | 1207 |
| .240 Weatherby Magnum | 1968 | .243 | 100 | 3395 | 3069 | 2766 | 2483 | 2520 | 2092 | 1699 | 1369 |
| .244 Belted Rimless Magnum (Holland & Holland) | 1955 | .244 | 100 | 3500 | 3230 | 2970 | 2755 | 2725 | 2320 | 1980 | 1677 |
| .250 Savage | 1915? | .257 | 100 | 2820 | 2504 | 2210 | 1935 | 1766 | 1393 | 1084 | 832 |
| .257 Roberts (+P) | 1934 | .257 | 120 | 2780 | 2562 | 2354 | 2156 | 2060 | 1750 | 1477 | 1239 |
| 25-06 Remington | 1969* | .257 | 120 | 2990 | 2730 | 2484 | 2252 | 2383 | 1986 | 1645 | 1351 |
| .257 Weatherby Magnum | 1948 | .257 | 120 | 3290 | 3074 | 2869 | 2673 | 2885 | 2519 | 2194 | 1905 |
| 6.5x54 Mannlicher-Schoenauer | 1900 | .263 | 159 | 2370 | 2090 | 1880 | 1680 | 1915 | 1545 | 1250 | 995 |
| 6.5x55 Swedish | 1894 | .264 | 156 | 2650 | 2374 | 2114 | 1872 | 2433 | 1952 | 1549 | 1214 |
| 6.5x68 | 1938 | .264 | 123 | 3450 | 2990 | 2600 | 2230 | 3255 | 2455 | 1860 | 1395 |
| .264 Winchester Magnum | 1959 | .264 | 140 | 3030 | 2782 | 2548 | 2325 | 2855 | 2407 | 2018 | 1680 |
| .256 Newton | 1913 | .264 | 140 | 3000 | 2824 | 2655 | 2492 | 2800 | 2492 | 2198 | 1932 |
| .270 Winchester | 1925 | .277 | 130 | 3060 | 2801 | 2557 | 2326 | 2704 | 2266 | 1888 | 1562 |
| .270 Winchester | 1925 | .277 | 150 | 2850 | 2584 | 2334 | 2097 | 2706 | 2225 | 1814 | 1465 |
| .270 Weatherby Magnum | 1943 | .277 | 150 | 3245 | 3036 | 2837 | 2647 | 3508 | 3072 | 2682 | 2335 |
| 7x57 Mauser | 1892 | .284 | 140 | 2660 | 2456 | 2261 | 2075 | 2200 | 1876 | 1590 | 1339 |
| 7x57 Mauser | 1892 | .284 | 154 | 2690 | 2491 | 2300 | 2118 | 2475 | 2122 | 1810 | 1535 |
| 7x57 Mauser | 1892 | .284 | 175 | 2440 | 2137 | 1857 | 1604 | 2314 | 1776 | 1341 | 999 |
| 7x57R | 189? | .284 | 154 | 2630 | 2435 | 2249 | 2071 | 2366 | 2028 | 1730 | 1466 |
| .284 Winchester | 1963 | .284 | 150 | 2860 | 2594 | 2344 | 2107 | 2725 | 2243 | 1830 | 1479 |

| Cartridge | Year | Caliber | Bullet Wt. | Vel. Muzzle | 100 yd | 200 yd | 300 yd | Energy Muzzle | 100 yd | 200 yd | 300 yd |
|---|---|---|---|---|---|---|---|---|---|---|---|
| .280 Ross | 1906 | .287 | 140 | 2900 | 2720 | 2540 | 2360 | 2610 | 2400 | 2010 | 1760 |
| .280 Jeffery | 1915? | .288 | 140 | 3000 | 2820 | 2630 | 2450 | 2800 | 2480 | 2160 | 1870 |
| .275 Belted Rimless Magnum Nitro-Express | 1913 | .284 | 160 | 2700 | 2550 | 2380 | 2230 | 2590 | 2310 | 2010 | 1780 |
| 7x64 (7x65R) | 1917 | .284 | 154 | 2820 | 2614 | 2418 | 2230 | 2720 | 2338 | 1999 | 1700 |
| .280 Remington | 1957 | .284 | 150 | 2890 | 2626 | 2376 | 2140 | 2783 | 2297 | 1881 | 1526 |
| 7x61 Sharpe & Hart | 1953 | .284 | 154 | 3060 | 2717 | 2398 | 2101 | 3203 | 2524 | 1967 | 1510 |
| 7mm-08 Remington | 1980 | .284 | 140 | 2860 | 2625 | 2402 | 2189 | 2543 | 2143 | 1794 | 1491 |
| 7mm Remington Magnum | 1962 | .284 | 160 | 2950 | 2728 | 2517 | 2316 | 3093 | 2645 | 2252 | 1906 |
| 7mm Remington Magnum | 1962 | .284 | 175 | 2860 | 2645 | 2440 | 2244 | 3179 | 2719 | 2313 | 1957 |
| 7mm Weatherby Magnum | 1944 | .284 | 160 | 3200 | 3004 | 2816 | 2636 | 3639 | 3206 | 2819 | 2470 |
| 7mm Weatherby Magnum | 1944 | .284 | 175 | 3070 | 2879 | 2696 | 2520 | 3663 | 3221 | 2825 | 2468 |
| .30-40 Krag | 1892 | .308 | 220** | 2000 | 1783 | 1590 | 1418 | 1970 | 1553 | 1235 | 985 |
| .300 Savage | 1920 | .308 | 180 | 2350 | 2136 | 1934 | 1744 | 2208 | 1824 | 1495 | 1216 |
| .30 Newton | 1913 | .308 | 172 | 3000 | 2804 | 2618 | 2439 | 3440 | 3010 | 2631 | 2287 |
| .303 British | 1887 | .311 | 174 | 2450 | 2250 | 2060 | 1850 | 2320 | 1960 | 1640 | 1320 |
| .303 British | 1887 | .311 | 215** | 2060 | 1879 | 1680 | 1510 | 2030 | 1680 | 1360 | 1050 |
| .30-06 Springfield | 1906 | .308 | 165 | 2800 | 2534 | 2283 | 2047 | 2873 | 2353 | 1911 | 1536 |
| .30-06 Springfield | 1906 | .308 | 180 | 2700 | 2468 | 2248 | 2040 | 2914 | 2436 | 2021 | 1663 |
| .30-06 Springfield | 1906 | .308 | 220 | 2410 | 2192 | 1985 | 1791 | 2838 | 2348 | 1926 | 1567 |
| .300 Holland & Holland Magnum | 1925 | .308 | 180 | 2880 | 2640 | 2412 | 2195 | 3316 | 2786 | 2325 | 1927 |
| .300 Holland & Holland Magnum | 1925 | .308 | 220** | 2350 | 2170 | 2000 | 1830 | 2700 | 2300 | 1960 | 1640 |
| .300 Winchester Magnum | 1963 | .308 | 180 | 2960 | 2745 | 2541 | 2345 | 3503 | 3013 | 2581 | 2198 |
| .300 Winchester Magnum | 1963 | .308 | 200 | 2830 | 2676 | 2528 | 2384 | 3558 | 3182 | 2838 | 2525 |
| .300 Winchester Magnum | 1963 | .308 | 220 | 2680 | 2448 | 2228 | 2020 | 3510 | 2929 | 2426 | 1993 |
| .300 Weatherby Magnum | 1944 | .308 | 180 | 3300 | 3077 | 2865 | 2663 | 4354 | 3785 | 3282 | 2835 |
| .300 Weatherby Magnum | 1944 | .308 | 220 | 2905 | 2498 | 2125 | 1787 | 4124 | 3049 | 2207 | 1561 |
| .308 Winchester | 1952 | .308 | 165 | 2700 | 2440 | 2194 | 1963 | 2672 | 2182 | 1765 | 1413 |
| .308 Winchester | 1952 | .308 | 180 | 2620 | 2393 | 2177 | 1973 | 2744 | 2289 | 1896 | 1556 |

*Cartridges existed in wildcat form for many years before being adopted as factory cartridges.

**Original loading; current loadings may exceed these figures.

Data are taken from published factory figures; bullets selected are of "average" shape for caliber and weight, i.e., not necessarily either the most or least aerodynamic. Many cartridges listed are obsolete, and figures used are historical and could not be verified.

# A SELECTION OF MEDIUM CARTRIDGES
## (current and obsolete)

| Cartridge | Date Introduced | Bullet Diameter (in.) | Bullet Weight (gr.) | VELOCITY (fps) | | | | ENERGY (ft-lbs) | | | |
|---|---|---|---|---|---|---|---|---|---|---|---|
| | | | | Muzzle | 100 | 200 | 300 | Muzzle | 100 | 200 | 300 |
| 7.9mm (8x57J) Mauser | 1888 | .318 | 227** | 2025 | 1830 | 1640 | 1460 | 2060 | 1590 | 1360 | 1040 |
| 8mm (8x57S) Mauser | 1905 | .323 | 196 | 2530 | 2199 | 1894 | 1618 | 2786 | 2105 | 1561 | 1139 |
| 8x68S | 1940 | .323 | 224 | 2850 | 2585 | 2336 | 2105 | 4041 | 3325 | 2716 | 2205 |
| 8mm Remington Magnum | 1978 | .323 | 220 | 2830 | 2582 | 2346 | 2123 | 3913 | 3257 | 2690 | 2203 |
| .318 Westley Richards | 1910? | .330 | 180 | 2700 | 2440 | 2190 | 1930 | 2920 | 2390 | 1920 | 1490 |
| .318 Westley Richards | 1910? | .330 | 250 | 2400 | 2210 | 2030 | 1850 | 3200 | 2720 | 2290 | 1910 |
| .333 Jeffery | 1911 | .333 | 250 | 2500 | 2300 | 2120 | 1930 | 3470 | 2940 | 2500 | 2070 |
| .333 Jeffery | 1911 | .333 | 300 | 2200 | 2030 | 1860 | 1700 | 3240 | 2750 | 2310 | 1930 |
| .33 B.S.A. | 1923 | .338 | 165 | 3000 | 2700 | 2410 | 2130 | 3300 | 2680 | 2140 | 1670 |
| .338 Winchester Magnum | 1958 | .338 | 225 | 2780 | 2572 | 2374 | 2185 | 3862 | 3307 | 2816 | 2385 |
| .338 Winchester Magnum | 1958 | .338 | 250 | 2660 | 2398 | 2152 | 1920 | 3929 | 3194 | 2571 | 2047 |
| .340 Weatherby Magnum | 1962 | .338 | 250 | 3000 | 2806 | 2621 | 2443 | 4997 | 4373 | 3814 | 3313 |
| .348 Winchester | 1936 | .348 | 200 | 2520 | 2215 | 1931 | 1672 | 2820 | 2178 | 1656 | 1241 |
| .35 Winchester | 1903 | .358 | 250 | 2200 | 1970 | 1760 | 1550 | 2690 | 2160 | 1720 | 1340 |
| .35 Newton | 1915? | .358 | 250 | 2975 | 2737 | 2512 | 2297 | 4925 | 4175 | 3500 | 2950 |
| .350 Rigby Magnum | 1908 | .367 | 225 | 2600 | 2360 | 2120 | 1880 | 3380 | 2790 | 2250 | 1770 |
| .400/.350 Nitro-Express | 1899 | .357 | 310 | 2000 | 1795 | 1610 | — | 2760 | 2220 | 1790 | — |
| .400-360 Nitro-Express | 1900 | .367 | 300 | 1950 | 1760 | 1580 | 1410 | 2540 | 2070 | 1670 | 1330 |
| .360 Nitro-Express No. 2 | 1905 | .367 | 320 | 2200 | 2110 | 1830 | 1660 | 3450 | 3170 | 2390 | 1970 |
| 9mm Mannlicher-Schoenauer (9x56) | 1900 | .356 | 245 | 2100 | 1870 | 1660 | 1460 | 2400 | 1900 | 1500 | 1160 |
| 9x57 Mauser | 189? | .356 | 247 | 2310 | 1940 | 1710 | 1550 | 2930 | 2050 | 1605 | 1320 |
| .358 Winchester | 1955 | .358 | 200 | 2490 | 2170 | 1875 | 1608 | 2754 | 2092 | 1562 | 1149 |
| .35 Whelen | 1987** | .358 | 250 | 2400 | 2198 | 2005 | 1823 | 3198 | 2681 | 2232 | 1845 |

403

| Cartridge | Year | Caliber | Bullet Weight | | | | | | | | |
|---|---|---|---|---|---|---|---|---|---|---|---|
| .358 Norma Magnum | 1959 | .358 | 250 | 2800 | 2504 | 2226 | 1966 | 4353 | 3480 | 2751 | 2147 |
| 9.3x57 Mauser | 190? | .366 | 286 | 2070 | 1819 | 1591 | 1390 | 2722 | 2103 | 1608 | 1227 |
| 9.3x62 Mauser | 1905 | .366 | 286 | 2360 | 2091 | 1840 | 1611 | 3538 | 2777 | 2151 | 1648 |
| 9.3x64 Brenneke | 191? | .366 | 286 | 2750 | 2240 | 1930 | 1730 | 4790 | 3180 | 2365 | 1895 |
| 9.3x74R | 190? | .366 | 293 | 2360 | 2160 | 1998 | 1870 | 3580 | 3000 | 2560 | 2250 |
| .369 Purdey | 1922 | .375 | 270 | 2620 | 2400 | 2190 | 1970 | 4120 | 3460 | 2880 | 2330 |
| 9.5mm Mannlicher-Schoenauer | 1910 | .375 | 272 | 2250 | 2040 | 1830 | 1630 | 3030 | 2500 | 2010 | 1590 |
| .375 Flanged Magnum Nitro-Express | 1912 | .375 | 270 | 2600 | 2280 | 1980 | — | 4060 | 3120 | 2360 | — |
| .375 Flanged Magnum Nitro-Express | 1912. | 375 | 300 | 2400 | 2105 | 1825 | — | 3850 | 2960 | 2220 | — |
| .375 H&H Magnum | 1912 | .375 | 270 | 2690 | 2420 | 2167 | 1929 | 4339 | 3513 | 2815 | 2231 |
| .375 H&H Magnum | 1912 | .375 | 300 | 2530 | 2268 | 2022 | 1793 | 4265 | 3428 | 2725 | 2142 |
| .375 Weatherby Magnum | 1945 | .375 | 300 | 2700 | 2560 | 2425 | 2293 | 4856 | 3901 | 3100 | 2432 |
| .378 Weatherby Magnum | 1953 | .375 | 300 | 2925 | 2576 | 2252 | 1953 | 5701 | 4421 | 3380 | 2541 |

**Original loading. Data taken from original factory figures. Bullets selected are of "average" shape for caliber and weight, i.e., not necessarily either the most or least aerodynamic. Many cartridges listed are obsolete and figures used are historical and could not be verified.

# A SELECTION OF HEAVY CARTRIDGES
## (current and obsolete)

| Cartridges | Date Introduced | Bullet Diameter (in.) | Bullet Weight (gr.) | VELOCITY (fps) Muzzle | 100 | 200 | 300 | Energy (ft-lbs) Muzzle | 100 | 200 | 300 |
|---|---|---|---|---|---|---|---|---|---|---|---|
| .450/.400 3 1/4" Nitro-Express | 1896 | .411# | 400 | 2150 | 1960 | 1780 | 1590 | 4110 | 3410 | 2820 | 2300 |
| .450/.400 3" Nitro-Express | 1896 | .411# | 400 | 2125 | 1940 | 1760 | 1590 | 4010 | 3350 | 2760 | 2250 |
| .405 Winchester | 1904 | .412 | 300 | 2204 | 1897 | 1623 | 1384 | 3236 | 2399 | 1740 | 1290 |
| .411 K.D.F. | *** | .411 | 400 | 2450 | 2236 | 2035 | 1847 | 5330 | 4439 | 3678 | 3030 |
| .416 Taylor | | .416 | 400 | 2350 | 2117 | 1896 | 1693 | 4905 | 3980 | 3194 | 2547 |
| .416 Rigby | 1911 | .416 | 410 | 2370 | 2108 | 1864 | 1640 | 5115 | 4048 | 3165 | 2449 |
| .416 Remington Magnum | 1988 | .416 | 400 | 2400 | 2175 | 1962 | 1763 | 5117 | 4203 | 3420 | 2761 |
| .416 Weatherby Magnum | 1989 | .416 | 400 | 2700 | 2391 | 2101 | 1834 | 6476 | 5077 | 3921 | 2986 |
| .425 Express | *** | .423 | 400** | 2400 | 2160 | 1934 | 1725 | 5115 | 4145 | 3322 | 2641 |
| .404 Jeffery (10.75x73mm) | 1910? | .423 | 400** | 2125 | 1930 | 1750 | 1580 | 4020 | 3310 | 2730 | 2200 |
| .404 Jeffery (10.75x73mm) | 1910? | .423 | 401(RWS) | 2330 | 2010 | 1800 | 1650 | 4840 | 3585 | 2885 | 2430 |
| 10.75x68mm | 192? | .423 | 347 | 2260 | 1910 | 1640 | 1440 | 3930 | 2800 | 2075 | 1620 |
| .425 Westley Richards Magnum | 1909 | .435 | 410 | 2350 | 2120 | 1910 | 1710 | 5010 | 4100 | 3330 | 2660 |
| 11.2x60 Mauser | 191? | .440 | 332 | 2450 | 2170 | 1650 | 1430 | 4430 | 3480 | 2010 | 1510 |
| .45-70 Government | 1873 | .458 | 405 | 1330 | 1169 | 1057 | 978 | 1591 | 1230 | 1004 | 861 |
| .450-3 1/4" Nitro-Express | 1898 | .458# | 480** | 2150 | 1900 | 1665 | — | 4930 | 3860 | 2960 | — |
| .500/.450 Nitro-Express | 1899? | .458# | 480** | 2175 | 1987 | — | — | 5050 | 4220 | — | — |
| .450 No. 2 Nitro-Express | 1903 | .458# | 480** | 2175 | 1904 | — | — | 5050 | 3900 | — | — |
| .458 Lott | *** | .458 | 500 | 2300 | 2062 | 1838 | 1633 | 5873 | 4719 | 3748 | 2960 |
| .450 Ackley | *** | .458 | 500 | 2320 | 2081 | 1855 | 1649 | 5975 | 4805 | 3820 | 3018 |
| .458 Winchester Magnum | 1958 | .458 | 500 | 2040 | 1823 | 1623 | 1442 | 4622 | 3690 | 2924 | 2310 |
| .460 Weatherby Magnum | 1958 | .458 | 500 | 2700 | 2425 | 2166 | 1924 | 8096 | 6530 | 5211 | 4111 |

405

| Cartridge | | | | | | | | | | | |
|---|---|---|---|---|---|---|---|---|---|---|---|
| .500/.465 Nitro-Express | 1907? | .466# | 480** | 2150 | 1830 | 1620 | — | 4930 | 3580 | 2800 | — |
| .470 Nitro-Express | 1907? | .475 | 500 | 2150 | 1897 | 1664 | 1455 | 5133 | 3995 | 3073 | 2352 |
| .475 Nitro-Express | 1907+? | .476# | 480** | 2175 | 1930 | 1700 | 1490 | 5030 | 3970 | 3090 | 2360 |
| .475 No. 2 Nitro-Express | 1907+? | .483# | 480** | 2200 | 1925 | 1680 | — | 5170 | 3960 | 3020 | — |
| .475 No. 2 Jeffery | 1907+? | .488# | 500** | 2150 | 1880 | 1635 | — | 5140 | 3930 | 2970 | — |
| .476 Westley Richards | 1907+? | .476# | 520** | 2100 | 1925 | 1760 | — | 5085 | 4295 | 3585 | — |
| .500-3" Nitro-Express | 189? | .510# | 570** | 2150 | 1890 | 1650 | — | 5850 | 4530 | 3450 | — |
| .500 Jeffery | 192? | .510# | 535*** | 2400 | — | — | — | 6800 | — | — | — |
| .505 Gibbs | 191? | .505# | 525*** | 2300 | 2020 | 1790 | 1550 | 6180 | 4760 | 3740 | 2810 |
| .577-3" Nitro-Express | 189? | .585# | 750 | 2050 | 1730 | 1450 | 1210 | 7020 | 5000 | 3510 | 2440 |
| .600 Nitro-Express | 1903 | .622# | 900 | 1950 | 1690 | 1450 | 1250 | 7610 | 5720 | 4210 | 3130 |

**Original loading.

***Wildcat cartridge. May be available from smaller ammunition manufacturers such as A-Square.

#Most common groove/bullet diameter. Always slug the bore of a Nitro-Express rifle to ensure that proper bullets are used.

406

# APPENDIX 5

## Care and Transport of Firearms on Safari

R egardless of which rifles you take on safari, they won't do you much good if you don't get them to Africa, through whatever customs you must pass, and to camp in good working order. Once there, of course, you must keep them working—but that's quite simple compared to the potential problems that can arise when traveling with firearms.

The first and most important rule is to plan your safari as far ahead as possible—and include your choice of firearms as part of that initial planning. Some countries are easier to get firearms in and out of than others. South Africa and Zimbabwe, for instance, require no prior paperwork; all that's needed is to register the serial numbers and obtain a permit right at the airport customs. Cameroon is at the other extreme, with unusual amounts of paperwork and a great deal of advance time required to obtain permits. Somewhere in between are Zambia, Botswana, Tanzania, Mozambique, and most other safari countries, all of which require permits to be obtained in advance.

Your professional hunter or outfitter will usually handle all the details of obtaining your gun permits if any are required. Normally, the client's primary function is to list the make, type, caliber, and serial number of the firearms, plus the amount of ammunition. The critical detail here is that the serial numbers must be correct—and once declared, should not be changed. As a writer, with obligations to try out and write about various firearms, I have more than once planned on taking some new rifle that turned out to not be ready at the last minute. Aside from the paperwork hassles of such last-minute changes, which create a professional hunter's nightmare, the risk of not getting your firearms to your final destination is greatly increased. Since such changes are usually transmitted via telex, FAX, or transoceanic telephone calls, there's always the chance of error. Once you've decided what firearms you're taking, and have communicated all the needed information, don't make any changes.

That means you must be sure of the firearms you're taking. If a new rifle is in order, get it in plenty of time, check it out and make sure everything works as it should—then, and not before then, send whatever information is needed. And stand by your choice.

When you're planning a safari, you should ask your hunter what he recommends, understanding that he may or may not have any real interest in firearms beyond their efficiency as simple tools. According to our survey (Chapter 36), the odds are good that he'll simply tell you to bring a .375. That isn't bad advice, but you may or may not wish to follow it. Whether you do or not, at least make certain the firearms you plan to bring are legal. Some countries do not allow semiautomatic firearms, while others prohibit

.22-caliber firearms. Many countries have specific caliber limitations for use on various classes of game, especially dangerous game.

Handguns can be easily imported into some countries and are totally taboo in others. I don't like to be encumbered with a handgun when I'm hunting with a rifle, so I rarely worry about it. On the other hand, I've done some handgun hunting in both South Africa and Zimbabwe and have enjoyed it immensely. If you wish to bring a handgun, make certain it's importation will be legal.

Ammunition can be subject to restrictions, and the exact amount you plan to bring is often stated on the gun permit. In Botswana, I have customarily had my ammunition counted on the way in, and in Tanzania you can expect to have it counted both coming in and going out. In rare instances, having cartridge headstamps that don't match the caliber of your rifle can be a real problem. For instance, a .416 Hoffman rifle using ammunition handloaded from necked-up .375 H&H cases, as absurd as it sounds, can be impossible to get into some countries. The gun permit says you have a .416, and it authorizes the importation of .416 cartridges—while the only ammunition you have is clearly headstamped .375. An alert customs official may well refuse entry of the ammunition, leaving you up the creek without your paddle and very little recourse.

Such restrictions vary tremendously from country to country, but all that's required is pre-hunt communication and common sense. These days, airline restrictions on the amounts of ammo they will carry are almost more serious than African importation regulations. Whichever airline you're flying, make certain you call a few days before your departure and ask someone in a responsible position what the current regulations and policies are for carrying ammunition. Each airline is a bit different, but a standard restriction is five kilograms of ammunition, usually required to be in original factory containers. Less common is the requirement for ammunition to be in a separate, locked, wood or metal container—but you can run into this.

Five kilograms, or 11 pounds, isn't much ammunition. A reasonable mix of ammo for one of my favorite batteries for a lengthy safari would be, let's say, 60 rounds of .30-06 ammo, 40 rounds of .375, and 20 rounds of .470 (with 30 soft and 10 solid for the .375, and 10 of each for the .470). On a little postal scale, I get about 15 rounds to the pound for 180-grain .30-06 ammo; about eight to the pound for 300-grain .375; and about five to the pound for .470. My 60 rounds of .30-06 weigh four pounds, the 40 .375 weigh five pounds, and the 20 big .470 cartridges weigh four pounds. With that modest amount of ammo, I'm over the five-kilo limit. And if the airline employees happen to make a point of it on that particular day, no amount of fluster, bluster, or finesse will get the extra ammo onto the plane.

The logical answer, in the face of shrinking airline ammo allocations, is to take fewer rifles. Sixty rounds for the light/medium rifle and 40 for the medium/heavy rifle is more than adequate for any sporting safari I can imagine, and that amount of ammunition will fall under the five-kilo limit. On the other hand, there is no way an ample supply of shotshells can be taken—so arrange to have them purchased locally.

In general, ammunition must be carried separately from firearms. I generally put mine in a metal military-type ammo can, then put the can inside my duffel bag, well-cushioned on all sides by clothing.

Which brings us, finally, to the problems of taking rifles on international flights. The first rule is to check in early; the handling of firearms can take extra time. Part of that time might be spent checking your firearms in with American customs.

Nobody will make you do this, but all firearms should be registered with customs before you depart the U.S. with them. It takes about two minutes, and the little form you receive (the same one you'd get for imported watches, cameras, expensive jewelry, etc.) is good for as long as you own the firearm.

And by all means, plan on plenty of time to make connecting flights. Speaking of connecting flights, if you're entering another country en route, you'll need to comply with any and all firearms restrictions of that nation. A possible option is leaving your firearms in bond at the airport, but make any needed arrangements in advance.

No matter how absurd the airline's rules may be, obey them. Firearms-related F.A.A. regulations are taken extremely seriously these days, and included among them is that firearms must be declared, and must be certified as being unloaded. Most airlines also require that firearms be locked in a case, so don't get caught short without a lock that works.

Passing through the customs of various countries is often greatly simplified by keeping the make and serial numbers of your firearms in your pocket, thus occasionally saving the necessity of opening the guncase.

Beyond such details, traveling with firearms is merely a matter of selecting as rugged a case as you can find, securing your guns carefully, padding them as well as you can, and entrusting the whole lot to the baggage-smashing gorillas. There are many good cases on the market today, including many that could stand up to being run over by a tank. However, I've now had three good gunstocks broken by airlines while in good cases. So buy the best case you can afford—but also carry good insurance!

Cases I like include McMillan's molded plastic case, a massive, indestructible case padded with thick foam that you cut out to the exact contour of your rifles. Another is the Texas-made Americase, interesting because it double-stacks two guns in top-and-bottom compartments rather than side-by-side. There are many others. Things to look for include a piano hinge on the back, reinforced corners, and sturdy locks that can't be broken off accidentally or easily pried off.

Far more important, to my mind, than the construction of the case is how it's packed. I've gone through a half-dozen good metal cases in the last dozen years, and in between I've used several very inexpensive plastic cases with equally good results. There aren't any real secrets to packing a gun case except to make certain there's adequate foam or other cushioning material to pad the rifle well and keep it immobile. I often augment a case's padding with rolled up T-shirts or clean socks, especially around the scope. Bolts are a serious problem with bolt-action rifles; if left in the rifle, they can cause a serious bulge—which, if the case is dropped, can result in serious damage. I am fairly certain this is how one of my rifles, a Weatherby Mark V, was shattered in a good stainless-steel case.

Instead, these days I take the bolt out and wrap it in a clean pair of socks. Some guys like to put their bolts in another bag to discourage theft. It's a sound idea, but it would be just my luck that that bag would go missing. I'm knocking on wood as I write this, but to date I have never lost any guns in transit—although I have had several delayed for quite some time. Last year, I did lose a duffel bag in transit while my gun case, which had been hand-carried (as the airlines are supposed to do), arrived safe and sound. The ammunition was in the duffel bag, and it was a scramble to find some in Johannesburg. But if the bolt to my .375 had been in that duffel bag, there would have been little point in shopping for ammo!

Once the rifles arrive safely in camp, African hunting is generally not as hard on them as most American game country. In most areas, dust and grit are constant, so regular cleaning is absolutely essential to ensure proper functioning. Rust prevention is also extremely important. In dry weather, sweating hands cause rust overnight, and the effects in wet weather are obvious. Most camps will have a cleaning rod and some oil, but the wealth of excellent gun-care products we have in America are unheard of over there. Take a spray can of Rem-Oil, WD-40, or whatever lubricant you prefer, and a minimal cleaning kit that includes a good jointed cleaning rod. The flexible pull-through type of rod is fine for cleaning, but if you take a spill and lodge some debris in your muzzle you simply must have a solid cleaning rod to get it out.

You should also have a good gunsmith's screwdriver that fits the action screws of your rifle so you can pull the action out of the stock in case it gets really soaked, and of course screwdrivers that fit the mounts of your scope. Speaking of scope mounts, alternative sighting equipment is absolutely essential. Auxiliary iron sights are one approach, and they'll surely do in a pinch—so long as you've checked them out before the hunt. Another option is to carry an extra scope already mounted in rings that will fit the bases on at least one of your rifles.

In your emergency repair kit, carry along some Superglue and the best plastic tape you can find—you'll be amazed what you can do with it. Just last season I arrived at a deer camp in Georgia at midnight only to find my riflestock broken in two at the pistol grip. We rustled up some Superglue and tape, and with liberal doses of each I got the stock put back together. I fired only three shots with it before I sent it in for a new handle. One shot was fired to check its zero, which hadn't changed. The other two were used to take two nice whitetail bucks with one shot each.

Which brings up one last point: Before you leave any airport anywhere in the world with rifles, open the guncase and check them out. If there's damage, you may have a legitimate claim against the airline for repairs—but you must check before you leave the airport.

# BIBLIOGRAPHY

Aitken, R.B. *Great Game Animals of the World.* New York: The Macmillan Company, 1968.

Askins, Colonel C. *Asian Jungle, African Bush.* Harrisburg, Pennsylvania: The Stackpole Company, 1959.

——, *African Hunt.* Harrisburg, Pennsylvania: The Stackpole Company, 1958.

Barnes, F.C. *Cartridges of the World, Revised 5th Edition.* Northbrook, Illinois: DBI Books, Inc., 1985.

Barrett, P. *A Treasury of African Hunting.* New York: Winchester Press, 1969.

Bell, W.D.M. *The Wanderings of an Elephant Hunter.* Suffolk, England: Neville Spearman, 1981.

——. *Bell of Africa.* Suffolk, England: Neville Spearman, 1983.

——. *Karamojo Safari.* Suffolk, England: Neville Spearman, 1984.

Blixen-Finecke, Baron B. Von. *African Hunter.* New York: St. Martin's Press, 1986.

Blunt, Commander D.E. *Elephant.* London: The Holland Press, 1985.

Boothroyd, G. *Gun Collecting.* London: The Sportsman's Press, 1987.

Bull, B. *Safari—A Chronicle of Adventure.* London: Viking, 1988.

Bulpin, T.V. *The Hunter is Death.* Long Beach, California: Safari Press, 1987.

Burrard, Sir Gerald. *Notes On Sporting Rifles.* London: Edward Arnold (Publishers) Ltd., 1958.

Carmichel, J. *Jim Carmichel's Book of the Rifle.* New York: Outdoor Life Books, 1985.

Clark, J.L. *Good Hunting.* Norman, Oklahoma: University of Oklahoma Press, 1966.

De Haas, F. *Bolt Action Rifles.* Northfield, Illinois: DBI Books, Inc., 1984.

Donnelly, J.J. *The Handloader's Manual of Cartridge Conversions.* South Hackensack, New Jersey: Stoeger Publishing Company, 1987.

Foa, E. *After Big Game in Central Africa.* New York: St. Martin's Press, 1989.

Haggard, H.R. *King Solomon's Mines.* New York: Dover Publications, Inc., 1951.

Hemingway, E. *Green Hills of Africa.* New York: Charles Scribner's Sons, 1935.

Ker, D.I. *African Adventure.* Harrisburg, Pennsylvania: The Stackpole Company, 1957.

Kittenberger, K. *Big Game Hunting and Collecting in East Africa 1903-1926.* New York: St. Martin's Press, 1989.

Lott, J. *Big Bore Rifles.* Los Angeles, California: Petersen Publishing Company, 1983.

Lyell, D.D. *African Adventures—Letters from Famous Big Game Hunters.* New York: St. Martin's Press, 1988.

Matunas, E.A. *Shooting.* New York: Outdoor Life Books, 1986.

Matthews, C.W. *Shoot Better.* Lakewood, Colorado: Bill Matthews, Inc., 1984.

———. *Shoot Better II.* Lakewood, Colorado: Bill Matthews, Inc., 1989.

Maydon, H.C. *Big Game Shooting in Africa.* London: Seely, Service & Co. Ltd., 1957.

Mellon, J. *African Hunter.* Long Beach, California: Safari Press, 1985.

Nobel. *Sporting Ammunition.* London: Nobel Industries, Ltd., 1925.

Nosler Bullets. *Nosler Reloading Manual Number Two.* Bend, Oregon: Nosler Bullet, Inc. 1981.

O'Connor, J. *The Big Game Rifle.* New York: Alfred Knopf, 1952.

Pardal, J.C. *Elephant Hunting in Portuguese East Africa.* Long Beach, California: Safari Press, Inc., 1990

Patterson, L. Col. J.H. *The Man-eaters of Tsavo.* New York: St. Martin's Press, 1986.

Ruark, R.C. *Horn of the Hunter.* Garden City, New York: Doubleday & Company, Inc., 1953.

———. *Something of Value.* Garden City, New York: Doubleday & Company, Inc., 1955.

———. *Use Enough Gun.* New York: The New American Library, 1966.

Rushby, G.G. *No More the Tusker.* London: W. H. Allen, 1965.

Sanchez-Ariño, T. *On the Trail of African Elephant.* London: Rowland Ward, 1987.

Sierra Bullets. *Sierra Bullets Reloading Manual Second Edition.* Santa Fe Springs, CA: *Sierra Bullets,* The Leisure Group, Inc., 1978.

Speer Omark Industries. *Reloading Manual Number Ten.* Lewiston, Idaho: Omark Industries, 1979.

Stigand, Captain C.H. *Hunting the African Elephant.* New York: St. Martin's Press, 1986

Taylor, J. *African Rifles & Cartridges.* Harrisburg, Pennsylvania: The Stackpole Company, 1948.

———. *Big Game and Big Game Rifles.* London: Herbert Jenkins, 1948.

Truesdell, S.R. *The Rifle—Its Development For Big Game Hunting.* Harrisburg, Pennsylvania: The Military Service Publishing Co., 1947.

White, S.E. *The Land of Footprints.* London: Thomas Nelson and Sons, 1925.

Wynne-Jones, A. *Hunting—On Safari in East and Southern Africa.* Johannesburg, South Africa: Macmillan South Africa (Publishers) (Pty) Ltd., 1980.

# Index

419

420

Lyell, Denis   134, 136
Lyell, Malcolm   92, 134, 136, 362-363
Lyman   218

## M

Machakos District   90
machan   277
Mag-Na-Port   212
magnum   20, 22-23, 27-28, 30-32, 37-39, 41, 45, 48-49, 51-52, 60-61, 63-64, 66, 70-71, 75, 95-96, 129, 143, 175-176, 179, 181, 184, 187, 196, 223-224, 259-260, 267-268, 273-274, 278, 302, 312, 320, 353, 356-357, 369-375, 378-379, 381
mamba   261
Manners, Harry   54, 166, 175, 294
Mannlicher   53, 59, 75, 96, 134-136, 139, 171-175, 180, 203, 355, 360-365, 376
Mannlicher-Schoenauer   53, 96, 171, 173-175, 180, 376
Mannlicher-Steyr   59, 96, 171, 173, 361
Marlin   46, 60, 69, 76-77, 194-195, 266, 280
Martini-Henry   76, 171, 191
Masailand   25, 32, 61, 74, 261, 266, 301
Matetsi   73, 320, 381
Mauser   21, 26, 34, 41-42, 44, 46, 59-61, 66, 70, 79, 129-130, 132-134, 146, 171-177, 179-180, 182-183, 185-186, 188-190, 205, 218, 363-365, 376
Maydon, H.C.   87, 129, 172, 364
Maynard   60
Mellon, James   195

metrics   22, 26, 41, 71, 95-96, 130, 132
Millais, John G.   96, 362
Miombo forest   301
Monte Carlo comb   210
moose   13, 24, 45-47, 66, 72, 76, 145, 224, 381
mopane woodland   301
Mosse, Captain A.H.E.   364
Mount Kilimanjaro   166, 305
mountain goat   142
mountain nyala   36, 50, 181, 271, 305
Mozambique   61, 90, 92, 293-296
muzzle brake   212-213

## N

Nairobi   356, 370, 376
Namibia   25, 181, 275, 369, 376
Neumann, Arthur   135, 360-361
Newton   17, 21-22, 36, 45, 176, 212, 363
Nile   287, 295
nilgai   142, 144
Nitro-Express   19, 27, 42-43, 53-54, 59, 61, 69-72, 74-76, 78-93, 95, 132, 135-136, 145, 147, 155-159, 161-164, 167, 169, 175, 192, 198, 200, 212, 288, 355-356, 361, 365, 380, 382
Norma   37, 43, 45, 51-52, 61, 93, 95, 274, 277, 302, 319-320
North American game   14, 32
Nosler   30-32, 49, 51, 55, 58, 130, 143-144, 268, 273, 278, 286, 370, 378, 380
nyala   36, 50, 57, 181, 267, 271, 305

426

427

These fine books are also published by SAFARI PRESS and are listed in chronological order. Numbers 2, 3 and 6 are out of print.

All books available from specialty retailers nationwide. For information on the above, direct your inquiries to the publisher. If you would like to receive our catalog, please send us a card giving your name and address.